THÉOPHILE GAUTIER

BY THE SAME AUTHOR

Fanny Brawne

Rachel

Théophile Gautier. From a photograph by Nadar, about
1856 (*Hulton Picture Library*)

THÉOPHILE
GAUTIER

HIS LIFE & TIMES

by

Joanna Richardson

MAX REINHARDT
LONDON

© Joanna Richardson 1958
Printed and bound in Great Britain for
MAX REINHARDT LTD
10 Earlham Street, London w.c.2
by Wyman & Sons Ltd, Fakenham
Set in Monotype Plantin
First published 1958

A

Alice Théo Bergerat

ET

Pierre Théophile Gautier

JE DÉDIE CETTE VIE

DE LEUR AÏEUL

EN TÉMOIGNAGE DE GRATITUDE

ET D'AFFECTION

Toute vie contient son roman, il s'agit de savoir le dégager, et ce roman est souvent l'histoire.

Théophile Gautier, *le Moniteur universel*
7 January 1854

CONTENTS

PART FOUR

La Comédie de la Mort

Appendices

ILLUSTRATIONS

Foreword

'I AM not one of those whose houses are marked by commemorative plaques,' wrote the author of *Mademoiselle de Maupin*. The comment was over-modest when it was made; it is untrue today, for on the walls of his house in the rue de Longchamps at Neuilly a marble slab reminds us of Théophile Gautier, *poète*.

Yet it is perhaps symbolic that the plaque remains upon a house that is otherwise forgotten, a house in which no relics have been gathered together, a house to which even those in the rue de Longchamps cannot always direct you. For Gautier, like his last house, is abandoned: posterity remembers the rose-coloured doublet, remembers the name from the programme of *Giselle*; the student has read, it may be, one of the travel books, *Mademoiselle de Maupin*, *le Capitaine Fracasse* and *Emaux et Camées*. But the rest of the three hundred volumes that Gautier filled with his poems and his travels, his novels and short stories, his plays and his forty unremitting years of journalism: these are forgotten in libraries, or hidden in the Press of a century ago, buried as deep as Tahoser in her tomb. And Gautier's correspondence is even more inaccessible: the vast bulk of it remains in the library of the Institut de France, the Collection Spoelberch de Lovenjoul at Chantilly. And here, more than eighty years after the poet's death, his most intimate letters are still being withheld. Twice I went to Chantilly and twice I was forbidden to consult them; and only after several years of research, through the generosity of two distinguished *gautieristes*, was I able to see what I believe to be copies of this vital correspondence. Small wonder that there is no good Life of Gautier in his own language, and that until now there has been no Life of Gautier in English. He still deserves the title that Adolphe Boschot gave him years ago: *le grand méconnu*.

Misunderstanding by itself is, of course, no adequate reason for a biography. But I think that Gautier also has his claims to greatness. His two major novels must be examined in any survey of the nineteenth-century French novel; and as a poet he is not only distinguished but influential. As a chronicler of the contemporary French theatre he is incomparably the most gifted, the most accurate and the most picturesque; as a critic of art he is original and penetrating. As a writer of travel books he is, at his best, a model. As a correspondent he is charming. His life is a vivid part of the nineteenth century, and as a nineteenth-century figure he is brilliant, exotic, Romantic, ubiquitous and, for all his evident faults, strangely endearing.

I have, then, written the Life of Théophile Gautier because I have long held him in particular affection and because, to my mind, his Life demanded to be written. The house in the rue de Longchamps remains forgotten; and, as Gautier wrote in his foreword to *le Capitaine Fracasse*, 'we had to build a home for the wandering ghost'.

I should like to record my gratitude to those who have helped me in the research for this book: first, and not least, the librarians and staff of the British Museum Reading Room, the British Museum Newspaper Library, the Bodleian Library, the Library of the Taylor Institute, and the Bibliothèque Nationale. I am grateful to M. Jacques Bardoux, of the Assemblée Nationale, M. Georges Lecomte, of the Académie-Française, and M. Marcel Bouteron, of the Institut, who enabled me to consult the Collection Spoelberch de Lovenjoul at Chantilly; and to M. Jean Pommier, curator of the Collection, who gave me access to certain unpublished notes and correspondence. I am also indebted to M. Jean Tild, and to Mme Meyer-Zundel, the friend of Judith Gautier, who read me passages from the unpublished volume of *le Collier des Jours*. I am glad to thank Dr Peter Green for his encouragement and excellent criticism, and I am profoundly grateful to M. Emile Henriot, of the Académie-Française, who so generously allowed me to use the letters of Gautier to Carlotta Grisi. I owe much to my mother for her patient interest in my Gautier studies, and for all her constructive comments on this biography.

My greatest debt is too large to be paid in a Foreword. I acknowledge it most gladly in the dedication of this book.

Oxford-Chantilly-Paris-London   J. R.

1953–1958

Introduction

THÉOPHILE GAUTIER cannot make his official, flamboyant, rosy-doubleted entrance until we have raised the curtain on the nineteenth century. A man must perform within the *décor* of his times, his part must integrate with the contemporary play.

One might almost say that *Hernani* was Gautier's cue, it so perfectly suited him. It is, however, a common fallacy to date the Romantic movement from 1830: in fact, Romanticism might be traced back far earlier: as far, perhaps, as *la Nouvelle Héloïse* in 1761. Rousseau and Chateaubriand, between them, had introduced many elements of Romanticism by the turn of the century: morbid introspection, the sense of isolation, pantheism and the return to nature, the love of the exotic, a passionate, fluent, highly-coloured style. In the *Méditations* of Lamartine, published in 1820, the poetry of Christendom, the power of lyricism were revealed. Napoleon's campaigns had revived an interest in Egypt, Italy, Spain; in a thousand *chinoiseries* in bric-à-brac shops lay another source of inspiration only waiting to be revived. And before the *bataille d'Hernani* was fought in 1830, Dumas *père* had tossed off his passionate historical dramas *Christine de Suède* and *Henri III et sa Cour*, and Victor Hugo had written the unactable *Cromwell*, with the preface that was to become the credo of the new school.

On 25 February 1830 there were, then, many Romantic glimmerings in a Romantic firmament; all that was needed was a brilliant planet: or, rather, a pole star to which new writers might turn for constant guidance. For many years the old order had been changing; it remained for the new, by some splendid *coup-d'état*, to impose itself.

Hernani, first performed on this February night, nearly a hundred and thirty years ago, was to be the most deliberate, most celebrated *coup-d'état* in literature. The first night was expected to be (and proved to be) a literary battle; and night after night, of course, the battle was repeated. But when *Hernani* was accepted by the public, the days of classical revival and classical pastiche were ended, and the Romantics were resplendently enthroned.

Romantic drama was a notable failure: psychology and neat construction were conspicuously lacking. The fiasco of Hugo's *les Burgraves* in 1843 meant the death of Romantic drama after thirteen years. But the passion, the unrestrained lyricism that had proved the undoing of drama were triumphant in poetry; and the historical sense, the love of the exotic and the adventurous that had failed to save *les Burgraves* inspired Romantic poets and novelists for years. Much of the stock-in-trade was, of course, bound to date. Byron would not have been happy in 1850. The extremely personal element in Romanticism was followed by the

extremely impersonal element in the Parnassians; the fantastically im-
probable novels of Sue were followed by the clinically realistic novels of
the Goncourts. The beginning of the century had seen Chateaubriand's
René. The end of the century saw Zola.

The change from personal to impersonal, from fantasy to realism, and,
one might add, from the effervescent to the contained, the uncontrolled
to the precise, is, at first glance, very striking. But it was, of course, a
very gradual process. And when we look for literary influences, when
we try to trace naturalism and realism to their sources, we come back
to the long-haired, familiar figure in the rose-coloured doublet on the
first night of *Hernani.*

Théophile Gautier was, no doubt, a flamboyant youth; but he soon
cast off his Romantic excesses. Basically, like Flaubert, he remained
Romantic; but while the rest were still enthusing over the Gothic in
1830, he was already worshipping the Greek ideal of beauty. And while
the rest might continue to pose as misunderstood geniuses, Gautier
understood that though art must be practised for its own sake, it must
be related to life if it were to survive.

The creed of Art for Art's Sake, of which he became the chief and
most fervent apostle, was not, as is commonly believed, an impractical,
affected and highfalutin creed. It was the recognition of absolute and
independent standards for art: the only standards, indeed, by which art
may be judged. It meant that art was set above the artist, was set above
conventional morals or religions, that art was a religion in itself. But
Gautier insisted, time and time again, that art must be brought into the
home: that public taste in all forms of art must be improved; and this
insistence is among the most striking facts in his criticism.

It is appropriate that the creed of Art for Art's Sake should have been
taught by one who had himself intended to be a painter. It is also understandable that Gautier's other great claim to distinction is that he
endowed literature, as surely as Baudelaire, with *un frisson nouveau.* It
was not, merely, a new excitement, but a new dimension, an undiscovered sense. For it was Gautier, the one-time artist, who made writers
permanently aware of the visual. 'My whole distinction,' he told the
Goncourts, 'is that I am a man for whom the visible world exists.' It
was not his whole distinction; but we may trace a large part of his
influence in the visual, three-dimensional, coloured and accurate writing
that he inspired. The artistic approach to literature and the religion of
Art for Art's Sake: these are his legacy.

Yet to say this is but to repeat what critics have said for over a
century. What critics have not discussed, or even known, is Gautier the
man. The *décor* has been sketched in; the actor must make his entrance.

PART ONE

The Son of Artagnan

1. The Son of Artagnan

TOWARDS THE end of 1810 Pierre Gautier, a minor tax-official, and his wife, the former Antoinette-Adélaïde Cocarde, spent their honeymoon and early married life at the Château d'Artagnan that was one day to figure in a novel. Then they made their way south-east, to the town of Tarbes, near the Spanish border: a town, indeed, so near the Pyrenees, that one could hardly escape the blue vista of mountains at the end of a street. They installed themselves, it is said, in shabby rooms where the previous tenants, an itinerant troupe of actors, had left some properties to settle their debts: the tawdry, tinsel accessories of pantomime. Among them (for the nomads acted Perrault) was Cinderella's throne. And to this throne, for want of a bed, Mme Gautier clung on the night of 30 August 1811. It was on this throne (according to the legend, a tempting legend that one hopes is true) that she gave birth, next day, to the child she had probably conceived at the Château d'Artagnan: to her first child and only son, a born Romantic: Pierre-Jules-Théophile.[1]

For the first few years of his life Théophile and his parents lived in this southern town where the sun cut out the shadows with sharp scissors and fell heavy in the summer on brown backs and brown faces. Théophile looked a southern child, with his dark hair, dark eyes and dusky skin, with his indolence, his momentary moods of elation and depression. And when he was three and a half, and his father's nomination as receiver of taxes led them to Paris, Théophile made no secret of his temperament. He recalled years later (though perhaps the account was exaggerated) that his regrets for the South made him suicidal: that he hurled his toys out of the window and would have followed had he not been restrained. Parisian French seemed to him a foreign tongue; and once, in a Paris street, as he heard some passing soldiers speaking the familiar Gascon, he tugged his nurse's hand: 'Come on! Let's follow them! They're ours!' Though he spent nearly all the rest of his life in Paris, Théophile Gautier remained a southerner: 'The memory of blue mountains in silhouette at the end of every alley has never left me, and has often touched me in my pensive moods.'

This frail and gentle child, who looked 'like some little Spaniard from Cuba, chilly and nostalgic,' lived 'in the most serene, most chaste of surroundings. It is hard to imagine an existence so purely enshrined as mine. My years flowed past, in the shadow of my mother's chair,

B

with my little sisters and the dog. I saw nothing round me but the good, kind tranquil faces of old servants, heads grown white in our service; friends and relations, grave and devout, clad in black, who put their gloves down separately on the brims of their hats; a few aunts, of a certain age, nice and plump, and neat, discreet, with dazzling linen, grey skirts, string mittens, and their hands folded in their laps, like pious people.'[2]

He could read at the age of five. They had taught him for months, with small profit, how to spell; but one day he was given a well-bound, gilt-edged copy of *Lydie de Gersin*. 'Keep it for next year,' said the donor, 'since you can't read yet.' 'I *can* read,' stammered Théophile, pale with anger, and retired into a corner; he made such efforts of will and intelligence that he deciphered the book from cover to cover and narrated it when the visitor next called. The door was unlocked. He turned to *Robinson Crusoe*. He could dream of nothing but desert islands and returns to nature, and stayed for hours in his cabin under the drawing-room table. He went on to *Paul et Virginie*, to find an intoxication which (so he declared) he found in no book in his maturity. He learned Latin from his father, a good humanist; and he spent his leisure copying etchings of Greek triremes: 'How many hours I spent shaping a log and hollowing it out with fire like the savages! How many handkerchiefs I sacrificed for sails! Everyone thought I was going to be a sailor, and my mother grew desperate at the idea of a vocation which in time would take me far away.' The triremes were succeeded by model theatres, and the décors turned the boy's thoughts towards painting. But it was time to begin his formal education. On 9 January 1822, at the age of ten years and three months, he entered the Collège Royal de Louis-le-Grand.[3]

It was a grim change from the familiar and grateful warmth of home, his father's kindly tuition, his mother's enveloping devotion, the wide-eyed admiration of his younger sisters Lili and Zoé. He was, of course, miserable. His fellow pupils, rough and turbulent, filled him with horror. He felt he would die of cold, boredom and isolation inside the high, grim walls. He was terrified by the college watchdog. The food his mother gave him mouldered in his pockets, he could not eat the food he had at school, and he grew so thin (he recalled) that the college became alarmed. On 23 April, after three brief months, his childish aspirations were realized and he was taken away by his family. 'During his unduly short stay at the College,' went the report, 'he showed himself gentle, sensible, and very well disposed. We have had nothing to reproach him for, except a little frivolity during the last days.'[4]

*   *   *

So it was that Théophile Gautier finished his education at the Collège Charlemagne as a day boy, an *externe libre*, a title which he inscribed with enormous pride on all his written exercises. He made few friends except Eugène de Nully and Gérard de Nerval (who had already distinguished himself by publishing a book of *Odes nationales*); he did not entirely satisfy his teachers, for at times he imitated the style of the Latin decadents; and once, congratulated on his perfect prose, he answered unpleasantly that there was no cause for congratulation: he had made a deliberate mistake and the Latin master had failed to observe it. He also studied old French authors, especially Villon and Rabelais, whom he knew by heart, and he attempted a poem, *le Fleuve Scamandre*, translations from the Greek, and a poem on Helen of Troy in decasyllabic verse: all of which have been lost. 'I have no pleasant memory of my college years,' he wrote, 'and I should not like to live them over again.' But long after he had left the Collège Charlemagne, one not unpleasant memory came to mind: 'It was Saint Charlemagne's Day, and our college had asked the Français for a performance of *Andromaque* with Talma playing Oreste. Overexcited by our wine-and-water (a little more purple, a little less watery than usual) we were almost delirious at the thought that we should see the famous actor; and the moment the doors opened, we were all of us sitting down in the pit, under the eye of our ushers. We must admit that *Andromaque* did not greatly amuse us. No doubt, although we were still in the sixth, nature had deposited some fatal germs of Romanticism within us; but what enchanted us was Talma's buskin, made of red crossed-over bands which went between his big and second toes. His flesh-coloured tights had toes as a glove has fingers, and that was far more amazing than the sublime manner in which he made his *s*'s vibrate when he thought he saw the Furies. Alas! the passion for local colour was already aflame within us!'[5]

* * *

The unorthodox *collégien* spent his holidays at Mauperthuis, and it was at Mauperthuis, it seems, that he read *The Mysteries of Udolpho*, the *Confessional of the Black Penitents*, the *Château des Pyrénées*, 'and with what anxiety we read them all, what anguish, what nervous shudders, what cold sweats down our back, especially if it were evening, and the rain whipped the windows, and the winter wind groaned in the chimney, and the weathercock screeched on the gables like a bird of night!'[6]

The frail and Spanish-looking child was growing sturdy: when he was free from the classroom he went to the Ecole Petit to learn swimming, sometimes he spent the whole day in the emerald Seine. It was his ambition to be a strong swimmer, to wear scarlet drawers, a *caleçon rouge*: it was, he added later, 'the only one of my ambitions to be realized'. Nor was swimming his only deviation from the curriculum: before he finished his course, he was learning painting in Rioult's studio in the nearby rue Saint-Antoine. It was here that he learned the art of close observation, developed his sense of form and colour; he owed to Rioult, he recorded, his ability to see and appreciate. And he owed, perhaps, to the little, ugly, paralysed master in the rue Saint-Antoine, to the artist whose own painting has been forgotten, the quality that would dominate and distinguish his prose and poetry and, through him, profoundly affect the course of French literature: the quality he would signify to the Goncourts when he told them: 'I am a man for whom the visible world exists.'

His short sight and his merely conventional canvases may have indicated to Gautier that painting was not his vocation. But in 1829, in the rue Saint-Antoine, the decisive revelation was accorded him.[7] 'On a single circumstance, a picture seen, a volume read, a piece of music heard by chance, a destiny may depend . . . I should probably have turned artist had it not been for a book by Victor Hugo which fell into my hands in the studio; it was *les Orientales*.'

> *. . . Alors s'en vont en foule et sultans et sultanes,*
> *Pyramides, palmiers, galères capitanes,*
> *Et le tigre vorace et le chameau frugal,*
> *Djinns au vol furieux, danses des bayadères,*
> *L'Arabe qui se penche au cou des dromadaires,*
> *Et la fauve girafe au galop inégal!*
>
> *Alors, éléphants blancs chargés de femmes brunes,*
> *Cités aux dômes d'or où les mois sont des lunes,*
> *Imams de Mahomet, mages, prêtres de Bel . . .*[7]

The vision might die to Hugo in *les Orientales*, but it was to remain with Gautier for life. 'From that moment the master played a more important part in our existence than the most intimate of our friends.'

In the summer of 1829, the eternally nomadic Gérard de Nerval and the wild and fascinating Petrus Borel offered to introduce Gautier to Victor Hugo, the condescending idol of Romanticism.[8] The young visitor arriving at the rue Jean-Goujon was so overcome that he sat for more than an hour on the stairs, summoning composure. Still speechless, he was shown into the presence. Hugo, from the height of his twenty-seven years, 'deigned to smile and speak a word or two of encouragement'. Gautier left to spend his holidays again at Mauperthuis, but he was no longer just a student of art. He was already a student of literature. And when, on 29 October, he attended the first night of Vigny's *le More de Venise*, he was 'still almost a child, but already loving art with a love that has not left us'.[9]

*   *   *

On 25 February 1830 some of the audience in the Théâtre-Français pointed out to each other, with horror, M. Théophile Gautier. 'His flamboyant waistcoat shone that evening over pale grey trousers with black velvet bands down the seams, his hair cascaded from beneath his flat broad-brimmed hat. The impassibility of his pale and regular features and the sang-froid with which he surveyed the good folk in the boxes proved to what degree of abomination and desolation the theatre had fallen.' It was the first night of *Hernani*: the night that was to decide the prestige—one might almost say the supremacy—of the new Romantic literature. Hugo's garish troops had been waiting for six or seven hours for the decisive fight between traditional and progressive, past and future, Classicism and Romanticism. 'A rising storm was grumbling in the auditorium, it was time for the curtain to rise; and people might have come to blows before the play, so great was the animosity on either side. At last the three raps sounded. Slowly the curtain drew back and there, in a sixteenth-century bedroom, lit by a little lamp, we saw Doña Josefa Duarte, an old woman dressed in black, her skirt sewn with jade in the style of Isabella the Catholic, listening for the knocks that the expected lover should knock on his mistress' secret door:

> *Serait-ce déjà lui?—C'est bien à l'escalier*
> *Dérobé . . .*'[10]

The *enjambement* had been made and the *bataille d'Hernani* had begun.

If *Hernani* had been produced in London that evening, it would have created small stir outside the theatre; broad vocabulary, elastic syntax, freedom from unities of time and place: these were taken for granted by the compatriots of Shakespeare. To the compatriots of Racine it was otherwise. Hugo's freedom of speech, his *enjambements*, his rejection of the unities amounted to iconoclasm. In *Hernani* he was attacking the sacrosanct traditions of the theatre; and he was doing so, moreover, in the holy of holies, the Théâtre-Français. And in France, where litera-ture, and particularly the theatre, is a matter of constant and lively public concern: in France, where literary traditions are fiercely re-spected, and the public is Classical, not Romantic, at heart, *Hernani* was epoch-making. It was as if a public schooled for generations on

Pope and Dryden were suddenly given the *Ode to a Nightingale*. *Hernani* imposed a new way of thought, a new and successful literary religion.

'The twenty-fifth of February 1830!' wrote Gautier, not long before he died: 'The date remains written in flame in the depths of our past: the date of the first performance of *Hernani*! That evening decided our destiny. There we received the impulse that spurs us on, even now, after so many years, the impulse that will make us march on until the end of our days. Many years have passed, but we still feel all the fervour of our youth, and whenever we hear the enchanted echo of the horn, we prick up our ears like an old warhorse ready to begin the battles of long ago.'[11]

*   *   *

Five months after the victory of Romanticism came the July Revolution: two days of street fighting in Paris which ended in the exile of Charles X and the accession of Louis-Philippe. The bourgeois monarchy had begun. And as the cannon-smoke wafted down the Passage des Panoramas, there appeared, in the window of Mary, the publisher, a small rose-bound volume printed at the expense of Monsieur Pierre Gautier: forty-two poems, written between 1826 and 1830, the *Poésies* of his son.

Poésies is evidently a first book; there is something timid, even virginal about it. It is written by a youth far less observant, far less vigorous, far less exuberant, than the Gautier who, a few years later, will write *Mademoiselle de Maupin*. It is the work of a writer who has not yet found himself: who still refers to eyes as *soleils jumeaux*, *ardens miroirs*, still rhymes *madame* with *flamme*, still uses all the Gothic impedimenta of stained-glass windows, moonlit basilicas, corpses on gibbets, birds of prey, death's heads and cataracts. Byron is openly imitated, and 'our dear authors, Victor and Sainte-Beuve' are not far distant. *Poésies* is no brilliant beginning, but it shows a gentle, boyish poet not to be found in later anthologies: a poet who does not yet see every landscape as an unframed picture or as a poor substitute for art, though he is, none the less, already preoccupied with the visible world.

Whatever its merits, *Poésies* passed almost unnoticed in the cannon-smoke of 1830. But the author was not deterred. He was living with his family at 8, place Royale, a corner house in the graceful square now known as place des Vosges; and soon after the Revolution Victor Hugo had moved next door. And there, in the place Royale, in that springtime of the nineteenth century, while the swallows nested in the eaves above, and the chestnuts slowly opened into candles in the square below, master and pupil, lord and vassal, talked literature from window to window. And slowly Gautier's painting was abandoned, quietly his writing increased. Hugo liked him well enough, encouraged his admiration, let him 'sit like some familiar page on the steps of his feudal throne'. Drunk with such favour, Gautier sought to deserve it, and wrote the legend of *Albertus*. It appeared, with his published *Poésies*, a score of new poems, and a lithograph by Célestin Nanteuil, late in October 1832.

Albertus (it might equally well be called *Véronique*) is the tale of a witch turned woman who persuades her lover to sell his soul to the devil. Albertus consents, Véronique turns witch again and Albertus dies. The theme is simple and familiar, it is carried through more than a hundred stanzas, and both theme and accessories are supremely Romantic. *Albertus* is an achievement for a poet of twenty, a lively advance on the *Poésies* of 1830, it shows a wide technical vocabulary, developing consciousness of visual detail, and anticipates a little of the vigorous description of *Mademoiselle de Maupin*. It is, however, far from being successful: it is self-conscious, and the style continually distracts from the subject. Gautier's facility is both an excuse and a warning. And (though he could not have read *Lamia*, even in translation) *Albertus* inevitably suggests the Keatsian poem with which, for feeling, language or technique, it could not stand comparison.

Hugo's bounty had inspired Gautier to write *Albertus*, Hugo's introduction led him to write his first short stories; for it was at 6, place Royale that he met Eugène Renduel, the publisher who sped about Paris in a cabriolet of steel and ebony, the great Romantic publisher who boasted Balzac and Hugo on his lists and seemed to possess a flair for divining glory. Renduel found Gautier 'droll' and asked him to write something for him. The first result was a kind of *Précieuses ridicules* of Romanticism, *les Jeunes-France*.[12]

And *les Jeunes-France* surely fulfilled all Renduel's expectations; it is a collection of satirical short stories which shows Gautier at his youthful best: vigorous, facile, original, paradoxical, gay. The stranger excesses of his artistic contemporaries are parodied in *Onuphrius : ou les vexations fantastiques d'un admirateur d'Hoffmann*. The medieval cult is exploited in the most sympathetic, most poignant of his tales: *Elias Wildman-stadius*; while *Daniel Jovard ou la Conversion d'un classique* is a devastating manual for all who would qualify as '*maître passé en la gaie science du romantisme*'. *Celle-ci et Celle-là, ou la Jeune-France passionnée*, already shows the Gautier of *Fortunio* and *Mademoiselle de Maupin*: sensual, assured, appreciative, Romantic, and, as he repeatedly tells us, Turkish in his sexual freedom. These tales, which more than once satirize the author himself, carry weight because they are written with

sympathy as well as amusement; they are sparkling forerunners of the
Panthéon Nadar. They are some of the best of Gautier's early writing,
they remain among the most spirited of his works.

2. The Green Season

AT THE end of 1834 Pierre Gautier was appointed receiver of taxes at
Passy. To move from the place Royale to the very bounds of Paris
would, to Théophile, have been exile; and for two hundred and fifty
francs he rented two tiny rooms in the Impasse du Doyenné and enjoyed
his first independence.

The Impasse du Doyenné was a dead-end of dilapidated buildings
in a corner of the Carrousel, a few yards from the Louvre. It was all
that remained of a *quartier* being demolished, and the houses seemed to
Balzac like living tombs. The end of the Impasse was marked by
weatherbeaten planks salvaged from boats; on the rue de Richelieu side
was a marsh, on the Tuileries side rose dumps of unused paving-stones,
on the side of the old Louvre spread the rubble and wreckage of
demolition. The ruins of the church of Saint-Thomas-du-Louvre,
which, in the eighteenth century, had collapsed, killing six canons in
its fall, added to the general desolation.

The gloom was pleasing to the Romantic mind, and, to Gautier, the
ruins assumed a charming aspect in moonlight. And if his own foothold
in the Impasse were small, he was living next door to Camille Rogier,
the artist, and his endearing friend from the Collège Charlemagne:
Gérard de Nerval. They had installed themselves in a large apartment,
where Rogier had embellished the walls with a portrait of Neptune
strangely like himself, while Gérard had provided tapestries, two
Fragonard panels, two sideboards, and a Renaissance bed for some
nebulous divinity (he himself slept in a tent on the floor). In this strange
oasis they were woken each morning by the door-keeper's cocks, crow-
ing in the grass around the Louvre. And Paris awoke to the Impasse du
Doyenné when the occupants gave a fancy-dress ball which made its
mark in history. The refreshments were visual: Adolphe Leleux, the
painter of Bretons, produced a bacchanal in the style of Velasquez,
Nanteuil abandoned engraving to paint a romantic naiad, Chassériau,
the pupil of Ingres, presented a Diana, and Corot dashed off a pair of
Italian scenes. Gautier, the pupil of Rioult, already attracted by the
eighteenth century, offered a *déjeuner sur l'herbe* in the manner of

Watteau, while Gérard, engagingly immaterial, contributed the advice that they should wreathe themselves with flowers.

The colony and festivities grew: Arsène Houssaye, the future director of the Comédie-Française, installed himself with Gérard, paying his rent by dinners at the Provençaux in times of opulence; Eugène Piot, the local Maecenas, photographer and collector of antiques, established himself on the opposite side of the landing. It was the time of Musard's intoxicating music, the time of febrile carnivals; they gave their balls in the Doyenné ('our Louvre,' as Gérard said) and danced till morning, when they sallied out in daylight, in fancy-dress, to breakfast in the Bois de Boulogne; and sometimes, wildly, they danced at La Chaumière, where Gautier distinguished himself in the *galop*, his Merovingian hair flying loose in the wind of his speed.

It was an easy-going, energetic, independent world, an enchanting vernal world that they would long recall, Gérard in his *Petits Châteaux de Bohème*, Houssaye in his *Confessions*, his *Souvenirs de Jeunesse* and even in poetry:

> *Théo, te souviens-tu de ces vertes saisons?* . . .
> *Retournons un instant à cette belle année :*
> *Traînons les vieux fauteuils devant la cheminée ;*
> *Prenons un manuscrit pour rallumer le feu,*
> *Appelons nos deux chats et devisons un peu.*
>
> *Que dit-on par le monde? Eh! qu'importe? nous sommes*
> *Dans la verte oasis, loin du désert des hommes.*
> *Laissons-les s'épuiser avec les vanités,*
> *Notre rêve vaut mieux que leurs réalités* . . .[1]

And Gautier hardly needed Houssaye to remind him. Again and again he recalled the green Parisian oasis where art was enjoyed for the sake of art and life for the sake of life; again and again he recalled 'the wild young men who live on their wits a little haphazardly and from day to day: artists, musicians, poets, journalists, who love pleasure better than money, and prefer to all things, even to glory, their indolence and liberty. They are a pleasant and a facile race, full of good instincts, prompt to admire, swept away and diverted by trifles, forgetting to-morrow's bread for this evening's conversation. To that Bohemia we all belong, more or less, or we have belonged to it. Oh! happy time when you thought yourself in debt for a few hundred francs, always paid twice over, when you grew drunk with youth if you drank a glass of

water, when you thought yourself Don Juan because your neighbour
had smiled at you over her mignonette and sweet peas! How many fine
dreams we have spun through tobacco smoke! What splendid stanzas
recited, what fine pictures seen! What exchanges, what combinations of
formal clothes when it came to a soirée! One of us, obliged to go to a
minister's, could only find, in all Bohemia, a cutaway coat in garnet
velvet that an artist friend had ordered for some Pompadour whim that
had once passed through his mind on a prosperous day! . . . We raise
our glass, and cry both loud and clear: *Vive la Bohème!*'[2]

*　　*　　*

In this Bohemia, in his microscopic writing, Gautier scribbled away.
His renown was already spreading. The pupil of Rioult had begun to be
known as a Salon critic with his articles in *la France littéraire*. The
author of the *Poésies, Albertus, les Jeunes-France* was the elated owner of
a letter from Hugo: 'I am very proud, dear Albertus, proud of your
friendship, proud of your talent . . . You are a great poet and an excellent friend.'[3] And Gérard, on his foreign peregrinations, wrote home to
Renduel: 'If you see Petrus and Théophile, tell them they're read in all
the reading-rooms of Italy.'[4]

Gautier was certainly read in the reading-rooms of France, for *les
Grotesques*, his studies of 'grotesque' and unfamiliar French poets, had
begun in *la France littéraire*, in January 1834, with an article on Villon.
It was, for the times, an audacious article: a few years earlier, Sainte-
Beuve had accorded Villon prudent and moderate praise. Now Gautier
wrote not only with sympathy but with enthusiastic admiration: an
admiration that would do much to resurrect Villon in France. The
immediate result was that Théophile Gautier and *la France littéraire*
had both been attacked by *le Constitutionnel*; and in May 1834, enlarg-
ing his diatribe against *le Constitutionnel*, Gautier had demolished
utilitarian literature and the whole tribe of journalists and critics,
recited the creed of Art for Art's Sake that he would profess all his life
and, with all the unrestraint and fire of a passionate youth in a wildly
exciting age, produced the finest example of rhodomontade in French
literature. It was the Preface to *Mademoiselle de Maupin*.

'. . . Nothing beautiful is indispensable to life. If you suppressed the
flowers, the world would not materially suffer; yet who would wish
there were an end of flowers? . . .

'. . . What is the use of music? What is the use of painting? Who
would be mad enough to prefer Mozart to M. Carrel, and Michelangelo
to the inventor of white mustard?

'Nothing is really beautiful unless it is useless; everything useful is ugly, for it expresses a need and the needs of man are ignoble and disgusting, like his poor weak nature. The most useful place in a house is the lavatory.

'For myself, I am one of those to whom the superfluous is necessary . . . I should most joyfully renounce my rights as a Frenchman and a citizen to see an authentic picture by Raphael, or a beautiful woman naked—the Princess Borghese, for example, when she has posed for Canova, or Julia Grisi when she enters the bath . . .

'Instead of creating a *prix Monthyon* for the recompense of virtue, I should prefer, like Sardanapalus, that great philosopher who has been so misunderstood, to give a handsome prize to the man who invented a pleasure; for enjoyment seems to me to be the end of life, and the only useful thing in the world. God has willed it so, He who created women, perfumes and light, lovely flowers, good wines, lively horses, greyhounds and Angora cats; He who said not to His angels: "Be virtuous," but "be loving," He who has given us a mouth more responsive than the rest of our skin that we may kiss women, eyes looking upwards that we may see the light, a subtle sense of smell to draw in the souls of flowers, strong thighs to grip the flanks of stallions and fly as swift as thought, sensitive hands to caress the long heads of greyhounds, the velvet backs of cats, and the satin shoulders of creatures of little virtue, and Who, in short, has given us alone the triple and glorious privilege of drinking without thirst, of striking light, and of making love in every season, which distinguishes us from the brute far more than the habit of reading papers and making charters. . . .'

The vibrant love of beauty, the passionate love of pleasure, the capacity for enjoyment, the question of Art for Art's Sake, all is there in embryo; despite the outrageous manner, the glittering pyrotechnics, the enormous paradoxes, the astonishing, constant rain of conceits, the Preface to *Mademoiselle de Maupin* contains much that stayed deep in Gautier's soul all his days. And it contained, too, much that had an unconscious irony:

'You only become a critic when it is well proved in your own eyes that you cannot be a poet. Before you degrade yourself to the wretched task of looking after the coats and noting the moves like a billiard-boy or a ball-boy, you have long courted the Muse, you have tried to possess her; but you lack the strength for it. Breath has failed you, and you have fallen weak and pale at the foot of the holy mountain.

'I understand this hatred of critic for poet. It is oppressive to see someone else at the banquet to which you yourself are not bidden, someone else sleeping with the woman who has rejected you. From the depths of my heart I sympathize with the unfortunate eunuch obliged to watch the sport of the Grand Signor.'

*   *   *

Many of Gautier's theories as a critic of literature (and, indeed, as a critic of the arts in general) are found in the Preface and text of *Mademoiselle de Maupin*. The Preface bears little relation to the novel, and is probably included on its own brilliant merits as a polemic. To posterity it has more than polemical interest; for when Gautier derides the whole conception of utility and declares, with all the ardour of his early manner, all the categorical certainty of youth, that 'nothing is really beautiful unless it is useless', he is for the first time professing the creed that he will profess, as poet and as critic, throughout his life. The Preface to *Mademoiselle de Maupin*, written at the outset of his career, is an impressive declaration of the creed of Art for Art's Sake, of the sovereignty of art, of its independence of moral and social conditions. It insists upon the supreme importance of beauty; it is an early expression of the philosophy that Gautier will express, more than twenty years later, in *la Nue*: '*Aime! c'est l'essentiel!*'

It is only this belief in beauty and in love that relates the Preface to *Mademoiselle de Maupin*. The novel is, in fact, much less a novel than an admirable series of visual descriptions, an honest, full-blooded likeness of Gautier in his early twenties, a Gautier already possessing many of the beliefs and emotions that will inform his criticism. The story is the least important part of the book: it is only important in so far as the equivocal position of the heroine, her ability to arouse a double passion, enables Gautier to suggest that beauty may be loved independently of sex, and for its own sake. His personal worship of loveliness is seen here not merely in his delicate and emotional portraits of women, but in his lyrical invocation to ideal beauty ('Whomsoever thou be, angel or demon, virgin or courtesan . . .') and in his hymn to beauty, 'pure personification of the thought of God'. Time and again in *Mademoiselle de Maupin* we are made aware of the author's religion of beauty, his Greek worship of loveliness. 'I entirely understand the wild enthusiasm of the Greeks for beauty,' he declares; it is the explanation of his assertion that 'Christ did not come for me; I am as pagan as Alcibiades and Phidias'. In his attitude to beauty, Gautier is pagan indeed; and there remains profound truth in his comment: 'I have looked at love in the classical light, as a more or less perfect piece of sculpture.' If he could consider a woman as her sculptor, this showed no inhumanity: it showed, rather, the Greek attitude, the attitude of the artist and idealist. And in his search for beauty and love, Gautier was a confirmed idealist: 'There is something great and fine in loving a statue,' he proclaims in his novel. 'The impossible has always pleased me.' This Romantic love of the impossible recurs throughout his work and dominates his life. It is the love he describes when he writes: 'If Don Juan had once found his ideal, he would have been the most faithful of lovers; but his greatness was in not meeting it, for he sought absolute beauty, and absolute beauty is God.'

*   *   *

Mademoiselle de Maupin was published by Renduel late in 1835. It is a version of *As You Like It* written with all the *naïveté* of a Romantic in his early twenties. It is based on a premise that does not bear the scrutiny of reason: that a woman could pass among young and old, men and women, amorous and experienced, month after month, as a man. Once this wild impossibility is accepted, we accept every conceivable *quid pro quo*; perversion becomes innocent or mitigated, love grows hesitant or guilty, and morality becomes strangely contorted. It is not surprising that the novel shocked contemporary opinion: the emotions it revealed were far from the conventional, idealised emotions of *la Nouvelle Héloïse*. Yet *Mademoiselle de Maupin* is more than an exploration of forbidden pleasures. If it impresses us by its unrestrained sensuality, its detailed, appreciative physical description, it impresses us, too, by its impulse and enthusiasm: its fire, momentum and vivacity transform it into a testament of youth. *Mademoiselle de Maupin* is a book that is written once in a lifetime, when dreams have not dissolved and disillusion is still unknown. None of Gautier's later prose is driven by the same energy; no novel better embodies the careless rapture of the young Romantic. And the book is more than a Romantic novel, more even than a testament of youth: it is a profession of faith. It is this eager profession that gives *Mademoiselle de Maupin* both lyricism and dignity. If the Preface is a *tour de force* as much as a declaration of the principle of Art for Art's Sake, the text itself has a higher status. It is a brilliant though unconscious development of the Keatsian theme: 'I have lov'd the principle of Beauty in all things.' It shows, already, Gautier's passionate idealism, his eager, wholehearted worship of beauty. 'I adore above all things the beauty of form; beauty, for me, is visible Divinity, palpable happiness descended on earth . . . Beauty, which alone of all things cannot be acquired; frail and ephemeral flower that grows without being sown, pure gift of heaven! Oh beauty! the most radiant diadem with which chance may crown the brow— thou art admirable and precious like everything beyond the reach of man, like the azure of the sky, the gold of stars, the perfume of the seraphic lily! One may change a footstool for a throne; one may conquer a world, many indeed have done so; but who could not kneel

before thee, pure personification of the thought of God!' Seen in this
spirit, *Mademoiselle de Maupin* has an aesthetic significance. It is not
merely the earliest and best-written of Gautier's novels. It is the first,
the most sustained, and one of the most brilliant of Gautier's profes-
sions of his creed.

*   *   *

The year of *Mademoiselle de Maupin* was an exciting year: 'Come and
dine one of these days in your old corner of the place Royale,' wrote
Hugo to his disciple in January. 'There is a swallow's nest over one of
your old windows which always makes me think of you. You should
certainly do as the swallow, and come back and lodge there in the
month of April.'[5] And then, one morning, a young man of distinguished
appearance crossed Gautier's threshold in the Impasse du Doyenné:
Jules Sandeau, an emissary from Balzac. Balzac had read *Mademoiselle
de Maupin*, much admired the style, and wanted Gautier to collaborate
on his paper *le Chronique de Paris*.

For all his literary success, the author of *Mademoiselle de Maupin* felt
apprehensive when, for the first time, he went to meet the author of
la Peau de Chagrin, *Eugénie Grandet* and *le Père Goriot*. Balzac had
already achieved enough to found half a dozen reputations. It was with
something of the nervousness he had known, six years ago, when he
had first met Hugo, that Gautier introduced himself. Bull-necked,
fiery-eyed, wearing the white flannel robe that symbolized, perhaps,
his cloistered life, Balzac had risen at midnight and worked until his
visitor's arrival, but he showed no sign of tiredness, indeed throughout
the lunch he was wildly gay. The conversation veered towards literature; by the time they had finished the *foie gras* (with forks especially
borrowed from Balzac's publisher), Gautier had promised to write for
the *Chronique de Paris*. He had also formed a friendship that was to last
until the death of Balzac, fifteen years later.

*   *   *

In July 1836, with the restless Gérard, Gautier set out on his first
journey abroad: to Belgium, 'to seek the reality of Rubens paintings.'
The Hôtel de Ville in Brussels was to him a revelation of the Middle
Ages, and the Gothic palace opposite was so dramatic in moonlight
that he waited for the entry of that passionate Romantic actress, Mme
Dorval. Then he and Gérard went on by train to Antwerp, through a
landscape 'perfectly flat and perfectly green; here and there the white
houses of Laeken, like marguerites, blossomed on rich emerald carpets
dotted with heavy oxen which swam in grass up to the belly; English
gardens with yellow alleys, sleepy rivers with pewter and quicksilver
waters, Chinese bridges illumined with brilliant colours, passed to left

and right; tall thin poplars filed past at a gallop; towers rose up on the edge of the horizon, great pools of water, the scattered scales of some gigantic fish, mirrored here and there on the brown earth. In the numerous hollows by the edge of the railway, a few taverns, with *Verkoopt men dranken* in letters a foot high, smiled sweetly from the bottom of their tiny hop-gardens, and made a thousand advances to the traveller, inviting him to get down and drink a good glass of strong Flemish beer, and smoke a pipe of patriotic Belgian tobacco: useless advances, for on a railway you cannot stop, even to drink—which, to my mind, is one of the gravest disadvantages of trains.'

*　　　*　　　*

And sensual, enthusiastic, young in heart, still the Gautier of *Mademoiselle de Maupin*, Gautier returned to France in August, to take the most momentous step in his life. Until now he had been a poet, a novelist, writing gaily and not too often in lesser journals. On 26 August 1836 his article on the paintings in the Throne Room of the Chambre des Députés appeared, with the signature 'Gauthier' he so deplored, in *la Presse*. Emile de Girardin, the editor, promptly asked him to write on the art of the French School in Rome.[6] The second article appeared on 30 August. Girardin declared: 'Your place, Monsieur, is assured by the article you have written, for all the articles you write.'[7]

And so, the day before his twenty-fifth birthday, the green season of life was ended. Théophile Gautier entered the newspaper world. His journalism would take him from Salon to concert to theatre, among the most distinguished men and women of the age; it would carry him to London, Munich and Berlin, to Spain, Algeria and Italy, to Turkey, Denmark, Russia, Greece, and Switzerland and Egypt. It would produce a ceaseless flood of novels and short stories and more than two thousand articles for the next thirty-six years. It would shape and fill his life. It would weigh upon his shoulders all his days.

PART TWO

Fortunio the Critic

3. Fortunio the Critic

EMILE DE GIRARDIN, five years older than Gautier, was the natural
son of Alexandre de Girardin, General, and Grand Veneur to Charles X,
and Mme Dupuy, the wife of a counsellor at the Cour royale in Paris.
'He was an imposing figure in an imposing age. At every step you walk
into this cold, swift man, this suppressed volcano, this marble beacon
which flames on all the horizons of the intelligence. You will meet him
on the rostrum, you will meet him in the Press, always rejected, always
victorious, taking by assault the place that is refused him, fearful
adversary, feared ally . . .'[1] Dickens would be awestruck by Girardin's
arsenals of cigars, Rachel would be one of his mistresses, the royalty
of art and letters were already among his guests and contributors, if
not among his friends. He had chosen the newspaper industry as he
would have chosen mining if his tastes had led him to metallurgy; and
he had founded and now edited *la Presse*. He professed constant scorn
(it was said) for literature pure and simple. He was, above all, tough,
disciplinarian and businesslike: some declared he rose at four to begin
his day. It has been rightly said that the chief of Gautier's editors was
more American than French. He was certainly the antithesis of
Gautier. He was the supreme example of the self-made man, the nineteenth-century precursor of Citizen Kane.

But if Emile de Girardin was an exacting employer, his wife was the
most graceful of presiding deities. Under the pseudonym of le Vicomte
de Launay, Delphine de Girardin contributed engaging gossip-columns
to *la Presse*; she was to write more than one play for Rachel. Her conversation, her presence, her influence were alike delightful. In her salon
in the rue Saint-Georges, Lamartine spoke of poetry to Hugo, Gautier
and Balzac spun their verbal fantasia. And just as her salon lent charm
to Gautier's life, so her influence gently smoothed his professional
path. It is said that she had advised her husband to make him the literary
editor of *la Presse*. But among the contributors was Balzac: far less
amenable as journalist than he had been as host or guest; and Gautier
found diplomacy difficult. 'My lovely queen,' went his note to Mme de
Girardin,[2] 'if I'm to go on getting caught between Emile the anvil
and Balzac the hammer, I shall resign my office. I'd sooner plant
cabbages or rake the paths in your garden.' 'I have a very satisfactory
gardener, thank you,' answered Mme de Girardin. 'Go on keeping
order in the palace.'

She counted Gautier among her closest and most favoured friends, she treated him with tact, charm, affection; and in her presence, when he wrote to her, he showed his happiness: 'Madame, I regret I have an engagement today,' goes a letter in his hand, 'but I shall come this evening and be there when the fireworks are let off after dessert. Like the urchins on public holidays I shall go home with five or six rockets. At your feet.'

* * *

The poet who charmed Mme de Girardin had a strong and unsurprising fascination for women, and had already charmed them with effect. We do not know where he met Eugénie Fort: perhaps in literary circles, for she had certain literary pretensions, and could turn her hand to translation. We know little about her save that she came of good family, was passionate by nature and Spanish in appearance. But what more was needed to attract the partisan of *Hernani*, the future author of *Voyage en Espagne*? Eugénie grew wildly enamoured of his poetry and of himself; and Gautier, who wrote her *Déclaration* and *Après le bal*, who had made her the heroine of *Onuphrius* in *les Jeunes-France*,[3] grew enamoured of Eugénie:

> *Par un caprice poétique,*
> *Notre climat para*
> *D'une grâce au charme exotique*
> *Cette autre Petra Camara.*

> *De chaudes teintes orangées*
> *Dorent sa joue au fard vermeil;*
> *Ses paupières de jais frangées*
> *Filtrent des rayons de soleil.*

> *Entre ses lèvres d'écarlate*
> *Scintille un éclair argenté,*
> *Et sa beauté splendide éclate*
> *Comme une grenade en été.*

> *Au son des guitares d'Espagne*
> *Ma voix longtemps la célébra.*
> *Elle vint un jour, sans compagne,*
> *Et ma chambre fut l'Alhambra . . .*

On 27 November 1836 Eugénie gave birth to Théophile Gautier *fils*.
According to Arsène Houssaye,[4] that happy spinner of tales, her

brother promptly offered Gautier the alternatives of marriage to Eugénie or a duel. Gautier (so legend continues) replied that he would accept the lesser of the evils, chose Houssaye and Eugène Piot as his seconds, and went next morning, at daybreak, to the gardens of Saint-Ouen, near Montmartre. The duel began. Then he had a change of heart, and agreed to recognize his son.

And what of Eugénie? Houssaye records that Gautier 'tore up this chapter in his life'; Eugénie herself implies in her diary that she refused a proposal from this poet of inadequate means. Did Gautier ever propose to Eugénie? He says that he had oriental ideas about women: that he would have preferred to be faithful to several wives rather than deceive a wife with several mistresses. Perhaps he could not have borne the idea of final or exclusive commitments. Perhaps he continued to wait, like d'Albert in *Maupin*, for some impossible Romantic ideal. Whatever the truth, he might have been much happier had he married Eugénie now; and he often professed to regret that he had not done so.

Meanwhile, Eugénie forgave him for his misdeeds, brought up *le petit Fortunio*, and earned the lasting devotion of Gautier's two sisters, Lili and Zoé, who addressed her persistently as 'Madame Gautier'. And while she retired, for the moment, into the shadows of his life, Gautier himself fell under the spell of Victorine, 'a beautiful brown girl, crimson mouth and hellfire eyes.' She seems to have been a *grisette* with little but physical attractions. Fierce and unscrupulous, she remained his mistress until, in 1841, he fell in love with the unattainable Carlotta Grisi.

* * *

Théophile Gautier, this selfish, attractive Romantic, was sometimes seen in Paris in Egyptian costume ('one or two women, knowing I only knew Arabic, even declared that I was very fine').[5] This original journalist, this engaging conversationalist, would have been Balzac's chosen companion in Italy in the spring of 1837; but 'my disappointments began with the loss of my travelling companion', wrote the novelist to Mme Hanska on a rainy Florentine day.[6] 'Gautier was to share the expenses of the journey and write a serious sequel to his Belgian travels; but the need to do the exhibition and write accounts of all the wasted canvas at the Louvre, obliged him to stay at home. Italy is the loser, for he is the only man capable of saying something new about it and of understanding it; but next time I make the journey, he will come.'

And so Balzac consoled himself in Italy, while Gautier remained in Paris, assessing the influence of Ingres and Delacroix, the brilliant advance in landscape painting, the future of sculpture, 'that art so royal, so divine',[7] and waiting for the imminent publication of *Fortunio*.

Fortunio is written with something of the fire and vigour of *Mademoiselle de Maupin*; it is the story of an impeccably beautiful courtesan who kills herself for love of a flawlessly handsome, dazzling, and largely indifferent young man. Fortunio (like d'Albert in *Mademoiselle de Maupin*) has many characteristics of the young Gautier, many qualities that Gautier dreamed of possessing. Fortunio, in his early twenties, is nonchalant, yet suggests a hidden vivacity and strength. He looks more Spanish than French, more Arabian than Spanish, his complexion is sallow, his hair is black and long; his hands (and Gautier was proud of his hands) are of 'inimitable perfection'. He is a fine conversationalist, a man of the world, an irresistible lover, an admirable horseman, a youth of fabulous wealth who demolishes part of Paris to build his Eldorado, the golden glass-domed palace of his dreams. *Mademoiselle de Maupin* had been a hymn to beauty; *Fortunio* is a fitting sequel, a cantata in praise of wealth, the splendour that surrounds it and the splendour that it brings.

*   *   *

'The feeling for poetry is not so dead in France as certain critics say,' wrote Gautier happily in January 1838, on the revival of *Hernani*. 'Art is still loved; and we are not just reduced to the whipped cream of the Vaudeville.'[8]

On 10 February his words were put to the test: his new book of poetry, *la Comédie de la Mort*, was published by Désessart. 'What! Théophile Gautier a poet!' cried Mme de Girardin with feigned surprise.[9] 'This prince of mockers, this master of irony, this great iconoclast, is also a dreamer of cascades, a melancholy inhabitant of the floating kingdom of clouds! Gautier, the brilliant contributor to *la Presse*!' The astonishment recorded in the *Lettres parisiennes* was expressed, less kindly, in *l'Artiste*: 'Never [that journal declared] never did man have fewer pretensions to serious thought than M. Théophile Gautier. If, in his productions, you perceive an apparently moral or philosophical opinion, be well assured that, when you come closer, you will only find the strangest paradox sustained with sang-froid and ending in monstrous fancy . . . As soon as M. Théophile Gautier abandons the realm of thought, where he sees nothing but chaos, to concern himself exclusively with the transient sensations of each day, he writes with verve and magnificence. Every fine form and graceful image, everything bright and beautiful, shining and splendid, is found in his poetry . . .'[10]

La Comédie de la Mort is based on the Romantic theme of life in death and death in life: the poet, wandering about the cemetery, imagines the agony of the dead who have not died, who have discovered

the inconstancy of their lovers, the indifference of their relations, grown
bitterly aware of the world's forgetfulness. And then, returning to the
living world, the poet turns to those who suffer from *le néant invisible,*
from the inner, spiritual death that no one mourns and no one sees;
and in a final passage that touches a new height of poetry, he pleads with
death to spare him:

> *Je suis trop jeune encor, je veux aimer et vivre,*
> *O Mort! . . . et je ne puis me résoudre à te suivre*
>   *Dans le sombre chemin;*
> *Je n'ai pas eu le temps de bâtir la colonne*
> *Où la Gloire viendra suspendre ma couronne;*
>   *O Mort, reviens demain!*

> *Vierge aux beaux seins d'albâtre, épargne ton poète,*
> *Souviens-toi que c'est moi qui le premier t'ai faite*
>   *Plus belle que le jour;*
> *J'ai changé ton teint vert en pâleur diaphane,*
> *Sous de beaux cheveux noirs j'ai caché ton vieux crâne,*
>   *Et je t'ai fait la cour.*

> *Laisse-moi vivre encor, je dirai tes louanges;*
> *Pour orner tes palais, je sculpterai des anges,*
>   *Je forgerai des croix;*
> *Je ferai dans l'église et dans le cimetière*
> *Fondre le marbre en pleurs et se plaindre la pierre*
>   *Comme au tombeau des rois!*

> *Je te consacrerai mes chansons les plus belles:*
> *Pour toi j'aurai toujours des bouquets d'immortelles*
>   *Et des fleurs sans parfum.*
> *J'ai planté mon jardin, ô Mort, avec tes arbres;*
> *L'if, le buis, le cyprès, y croisent sur les marbres*
>   *Leurs rameaux d'un vert brun.*

> *J'ai dit aux belles fleurs, doux honneur du parterre,*
> *Au lis majestueux ouvrant son blanc cratère,*
>   *A la tulipe d'or,*
> *A la rose de mai que le rossignol aime,*
> *J'ai dit au dahlia, j'ai dit au chrysanthème,*
>   *A bien d'autres encor:*

> *Ne croissez pas ici! cherchez une autre terre,*
> *Frais amours du printemps; pour ce jardin austère*
> *Votre éclat est trop vif;*
> *Le houx vous blesserait de ses pointes aiguës,*
> *Et vous boiriez dans l'air le poison des ciguës,*
> *L'odeur âcre de l'if.*
>
> *Ne m'abandonne pas, ô ma mère, ô Nature,*
> *Tu dois une jeunesse à toute créature,*
> *A toute âme un amour;*
> *Je suis jeune, et je sens le froid de la vieillesse,*
> *Je ne puis rien aimer. Je veux une jeunesse,*
> *N'eût-elle qu'un seul jour! . . .*[11]

But death comes, unrelenting.

La Comédie de la Mort is technically far in advance of *Albertus*. Gautier has lost his stylistic self-consciousness, he is borne along by his theme; and he is already deeply troubled by doubts of the life to come. He is not only terrified (as he will always be) by the thought of physical decomposition, he is already profoundly saddened by the thought of spiritual death: the death which, to him, is far worse than the death of the body. He can only counsel, in the words of Faust, in the words that he himself will echo in *la Nue*, some thirty years later, '*Aimez! car tout est là!*' He believes in delighting in life. He would like to believe in a consolation after death, but he cannot; and he will never be able to accept the Catholic belief in the life to come. Gautier will always venerate all religions; he will constantly practise many of the Catholic virtues. And whatever his cynicism, it will always hide a Romantic thirst for the impossible, the longing implicit in *la Comédie de la Mort*: the longing to believe, the longing for Christian faith that is not satisfied.

*   *   *

And then there must be a footnote, for Gautier is not wholly portrayed in *Fortunio* and in his poetry. And in the turning pages of memoirs and correspondence he passes before us, like a shadow show, the author of *la Comédie de la Mort*, the wild, engaging Gautier of 1839: harassed by the authorities for failing to mount guard with the *garde nationale*,[12] dispatching his Abyssinian servant, Abdallah Pergialla, to collect his dues from his editors,[13] boosting Balzac, that literary Briareus, in *la Presse*,[14] and receiving from Balzac the dedication of *Une Princesse parisienne*.[15] He watches Mlle Grahn taking over *la Sylphide* from Mlle Elssler, and decides she has 'earned her place among the most brilliant hopes of the Opéra; her feet already speak French very well'.[16] He sends an urgent request to Girardin: 'Please give 100 francs or more to the bearer of this note, be kind enough to do what I ask for without money I should die of hunger in the tyrant's cells—I will settle the debt with quick and copious copy—come and see your unfortunate contributor under lock and key.'[17] And then, out of prison, there is a gay glimpse of him in the *salon* of the 'docte Uranie,' the Princess Belgiojoso:[18] passing through the 'veritable string of catafalques' in the rue d'Anjou-Saint-Honoré, the décor which would have done credit to the Théâtre de la Porte-Saint-Martin. A turbaned negro in a brocade skirt, out of Veronese, leads him to the Gothic oratory decorated with death's heads, then into the *salon* hung with silver-starred black velvet, where the princess lies receiving her guests. Pale as a risen corpse (her pallor carefully maintained) the 'nouvelle Julie' limply reclines on a sofa, a nargileh between her lips and a wreath of fuchsias about her brow, welcoming Gautier, Heine, Houssaye, and a multitude of artists and dandies, madrigals and compliments.

4. Don Teofilo

IN MARCH 1840, on the eve of the *Salon*, Gautier demanded a rise from *la Presse*. 'It is painful to discuss remuneration for intellectual work because I have to vaunt my abilities, but I cannot do this work for so little: I have always found the payment inadequate . . .'[1] The letter clearly, pathetically shows that Gautier lacked the toughness of the journalist. Girardin recognized the fact and underpaid him, while he considered him an imbecile for not selling his soul to the theatre managers and raising his income from 3,000 to 40,000 francs. It seems unlikely that Gautier was given the increase for which he asked; and within a week or two, as so often happened, he had found a means of expressing his feelings to his readers. The pretext was a performance of Vigny's *Chatterton*:

'. . . Poor Chatterton, it seemed hard indeed to work for your living, to sell your immaterial thoughts, to be driven on by a bookseller! You preferred to empty your phial of opium rather than finish your task uninspired. Today you would drink three cups of black coffee to have fever for want of inspiration, if you were a journalist like us, obliged to concern yourself always with the thoughts of others, obliged to follow their dreams and not your own, to improvise without rest, to write night and day, about everything, about nothing, with no time to study, to correct, obliged to sacrifice every morning what is dearest to man, literary self-respect . . . You are rich, you are loved, what more do you want? Egoist! When you died you did not think of Kitty Bell; when you burnt your poems, you did not think of posterity, that pale comforter of the great and misunderstood.'[2]

*   *   *

Some time that April, when the restlessness of the spring was upon him, Gautier remarked that he wanted to visit Spain. The stray remark, so he tells us, was taken for an intention, and soon his friends were asking when he would leave and expressing surprise to see him still in Paris. He did not need much persuasion to depart; for if spring fever drew him towards the Pyrenees, he also longed to break the chain of journalism, to refresh his mind, to make a voyage of discovery, to see for himself the inspiration of *Hernani* and some of *les Orientales*, to search for the Toledo swords of Romantic oratory. And this last motive, indeed, was more than metaphorical; for as Eugène Piot, his companion, pointed out, Spain was impoverished by the Carlist Wars and Spanish antiquities should be cheap to buy. On 5 May, bearing a primitive camera and high Romantic hopes, they left on the Bordeaux diligence on the first stage of their journey.

At last they came to the bridge of la Bidassoa, half in France and half in Spain; another few turns of the wheels, and Gautier might lose an illusion, see the flight of the Spain of his dreams, the Spain of the romancero, the Spain of the ballads of Victor Hugo, the Spain of the tales of Mérimée and the *contes* of Alfred de Musset. As he crossed the border he remembered the pleasant challenge of Heine: 'How will you talk about Spain once you have been there?'

*   *   *

On one side of the bridge stood a gendarme, grave and upright; on the other, a Spanish soldier lazed in the grass. Already the undulating roofs, the whitewashed walls of Irun had a touch of the Moorish about them; the horses were unharnessed and replaced by mules. A *zagal* in pointed cap with velvet stripes came to look after the carriage, and two *escopeteros* sat on the box to scare the bandits. Then off they galloped, while beggar children tossed flowers and wild strawberries into the carriage.

At sunset next day the exotic procession entered Vittoria. Gautier shuffled off the lethargy of Paris like a chrysalis, and flew from customs to church, from church to supper, from supper to a theatre to see a *baile nacional*. A few hours later they set off for Burgos, where the magnificence of the cathedral filled him with despair: 'Utter sadness falls upon me when I visit one of these prodigious buildings of the past,' he was to write. 'A vast discouragement takes hold. And all I want is to retire into a corner, set a stone beneath my head, and await, in the immobility of contemplation, the final immobility of death. Why labour, why bestir oneself? The most violent human effort will never excel it . . . When I think that I've spent the best part of my life rhyming ten or twelve thousand lines, writing six or seven poor volumes in 8vo, and three or four hundred bad newspaper articles, I am ashamed of myself and of my times.'

They left Burgos in 'a fantastic coffer with all sorts of queer-shaped windows, and furnished inside with little satin-covered cushions which might have been pink once upon a time . . . This respectable carriage was trustingly slung on ropes, and tied together in dangerous places with esparto cords'. They drove off as if the devil followed and, sure enough, as Gautier revolved some hemistich in his mind, they came to sudden grief. Pink cushions covered the road, the mules had vanished, and in an even more dubious vehicle they sped on to Valladolid to watch a Spanish translation of *Hernani*. Doña Sol, noted Gautier, 'was almost as *young* as Mlle Mars, and lacked her talent'.

The acidity of the remark belied his mood: free of journalism, of the petty cares of daily existence, he was not merely happy but exalted; and on the way to Madrid, when they were forced to dismount and follow the carriage on foot across the mountains, he was drunk with the pure, sharp air: 'I felt so lighthearted, so joyful, so full of enthusiasm, that I cried aloud and capered about like a young goat; I wanted to throw myself head first into all these charming chasms, so azured, so vaporous, so velvet; I should have liked to roll in cascades, bathe in every stream, take a leaf from every pine, wallow in sparkling snow, mingle with all this nature, and melt like an atom in this immensity.' The high peaks glinted and seethed with light like dancers' skirts in their rain of silver spangles; at times it was hard to know where mountain ended and heaven began. And sometimes they met Valencians, as brown as Florentine bronze, leading convoys of mules bedecked with bells and fringes and striped coverings. Then they descended the mountains, crossed a dry and desolate landscape, entered Madrid, settled in *la fonda de la Amistad*, and sent the servant for tickets for the next bullfight.

*　　　*　　　*

As he waited for the bull to burst into the huge arena on that sunlit summer day in 1840, Gautier experienced one of the strongest emotions he had known. The colour and savagery, the skill, the audacity of the *corrida* swept him into a Romantic heaven, so impressed him that in later life he would wait five hours in Mediterranean heat for a fight,

or ride thirty leagues to see Montès wield his sword. Of all the myriad
spectacles he had witnessed in Paris and was to witness in many parts
of the world, none so excited him, none so possessed him.

And Gautier's impressions of Spain show a gaiety and *entrain* that
none of his later travel books recaptures. He was twenty-eight, free and
vigorous, the full weight of journalism, of deception and unhappiness,
had not yet fallen upon him, he was not yet suffering from debts and
persistent creditors. In Spain, in this summer and autumn of 1840, he
recaptured some of the joyousness of the Impasse du Doyenné. He
was only to know it once more in his life.

Night after night he wandered down the Prado at Madrid, admiring
the women with their heart-shaped mouths, like so many Regency
portraits, and looking (amateur of the picturesque) for a *manola*, one
of a vanished race; and 'once, as I crossed the Rastro quarter of
Madrid, I found myself in a tiny deserted alley; and there, for the first
and last time, I saw the *manola* I wanted. She was a big strapping girl
of about twenty-four, with a swarthy complexion, a sad and steady
gaze, a rather full mouth, and something indefinably African in her
face. An enormous tress of hair, so black that it was blue, was swathed
round her head and held up by an elaborate comb; bunches of coral
hung from her ears and round her sunburnt neck; a red fan trembled
like a cinnabar butterfly in fingers that were weighted with silver rings.
Then the last of the *manolas* turned the corner of the alley and disappeared from my astonished gaze. I had this once, in the real and living
world, seen a dress of Duponchel's, a costume from the Opéra!' The
Madrid of 1840 is caught in the amber of *Voyage en Espagne*: the water-
sellers bearing sunburnt barrels on their backs, the fire-sellers, with their
cry of *fuego, fuego*, offering lights for cigarettes and Havana cigars, the
cafés where the visitor regales himself with almond drinks and *spumas*;
and, late at night, when the city is otherwise silent, the choirs of chirp-
ing crickets hung in cages outside the windows.

And vivid, too, in its contrast, is Gautier's impression of the Escurial:
huge, bleak and terrible. In the chapel of the Escurial he felt so downcast, so crushed, so firmly in the hold of some inflexible, unseen power,
that prayer seemed useless. When he climbed to the palace roof, he
felt he stood on some monument of the Pharaohs; when he paced the
corridors, he moved in some architectural nightmare. 'I advise those
who have the fatuity to believe themselves depressed to go and spend
three or four days at the Escurial; there [he wrote] they will learn the
real meaning of spleen, and all the rest of their lives they will enjoy
the thought that they might be in the Escurial and they're not.'

When Madrid had been exhausted, he and Piot left for Toledo, 'the

town of fine swords and Romantic daggers'; and from the top of the
ruined Alcazar, which seemed to realize Piranesi's dream, Gautier
admired the sunset. He bathed in the Tagus, explored the cathedral
conscientiously to fulfil his 'humble mission of literary daguerreotype',
and returned to Madrid to catch the diligence for Granada.

*   *   *

Granada brought some of the highlights in his Spanish travels:
some, indeed, of the most enchanting moments in his life. The Alameda
was to him one of the most pleasant places in the world, with its fountains, its vast flowerbed filled with myrtle, roses and jasmine, its evening
procession of young women in mantillas, wearing flowers in their hair
and satin shoes on their feet; and

'a spectacle which the northern peoples cannot conceive is the Alameda
at Granada at sunset: the Sierra Nevada takes on unimaginable tones.
All the steeps, the summits struck by light, turn roseate: a dazzling
rose, ideal, fabulous, glazed with silver, shot with purple and reflections
of opal, that would make the clearest colours on the palette seem muddy;
tones of mother-of-pearl, transparencies of ruby, veins of agate and
aventurine to defy all the fairy jewellery of the *Arabian Nights*. The
valleys, the crevices, the roughnesses, all the places beyond the reach
of the setting sun, are of a blue to vie with the azure of sky and sea, of
lapis-lazuli and sapphire; this contrast between the light and shade is
prodigious in its effect: the mountain seems to have clad itself in a
measureless robe of shot silk, spangled and ribbed with silver; little by
little the splendid tones dissolve and melt into violet half-tints, the
shadow invades the lower ridges, the light withdraws towards the
summits, and when all the plain has long been in obscurity, the silver
diadem of the Sierra still sparkles in the serenity of heaven beneath the
kiss of farewell of the sun.'

For the Alhambra itself Gautier conceived a passion; and a kind
authority allowed him to live there for four days and four nights which,
he said later, were the finest he had known. In the huge, marble-
pillared Court of Lions he made his home, with two mattresses, a
copper lamp, an earthenware jar and a few bottles of Jerez wine which
he left to cool in the fountain. It was in this fountain that the thirty-six
members of the Abencerrage family had been decapitated by their rivals,
and tradition said that the red stains at the bottom were not rust.
Apprehensively he watched the moonbeams on the water; and once
he woke abruptly from his sleep, and reflected: 'The hour will come

when you will be lying down as you are now, and you will rise no more.'
One can understand that he found the real charm of the Generalife in
its gardens and their fountains.

And in the midst of one of these fountains bloomed an immense
oleander of incomparable brilliance, 'like an explosion of flowers, the
bouquet of a floral firework; with a splendid and vigorous freshness,
almost clamorous, if the word may be used of colours, enough to make
the reddest rose seem pale. Its fine flowers burst with all the ardour of
desire towards the pure light of heaven; its noble leaves, formed expressly by nature to crown the glorious, washed by the drizzle of the
water-jets, sparkled like emeralds in the sun. Nothing has ever given
me a more lively feeling of beauty.'

> *Dans le Généralife, il est un laurier-rose,*
> *Gai comme la victoire, heureux comme l'amour.*
> *Un jet d'eau, son voisin, l'enrichit et l'arrose;*
> *Une perle reluit dans chaque fleur éclose,*
> *Et le frais émail vert se rit des feux du jour.*
>
> *Il rougit dans l'azur comme une jeune fille;*
> *Ses fleurs, qui semblent vivre, ont des teintes de chair.*
> *On dirait, à le voir sous l'onde qui scintille,*
> *Une odalisque nue attendant qu'on l'habille,*
> *Cheveux en pleurs, au bord du bassin au flot clair.*
>
> *Ce laurier, je l'aimais d'une amour sans pareille;*
> *Chaque soir, près de lui, j'allais me reposer;*
> *A l'une de ses fleurs, bouche humide et vermeille,*
> *Je suspendais ma lèvre, et parfois, ô merveille!*
> *J'ai cru sentir la fleur me rendre mon baiser ...*[3]

* * *

Invigorated by such beauty, by his Spanish happiness, Gautier
climbed the Mulhacen, wrote a poem near the summit, and set off for
Malaga, where the new arena was to be inaugurated and Montès de
Chiclana, the most brilliant of matadors, was himself to perform. To
leave Spain without seeing Montès was as uncivilized as to leave Paris
without seeing Rachel; and on a torrid day when an excited rumour
hung about the town like a haze of sound, he made his way through the
narrow streets of Malaga. 'Oh singers with golden voices, dancers with
fairy feet, actors of every kind, emperors and poets, you who imagine
you have roused enthusiasm, you have not heard them applauding

Montès!' That evening he went to a theatre: they were performing
Lope de Vega to a deserted auditorium.

It was through Cordova and Seville (whose cathedral seemed to him
like a hollow mountain) that Gautier, with Piot, made his way home
towards France. It was from Cadiz that he sailed round the Spanish
coast. It was at Port-Vendres that he set foot again on French soil.
Spain had given him inspiration for a book of poems, *España*, for one
of his happiest travel books, *Voyage en Espagne*; he would write them,
as he would write so much besides, with a quill fallen from an eagle
one white and azure day on the Sierra Nevada.[4] And if he confessed
that 'people who go to Spain to buy curiosities are very disappointed'
he had discovered something as durable as any Toledo sword: Spain
was one of his spiritual homes. 'Nor Italy, nor Africa, nor Asia, nor
Greece, for all their marvels, ever excited in us the nostalgic regret
that makes the cachucha a sort of *Ranz des vaches* unbearable to
hear.'[5]

5. *Giselle* and *la Péri*

'MY DEAR HENRI HEINE,

'A week or two ago, as I was turning over the pages of your fine book
l'Allemagne, I came across a charming passage—one only needs to open
the book to do so—it's the part where you speak of the elves in white
tunics whose hem is ever damp, of the water sprites who show their tiny
satin feet on the ceiling of the bridal chamber, of wilis the colour of snow,
with their unrelenting waltz, and of all those delightful apparitions you
have met in the Hartz and on the shore of the Ilse, in the velvet mist
of a Teutonic moonlight; and I could not help exclaiming: "What a
ballet it would make" In a fit of enthusiasm, I even picked up a large
sheet of white paper and wrote at the top, in an admirable, careful
hand: LES WILIS, *ballet*. Then I began to laugh and threw the paper
away without more ado, telling myself that this vaporous, nocturnal
poetry, this voluptuously sinister phantasmagoria, all these legends and
ballads so foreign to our customs, could not possibly be translated into
theatre. That evening, at the end of a corridor at the Opéra, while my
head was still bursting with your idea, I met the gifted man who brought
into ballet all the fantasy and caprice of *le Diable amoureux* (and much
of his own, besides): all the fantasy and caprice of Cazotte, the great
poet who discovered Hoffmann in the middle of the eighteenth century,

in mid Encyclopædia. I told him the legend of the wilis. Three days later the ballet *Giselle* was written and accepted. At the end of the week, Adolphe Adam had composed the music, the scenery was almost finished, and rehearsals were in full swing.'[1]

Giselle was first performed at the Opéra on 28 June 1841, and the public, 'who still regretted Taglioni and still counted on the return of Elssler, *la sylphide* and *la cachucha* incarnate, were consoled in an evening and no longer envied St. Petersburg or America. A dancer had been revealed'.

Carlotta Grisi had already appeared in *la Favorite* and *Zingaro*, but she was indeed revealed to the world this night, in the ballet that Théophile Gautier had written; and through his lorgnette, this summer evening, he watched the first performance of the most popular of all his works, the greatest triumph of the 'blonde Italian with forget-me-not eyes', of Carlotta, whose feet 'would be the despair of an Andalusian *maja*, who could wear Cinderella's slippers over her ballet shoes. Her legs are slender, elegant, responsive, the legs of Diana the huntress, they would follow the anxious deer with ease through the thickets . . . We could give no better idea of her complexion than by comparing it with the softest rice-paper from China or the inner petals of a camellia just in flower. . . .'

Gautier's adoration for Carlotta is evident from this moment. His original tepid interest has turned to passionate admiration: 'When from time to time the tip of her little white foot skims the ground,' he wrote of her Beatrix in *la Jolie Fille de Gand*, 'you know that it is entirely out of kindness, not to cause too much despair to those who have no wings. . . . Never did pearl more divine fall from the necklace of heaven upon the common earth.'[2] He noticed every detail of her appearance: her tunic starred with silver, when she appeared as Diana, the crescent of jewels in her hair, the quiver slung from her shoulder. Whether she were convalescing from cholera or posing for a statuette, whether she were touring the provinces or touring abroad, he cast his rain of flowers at her feet. Countless appreciations and asides scattered throughout his criticism reflect the love that shines from his ballets and his poems, from *Spirite* and from his letters: the love that, as he told her, a quarter of a century after *Giselle* had been born, was 'the true, the only love of my heart'.

And when, in so many of his works to come, he wrote of a passion ideal, impossible, the love of a statue, a spirit, a woman far removed in place and time, the Romantic love of the unattainable, it was not only the Romantic love of *Mademoiselle de Maupin*: it seemed a reflection, now, of his own predicament. Carlotta had married Jules Perrot, her master and partner: it was for her a marriage of pure convenience. But when in time she chose a lover, bore his child, accepted his villa on the shores of Lake Geneva, she chose a Polish nobleman, Prince Radziwill. To Gautier she was the statue that never came to life; and she rewarded her Pygmalion for his devotion, for ballets, poems, novel, for creating her career, with that bitter consolation: lasting affection.

'I sometimes spoke, quite alone, under the chestnut trees, with the Lady of the Violet Eyes,' wrote one who had known her, at the end of the century, when Carlotta Grisi had died.[3] 'We spoke of the master in whom she had inspired a love so profound that it dominates his work and drew his last sigh from him. We talked of him in low voices, as if in a ruined chapel, and she was flattered that she had been the object of his passion, but less flattered than astonished. . . . No one, indeed, had a less romantic soul than Giselle, the Wili of the Hartz imagined by two poets and realized by a little Balzacian bourgeoise of the Maison du Chat-qui-pelote. What touched her most was the memory of the works he had written, not about her, but for her, the works that had brought her the finest triumphs of her career. For the rest, she was only coy and modest about an over-zealous friend who had mistaken his altar. . . . And I saw how unreliable it is, the axiom that all women are aware of the love that they inspire.'

*   *   *

One night in January 1842, at the Porte-Saint-Martin, Théophile Gautier, greatly astonished and slightly apprehensive, saw, on stage, a vaudeville vision of the twentieth century. 'On all sides the houses rise in Babylonian magnificence . . . At night the beacons of sideral gas shed a blue light throughout the town, a light as brilliant as that of the sun . . . There are women lawyers, women artists, women writers . . . Steam tilburies are passing in all directions . . . A trumpet sounds, the omnibus for China's about to leave . . .'[4] And then, in the way of the world, something that might have seemed equally impossible to the partisan of *Hernani*, the author of *Mademoiselle de Maupin* and *Fortunio*, happened in real life to Théophile Gautier. The previous year he had been appointed secretary to the commission for Napoleon's monument: a commission which included Ingres, David, and an imposing array of officials from the Beaux-Arts.[5] Now, on 16 January, over his signature, the commission published its report. On 17 January 'M. Théophile Gautier, *homme de lettres*', became Chevalier de la Légion d'honneur.[6]

It was the beginning of respectability: the beginning, it seemed, of a slightly more conventional career. And yet (one records the story with a certain pleasure) it was far from marking complete reform. It is said

D

that when the official called to pin on the decoration, he found M. Théophile Gautier, *homme de lettres*, swathed in gay but amorphous drapery (perhaps his old Egyptian costume) with no lapels.

*   *   *

Constantly, in his dress, in his work, and in his travels, Gautier escaped from nineteenth-century Paris. One morning this March, having spent the night at a fancy-dress ball, he tore off his caftan and daggers (so he tells us) and determined to cure his hangover by a visit, his first visit, to London. It might be more accurate to say that he departed to help stage *Giselle* for Carlotta at Her Majesty's Theatre.

He crossed from Boulogne on the *Harlequin*; after two or three hours, 'a white line rose from the sea like a cloud: the coast of Albion, on which the vaudeville-writers have written so many couplets'. The *Harlequin* puffed past the well-groomed Kentish landscape into the Thames Estuary, where the cosmopolitan multitude of sunlit boats, crossing and passing 'with orderly confusion', appeared 'the most prodigious spectacle that human eye could see'. The East India Docks were, Gautier thought, 'enormous, gigantic, fabulous, exceeding human proportions', the forest of rigging would have shamed the virgin forests of America, and by the time he disembarked he had decided that water was the Englishman's native home.

Next morning he set off to explore the city: observing the soot-dark statues, the Duke of York like a negro on his pillar, George III, an equestrian chimney-sweep. He noticed 'gin-temples,' drunken beggars sadder than Goya's *Caprices*, the sentimental pictures and pungent caricatures of royalty in the printsellers' windows, the hoardings in Trafalgar Square where Nelson's Column would rise. He admired the policemen with batons and numbered top-hats, he studied the birds on the lake in St. James's Park, he noted his impressions of Her Majesty's Theatre, sharp, bright, naïve as a Victorian print. The audience seemed like illustrations in keepsakes: 'Here indeed are the long-lashed eyes, their gaze sunk in the distance, the spirals of fair hair caressing the white shoulders, and the white breasts generously displayed.'

And then, for the first time in London, the curtain rose on *Giselle*, 'the ballet which [remembered *The Times*] created such a sensation at Paris . . . Carlotta Grisi is the heroine, and very beautifully does she give the character of Giselle . . . Poor Perrot had hurt his leg, and posted notices to that effect about the theatre, but he sprang about with his usual rapidity as the Duke, and his apology seemed altogether superfluous.'[7] So, too, thought the new manager of Her Majesty's Theatre, Mr. Benjamin Lumley: 'The charming ballet *Giselle*, with the truly captivating music of Adolphe Adam, was admitted [he recalled] to be vastly pretty. The production may be regarded as the main element of attraction on the opening of my first season.'[8]

Gautier returned to France with the confirmation of his greatest theatrical success. He took away, too, a lively first impression of London that was not to be altered on his later visits. He might indulge in the expected quips about weather, food and clothes, yet 'despite these criticisms of detail, the general appearance of London has something that astonishes and almost stupefies. London [he wrote] is very certainly a capital in the sense in which civilization understands the word'.

*   *   *

The new year, 1843, opened with Rachel's first performance in the part that was to be her supreme achievement. Even Gautier, with his Romantic disapproval of Racine, was spellbound by her classical beauty, her passionate Greek interpretation of Phèdre. The year was indeed to be memorable in the theatre: in March came the ponderous, unmanageable Hugolian drama which spelt the failure of the Romantic theatre.

But if Romantic drama had ended in laughter (in les Hures at the Palais-Royal and les Buses graves at the Variétés), Gautier's own dramatic ventures were flourishing. January brought the announcement of a new ballet 'attributed to an author for whom we have the greatest respect, an author whom we would not venture to criticize in the least, as he happens to be none other than ourselves. According to well-informed people, the subject of this choreographical work is taken from Oriental legend'.[9] In an open letter to Gérard de Nerval, the greatly respected author was more explicit:

'I should so have liked to join you in Cairo, as I'd promised, but as I couldn't follow you, I've made my own Orient at the Académie royale de musique et de danse . . . I am a Turk, myself, not from Constantinople but from Egypt. It seems to me that I've lived in the East; and when I disguise myself in the carnival with a caftan and a tarbouch I feel I am wearing my real clothes again. I have always been surprised not to understand Arabic fluently. I must have forgotten it.

'It was with this Oriental preoccupation, one grey, rainy day when the wind was keen, that I began something like a little Turkish or Persian poem; and I had already written twenty lines, when the judicious idea fell from heaven that if I wrote any more, no one would ever read them. Poetry is the language of the gods, and gods alone read it, to the great despair of publishers. So I threw the stanzas into the waste-paper basket, and, taking a sheet of paper, I entrusted my subject to the feet which, out of four lines of Heine, created the last act of *Giselle*.'[10]

The result was *la Péri*. It was first performed at the Opéra on 17 July 1843, with 'immense success'. 'We should be very tempted to attack the critic of *la Presse* for abandoning the literary tourney to limit himself to ballets [said *la France littéraire*]. But how could we not forgive the author of *Giselle* and *la Péri*? This new ballet touches perfection.'

La Péri is a development of d'Albert's quest for ideal beauty in *Mademoiselle de Maupin*. It also strangely anticipates *Spirite*, the novel that Gautier would write twenty-two years later: it has the same theme of the love of mortal and spirit. And in the ballet as in the novel, one seems to see the author himself: the youth who has exhausted temporal pleasures and, 'like all great voluptuaries, fallen in love with the impossible'.

But all symbolism was forgotten in Carlotta's dancing; however charming the Oriental *péris* might be with their gold-striped trousers and jewelled bodices, their parrots' wings, their black-tinted eyelids and scarlet hands, they could hardly, Gautier considered, be lovelier than she. And when she floated from the cloud-tops into her lover's arms, as light as a dove's feather: 'What marvellous dancing! You would think her a rose-leaf borne on the wind.' Nine columns he filled with adulation: 'If my name were not on the posters,' he ended simply, 'what praises I should sing of this enchanting Carlotta!'

*   *   *

And within a few weeks came another dramatic success. *Un Voyage en Espagne*, a three-act vaudeville by Théophile Gautier and Paul Siraudin, was first performed at the Variétés on 21 September. This crazy series of abortive love-affairs, arrests, capture by brigands and involvement in the Carlist Wars scored a notable success. 'My dear Théophile [wrote Roqueplan, director of the Variétés], you have allowed all your fancies to disport themselves, and the people who constantly ask for novelty ought to show me some gratitude for recruiting you as a writer of vaudevilles.'[11]

Un Voyage en Espagne brought Gautier more than a tribute from Roqueplan: it brought him the favours of one of the most endearing courtesans of the time: Julie-Justine Pilloy, better known as Alice Ozy. She had a small part in the vaudeville and was much afraid that it would be taken from her. Someone advised her to see Gautier, and Gautier invited her to dinner. It was that evening (so it is said)[12] that she inspired the quatrain:

Pentélique, Paros, marbres neigeux de Grèce,
Dont Praxitèle a fait la chair de ses Vénus,
Vos blancheurs suffisaient à des corps de déesse.
Noircissez, car Alice a montré ses seins nus![13]

Henceforward it was Alice who sat in the critic's box when she was not admired on the stage. It was Alice, some ten years later, who reserved the privilege of taking his arm and pricked the jealousy of Marie Mattei; it was Alice who wrote to Gautier: 'Give me a part at the Vaudeville, and I will refuse you nothing.' Their relationship, more or less amorous, lasted the rest of his days.

*   *   *

Yet Alice Ozy remained of comparative insignificance in Gautier's life. 'The invention of Apollo surrounded by the nine Muses is a symbol realized by every poet today, married or not,' wrote Arsène Houssaye, with a certain justice. 'While Mme de Lamartine paints water-colours, Lamartine might count up the *belles mondaines* among his followers. Victor Hugo has just been noticed with his third Muse. Alfred de Musset is in love with a princess, a woman of the world and a female novelist, not to mention Mme Mimi Pinson . . . Théophile Gautier is in love with the three Grisis.'[14]

Gautier's admiration of the beauty of Julia Grisi shines from the Preface of *Mademoiselle de Maupin* and the lines of *la Diva*. Gautier's adoration of Carlotta, the presiding, unattainable divinity, is evident in his writing from *Giselle* to *Spirite*, in a multitude of letters, in reviews; in the record, in later years, of his constant pilgrimages to the Villa Grisi-sur-Saint-Jean. But it was neither la Diva nor Giselle who was to dominate his daily existence for the next twenty years: it was the sister of Giselle, Ernesta Grisi.

Her fine Italian profile remains on a medallion; sallow and large-eyed, seductive, a blossom-wreath on her dark hair, she watches posterity from Riesener's portrait. Was it her likeness to Carlotta that first drew Gautier? Was it her passionate contralto as she sang at the Théâtre-Italien? Was Gautier drawn to her purely by physical attraction? All these reasons may help to explain why, by 1844,[15] he had become the lover of this fiery singer: of this capable housewife who took him in her charge as his mother had taken charge of a spoilt child. But probably the strongest influence was Ernesta's comforting and practical nature. Gautier, impractical and often weak, needed a firm maternal hand to guide him. Ernesta was, above all, motherly; she knitted his socks and scarves, she mended his clothes, she served him his favourite *risotto à la Milanaise* and *risotto à la Bisque*. She gave him the old domestic security, the pampering he had known as a boy. She was not merely attractive; unlike Eugénie Fort, she had a strong will and made herself domestically essential.   That was why the liaison was marriage in all but name, and lasted for two decades.

*   *   *

Whatever Gautier's triumphs with Alice Ozy, his future successes with Ernesta Grisi, the year of *la Péri*, of *Un Voyage en Espagne*, was to bring him dramatic triumph in full measure, not only at home, but abroad. On 30 September 1843 the Theatre Royal, Drury Lane, opened for the season with the opera *The Siege of Rochelle*, 'after which [first time in this country] the ballet of *The Péri*'.[16] It was another international success for Gautier and Carlotta. The ballet (recorded *The Times*) 'was just as successful as the opera had been unlucky. We never saw an audience so completely turned round from an ill-humour to a state of perfect delight.'[17] The applause was 'a perfect storm that has rarely been equalled', *la Péri* earned the tribute of parody, as in Paris, and the audience at the St James's Theatre were soon applauding the Castelli children in a new ballet, *le Rêve de Pygmalion*, 'emulating the celebrated leap: both Mlle Eliza and Mlle Rosette leaping from a raised platform at the back of the stage into the arms of the Pygmalion'.[18] And, as if this were not enough, the Princess's Theatre opened with a revival of that 'grand ballet entitled *Giselle, or The Wilis*.'[19] It was 'very beautifully put on the stage, and Gilbert and Miss Ballin were the Duke and Giselle, and danced to the loudest applause'.[20]

It was small wonder that Gautier was tempted again across the Channel. It was from 48, Haymarket that he wrote, on 7 November, to Noël Parfait, asking him to confirm Carlotta's triumph in *la Presse*.

6. *Hernani* and Others

AS THE YEAR 1843 drew to its close, Théophile Gautier found himself renowned as the author of a vaudeville and of two much applauded ballets, one of them a classic. He was also well established as the dramatic critic of *la Presse*.   And while he sits happily in the Theatre Royal, Drury Lane, observing his international success, posterity may perhaps turn aside for a moment and consider his dramatic criticism.

And since posterity may see his future as well as his past, it may recall his comment in 1856 that his greatest pleasure, after that of seeing, had been to transpose visual art into literature. Such a transposition (naturally enough, for a pupil of Rioult) was among his chief purposes as a critic of the theatre; and his clearest statement of this purpose may be found in his article on Mlle Georges' benefit perform-ance in 1849, when he was led to reflect on the transience of the actor's art:

'[Dramatic criticism] must become a kind of theatrical daguerreotype recording every pose and aspect of the actor; a sentence even more responsive than the thin silver plate covered with iodine should repro-duce the vocal inflexions, the facial expressions, the poses, gestures, the walking, attitudinizing, coming in and going out, the standing and the sitting, of all great actors . . . All their parts should be preserved like this, their every sound recorded with the religious care of a master's score!' [1]

This idea of the critic's purpose was inspired by the wish to immor-talize that would inspire the poet of *l'Art*. And poetic feeling also inspired Gautier's conception of the theatre itself:

'The theatre is the focal point of modern civilization; there, then, we must bring together every comfort, richness and splendour, make it a joyous and resplendent centre where the spirit may forget the sadness of existence, where the body may rest from its fatigues in the satisfac-tions of well-being and lend to thought the sympathetic attention that masterpieces need. As soon as you cross the threshold of this magic world animated by the creations of the poets, a fresh, warm atmosphere should envelop you like a caress and dispose you to ideal life . . . Nothing is too rare, nothing is too sumptuous for the sanctuary of the Idea.' [2]

The serious theatre remained, to Gautier, throughout his career, the sanctuary of the Idea, the temple where one might practise the religion of beauty and live the life of the ideal.

*   *   *

Gautier's lofty conception of the theatre, his profession of the religion of beauty, is seen in many forms in his dramatic criticism. It is seen, in the first place, in his preoccupation with appearance: to Gautier, since every element in the theatre was a potential expression of beauty, a play must be physically beautiful. This 'passionate and intelligent love of beauty' [3] is evident from his earliest memories of the stage, his first articles on the theatre, nor can we be surprised to find such a 'sculptor's temperament' in an artist turned critic. It is significant that his earliest recollection of the theatre should have been a vividly detailed remem-brance of Talma's costume. [4] Even before he wrote for *la Presse*, he considered an actor's appearance an integral and important part of a play, and insisted that it was as liable to criticism as language, plot or

performance. We find the same concern with appearance throughout
Gautier's criticism. He deplores shabby scenery,[5] he feels that the
money lavished on salaries would be better spent on production.[6] He
decides that 'after all, the only purpose of dancing is to show lovely
figures in graceful positions and to develop lines that please the eye;
it is a silent rhythm, a visible music'.[7] He rebukes Julia Grisi for dis-
torting her face as she sings;[8] and, describing the return of Cornélie
Falcon to the Parisian stage, he audaciously reasserts the supreme
importance of appearance: 'Her beauty has been preserved, what does
her voice matter?'[9]

Such concern with physique degenerates at times into a *boutade*, and
when Gautier blandly writes of the matador: 'An elegant death is an
important part of the art,'[10] one feels that he is writing for effect. None
the less, this interest in appearance inspires some of his most valuable
criticism, some of the criticism on which he himself set much store,
and we owe to it his brilliant likenesses of contemporaries. Constantly
the critic practises his creed and draws his dramatic criticism towards
the visual art which he has abandoned. Constantly he takes coloured
photographs of the theatre. Henri Monnier, Frédérick Lemaître,
Marie Dorval are three-dimensional, living figures recalling his belief
in the 'theatrical daguerreotype'; his vibrant likenesses of Rachel remain
the most convincing, most beautiful portraits of her that we possess;
and the grandiose, pathetic bulk of the ageing Mlle Georges rises from
his pages, recalled with the power of an artist and a poet.'[11]

Yet Gautier's concern with appearance produced much more than
superlative verbal photographs, possessed even more than aesthetic
implications, showed even more than his lasting search, as poet and as
artist, for beauty. It emphasized his dislike of the social trends of the
time. If beauty were 'the first talent of a woman,'[12] distinctive appearance also asserted the significance of the individual in an age when men
were reduced to uniformity. Throughout his career, Gautier justly
proclaimed the supreme importance of the individual; for individuality
was, to him, one of the signs by which the artist distinguished himself
from the bourgeois. And distinctive appearance, like style in painting
or writing, was not only the artist's hallmark but his duty.

Just as the appearance of Liszt and Ingres proclaimed the distinction
of the artist, setting him apart from a uniform bourgeois world,[13] so a
brilliant theatre represented a challenge to the dull uniformity, the
democratic levelling of the reign of Louis-Philippe; and Gautier believed that those who dressed splendidly, like those who paraded their
wealth, did a service to those who dressed in sombre clothes. The
historical figures at the Cirque-Olympique in the early 1840's sym-

bolized, to him, the brightly coloured ideal in the face of dreary reality;[14] and it was something of the same far-away, unreal brilliance that, understandably, he admired in the multi-coloured historical dramas of Dumas *père*.[15]

A poet and artist himself, Gautier naturally deplored in his country-men what seemed a prosaic nature, a lack of artistic sense: their inability to content themselves with the 'plastic forms of poetry, painting, music and dancing. They also demand a meaning and a moral', he complained. 'Few of us look at a picture, read a book, listen to a tune for the beauty of the colours, the language, or the sounds: in short, for its personal charm. This is at once our failing and our merit.'[16] It was this demand for moral and meaning that so sharply distinguished the French in general from Gautier himself, that made it difficult for them to enjoy art for its own sake. It was this rationalism, he recognized, that had led them to produce a rational dramatic literature and occasionally made them unjust to such purely artistic entertainments as the ballet. For such unfortunate rationalism he himself made amends in some of his most heartfelt articles. The critic who had stood at an easel in Rioult's studio enjoyed the ballet for its plastic qualities: saw it, above all else, as the visible realization of a dream: 'It is the ideal made palpable,' wrote the author of *Giselle*. 'It is love translated into pictures, rhythmic grace, harmony condensed into figures, music carried from sound into sight. It is a wordless hymn to the rotation of the spheres and to the movement of the worlds . . . One could not spend too much care on the accomplishment of so difficult, so highly responsible a task.'[17] And Gautier could not spend too much affection and care on his articles on ballet. They are some of his finest transpositions of art. Carlotta Grisi takes pride of place, but Taglioni, Elssler, Grahn and Cerrito dance in and out of his reviews: individual, charming, and visually convincing.

*   *   *

If Gautier considered the actor's appearance as an integral part of a play, he also insisted, frequently, on the importance of décor. He be-lieved, and with reason, that décor was not only the background of the picture that poet and artist painted, a factor in the all-embracing art of the theatre, but an art in its own right.[18] And he went further, treating the scenic art with a new seriousness: the seriousness, again, of one who remained an artist himself. Repeatedly he declared that décors were often superior to pictures,[19] and pointed out, too, the erudi-tion and versatility necessary to the scene-designer. Just as he deter-mined to record the transient art of the actor, so he determined to leave a just and permanent record of the passing art of scenic design.[20]

Throughout his dramatic criticism he described and criticized décors with the diligence of an artist bent on perfection; and he did not merely pass strictures on inaccurate scenery[21] and anachronistic costume,[22] but even on incorrect wine-glasses in a drinking-scene.[23] And since perfect production demanded practicability as well as aesthetic pleasure and accuracy, he emphasized, often, the need for scenic reform, and fought the stubborn conservatism of scene-designers with his own enlightened good sense.[24]

Nor was it only the appearance of actor and of décor, the practical demands of scenery, that he considered his province. His interest in the visual aspects of the theatre extended, naturally enough, to theatrical design. The physical discomfort of the spectator was a theme to which the critic often returned. He was quick to see external influences on the development of the theatre, and, as Haussmann's Paris rose over the old city, Gautier urged the theatre to keep pace with civic improvements, and asked for a generous use of space and money.[25] In his travel books he minutely described theatres, inside and out; in the articles sent from London in 1849 he recorded, photographically, the appearance of Her Majesty's Theatre and of Covent Garden. When a statue of Mercury was set in the foyer of the Opéra, he urged that other theatres should be embellished with statuary and paintings;[26] and with Garnier's help he devoted detailed articles to the building of the new Opéra.[27] His dramatic criticism confirms his devoted interest in 'the sanctuary of the Idea' and suggests that as a dramatic critic he understood the importance of the theatre itself: a building in which material comforts were duly remembered and the dignity and splendour of drama were enhanced and recognized.

*   *   *

Gautier's lofty conception of the theatre was shown not only in his artistic concern with appearance, but also in his poetic concern with style. He constantly tried to bring literary—indeed, poetic—standards to the stage. He considered style indispensable to the serious theatre. Poetry was to him the language of the gods, a means of idealization, and as clearly as the footlights it divided the stage from the real, prosaic world:

'This figurative, conventional language . . . that is not used in real life by the people who use it on the stage, is perspective, remoteness, illusion, ideality. Like the fiery cordon of footlights, it divides the fictitious world from the world of reality, and creates the vagueness indispensable to the poet's creations . . . Art is not life.'[28]

It was the belief that Sarcey professed, years later, when he wrote that 'if great ideas and noble passions are to move the multitude, they must be heightened by style . . . In works of art there must be a touch of another world.'[29] And poetic illusion was, to Gautier, not merely the property but the duty of the theatre; and in criticizing a play which had shown the life behind the scenes, he made this clear:

'The footlights are a frontier of fire dividing the auditorium from the stage, the real world from the world of imagination; the audience must not be allowed to cross it. Beyond this frontier reigns illusion; perspective creates new depths, light creates enchantments; tinsel seems gold; rouge seems the freshness of youth; the characters, like the decorations, are painted, and from this collection of harmonious lies emerges relative truth, which is the truth of art.'[30]

Years later he emphatically reminded his readers of 'this harmony of lies, this solidarity of illusion which are some of the liveliest pleasures of the theatre and, let us be frank, the only end of art.'[31]

Gautier's idealism, his longing to bring poetry to the stage, made him out of sympathy with his time. In the very years in which he began his dramatic criticism, Heine observed that since the July Revolution the French were no longer themselves, that they 'never indulged in nebulous, twilight thoughts and feelings, either in art or in life,' that they were all 'more or less materialistic according to whether they have received more or less of this French education, the product of materialistic philosophy.'[32] The Revolution of 1830 and the advent of a bourgeois monarchy had indeed made the public aware of the virtues of quiet domesticity; and, intent on the present, they asked not for history but for a photographic likeness of themselves, an expression of their absorbing domestic interests. As early as 1838 Gautier observed that there was no modern theatre in the highest sense of the term.[33] Romanticism, after all, had expressed the feelings of an artistic minority; and the majority, the bourgeois public, were dictating their entertainment. The most popular dramatist of the period (and, aided by a host of collaborators, his prolific triumphs continued through Gautier's career), was Eugène Scribe. One may pause to consider Scribe for a moment, as to Gautier he was a symbol.

Gautier has been roundly condemned by Scribe's biographer because he criticized Scribe for lack of style. 'To deplore the lack of poetry and style in Scribe's plays is [so we are told], as much beside the point as it would be to berate Racine for not having written as brilliant comedies as Beaumarchais.'[34] It was not, however, beside the point that Gautier consistently made, a point that the platitudes of *la Calomnie*, the tortuous melodrama of *Adrienne Lecouvreur* prove to be incontrovertible: that style is indispensable to a lasting theatre. Scribe represented, to Gautier, the triumph of mediocrity, the victory of the bourgeois over art, he was diametrically opposed to all that as artist, poet and critic, Gautier maintained; he showed in his work 'the complete absence of any art or literature'. 'His ideas are those of the crowd,' lamented Gautier, 'so he is understood by everyone except by poets and artists ... Personally we prefer Phaeton hurled from Heaven, Icarus falling in the sea because he did not want to fall in the middle regions. It is finer to fall from the chariot of the sun than to trundle safely home in a cab.'[35]

*   *   *

The intellectual and spiritual apathy of the public, which made the fortune of Scribe, created an atmosphere in which lasting dramatic art could hardly be produced. The time was certainly ripe for the critic, in Arnold's phrase, to establish an order of ideas and make the best ideas prevail. To make such a change of climate was indeed Gautier's purpose; and believing, like Shakespeare, like Hugo, in the universal nature of the theatre, he set out, with all the fervour of an artist and a poet, to achieve his purpose.

Constantly he criticized the uninspiring public. Already in 1837[36] he complained of Parisian apathy and its ill effects on the stage: directors of theatres were, he declared, not interested in fostering new actors and dramatists; actors continued playing the same part in different plays, and some parts were merely mosaics of old successes. In the 1840's, while Musset wrote plays with no thought of the stage, and poets turned from the theatre, Gautier deplored the apathy of Parisians watching the ballet as a means of avoiding intellectual effort, and he saw, regretfully, in the decline of melodrama, the fashion for cynicism and indifference.[37] Considering a vaudeville towards the end of 1843 he felt indeed that boredom might be the motive force of the time;[38] and reviewing *la Camaraderie* in 1844, he recalled the enthusiasm of the Cénacle for Hugo, the enthusiasm that still remained in his own heart long after the *bataille d'Hernani*: 'But there are no comrades or enemies now, we have lost the strength to love and hate,' he ended sadly. 'The great misfortune of the age is indifference.'[39] Some twenty years later he still needed to deplore the general apathy and the increasing triviality of public taste.[40]

Nor was it only apathy that Gautier attacked, and attacked so rightly. He deplored misplaced enthusiasm. 'Poor great Shakespeare!' was his comment in 1846, on a visit to England. 'Our civilization, stupefied by vaudevilles, tragedies and music, can no longer bear works of so strong a savour, of a genius so free and original, a variety so inexhaustible.'[41] The comment, applied to England in the age of Macready, was not entirely fair; but it might well have been applied to Paris in 1855, when

Gautier's faith in the 'sympathetic welcome' of the Parisian public was promptly destroyed by their reception of the English actors who had come over for the International Exhibition, and he was forced to admit that 'the fashion is for tragedy, not for drama.'[42] Gautier, to whom *Macbeth* was 'a sort of mimed symphony,' was not, perhaps, the best qualified of Shakespeare's supporters, but his admiration, partly based on the precepts of the *Préface de Cromwell*, was ardently sincere; and unfortunately his words on dramatic fashion were justified. Fashion, like boredom, was a motive force in the nineteenth-century theatre. Rachel had brought tragedy into fashion, but the fashion was to die with her in 1858. And more often fashion lacked the justification of genius; in 1844 Paris had been swept off its feet by the polka: a craze which Gautier had deplored as a sign of gregarious admiration, a symbol of decadence.[43] A dance which, to casual spectators, seemed harmless enough, appeared to him yet another mark of an unoriginal age, a sign of uniformity, a clear sign of a twisted sense of values. His feelings might well be applied today to infatuations for popular singers and film-stars. They have their permanent validity.

With this lack of proportion, this lack of lofty thought or poetic feeling among the Parisian public, went a fierce conservatism in matters of detail that Gautier often deplored: 'You will change the government twenty times, but you'll never change the scene at the Comédie-Française.'[44] Blind conservatism was incompatible with his belief in the absolute freedom of the theatre and the progress of dramatic art; and the revival of *la Sylphide* brought an attack on the 'Gerontiuses of opinion' whose appreciation was crippled by recollection.[45] Gautier attacked obstinate conservatism all the more fiercely as he saw it, at times, as envy in disguise, as a means of avoiding praise for one's contemporaries.[46]

Nowhere in Gautier's criticism is it clearer than it is in his reviews of the theatre that he pitted his poetic nature, his religion of beauty, against an apathetic and prosaic age:

'The French, who are indifferent to poetry, pre-eminently anti-lyrical, unappreciative of metaphors, but gifted with admirable practical sense, like the theatre where everything is real, palpable, symmetrically arranged, conducted logically according to rules that it is always danger-ous to infringe. The finest books may pass unnoticed; every Monday twenty articles are devoted to the slightest vaudeville.'[47]

It was this unpromising public, pedestrian when he was poetic, didactic when he was artistic, apathetic or flippant when he was inspired, timid and conservative when he was bold and progressive, that Gautier set out to instruct in the scope and purpose of the theatre.

*   *   *

But in his struggle to improve the climate of the stage, Gautier did not criticize the public alone; he also vigorously expressed his Romantic disapproval of all restrictive practices and all authorities who seemed to hinder the development of the theatre. The *comité de lecture* appeared to him instrumental in keeping authors of promise away from the stage;[48] to him it seemed that only two judgments were possible: the judgment of a single arbiter or that of the public. It was evident, he insisted,[49] that the work of the committee was sometimes illusory, that a play by Hugo or Dumas would always be accepted; besides, refusals had a sort of official sanction about them that harmed a literary reputation. The director of the theatre should be sole judge. Nor did directors entirely escape his censure: in one of his earliest articles, regretting that Hugo and Dumas had produced no school of drama, Gautier insisted that directors were largely to blame: 'We believe that people who might have written remarkable plays have not done so through discouragement, or because they found it repugnant to accept trivial requirements.'[50] The critic who wanted to see the poet spread his wings in revues where no rules or traditions oppressed him, in which his imagination and caprice might have full rein, saw him rejected by the timidity of the director; and even less justified were the arbitrary decisions of government censors. Naturally and rightly the apostle of Art for Art's Sake attacked the authorities who denied the sovereign independence of art and judged it by invalid criteria:

'The theatres are in a serious position [he wrote in 1849]. They stand between suppression and censorship: suppression seems to us the lesser of the two evils, because you don't accept it, you undergo it; it is a brutal fact, and that is all. But to go and humbly present the censors with manuscripts that they can scratch out with their scarlet claws is to recognize an illegal authority and to give legal power to an abuse.'[51]

Sometimes it seemed that the theatre defeated its own purpose, that actors and dramatists prevented dramatic progress by their stubborn refusal to clear the path for new talent. Even Rachel did not escape Gautier's criticism when he noticed her dislike of contemporary work and considered that she hindered modern drama; he curtly observed that 'the author cannot be sacrificed to the susceptibilities of the actress.'[52] Every tendency in the actor that contradicted the full and free development of the theatre, Gautier deplored: he attacked the mistaken individualism in acting that split a tragedy into parts instead of fusing it into a whole; he frequently expressed his dislike of specialization, for he earnestly believed that actors, like dramatists, indeed like the exponents of every art, should be free to use all their powers. He recognized the acceptance of specialization as a sign of apathy, a means of avoiding the formation of new opinions, as a sign that those who judged mistrusted their own judgment. He saw that specialization had not existed at the most brilliant periods in the history of the arts. He saw it, and rightly, as an atrophying force; and he saw it, in particular, as the strait-jacket that had cramped and restricted seventeenth-century tragedy and made it an incomplete, unfulfilled art. 'People will object that Corneille and Racine have written masterpieces despite these fetters,' he wrote in 1850, discussing the unity of place. 'Yes, but we do not know what they would have done had they been free.'[53]

At this highly controversial point we may, of course, well remember the critic's admission that 'others are deeper than I am';[54] we may argue that he was not sufficiently intellectual to appreciate the subtleties of Racine, to appreciate an entirely inward drama. We may criticize Gautier for failing to see that the unity of time is vital to a study of psychological conflict, that restrictions may intensify art, that indeed it is sometimes 'pastime to be bound'. Yet perhaps in making these criticisms we should be asking for the impossible from a born Romantic, a Romantic of 1830. It would be wiser to recognize, yet again, in Gautier's criticism of seventeenth-century tragedy, the assertion of that chief and familiar principle: the absolute freedom of the theatre. Gautier is expressing the Shakespearean view, the view that Hugo, in the *Préface de Cromwell*, the decalogue of Romanticism, and again in the preface to *Marie Tudor*, expressed with conviction: it is the natural view for a Romantic poet, the partisan of *Hernani*. His instinctive satisfaction with much of Corneille and Racine is not a narrow prejudice, a stubborn, unthinking refusal to admire, but a whole-hearted regret of limitations in art. 'Tragedy,' he writes, 'is a dated form, not because it is old, but because it is exclusive.'[55]

Throughout his career as a critic, Gautier expressed his admiration of Corneille; and, whatever his outbursts at the Magny dinner, he was not blind to the beauties of Racine. It was not the dramatists whom he attacked, but the Academicians of their time; it was not the genre that he deplored, but the etiquette that he could not bring himself to accept. When, in 1844, the English actors brought Shakespeare to Paris, Gautier's conviction became yet stronger: 'Let us say here, once and for all, that without changes of scene the modern theatre is impossible.'[56] Modernity of feeling and expression was essential to a progressive theatre, and the theatre must progress if it were to survive. 'We may no longer paint like Masaccio, write like Jodelle or Du Bartas, sculpt like the carvers of images in the thirteenth century. . . . March forward: like Lot's wife, every retrospective spirit sets and becomes a statue.'[57] If Gautier attacked the tragedy of the seventeeth century as a national superstition, if he announced that he would rather stay in a dark and empty cellar for five hours than watch a performance, he enlarged thoughtfully on his reasons: 'People may think, because of this, that we loathe tragedy: not at all. It is our love for tragedy that makes us speak in these terms. Tragedy, as the Greeks understood it . . . with its grandiose proportions, its religious meaning, its full-throated lyricism, its choirs with their skilful evolutions, its continual chants, its splendid décor and spectacle, in no way resembled what the moderns call by this name; the Opéra gives the most accurate idea of ancient tragedy, and, as will be seen, there is a great difference between these brilliant performances to which all the arts contribute, and the cold and barren poems declaimed in the rue de Richelieu.'[58] When tragedy was untrammelled and allowed to embrace poetry, music and visual beauty, when lofty conception was matched by full and free expression, when tragedy became a synthesis of the arts, it was, to Gautier, an ideal dramatic form.

Indeed, all Gautier's dislikes spring from this single motive: his determination to encourage a free, progressive and enduring theatre. It was this determination that led him to condemn what seemed an exclusive fetish for Corneille and Racine. It was this interested conservatism, this atrophying admiration among the general public, that led him, for a moment, to condemn Molière with excessive vigour.[59] It was the same belief in the absolute freedom of the theatre, in the sanctuary of the idea, that led him to exactly the opposite extreme: to regret the heavy editing of Molière and, this time, to praise him as 'the greatest man that nature has produced.'[60] It was this belief in the liberty of art that caused the critic to insist again, and indignantly, that plays should be revived intact. And demanding, repeatedly, that dramatic art must be kept untouched, independent of fashion and convention, he deplored the theatre used as a hustings or a pulpit, the political play dependent on topical attraction.[61] To Gautier art and poetry had their own morality, and if the artist and poet had charge of souls, it was because beauty taught its own implicit lesson. To Gautier, the theatre remained an art to be practised for its own sake, and according to its own code. It was characteristic of the apostle of Art for Art's Sake that when in 1863 he came to discuss the freedom of the theatre, he made a single request: 'Among the theatres which will spring from the earth

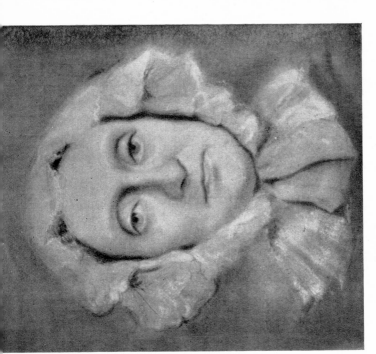

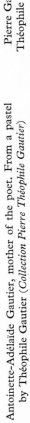

Pierre Gautier, father of the poet. From a pastel by
Théophile Gautier (*Collection Pierre Théophile Gautier*)

Antoinette-Adélaïde Gautier, mother of the poet. From a pastel
by Théophile Gautier (*Collection Pierre Théophile Gautier*)

Théophile Gautier, in the costume he wore at the *bataille d'Hernani*. From the self-portrait in oils, painted in 1830

The first known photograph of Théophile Gautier, taken in 1849 *(Photo : Le Gray)*

like the wall of Thebes at the sound of Amphion's lyre, we should like
to see three devoted to pure art.'[62]

*   *   *

It is among the tasks of the dramatic critic to interpret the past to
the present: to be what Brunet called the organ of revivification. It is
clear that Gautier devotedly admired Greek tragedy. Often he insisted
on the importance of translation: his enthusiastic review of the *Antigone*
in 1844[63] becomes a warm defence of what he considers a neglected
art, an art that the most celebrated foreign authors had practised and
that the poets of France might well practise too. As he fostered the
theatre of ancient times, so he showed his appreciation of the medieval
theatre, and delighted in the unrestrained comedy of *l'Avocat patelin*.[64]
He appreciated early tragedy as well as early comedy: the romantic,
pre-Cornelian tragedy *Saint-Genest* called forth a vigorous apology for
Rotrou.[65]

Corneille himself was one of Gautier's heroes. We have seen that the
critic considered him an unfulfilled genius: repeatedly he insisted that
if Corneille had been allowed to develop completely, he might have
risen to Shakespearean stature:

'If he had been allowed to follow his entirely Spanish temperament,
Corneille would have developed with incredible vigour, passion and
splendour, and France would have had a poet to oppose to Shakespeare . . . Compelled to make his characters converse face to face with
each other, he wrote long speeches followed by replies where he would
have naturally drawn his sword and engaged in furious action . . . This
does not in the least diminish the respect we feel for the great Corneille;
we just believe that he did not give his measure.'[66] Cornelian figures
seemed to Gautier like statues by Michelangelo, making gigantic but
immobile efforts to lift invisible burdens.

This comment on Corneille's 'entirely Spanish temperament' contains much that is significant in Gautier's appreciation of the dramatist.
It was the Spanish, indeed Romantic, element in Corneille that won his
sympathy: in fact when *Hernani* was revived in 1838, Gautier described
Hugo's poetry as Cornelian, his drama as a cousin of *le Cid*. His appreciation of Corneille developed over the years. By 1863, when he saw
the disuse of tragedy as a terrifying sign that poetry might vanish from
the theatre, he recognized in Corneille not merely grandiose Romanticism, but a lofty concept of life that would raise the public spirit by
its example;[67] and by 1870 he had set him up as an heroic symbol:

'It is good to lead distracted and forgetful spirits towards the sacred
ideal, and to pour libations on the white marble altar of the heroes.
The heroes! . . . those divine geniuses, spearheads of humanity . . .

E

Homer, Aeschylus, Shakespeare, Michelangelo, Raphael, are heroes like Alexander and Caesar, and no one is worthier than Corneille of entering the immortal phalanx. He has had a truly heroic influence upon men.'[68]

Gautier was not blind to the beauties of Racine, but he was never wholly sympathetic to him. His lack of sympathy was frankly expressed in his early criticism; and while he was understandably swept off his feet by Rachel's interpretation of Phèdre, he was careful to remark that if Phèdre was the finest woman's rôle in tragedy, it was also the most Greek of Racine's characters: it was not so much Christian as pagan.[69]

And here, it seems, we find a significant parallel to Gautier's early appreciation of Corneille. What he admired in both dramatists were the qualities by which they differed most from the seventeenth century: Romanticism in Corneille, classicism in Racine. It is a theory borne out by his comment on Phèdre, 'this Greek character . . . that Euripides would not disown as a daughter'; it is borne out, too, by his admiration of Rachel: with wonderful instinct, so he wrote, she inspired 'a Greek and entirely new meaning in the fine French tragedy'.[70]

It is true that Gautier's appreciation of Racine, like his appreciation of Corneille, changed with time; but it must be emphasized that even in the 1860's his sympathy was less for Racine than for tragedy, and that if, in 1863, he defends Racine, it is, again, because he fiercely defends tragedy itself as the last foothold of poetry in the theatre, the only means of training the actors of the future in the great tradition of literature.

'Though one may prefer the supple, varied manner of Shakespeare, profound and free, tragedy is still among the noblest forms that has clothed the thought of man. By the sobriety of its composition, the purity of its lines, the rhythm of its attitudes, the loftiness of its style, unencumbered by any detail, and by the balanced progress of its hexameters, it attains the serene loveliness of ancient bas-reliefs. The coldness for which we reproach it is only the snowy paleness of marble. And so we must lament the disappearance of tragedy. With it there disappears that language of the gods "that the world understands and does not speak" . . .

'People may be astonished at the solicitude that we, an old Romantic, show for tragedy; but we are afraid to see serious poetry vanish from the theatre . . .

'Great art is never entertaining in the vulgar sense of the word. To look at a fresco by Michelangelo, to listen to a tragedy by Corneille is a serious pleasure that seems like work, for it needs a spiritual effort to rise to the comprehension of these virile beauties; but what a noble use of human faculties! To understand beauty is almost to equal it! The frequent, easily impassioned study of the masters would make our spirits lofty again. Actors would shape themselves by performing them frequently; actors and public would be ready when some poetic master-piece, some great unknown work, some classic of the future, made its appearance. And that cannot fail to happen if the poets feel themselves to be interpreters. . . .'[71]

It is a remarkable apology from the Romantic of Romantics, yet it is typical of Gautier and well suggests his poetic breadth of view.

No such outside pressure was needed to make him express his affec-tionate admiration for Molière. The enthusiasm which he showed in 1838, reviewing *l'Ecole des Maris*, informed his detailed interpretations of individual characters in the 1860's. Molière alone, of the great trinity of the seventeenth century, did not seem, to Gautier, to have been impeded by conventions; and he found in Molière not only romantic audacity carried to its extreme, but the honest, whole-hearted humour he enjoyed in *l'Avocat patelin* and the Shakespearean mixture of tragic and comic, of grave and gay which he believed essential to dramatic art. He enjoyed both the wisdom and the *naïveté*.

The variation of mood that Gautier admired in Molière he admired even more fervently in Shakespeare; and his abiding admiration of Shakespeare (even though he could only read him in translation) shows Gautier to be not only a typical Romantic, but to be well in advance of the French public. As early as 1842 he urges the Odéon to produce translations or verse imitations of Shakespeare and other foreign dramatists: 'The moment has come; the modern genius identifies itself easily with the creations of every country; we no longer live in the days when translators suppressed the passages in their authors that did not suit French taste, and deprived a work of precisely everything that gave it charm and curiosity, everything that gave it colour and style.'[72]

Gautier's optimism was not justified by the reception of the com-pany who brought Shakespeare to Paris two years later. Macready's diary suggests that although the venture was acclaimed in literary circles, the public was not entirely sympathetic. But Gautier did not notice this lack of sympathy: 'Save for a few small cuts which have always been made, *Othello* has been performed in its entirety,' he wrote eagerly. 'The Parisians of 1844 have been able to take pure Shakes-peare.'[73] Like Hugo, in the Preface which was part of Romantic doc-trine, Gautier used Shakespeare as an infallible weapon in his battle for the freedom of the theatre, a brilliant proof of what might be achieved when no linguistic rules, no unities of time and place were imposed.

*   *   *

The contrast between Shakespeare and French seventeenth-century tragedy was an established theme in Gautier's criticism; it was, perhaps, their 'secret relationship to the women in Shakespearean comedy'[74] that drew him towards the heroines of Marivaux. He revelled in the speed and subtlety of Marivaux's conversation, which recalled that of Beatrice and Benedick, and recalled, too, that eminently eighteenth-century quality, *l'esprit*. Long ago Gautier had insisted that *l'esprit* was among the most important qualities in art and literature, and that his compatriots unjustly disdained it. It was this affection for wit and poise, gaiety and elegance that inspired his happy appreciations of *le Jeu de l'Amour et du Hasard*[75] and *les Fausses Confidences*,[76] and brought him to make his apology for the *maniérés*. He writes here with the brio that he shows in his articles on eighteenth-century art; the instinctive sympathy, the delicate understanding are evident. And a like sympathy inspires his exact appreciation of Beaumarchais as 'a man of the world who writes',[77] and of Regnard, who shows a similar joy of living and ease of manner. Reviewing *le Joueur*, Gautier sums up Regnard in a few pertinent and visual phrases; and one sees in the swiftly-drawn portrait a reminiscence of Fortunio, a character that Gautier himself would have liked to be.[78]

*   *   *

But criticism (and Gautier would have been the first to admit it) is not only the interpretation of past to present: it is also the interpretation of the present itself; and of all the many functions that the critic must undertake, this is probably the most exacting. For if it is comparatively simple to pass judgment on an author whose renown has been established by the years, it is a delicate matter to distinguish fashion from permanent values. It is also among the most important of the critic's tasks.

And it is a task that, in writing of the contemporary theatre, Gautier performed with admirable discrimination. It is true that, being naturally benevolent, he sometimes overpraised; it is also true that he rarely underestimated a performance or a play that is recognized as significant today. If it is a platitude to observe that he remained a Romantic all his life, at least his criticism suggests that from the first he was able to winnow the Romantic grain from the chaff. As early as 1836 he could write happily: 'The corpse is on the decline. *De profundis* upon it.'[79] In 1837 he produces a remarkable satire on the ultra-Romantics, *les*

Hommes de Génie.[80] And in his dramatic criticism he laughs at excesses: his account of *la Reine de Chypre* in 1841[81] implies that he has progressed since the days of *Hernani*; his review of *Paris le Bohémien* in 1842[82] shows affection but a certain amusement; and he can dismiss *Manoel le Soldat* as 'the sort of melodrama that is no longer written, or, rather, that shouldn't be written any more'.[83] Even Dumas is reminded that *Halifax* is 'a cloak-and-dagger play, somewhat displaced in our age when there are no cloaks or daggers.'[84] Surprisingly soon, Gautier outgrew the excesses of the Bousingos and the *bataille d'Hernani*; and even his admiration for Hugo could not persuade him that *les Burgraves* was a great play. He devoted two articles[85] to analysis and quotation: it was his usual means of kind evasion. He showed both his loyalty to Hugo and his discrimination.

Gautier often and wisely expressed his belief that art must progress with the times if it were to survive. He considered also that a play belonged not only to its author but to its age, that it possessed an inevitable period colour. He explained his theory in 1851, when he came to review a drama of Spanish inspiration that would have been in its element in the days of *Ruy Blas* and *Hernani*;[86] he repeated his belief in the latter days of the Second Empire, when he wrote so affectionately, so vividly, of the dating of Bouchardy.[87] Yet though he recognized Bouchardy as a period piece, though, even in Bouchardy's heyday, he had been aware of his Romantic excesses, the lack of style, Gautier expressed his genial pleasure in 'the Sophocles of the boulevard'; for whatever his weaknesses, Bouchardy undeniably created the illusion that the critic sought in the theatre; the wild impossibilities, the breathless excitement, the *naïveté*, and, above all, the dramatist's faith in his own work, redeemed him in the pedestrian age of Scribe, an age when the theatre was too often a mirror, not a picture, when monotonous themes were prosaically treated and cynicism was so frequently shown. And if he criticized Sue for a similar lack of style, Gautier admired him, likewise, for his Romantic vigour and fertility of invention: for sweeping the theatre away from reality with the adaptations of his novels. The immense vogue for Sue in the 1840's did not leave the critic untouched; and though at the end of his life he recognized that he had spoken with 'the reserve of the writer in love with poetry and high literature, against these prodigious fashions earned by tricks outside the province of art,' he maintained even then, when Sue was almost entirely neglected, when his name had disappeared like a meteor, that he had been 'a vigorous and powerful mind, prodigiously inventive, an artist with a rough touch.'[88]

Such audacity had always been, to Gautier, one of the qualities

essential to a dramatist: audacity and enthusiasm made the wildest
melodrama superior to the neatest comedy by Scribe, because, again,
they created the essential illusion and protested against the cynicism and
indifference, the prosaic nature of the age. The wholeheartedness of
Bouchardy and Sue was enough to mitigate many of their faults, it
was a hallmark on all Romantic productions; and, noticing the revival
of *la Nonne sanglante* in 1864,[89] the critic looked back regretfully across
years of dramatic sterility to the fertile years of Romanticism, and compared the Romantic era to the Elizabethan Age. The revival of Romantic
dramas in the 1860's only emphasized the modern lack of boldness and
imagination. *La Tour de Nesle* seems today a vigorous but strangely
naïve period-piece: a melodrama anticipating by a hundred years the
adolescent extravagances of Hollywood. Yet, revived in 1861, it showed
a grandiose conception which, understandably, to Gautier's mind,
dwarfed the stockbrokers of the contemporary stage. To the artist
and poet turned critic such spectacular resurrection of history was
greatly preferable to the photographs of contemporary life which he
was so often forced to see, and he welcomed the drama with a burst
of wild but intelligible Romantic enthusiasm.[90]

If his approval of Dumas seems excessive today, his enthusiasm for
Musset deserves our admiration. Musset, like Shakespeare, was to
Gautier an example of what might be achieved when poetry was
brought to the stage. To the critic, guided by 'his passion for lyricism,
style and form',[91] the divorce of poetry and theatre in the mid-nineteenth century remained an abiding regret: poetry, he insisted, maintained the theatre in the sphere of art, it was the language to use in the
sanctuary of the Idea where the soul might forget the sadness of
existence and enter a magic world animated by poetic creations. The
poet, even the lyric poet, could construct a drama: and poets need not
bow to technical conventions, rely on that *connaissance des planches* that
was given such undue importance by the admirers of Scribe:

'O poets—stay poets and yours will be the gain!—What we expect
of you are not dodges and theatrical devices, but thoughts, cries from
the soul, noble flights towards the ideal, observations that only dreamers
can make with their eyes that seem not to see, sparkling caprices, great
sweeps of passion, and, above all, and always, form and style.'[92]

The invocation might be addressed personally to Musset. With his
love of poetry and fantasy, Gautier had long pleaded Musset's cause
to a public 'accustomed to the bourgeois, ordinary manners of M.
Scribe,' a public 'that takes no notice of thought or observation,
poetry or style, and only sees in a drama a more or less skilful game of
chess ... M. de Musset has written a whole book of comedies and pro-

verbs, full of the most twinkling spangles of fantasy and the sweetest tears of sensibility,' Gautier had proclaimed in 1842. 'It's something as witty as Beaumarchais, as delicate as Marivaux, as capricious as Shakespeare. Well, none of that, say the experts, is worth anything in the theatre. What the devil are we going to see in the theatre? We are very curious to know.'[93] In 1843 Gautier pleaded eloquently in favour of *le Spectacle dans un Fauteuil*: a realization of the romanesque theatre of which he had dreamed in *Mademoiselle de Maupin*.[94] In 1845 he had again appeared in Musset's defence, deploring the clumsy adaptations of his work that had found their way into the theatre.[95] When Musset achieved his triumph in 1847 with *Un Caprice*, Gautier proclaimed his admiration[96]; and when, in 1848, Musset was performed at the Français and the Théâtre-Historique, the critic gave full rein to his enthusiasm: 'And people complained of the lack of comedies, while they had volumes of admirable plays at their elbow: plays which combined the delicacy of Marivaux with the fantasy of Shakespeare!'[97]

Long after Musset had been accepted by director and public, Gautier continued to support him pugnaciously; he now attacked the authorities not for negligence, but for bad judgment, deploring the choice of Musset's work that was made for the theatre. It was, he felt, a choice in which metaphysics were retained and poetry abandoned.

*   *   *

Just as Gautier supported Musset with vigour and discrimination, so, instinctively, he acclaimed and assessed Coppée and Banville. Ardently he welcomed the dramatic experiments of the new generation of poets. The stronger the poetry in an entertainment, the more eagerly he encouraged and defended it. From his earliest years as a critic, he expressed his love and respect for the mysterious. Those who chose to burlesque the Orient in vaudeville were taken to task; and reviewing *les Amours de Psyché*, a travesty of mythology, he saw fit to remind his readers that all forms of religion, whether practised or disused, should be respected. For poetry, to Gautier, did not only mean a literary form: it often meant the primitive and simple, the entertainment furthest from reality. It embraced the element of sublimity in the epic presentations of French history at the Cirque-Olympique: the pageants which ignored the passing fashions that drama dully reflected, appealed to the nobler instincts of the public and realized their dreams. Poetry, in its widest sense, included the pantomime; it included the brilliant unreality of fireworks, and inspired Gautier's charming apology for pyrotechnics. It was found in the bullfights which, again and again, he described with heartfelt pleasure. The critic who practised both verse and painting found poetry in appearance, thought and style.

And, though he looked first for poetry, he welcomed originality and dramatic sense wherever he found them. He delighted in *le Demi-Monde*,[98] the work of one of the most gifted dramatists of the second half of the century; and in 1861, when *Nos Intimes!* won a well-deserved triumph at the Vaudeville, he greeted Sardou with an enthusiasm which seems almost pathetically fervent.[99]

Gautier was rarely led astray: his sense of art was both catholic and discriminating. George Sand's reputation as a novelist did not blind him to her defects as a dramatist; and for all his admiration and friendship for Balzac, it is evident, likewise, from the measured praise in his articles, that he did not consider Balzac established in the theatre.

His generous but vigilant discrimination is seen, too, in his attitude to Ponsard who, early in 1843, was expected to be the long-awaited star in the dramatic sky. His wish to admire Ponsard was honest; nor did the failure of *les Burgraves* and Gautier's loyalty to Hugo, nor did the farcical reception of *Judith* and Gautier's loyalty to Mme de Girardin prevent his appreciating Ponsard's work. But he understood that Ponsard had been raised to the skies by Hugo's detractors, and he recognized in him not the awaited genius, but 'a clear, straightforward mind, full of good sense, sustained by a good education and, if he doesn't take this perfidious and overwhelming praise too seriously, capable of becoming a very good dramatic poet'.[100] And this seems, as we look at it now, not the cunning pleading of a Romantic with personal loyalties, but a more than generous assessment of the didactic dramatist of the *école du bon sens*: the school diametrically opposed to Romanticism (and, indeed, to Art for Art's Sake), the school which was distinguished by 'negative qualities: absence of lyricism and imagery, and banal moderation of matter and manner'.[101] Gautier's assessment of Ponsard remained his considered opinion when, twenty-six years later, after a triumphant career, the dramatist had died and *Lucrèce* was revived. Discussing the original impact of *Lucrèce*, Gautier wrote:

'Now all the tumult has died. The Romantic School is scattered. Ponsard, sanctified by death, enjoys the reputation that was due to him for his pure and honest, conscientious work. If he is not a genius, he is at least talent at its highest, and that is a glory with which, living or dead, one may be content.'[102] Purity, honesty, conscientiousness: these mid-Victorian virtues are all that the twentieth century may accredit to the dramatist; and Gautier's verdict calls for no criticism, except that it is perhaps a trifle too kind.

*   *   *

Gautier's dramatic criticism reflects not only the vicissitudes of the theatre but the changes in his own life. The bravado and verbal pyrotechnics of his early articles are replaced, in later years, by more sober views, more temperately expressed. The development may be partly due to the tolerance of middle age, and partly to the reticence that his work on the Government paper involved. It may also be due to a certain resignation, affected or sincere, to the inartistic age in which he lived. 'As you go on in life,' so he had written in 1841, 'you see the triviality of the things that impassioned you; you find that the people you detested are only ridiculous; you are bored to death by the vehement.'[103]

The vaudeville he had once dismissed so scornfully, the dancing which, when the polka swept Paris, he had condemned as a sign of boredom and gregarious admiration, came in time to be approved. He was now more prepared to make concessions, to give measured praise as well as criticism to an author he had formerly dismissed. He came to declare that Dennery, the popular dramatist, was not to be despised, that there were indeed reasons for admiring him. Such tolerance extended to Scribe himself. In 1856, insisting that classical masterpieces must not be performed at the expense of modern art: 'Are there then no more poets and authors capable of writing for the French stage? [asked Gautier] Have they thrown aside their pens, Scribe, Alexandre Dumas *fils*, Alfred de Vigny, de Musset, Ponsard, Augier . . . to quote only the famous?'[104]

It is surprising to find Scribe among the accepted authors; and it is both surprising and illuminating to compare the critic's original comments on *Une Chaîne* in 1841 with his comments on the revival of the play in 1856: 'M. Scribe, let us be honest, is not our author; that does not prevent us from recognizing his marvellous fecundity, his rare understanding of the stage, his extreme skill in handling difficult situations, and finally a continuity of successes which is not obtained without real merit . . . The public cannot be mistaken in its pleasures for forty-five years.'[105]

Defence of the public becomes, indeed, a recurrent theme with the sobering critic: 'Directors, critics, connoisseurs and so-called experienced people slander the public and mistrust it outrageously,' so he declares in 1855, insisting that the public would forgive technical innovations for the sake of originality.[106] The public has now become the 'indispensable collaborator' in every dramatic work, and 'if it does not want to lend a hand with the work, the work stays incomplete, and the success is compromised.'[107] When Bouilhet's *Madame de Montarcy* is performed: 'It was a pleasure to see this multiple spectator, this great collective soul, this critic more intelligent than all the writers of Monday

articles, educate the poet.'[108] By 1860 Gautier can sign a panegyric
of the public which, twenty years earlier, he could not have conceived.[109]

*   *   *

Yet it would be wrong to conclude from such tolerance, such concessions, such determined attempts to appreciate the fashions of his
time, that Gautier had sold his soul to a government paper, forgotten
his poetic and artistic standards. There is a sad depth of meaning in
his comment after nearly twenty years of dramatic criticism: a pathetic
fall from his enthusiasm at the *bataille d'Hernani*: 'The theatre, as
people understand it in Paris, is a hardship rather than an entertainment . . . It would be difficult to invent a torture more cruel than this
pleasure.'[110] The Goncourts observed him at a first night in 1859 in a
state of torpid resignation; and in 1856 the *Journal* records his comment
at another first performance: 'That's how I like the theatre: from the
outside . . . It's such a clumsy, abject art, the theatre.'[111] The theatre
continually disappointed him, continually frustrated his poetic and
artistic hopes by its prosaic reality. He deplored dramatic sterility, the
increasing triviality of public taste, the vogue for inferior entertainment, the fashion for realism; and to the end of his career, believing
in dramatic illusion, in the ideal, make-believe world of the theatre, he
regretted the frock-coated Parisian Narcissi, only absorbed in themselves:

'The modern public does not like historical drama, unless it lends
itself to some allusion [he lamented in 1870]. One might even say that
it no longer believes in the past, it is so absorbed by the present. . . .
What is the use of these heroes who did not speculate at the Bourse?'[112]

But if he continued to attack the weaknesses of dramatist and public,
to express his weariness and frustration, Gautier continued, also, to
maintain his constant ideals. He continued to support every poetic
tentative in the theatre. He insisted on the importance and art of décor,
the need for innovation in scenic art; he emphasized, still, the importance
of physique, of accurate historical detail. Again and again the 'partisan
of freedom in art'[113] pointed out the need for absolute freedom in the
theatre, maintaining that art was a law unto itself, its own religion,
independent of politics as it was independent of religion and morals.
Repeatedly he recorded his conception of a free and catholic theatre
that presented the plays of every country and of every age, and reconciled the stage to poetry; and he continued, poignantly, to hope for a
dramatic renaissance, to persuade himself that the theatre was merely
dormant, not sterile: 'Works of art take time, like the harvests, and
critics rather resemble the children who go ten times a day to see if

the plant they potted yesterday has grown yet. . . . Let us wait patiently
for the young generation to find their formula and discover the new
ideal in modern times.'[114]

A study of Gautier's dramatic criticism suggests that he possessed
the virtues by which any critic of any art is best served: wide enthu-
siasms, an abiding, indeed a religious belief in beauty of every kind,
and in Art for Art's Sake. And he possessed perception: a perception
which, in his case, was almost infallible. Gautier, as he reminds us so
often, was a poet, and he remained aware that if his immediate and
ostensible task was to write for his contemporaries, his ultimate
responsibility was to posterity: 'We are a poet, a prophet, and, gifted
with the gift of prophecy, we cannot stop ourselves, through all the
accounts of vaudevilles and melodramas, from thrilling with a thrill
of the future.' And to the tolerance and discrimination of the critic,
the enthusiasm, the standards and vision of a poet, Gautier added his
own peculiar ability as an artist: his own unique ability to transpose the
passing dramatic art into a detailed, visual and lasting record.

7. Son of the Prophet

THE YEAR 1845 opened sadly for the dramatic critic of *la Presse*. It may
be that as his own *Poésies complètes* were to appear in July, he was more
than ever conscious of his true vocation, and of the few consolations
that his daily work would bring. 'Journalists, those weekly *graciosos*, are
human after all, and they are sometimes sad; dreaming takes possession
of them as if they were poets.'[1] And as he considered the spring flower-
ing of poetry: 'The month of May is here,' he wrote despondently.
'The double cherries and poets are in flower. Let us talk a little of three
or four of these pleasant books. Do they not deserve a kindly look,
above all from a journalist who was once a poet himself?'[2] The demands
of a new serial, *la Croix de Berny*, kept him constantly busy, the landscapes in the *Salon* enticed him to distant climates, and he began to
feel the restlessness which grew so acute every spring and every summer:

> J'aime un fez écarlate,
> De sequins bruissant,
> Où partout l'or éclate,
> Où reluit le croissant . . .[3]

So learned the readers of *la Presse* at the end of April. It was an indica
tion of Gautier's thoughts.

For he was fascinated by the Oriental fashion.

'It is strange [he wrote], we believe we have conquered Algeria, an
Algeria has conquered us. Our women already wear scarves interwove
with thread of gold, streaked with a thousand colours, which hav
served the harem slaves, our young men are adapting the camelhai
burnous. The tarbouch has replaced the classic cashmere skull-cap
everyone is smoking a nargileh, hashish is taking the place of cham
pagne; our Spahi officers look so Arab one would think they had cap
tured themselves with a smala; they have adopted all the Oriente
habits, so superior is primitive life to our so-called civilization.

'If this goes on, France will soon be Mahometan and we shall see th
white domes of mosques rounding themselves on our horizons, an
minarets mingling with steeples, as in Spain at the time of the Moors
We should indeed like to live to see the day. . . .'[4]

He had, in fact, determined to go to Algeria. His original plan ha
been to visit Algiers and Constantine, Tunis and Tripoli, Alexandri
and Cairo, sail up the Nile to Thebes, cross the isthmus of Suez, trave
through Syria, visit Jerusalem and continue (by way of Rhodes) t
Smyrna, go to Athens and Nauplia, finish his tragedy *l'Orestie*, an
return to France by way of Trieste and Venice. This breathless itinerar
had been suggested by the late Duc d'Orléans, who had promised t
use his influence to make the journey successful. By July 1845 the rout
had somewhat contracted, and Gautier arranged to join Genera
Bugeaud's Kabylian expedition.[5]

*   *   *

Early that month, with promises of a sequel to his Spanish impres
sions, *Tra-los-Montes*, he left for Algeria, whence (predicted *l'Artiste*
hopefully) 'he will send us some of those vivid coloured pages s
worthily recalling the pictures of Decamps.' On July 7 Gérard de Nerva
took over in *la Presse*: 'M. Théophile Gautier,' he announced, 'is goin
to study and record this second France which was been won fron
barbarity and the desert.' M. Gautier himself was in Châlons tha
morning,[6] on his way to laze with Joseph Méry, the Marseillais poet
under the tamarind trees at les Aygalades, to listen to the click of th
cicadas and the delicious descent of Méry's conversation. Then h
embarked in the *Pharamond* at Marseilles; and on 22 July he sat i
Algiers, writing gaily to his ex-host: 'We are setting off tomorrow o
an expedition with General Bugeaud . . . How goes *la Croix de Berny*?'

He forgot his journalism happily as he visited French North Africa from Oran to Constantine. At Oran he met an engaging Arabian-looking figure, green-eyed, ironic, bearded, stepping off a felucca: Louis de Cormenin, poet, journalist, traveller, arrived from Spain. Together they journeyed through Mostaganem and Algiers to Constantine, where passing storks dropped snakes upon the rooftops. There is a glimpse or two of Gautier, this African summer, in *Loin de Paris*, there are sharp reminiscences throughout his writing. But though Noël Parfait, his second companion, took notes of Algerian costumes, the book on Africa never matured beyond Hetzel's advertisement: it is one of the sad miscarriages in Gautier's work.

And so it was left to Gérard de Nerval to create the charming mirage of Gautier on his journey; and in August, when Carlotta appeared again in *la Péri*, he took the opportunity: 'At this moment, our friend and collaborator is realizing the dream he spun when he wrote the ballet: he is seeing the true Orient, the clear sun reflected on the whitewashed walls, the emerald plants, the glowing rose of morning and of evening, the gildings and shining embroideries, the yellow, red and blue women of Don César de Bazan, and all the thousand pictures of changing colours whose ideal is not wholly confined to the canvases of Decamps and Marilhat.'

Gautier came home in September 1845, enveloped in a burnous against the autumn chill and (as Sainte-Beuve remembered, twenty years later) holding a small lioness upon his knees. As the diligence came in sight of the gaslit tiara of Paris, as the follower of Bugeaud became once more the dramatic critic of *la Presse*, Gautier asked himself what new genius had been discovered. Nothing had changed. The same engravings embellished the printsellers' windows; the identical cashmere, a little more faded and creased, hung in the drapers' shops; the dandies he had left on the boulevard de Gand, smoking their cigars, were standing there, the ash a little longer. And when, hale and tanned, he went to see his collaborator, Gérard reassured him: 'You might have stereotyped your old articles, they would do today. What you wrote about Carlotta when she danced in *Giselle* and *la Péri* would still apply to *le Diable à Quatre*. No second Félicien David has arrived from the East, unless you have brought him back in your trunk. And Ponsard the Great is still finishing his tragedy.'[8]

One event of importance had occurred in Gautier's domestic circle: an event which was to bring him yet further commitments and to add much to his sorrow and something to his glory. On 24 August, while he had been (somewhat callously, one feels) in Africa, Ernesta had given birth to his daughter, Judith.

And in his absence he had earned another title to renown. On 5 July
Charpentier had published the *Poésies complètes de Théophile Gautier*.
The volume, in Sainte-Beuve's opinion, would have a certain success
among those who were satisfied with colour and graceful fantasy.[9]
'What a pity,' he added, 'that an almost continual pretentiousness
spoils it all, and that true and simple sensibility is lacking!'[10] Yet even
Sainte-Beuve chose to copy out one of the poems: for to him *Fatuité*
faithfully expressed Gautier's manner and way of living, his bearing,
his very breathing. Every word revealed the ebullient vigour of the
author of *Fortunio*, the lover of Ernesta, the wayward, energetic Gautier
of the early 1840's: a Gautier almost insolently assured:

> *Je suis jeune; la pourpre en mes veines abonde;*
> *Mes cheveux sont de jais et mes regards de feu,*
> *Et, sans gravier ni toux, ma poitrine profonde*
> *Aspire à pleins poumons l'air du ciel, l'air de Dieu.*
>
> *Aux vents capricieux qui soufflent de Bohême,*
> *Sans les compter, je jette et mes nuits et mes jours,*
> *Et, parmi les flacons souvent l'aube au teint blême*
> *M'a surpris dénouant un masque de velours.*
>
> *Plus d'une m'a remis la clef d'or de son âme;*
> *Plus d'une m'a nommé son maître et son vainqueur;*
> *J'aime, et parfois un ange avec un corps de femme,*
> *Le soir, descend du ciel pour dormir sur mon coeur.*
>
> *On sait mon nom; ma vie est heureuse et facile;*
> *J'ai plusieurs ennemis et quelques envieux;*
> *Mais l'amitié chez moi toujours trouve un asile,*
> *Et le bonheur d'autrui n'offense pas mes yeux.*[11]

*   *   *

In his prime, in his mid-thirties, Gautier was indeed a superb and
arresting figure. Even Eugène de Mirecourt, that sharp and dubious
biographer, admired Gautier Pasha on his return from Algeria, 'walking
the boulevards in his burnous, half Parisian, half son of the Prophet.'
Even Mirecourt stopped to watch Gautier as he drove in his carriage,
drawn by a pair of dapple-grey ponies, Jane and Blanche, the ponies
that were painted by Rosa Bonheur,[12] across the place de la Concorde: a
massive Phoebus Apollo in the carriage of Tom Thumb. Gérard de
Nerval recorded with respect that at the opening of the Château-Rouge
Gautier registered 520 on the punchball: 'Such essays earn the critic

he blind respect of the masses.'[13] It was now, too, that Charles Mon-
elet first met him and recognized him as 'the most perfect incarnation
f Romanticism. His aspect did not destroy the image I had created of
he partisan of *Hernani*, the spectator in the legendary cherry doublet.'[14]
t was now that Feydeau observed him: 'His dark chestnut hair fell
iterally to his waist. He usually wore a black velvet jacket, footed
rousers and yellow slippers. Bareheaded, cigar in mouth, holding
iimself erect under a large umbrella when it rained, he ambled round
he streets, stopping at merchants' stalls, and he was not above chatting
vith the old biddies on the pavement.'[15] And a writer in the *Journal du
Dimanche*, meeting the son of the Prophet, was equally satisfied: 'I
ound M. Théophile Gautier crouching on cushions and surrounded
y cats. . . . There were cats of every colour, everywhere, even on the
helves of the bookcase. I must admit I was also much surprised (for
. was still ignorant about literature) by his exotic costume: it was a
:ostume only Gautier could wear, entirely foreign to our shabby
:ivilization. . . . Every word that fell from his lips was a topaz or a ruby,
iis sentences took on rainbow hues from the sun.'[16]

Such was Gautier when he lived at 14 rue de Navarin; it was a fine
'illa, said Mirecourt, and on the vast lawns in front of it 'sprawled
ur men of letters in footed trousers and grey waistcoats, amazing the
ieighbourhood by their eccentric poses, demanding inspiration from
heir cigars'. Such a villa was not easy to leave; and Gautier only left
t in 1847 to take a house near the Champs-Elysées: the house, of course,
nce inhabited by D'Orsay and Byron.

*　　*　　*

Théophile Gautier, this strange, impressive figure, moved in a magic
vorld. He shone with Hugo at the soirées of the Duc de Nemours,
ind when Bocage arranged an exhibition of art by men of letters (Mme
Sand, it was said, had promised an engraving), he showed his painting
it the Odéon.[17] *Le Corsaire-Satan* published his conversation; he dined
vith Gérard de Nerval and Léon Gozlan,[18] encouraged Dumas *père* to
uild the Théâtre-Montpensier,[19] he reviewed the young Saint-Saëns,
he prodigy who already so interpreted Beethoven that 'the whole
Conservatoire was desperate with envy'.[20] He ate hashish with Fernand
Boissard, with Balzac and Baudelaire, at the gilded Hôtel Pimodan on
he Ile Saint-Louis, '*une tombe dorée au bout du vieux Paris*',[21] he dined
vith Balzac at Hugo's in the place Royale. He impressed Sandeau with
iis paradox and his Merovingian hair at Arsène Houssaye's rooms in
:he rue du Bac. He hastened from Rachel's performance as Jeanne
l'Arc, in the rue de Richelieu, to the *Salon*, where he discussed the
uture of painting, the future of all art. 'Our duty,' he wrote, with the

fervour of *Mademoiselle de Maupin*, 'our duty is to visit the planet that God has given us for our habitation and to bring out its infinite beauties in works as perfect as possible. It is the duty of poets, painters and sculptors to write the commentary on creation; in a few years, the *Salon* should be the panorama of the world. From the discovery of steam there will date a new era in poetry. . . . The modern Pegasus will be a railway engine.'[22]

The modern Pegasus was indeed steaming in triumph through France; and no traveller was more intrepid, more enthusiastic, than Gautier. He boarded the first train of the Chemin de Fer du Nord, with 'all the great, the rich, the learned and the honourable of Paris. . . We were thrust in the ribs by a thoughtful diplomat, jostled by a first rank painter, our feet were trodden on by a millionaire'. Past Enghien Pontoise, they steamed resplendently, through fields where the poppies seemed like multitudes of sparks fallen by the wayside. They stopped at Amiens for an official speech (but Amiens, 'famed for its excellent duck *pâtés*, might have offered some to its guests'); then off again they shot at thirty miles an hour, to Lille, where the cannon thundered, the garrison turned out, and the visitors were compensated for absent *pâtés* by the banquet where twenty-six tables of fifty-two covers each were weighted with 'food as abundant as it was fine; the wines of Moët and Chandon flowed in waves, and the menu had been prepared by two of the most distinguished *officiers de bouche* in Paris'. They toasted the King of the French, the King of the Belgians, M. de Rothschild, while all the inhabitants of Lille filed past in admiration, 'as people did long ago at Versailles at the dinners of Louis XIV'. Then out they trooped to the Esplanade to hear Berlioz's *Symphonie héroïque* performed beneath a temple of coloured glass, and to attend a ball at the Hotel de Ville. 'M. de Rothschild was radiant, and really [considered Gautier] he was justified. . . . Brussels and Paris may take one another's hand, and here we are a couple of steps from the Rhine, the German Rhine that will soon be only the song by Alfred de Musset.'[23]

The new railway, naturally enough, had reminded him of his wanderlust; yet it was not to the Rhine that he made his next journey: 'Stay in London as long as you like,' wrote the patient Girardin on 29 June, 'but send me four or five articles immediately. . . . Tell us about Mlle Rachel, all the stars of the Parisian sky.'[24] The Parisian stars had indeed shot, comet-like, to London: Rachel was converting the most insular of spectators to Racine at the St James's Theatre; Cerrito was dancing at Her Majesty's (though, to Gautier's mind, she bore no comparison with Taglioni, Elssler or Carlotta Grisi); and Carlotta herself had promised to dance for Ernesta's benefit. Gautier stayed in

Théophile Gautier at St. Petersburg, early in 1859
(*Photo: Richebourg*)

'Un mélancolique Marino Faliero': Théophile Gautier,
about 1856 (*Photo: Nadar*)

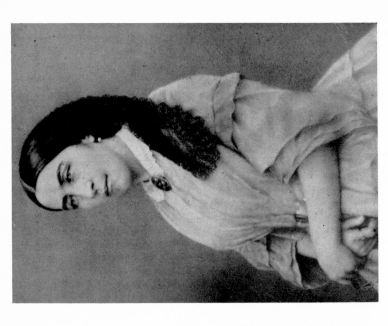

Théophile Gautier *fils*. From a photograph in the possession
of M. Pierre Théophile Gautier

Eugénie Fort. From a photograph in the possession of
M. Pierre Théophile Gautier (*Photo: Nadar*)

London for a month. He produced two articles. Then he returned to Paris, went the round of the summer theatres, and early in October, pursuing his vagrant fancy, impenitent as ever, he was on his way to Spain.

'Forgive me, *mon cher maître*, for taking flight to Madrid without any warning,' went his letter to the desperate Girardin. 'I hardly had time to throw a little linen and a pair or two of white gloves into my humble case, and as I have travelled sufficiently by now to know that nothing is less noticeable than absence, I got into the carriage happy enough about my escapade. Gérard had promised me to review *Pierrot valet de la mort* . . . As for *Militona*, which you have so kindly announced in *la Presse*, *Militona*, whose first pages lie interrupted on the table, it has a Spanish subject. Was there a better place to finish it than the Calle del Carmen, a stone's throw from the Puerta del Sol?'

It was not, of course, *Militona* that lured the vagabond critic across the Pyrenees. This was the time of the Spanish marriages, of Queen Isabella and Don Francisco d'Assise, of the Infanta Doña Luisa Fernanda and the Duc de Montpensier, and no *aficionado* could miss the bullfights held in celebration. So it was, after six years' exile, that Don Teofilo drove again through Burgos, where the cathedral 'held its stone arms to heaven with the same desperate ardour, and did not glance towards human affairs with one of its stained-glass eyes'; so it was he arrived, triumphant, at the Plaza Mayor in Madrid, which was already prepared for the *corrida*. Next day he saw the princes arrive in a sparkling cloud of officers gorgeous and streaming with gold: saw the wedding procession, a vision of carriages 'sparkling with gilt and coats of arms, thoroughbred horses of superb deportment, harnessed with wild splendour', and the Duchesse de Montpensier, dazzling in her pallor. And then, in the presence of thirty thousand spectators, the bullfights continued for three days, the great Montès de Chiclana showed his mastery, and the dramatic critic of *la Presse*, forgetting the labours and disappointments of Paris, forgetting all his responsibilities, recaptured some of his early enchantment.

*   *   *

He returned to the rue de Navarin to find financial troubles awaiting him. He wanted to write for more periodicals, and asked the manager of *la Presse* to make diplomatic enquiries of Girardin. The answer was (as one might expect) severe: if Gautier were suddenly gifted with fecundity and produced the articles he owed *la Presse*, he might write for any paper; if he published a single signed article elsewhere before he had acquitted his debts, the article would count as his resignation. He had agreed to write seventy-two articles a year for 10,000

F

francs; he had received the money but the articles were not written.
He had been to Algeria for two months (added Girardin) and was paid
as if he had continued to write; he had spent a month in London and
sent only one letter on the theatres; he had sent a single letter from
Spain, and that had arrived late. He had received 2,000 francs in advance for *Militona*, and Girardin had been waiting for the manuscript
since July. If such behaviour continued, he would be dismissed.[25]

Gautier, it seems, was not stirred by the letter; for his Oriental
lethargy continued, and in December Girardin needed to ask if a
heavy cold was any excuse for not writing *Militona*. And when at last,
five months late, Gautier set to work, he was not inspired by the sharp
and entirely justified remonstrances of Girardin. He owed his inspiration to hashish. He dashed off his Spanish story in ten days (he told the
Goncourts), with the aid of five grains of hashish morning and evening.
It gave him 'wonderful lucidity'.

*   *   *

Militona was acclaimed as its author would have wished: 'What a
pity,' commiserated the *Revue de Paris*, 'that criticism deprives poetry
and the novel of a pen of this metal, an imagination of this vigour and
versatility!' But before *Militona* was published, the most substantial
fruit of Gautier's Algerian tour was seen at the Porte-Saint-Martin.
La Juive de Constantine, based on a tale he had heard on his travels,
was the story of a Jewess, the mistress of a Christian, who had been
dismissed by her tribe as dead. In the cemetery she could read the
inscription on her own tomb; and, for the short remainder of her life,
she wandered about the streets, 'wiped by some tacit convention
from the face of the world'. As a poem by Vigny, *la Juive de Constantine*
might have triumphed. As a melodrama by Gautier, it was ill received.
When, in the fourth act, the curtain rose on the moonlit cemetery,
when the girl cast flowers on her mother's tomb and prepared to die,
the audience laughed heartily. 'Perhaps all the cypresses had made the
public good-humoured; yet at the dress rehearsal the act had moved
the firemen on duty, and a few scene-shifters' wives had dabbed their
eyes at the passages considered most amusing.' The basic act of *la Juive
de Constantine* was removed, one or two parts were cut, and the piece
was repeated without opposition. 'We had thought,' wrote Gautier,
'that a faithful impression of the diverse peoples in Africa might, plot
apart, have some interest for the French public. We have since discovered that the French public does not believe in Algeria; sixteen
years of possession have still not removed its doubts. It believes that
Algeria is populated by date merchants from the rue Vivienne.'

8. *Le Glas Intérieur*

'THE YEAR 1847 is beginning badly. There is Chaudesaigues, a poet turned critic for want of bread, like the rest of us, who fell dead, the other day, over the first page of his article.'[1] It was not the first time, nor the last, that Gautier published his discontent with his profession: he always considered himself a displaced poet. But on this occasion his lament roused Girardin to fury; and Girardin, in fury, did not consider writing a private rebuke. Next day, 2 February 1847, all the readers of *la Presse* learned of his disapproval: 'What was M. Gautier thinking of yesterday, when he pitied the writers who "wanted bread"? . . . Does not M. Théophile Gautier himself receive annually, from *la Presse*, more than the Presidents of the Chamber of the first *Cour royale* in the kingdom? If he were not a writer, a poet even, would he occupy a better place in the vast amphitheatre of society? Would any other function be more lucrative for him? Once and for all, at least in this paper, let us forget all the platitudes about great souls who die misunderstood and poets turning critics "for want of bread". They have only to write poems like *les Méditations* and they will lack neither bread nor publishers.'

The public correction was unnecessary and profoundly humiliating, and Gautier felt it. His only answer, he told Du Camp,[2] would be to resign from *la Presse*, but he could not afford to do so: a fact which was in itself confirmation of his words. 'Our Father Which is in Heaven does not give us our daily bread at all. And so we have to stay where the larder is full.'[3]

*   *   *

Despondently he continued his treadmill round, sat for nine hours watching *la Reine Margot*, the drama in five acts and fifteen tableaux with which Dumas inaugurated the Théâtre-Historique. 'Though we are not the good Homer, we may have nodded at times as we wrote our article, and dreamed as we leant against one of our columns.'[4] He was glad indeed when, in March, he was sent an invitation for the opening of another railway line. '*Théâtre de l'Odéon. Première représentation du chemin de fer.*' It was a first performance as good as any other, and at five in the morning he waited on the platform, the first to arrive for the journey. The miracle of the railway was still fresh to him. Early that morning they reached Rouen, then steamed on to le Havre, where all the population was afoot, the local *garde nationale* formed a guard of honour, ships were dressed overall, and a 'brilliant collation' was waiting at Frascati's. He paused on the beach to watch the leaden sea, the fishing-boats heaving under the wind, the solitary steamer trailing its feather of smoke: then returned to Paris to see the end of *l'Enfant de l'amour*, 'in which Virginie Déjazet was completely triumphant'.[5]

It seemed easier to triumph on stage than in art: Corot was rejected this year by the *Salon* jury, Ingres did not even enter,[6] and the most popular exhibit was the statue which achieved a *succès de scandale*. Clésinger's statue, *la Femme piquée par un serpent*: some remarked that it was the likeness of a woman experiencing an orgasm.

Remembering such triumphs, remembering his controversy with Girardin, Gautier might well ask what was the secret of success. More than once the question recurred to *le pauvre poète détourné de son art*.[7] And, superstitious as he was, he believed that the answer lay in the stars and not within himself. 'The world obeys unknown magnetic influences . . . An invisible pen adds or subtracts from the sum of probabilities . . . The important thing is to be fortunate. Endowed with fortune, you can commit every imprudence, every audacity; when you are fortunate, prodigality is more rewarding than thrift, dissipation more rewarding than labour; what should have been your perdition is your salvation, and however hard you cast your fortune through the door, it comes back through the window, drawn by an invincible attraction.'[8]

Gautier's despondency is Romantic, characteristic. It is sometimes a pose he strikes, and yet it is sometimes strange. Early in 1848 a journalist at a theatre noticed the dramatic critic of *la Presse*, 'shining like a star in the auditorium'.[9] Those who attended the royal fêtes at Versailles often observed him among their fellow guests[10]; and those who patronized Marquis, the Royal confectioner, found Gautier's poetry wrapped round their chocolate.[11] Every Monday thousands of readers enjoyed the verbal pyrotechnics, the sometimes cynical prose that hid much truth and feeling. 'He was recognized as a poet of high rank and a great prose-writer; newspapers, publishers and reviews demanded him; he lived in style, if not entirely according to his taste.'[12] Perhaps he had not thought of the future. In February came the Revolution.

*   *   *

It was the end of the bourgeois monarchy; Louis-Philippe and his Queen fled to England for sanctuary. It was also the end of Gautier's carefree existence: his contract with *la Presse* was annulled and left him in debt; he had received a few advances and no longer possessed the constant income with which to repay them. For the next decade he would struggle to provide for his family. In February, in the very month in which his life was broken, Ernesta again became pregnant. And then, on 26 March, his mother died.

She had shown him all the love that a mother shows an only son, a son who has earned European celebrity. And Gautier, who constantly needed maternal affection, who responded to her enveloping devotion, had adored his mother. Her death moved him profoundly: years later, at the funeral of Mme de Cormenin, when Maxime du Camp asked why he sobbed so bitterly, he answered: 'I am thinking of my mother.' Now he forced himself to write an article to pay for her funeral; he could only express his grief in *le Glas intérieur*:

> *Comme autrefois pâle et serein*
> *Je vis, du moins on peut le croire,*
> *Car sous ma redingote noire*
> *J'ai boutonné mon noir chagrin.*
> *Sans qu'un mot de mes lèvres sorte,*
> *Ma peine en moi pleure tout bas;*
> *Et toujours sonne comme un glas*
> *Cette phrase: Ta mère est morte!*
>
> *Au bois de Boulogne on me voit,*
> *Comme un dandy que rien n'occupe,*
> *Suivre à cheval un pli de jupe*
> *Sous l'ombre du sentier étroit.*
> *Même quand le galop m'emporte,*
> *Ma peine vole sur mes pas,*
> *Et toujours sonne comme un glas*
> *Cette phrase: Ta mère est morte!*
>
> *A l'Opéra, comme autrefois,*
> *Je tiens au bout de ma lorgnette*
> *La Carlotta qui pirouette*
> *Ou Duprez qui poursuit sa voix.*
> *A la musique douce ou forte*
> *Ma peine mêle son hélas!*
> *Et toujours sonne comme un glas*
> *Cette phrase: Ta mère est morte!*[13]

Troubled himself, he moved about the troubled city, seeking in art the consolation he could not find in life, urging poets and artists to rise above adversity: 'We must give the masses the feeling of art: without it the nations are but multitudes borne away on sombre tides into the chasm of oblivion. Beauty has enormous moral power. It touches those whom good alone could not attain. The beautiful and the good are two forms of truth.'[14] And in his first article on the *Salon*, passionately, he declared his belief in the power and necessity of art:

'Oh you who have the fortune to be young, do not fear your youth, let yourselves be swept away by fire, audacity, enthusiasm, love! May these four horses of flame draw your chariot of fire through the empyrean! Away with the timid, with their lamentable histories of Phaeton and Icarus, be not afraid of falling from the sky, it is already fine to fall from heaven. . . . By strength and perseverance in your studies, by the audacity and liberty of your work, deserve to be the artists of this colossal and climacteric century, of this great nineteenth century, the finest epoch seen by humankind since the loving earth fulfilled its revolution round the sun. Be worthy of the time when human genius has cancelled time, space and pain. . . . If you wish it so, what will they be beside our own, the vaunted centuries of Pericles, Leo X and Louis XIV? Will a great free people do less for art than a little town in Attica, a Pope and a king? . . .'[15]

*　　　*　　　*

Disillusionment and anticlimax persisted in Paris. Wanderlust and despondency overcame him, and Gautier remembered his African summer of three years ago. For 'the Orient is dangerous, above all the barbaric Orient; it causes a vertigo we can well understand. . . . Those embroidered tunics, those girdles bristling with arms, those saddles embossed with gold, the long guns ornamented with coral, the white burnouses with their majestic folds, the lithe and ardent horses with pink nostrils, manes tinted with henna: all trouble you, intoxicate you strangely. Few of those who have seen the sight, even among the most robust, resist it completely; everyone returns slightly Musulman at heart. And it sometimes happens, in Christian lands, on a rainy day, when the bourgeois look too ugly tramping through the mud, that one thinks of the minarets of Constantine, the fantasies of Arab douairs, and murmurs: There is no God but God, and Mahomet is His prophet'.[16] On 6 August Gautier drafted a letter to the Minister of War, asking for land in the Valley of Zer-Hamna, near Philippeville;[17] he would follow Petrus Borel, abandon journalism, and become a colonist in Algeria. He would live the rest of his life among 'the whitewashed walls, the emerald plants, the glowing rose of morning and of evening, the dusty ocean of desert.'

But the Romantic project was abandoned. He stayed in Paris. On 27 November Ernesta gave birth to a second daughter, Estelle, and his burden weighed yet heavier on his shoulders. And while he continued his incessant and distasteful task, December brought another new order to France. Louis-Napoleon was elected President of the Second Republic.

9. Marie

IN JANUARY 1849 the Académie-Française was called upon to elect two immortals, and *l'Événement* suggested Gautier as a candidate.

Gautier promptly refused to stand. Nearly two decades had passed since the *bataille d'Hernani*, but the wearer of the rose-coloured doublet, the Romantic who, on forty consecutive evenings, had applauded the audacious '*escalier dérobé*', could not now desert the ranks and become a *perruquiniste*. It is true that he made an occasional concession to orthodoxy: he attended the formal farewell dinner for the Paris correspondent of *The Times*.[1] But he remained incomparably happier watching *la Jeunesse des Mousquetaires*,[2] or spending an evening with Boissard and Delacroix at the Hôtel Pimodan;[3] and Maxime du Camp, who called on him in the rue Rougemont, would find him with the engaging nomad who flitted like some eternally restive sparrow round the city: Gérard de Nerval, curled up under a plaid and resting from his nightly peregrinations. And Gautier, quite surely, was gayest of all in the atmosphere of Montmartre: in the fifth-floor apartment at 16, rue Frochot where Mme Sabatier gave her Sunday dinners to Flaubert, devotedly affectionate, and to Baudelaire, who worshipped her in secret, in *les Fleurs du Mal*, as '*la muse et la madone*'. 'Her lovely hair, brown in shadow, gold in sun, brushes lightly over her brow, as if it were caressed by an amorous wind; her eyes gaze, fine and frank, her pink nostrils breathe in ardent life, her crimson lips seem half open for a smile or a kiss. . . .'[4] So Gautier described her himself. And *la Présidente*, as he named her, and as he himself implied, was no Madonna, but the most enchanting *demi-mondaine*. It was she who had posed for Clésinger's notorious statue, *la Femme piquée par un serpent*, the sensation of the *Salon* two years ago; and she owed her apartment to Hippolyte Mosselmann, brother of the celebrated Mme le Hon, mistress of Morny. And in this apartment, if she did not encourage Mosselmann's rivals, she presided, feminine and tolerant, over an uninhibited conversation.

Hostess, décor, conversation: all emphasized the truth: Gautier was determined not to be orthodox and unoriginal. 'As you go on in art and life, you should leave imitations and borrowed processes behind, and constantly accentuate your own character. Originality is the final manner of the poet and artist who understand life. In art it is not bad to have something shocking about you. The shocking, like the paradoxical which is only a virtue too forcibly expressed, is the result of premature beauty. The day when nothing is shocking in your work, do not congratulate yourself unduly, it means that the public is as strong as you are: that the public has caught up with you.'[5]

*   *   *

The question of progress in the arts occupied the new Government in these early months of 1849; in February the Ministers asked the City of Paris to help to subsidize the completion of the Louvre.[6] The Age of Haussmann was already beginning. The new President, determined to restore the sparkle to society, gave a 'gay, splendid, well-arranged, lively and pleasant ball' at the Elysée, where the orangery was turned into 'a redolent jardin d'Hiver, with occasional bosquets for flirtations', and, but for the 'apparition of Mme Victor Hugo, in a sort of wild sibyl-like coiffure, which attracted many smiling remarks, the whole fête presented the old scene of a *bal du grand monde* "under the tyrant"'.[7] Indeed it seemed that the monarchy had returned in thin disguise; and Parisian life returned to its old pattern.

But if political fever abated, spring fever increased. 'Let's bring this article to an end,' wrote Gautier on 21 May. 'It's very good of me to have dashed it off, for I might instead have gone to London on the famous excursion on which, for 175 francs, a highly intelligent, diligent organization looks after you for a week, takes you there, brings you back, beds you, boards you, escorts you to entertainments, museums and docks, to Richmond and to Hampton Court and Greenwich. . . .' That day he informed Ernesta he was going to London.[8]

Once, he reflected, it would have been quite a journey; now it was hardly an excursion. One could lunch *aux Frères Provençaux* and sup at Verrey's in Regent Street; if Roger were tired and not singing in *le Prophète*, one could console oneself with Calzolari at Her Majesty's. He himself found consolation at half a dozen London entertainments: among them *le Violon du Diable* at the Adelphi, *les Demoiselles de Saint-Cyr* at the Theatre Royal, where he considered Buckstone 'highly diverting'. Often though he complained of fatigue in Paris, in London he was tireless. He watched a harlequinade at the Royal Pavilion Theatre, an 'admirable' performance of *les Huguenots* at Covent Garden. And then he went to Ascot.

One sparkling morning in June, in a diligence drawn by four exemplary horses, the French expedition set off for 'le Chantilly de Londres'.

'As you go out of London, everything grows elegant, clean, well cared-for, picturesque. . . . You cannot imagine anything more charming, more inviting, better kept, than the long procession of houses, cottages and parks, greenhouses and nursery-gardens which begins beyond Hyde Park and never ends. As you pass these delightful houses it is difficult not to covet, and more than once, from the top of our diligence, we chose, in imagination, a retreat to which to retire from the exhausting turbulence of Paris.' The Victorian race-course, with its multitude of carriages brightly painted in yellow, red and white, and enhanced by golden ciphers on the doors, caught Gautier's imagination. He was fascinated by this immense Frith landscape: by the gargantuan consumption of sandwiches, hams and cakes, port, claret and champagne; by the women, on the boxes of their carriages, with their elegant dresses and furbelows of shot silk, their fringed parasols and brilliant hats; by the Queen's carriage with its red-and-gold clad postilions driving down the course. The signal was given. The jockeys' caps were soon a row of poppies, cornflowers and anemones on the horizon. And then came the winner, led to the Royal box, and Victoria Regina, 'inclining her pink bonnet, did honour to the noble animal with powerful withers and steaming nostrils which had just caused thousands of guineas to be lost and won. And you saw the living reality of the English sporting-prints with cherry-coloured horses, emerald fields and jonquil carriages which, in Ritner and Goupil's window, cast doubts upon English art. A visit to Ascot justifies them completely'.

And then he visited the Chinese junk moored at St Catherine's Docks, realized another dream: the dream that had taken shape in the steam of tea, as he had gazed at blue cups and lacquer coffers incrusted with mother-of-pearl. On the bridge of the junk stood a four-foot high pagoda; on the poop a gigantic chimerical bird, carved and coloured, spread its wings. And Gautier wondered why some company did not organize excursions to Egypt, Greece and China. 'At least man would not quit this earthly life without visiting his planet and dutifully admiring all creation. God has created him for that alone: man is the reader of the poem divine.'

Yet the most perfect stanza in creation, the finest work of the celestial artist, was not the vast rice-fields of China, nor the sluggish, stately Nile, nor even the Grecian landscape, grey with olive-trees. Gautier had always thought, and he would always believe, that the most perfect work of the artist of artists was woman. On his way to London he had met the charming, flirtatious but strictly married Régina Lhomme: Régina, dark-haired, pale-skinned, Spanish-looking, and her husband Alphonse, *le plus malin des bourgeois*; and with them he had started a

friendship to last his life. And in London, late in May, he had found
even more convincing proof of his theory. He had met the fiery, elegant,
slightly mysterious, entirely captivating Marie Mattei.

*   *   *

She was, it seems, about thirty: brown-haired, fine-featured, exquisitely pale, with Mediterranean eyes. She had been unhappily
married and paid heavily to regain her freedom, for she saw little of
her two children. She was Italian: her children were brought up in the
convent at Bastia, and she herself had a house at Monticello. She was a
nomad, for her letters show her in Lyons, Paris, Marseilles, Geneva and
Rome. She was known in papal circles, deeply religious, and (unlike
Ernesta) deliciously dressed: her correspondence is punctuated by the
names of fashionable modistes and coutouriers. She was charmingly
Bohemian, rolling her own cigarettes and delighting in stronger smoking: 'It makes me desolate to contradict you,' she would write to
Gautier, 'but I am not poisoning myself in the least with cigars. The
ones I smoke are so exquisite that I've often thought of sending you
some.'

She had all the passion of Ernesta, and far more than Ernesta's
intelligence. She appeared when Ernesta, domestic and familiar, was
busy with her career, harassed by the work of maternity. Gautier was
ready to fall in love. And though Marie Mattei hesitated to surrender,
she fell in love with him overwhelmingly: fell in love with all the passion
of the lonely. 'I shall never be able to describe the dreadful solitude
through which I dragged my life, the ennui that I always bore with me,
the baseless grief which so often made me long for death,' she wrote to
him. 'I saw love everywhere, except for me. . . . I swear to you that
when I fell so in love with you that I could kneel as you passed, I was
about to disbelieve in love.'

*   *   *

Gautier returned to France at the end of June to resume the round of
the theatres, write an appreciation of Henri Monnier, a dozen articles
on the *Salon*. Theatres and galleries seemed even more oppressive in
the summer sun, his wanderlust pulled him constantly from Paris.
Maxime du Camp, who frequently called on him, found him more
often than not in the studio high up in rue Rougemont, tranquil and
alone. 'In his firm round writing he covered the requisite number of
pages for his article, and, when his labour was over, he crouched like
a Turk on a divan, held a cushion against his breast, and went off for
hours into I know not what enchanted world.'[9]

One enchanted world, at least, might be discovered: as Gautier wrote
of the open-air theatres in Paris, his imagination raced to the arenas in

pain and his pen recorded his reminiscences. As he wandered round
the *Salon*, his attention was held by a painting of Bohemians near
Granada: 'How lovingly that gitana bends till her brown shoulders
touch the ground; the castanettes chatter, the panderos rumble and
thunder; the wild assembly cries out *ay* and *oh!* and in their faces, the
colour of orange-peel and Cordova leather, the eyes are twinkling like
black stars. . . . And in the background rise the blue crests of the Sierra
l'Elvira or the Sierra Nevada.'[10] In the last week of August Lord
Pilgrim announced in *l'Artiste* that 'Théophile Gautier is in Bilbao
first performance of *Une Course de Taureaux*).'

He was expected back in Paris about 9 September. And it was,
perhaps, then that he received an enchanting invitation: 'My dear poet,'
wrote Mme Dumas, 'how can one offer a vulgar cup of tea to you who
feed on an oleander's kisses? If, however, you would care to descend
for a moment from the blue clouds of your beautiful Spain, you would
find me at home on Wednesday evening.'[11]

Gautier's autumn dreams were less of Spain than of Marie Mattei.
It was on 15 October, in Paris, that she became his mistress.[12] 'It will
be three months tomorrow, dear beloved,' she wrote to him on 14
January, 'that you made the sun shine for me and awoke my soul from
its winter sleep. For that alone, and for your kindness to me, I shall be
at your feet all my life.'

10. The Sorrows of Fortunio

OCTOBER WAS was not a month of perfect happiness; if there were private rejoicing, there were also public and private regret. On the 28th,
Gautier attended a farewell dinner for Flaubert and Du Camp, who
were leaving next day to fulfil a dream of his own: to journey through
Egypt and Palestine. They dined at the Provençaux, where Flaubert
spoke of discovering the sources of the Nile, and Gautier urged Du
Camp to turn Moslem, so that he could wear silk clothes and kiss the
black stone at Mecca.[1] Next morning Flaubert left for Egypt; and the
author of *Une Nuit de Cléopâtre* set off to the Madeleine where, before
a congregation more conscious of their elegance than of their grief,
Chopin's funeral service was being held.

And at this time there is a thread of sadness in Gautier's writing.
Though eminence had come to him, though he was the sovereign
spectator in all theatres, though he created literary opinion, though

Clésinger had sculpted him, though Riesener would exhibit his portrait in pastel, at the next *Salon*, though Marie adored him with all the force of first rapture, his love of poetry remained frustrated. The eminence he had gained was not the eminence he desired: he was recognized as critic, he longed to be a poet. He tried to secure a government sinecure for which he was well fitted: the post of an Inspecteur des Beaux-Arts. It would give him time to devote himself to poetry and literature, to realize his life-long dream. But the Republic, like the monarchy which had passed and the empire which was yet to be born, disdained his services.

December came and went, bearing part of his life into nothingness. Carlotta danced her farewell to Paris in *la Filleule des Fées*. Marie, too, departed, drawn by her migratory nature and, perhaps, by commitments, to Marseilles, and letter after letter, too passionately written for punctuation, flew back to Paris: '*Monday midnight* . . . and Monday, as you know, was one of our days of joy.' She lit a candle in the church of la Pallud, before the statue of St Theresa. 'This St Theresa, dressed as a nun with her crown of roses, reminds me now of one thing alone: her feast day is 15 October.' And again she wrote to him:

'Dear beloved,

'It is only three days since I wrote to you, but I feel so desperate that I come to tell you my grief: you are so good and indulgent to me I can see quite well I'm becoming a boring abandoned woman. . . Yet I lean my head against your breast, which I adore, as you know. . . I should be the most ungrateful creature on earth if I ceased for minute to worship you, if I forgot the nothingness from which you brought me into life. . . . This evening I came across those ruffles that Gigoux gave me one night, as we were coming back from dinner. *Ti ricordi?* Do you remember that evening? I sat in contemplation of those ruffles, I saw you leaning back in that chair and looking at our bed with shining eyes. The very thought I shall see that look again is for me a joy beyond expression. . . .

'I shall see you again, with God's help, as surely as I love you; but tell me if you want to stop loving me. That will not stop my seeing you again. . . .

'How I have suffered! You can imagine I've been unspeakably jealous of Mme de Girardin. I dreamed you were in her box and I *saw* your lips touch lightly on her shoulder. I woke up crying real tears, I swear to you, and ever since I have thought—that I love you enough to lose my reason and my life and to exchange eternity for the hour you promised me when you return.'

. . . . .

And so Marie stayed in Marseilles, living in passionate recollection and in reverie. 'As you say, my dear darling,' she wrote on 11 March, 'as you say, my dear darling, it will be exactly two months tomorrow since you kissed me in the carriage at the Madeleine. I still keep that kiss: it was so *true*, so warm.' And again: 'I feel your love as if I saw it, and I've certainly seen you almost senseless with joy.' And later: 'Since I felt the coldness of your hands at the Hôtel Beauvau, since I saw you bereft of colour and of speech, I shall not dare to doubt you.' She alone, Marie, *l'Italienne*: she alone, of all the women Gautier had known, gave him the passionate, unfailing, dramatic love he needed.

*　　　*　　　*

The year 1850 opened conspicuously. Dumas produced a three-act comedy, *le Chandelier* was promised, Rachel appeared in Romantic drama, and a vast concourse invaded the Porte-Saint-Martin for Lamartine's *Toussaint Louverture*. Berlioz roused his audience with his *Symphonie Fantastique*, and Gautier had the personal satisfaction of recording Ernesta's success as Malcolm in *la Donna del Lago*. On 5 April, at the Théâtre-Italien, where her voice still echoed, his own words were heard: those of *le Sélam*, his 'descriptive symphony' of the Orient, set to music by his friend Ernest Reyer. 'It is all suave and exquisite poetry!' cried Méry. '*Le Sélam* is original and perfectly beautiful. . . . What a future for a young composer of twenty-five!'[3]

And what future would there be for the poet of thirty-eight? Gautier must have wondered despondently as he plodded home, night after night, to the fifth-floor rooms up the black stairs in rue Rougemont, after watching one of the endless trivial comedies on which his bread depended. 'It was only a little more than half-way through at midnight,' he wrote, dejectedly, reviewing a five-act *féerie*.[4] 'One came home red-eyed, hollow, stupefied. The passers-by were passing no longer. The gaslight, paling in the wan dawn, wavered and went out. The city was very strange, the market-gardeners were arriving on their carts of vegetables, the real Paris was asleep, the boulevards were deserted. . . . Under the sensible Paris, still in bed, there moved the workaday Paris of the shadows.' Both place and time seemed foreign; though Gautier enjoyed the luxuries that money would bring, he was the least materialistic of men, and he was out of place in what he called the century of the Rothschilds: the century when 'the fever of gold has invaded society, the gods have fallen powerless from their obsolete Olympus . . . and in the midst of the crumbling of arts, letters, religions and arms, only the stacks of banknotes remain'.[5] Arsène Houssaye, now director of the Comédie-Française, Houssaye, wealthy and practical, bought a small estate off the Champs-Elysées embracing the little house in the avenue Lord-Byron where Gautier had once lived. He offered him the house as loan or gift; but Gautier refused: 'I don't earn anything now-adays, 6,000 francs at most. Beaujon is too far away since I've sold my ponies. . . .'[6]

One morning late in June, as he finished an article on Ponsard, there came a letter that brought the full weight of melancholy upon him: a letter sent by Maxime du Camp, that amiable traveller and memoir-writer, from the second cataract of the Nile. 'Greetings, Fortunio! I wager you haven't 37° in the shade. Have you a great deal of fog and vaudevilles? When will you come and roam in the lands of the sun? . . . The Isle of Elephantine is for sale: 12,000 francs. I'm dying to buy it, and I'd always have a hammock to offer you under a palm-tree.'[7] 'I should rob the Bank of France and join you,' Gautier answered, 'for they pay so little for syllables it would be the only way. . . . I feel I am dying of nostalgia for Asia Minor, and if I didn't write a verse or two, I should abandon myself to the worms, though I find death still more hideous than life.'[8]

But if he could not go to the Isle of Elephantine, he decided, in July, on a more enchanting journey: he would sail to Naples with the Lhommes and Louis de Cormenin, write his first impressions of Italy (the impressions that Balzac had so long awaited), and spend part of the summer in the lotus city of Venice with Marie.

On 29 July, with the familiar personal touch, he announced his departure in *la Presse*: 'We had hoped to see *les Frères corses* on Satur-day; we shall have to content ourselves with the shores of the Mediter-ranean, Genoa, the Corniche road and the Roman Campagna.' To Eugénie Fort (with whom he now had a platonic relationship) he wrote, callously, next day, that he was leaving within twenty-four hours: 'It has been so suddenly decided and arranged that I haven't time to come and say good-bye.' Within the week he had left. 'It is by the common or garden railway,' wrote Gérard de Nerval, taking over his work, 'that Théophile Gautier has just departed for the country which the scene-designers of the Théâtre-Historique had half revealed to him. It is useless to cast the flowers of rhetoric after the train which is bearing him away to a lovelier world.'[9]

*   *   *

As he sped towards Italy, Gautier himself was casting flowers of eloquence at the feet of Marie. 'Before I caught the train I received your little note,' she answered from Geneva on 10 August. 'It gave me a glimpse of the heaven that is Venice, and I went my way with the joy that God reserves for lovers' hearts. Yesterday I found your second little note. Thank you a thousand times, dear love. No doubt you are

n Venice already, as it is the 10th. I'm leaving on Monday morning
or Domo d'Ossola where I shall arrive on Tuesday evening. I think I
hall reach Venice on Saturday, sooner if I can. I am still well, but a
ittle afraid of fatigue. Yet the longing to see you is so strong I shall
ardly stop on the way. Where shall I find you in Venice? I'm addressing
his note, which leaves before me, poste restante, where I hope you will
ind it, and I beg you to leave your address for me there. I'll go in
earch of your little note as soon as I arrive. I should write to you at
reat length, if I were not breathless at the mere thought of seeing you,
nd feeling myself beloved. May God make you happy, as I am, in
your affection. I love you, that you know.'

11. *Séjour à Venise*

EVERY MAN (it was one of Gautier's beliefs) has chosen a native country
n his dreams. Venice was one of his own elected homes, clearly con-
eived in the dark-room of his imagination. And on a stormy August
night in 1850, his train, like some nightmare hippogriff, crossed the
oridge into Venice, from dream to reality.

He was rowed round meandering canals: 'Strange resonant cries
echoed at the corners, a floating coffin, a shadow bent over it, slipped
rapidly past us; a window, narrowly skirted, gave a glimpse of an interior
starred by a lamp or reflection, like a Rembrandt engraving. . . . From
the tops of arches, forms that were vaguely human watched us pass,
like the dismal figures of a dream. . . . We felt we were travelling in a
novel by Maturin, Lewis or Ann Radcliffe, illustrated by Goya,
Piranesi and Rembrandt. The old histories of the Three Inquisitors,
he Council of Ten, the Bridge of Sighs, of masked spies . . . of execu-
ions at the Orfano canal, all the melodrama and romantic décor of
old Venice returned to us. . . . A cold terror, damp and black like all
around us, had taken possession.' Then the boat drew up at the steps
of the Giustiniani Palace, now the Hôtel d'Europe; and Gautier, from
his balcony, was soon watching the lanterns of gondolas coming and
going on the canals like sparks on burning paper.

*   *   *

Voyage en Italie might well be called *Séjour à Venise*: the larger part
of the book, the most animated, most brilliant pages are filled with
verbal photographs of Venice. Such a photographic task even Gautier
found demanding: 'What needs to be rendered is the effect, the colour

and movement, the stir of air and water, life itself,' he wrote, recalling
his first impressions of the Piazza San Marco.

'How can we express the rosy shades of the ducal palace, that seems
like living flesh; the snowy whitenesses of statues, drawing their contours in the blue of Veronese and Titian; the blushes of the Campanile
caressed by the sun; the flashes of distant gold, the thousand aspects
of the sea, sometimes mirror-clear, sometimes seething with sequins
like a dancer's dress? Who will paint this vague, luminous atmosphere
filled with sunshafts and vapours . . . the coming and going of gondolas,
barges, argosils, galiots; the red or white sails, the boats familiarly
resting their cutwaters on the quay, with their thousand odd and
picturesque flags and drying nets and lines; the sailors loading and
unloading boats, the crates being carried, the barrels rolled, the motley
strollers on the mole, Dalmatians, Greeks, Levantines and others, that
Canaletto would indicate in a single stroke; how can one show it all
together, as in nature? . . . The poet is less fortunate than the painter
and the musician. He has but a single line at his disposal.'

In the verbal panorama of Venice, in the multitudinous impressions
that Gautier absorbed and noted for fourteen hours a day, one does not
feel the restrictions of the writer's art. And if too many churches
demand his close examination, if too many pictures are reproduced in
detail, when the artist replaces the critic we are fully recompensed.
At a certain moment, the artist suddenly takes over the chronicle of
St Mark's, and Gautier records an impression of the cathedral, lyrical
and splendid. The artist traces the rococo façade of San-Moisè with
perfectly matched ebullience. And from the window of his new hotel
in the Campo San Moisè, he records, precise as Canaletto, the cortège
on the canal beneath his window: the boats from Fusina, burdened
with grapes and peaches, leaving their garden smell in the early morning air; the red funeral gondola bearing a corpse towards Murano,
the official gondola trailing the Austrian flag and carrying some 'cold
stiff dignitary, his breast bedecked with decorations', to his functions.
He watches the quarrelsome gondoliers as they brandish their oars,
the fishermen as they tow a dolphin in triumph. He catches the Piazza
San Marco alive with flower-sellers, ragamuffins, vendors of crystallized
fruit, itinerant musicians; he records the band of the Austrian invaders
playing the overture to *William Tell*, the voice of Girolamo as he sings
la Biondina in gondoletta and the verses echo down the dark canals.
From the moment the frigate fires its cannon at dawn until the sun sets
in fire behind San Giorgio Maggiore, Gautier catches the vivacity and

mystery, the colour and the adventure of Venice. These are among his happiest impressions of travel.

And some of this felicity he surely owed to the companion he so discreetly omitted to mention in his Venetian chapters, the apparition only recorded in the two final paragraphs of his book: the mysterious woman who 'greatly intrigued the cosmopolitan curiosity of Florence'. It is probably the most complete likeness of Marie Mattei. She sits alone and indolent in a brown barouche,

'draped in a big shawl of white crêpe de chine, its fringes almost touching her feet. Her Parisian hat, clearly made by Mme Royer, cuts a sharp halo round that fine and delicate profile, modelled like an antique cameo, a Grecian contrast with her completely modern elegance and a bearing so coldly distinguished that it is almost English. Her neck, so white it shows a tint of blue, the smooth rose of her cheeks, the clear blue of her eyes seem to mark her as a northern beauty; but the spark in those sapphire eyes is so ardent that it must have been lit beneath some southern sky. Her hair, pinned up in wavy bands, has those brownish tones, that brilliance typical of blonde women in warm climates; one of her arms is hidden in the folds of the shawl, like that of Mnemosyne, the other, enhanced by a striking bracelet, emerges half bare from the lace billows of a *manche à sabot*, and, with her little gloved hand, against her cheek, she toys with a camellia, a gesture of dreamy distraction that is evidently habitual. Is she English, Italian or French? No one can say for certain, as no one knows her. . . . Has she crossed Europe for some mysterious rendezvous?'

The answer to the Florentine question had already been given in Venice, in this summer of 1850, in an idyll that lasted from 17 August to 4 September; and the solitary woman in the carriage might be recognized as the mistress who had glided in a black gondola in waters that were 'black as the waters of Lethe', and had inspired the poem that Gautier had written in September in Louis de Cormenin's little notebook, the finest of his erotic poems: *Musée secret*.

* * *

Yet Venice was not a dream of unbroken felicity. One day as Gautier sat in a café in the Piazza San Marco, the waiter brought a copy of the *Journal des Débats*. It announced the death of Balzac: Balzac, whom he had laughed with, worked with and admired for fifteen years, since the days of *Mademoiselle de Maupin* and the Impasse du Doyenné: Balzac, who had so wanted him to come to Italy: Balzac, whose last, dictated

G

letter had ended with the words: 'I cannot read or write!' The past was breaking away. And the news touched Gautier all the more profoundly, as only that morning he had seen the soulless creatures lingering on in the madhouse at San Servolo. The decisions of destiny were hard to explain.

And the brief idyll had ended. 'Dead, exhausted, utterly broken,'[1] Marie had for the moment left him and returned to France. Their liaison was always swallow-like, and had its seasons. Nor was he only saddened by her absence: he was harassed now by the demands of his editors, the ceaseless problems of finance:

'Here is a colossal article on St Mark's [he wrote to the manager of *la Presse* on 14 September]. Another on the Ducal Palace is in progress and will be sent off soon. The last one will follow closely. Don't fail whatever happens to send me 500 francs at Florence because my money has very nearly run out. Don't fail. It is very urgent. . . . Try to make the money reach me by the twenty-fifth so that I don't die of hunger in some tavern corner and can leave for Rome. . . .'

And then, a pathetic comment on his commitments: 'When you have received the two articles . . . be kind enough to write to my father at Montrouge to come and take the 60 francs that are left—supposing that you have given 400 francs to Mme Grisi and 500 to me. . . . If you see *le patron* tell him I'm working like an ox, running like a stag, and that I'm thin as a lizard, all for the greater glory of *la Presse*.'[2]

It seemed ironical that as he sat in Venice, writing against inclination, begging for money to be sent to him, *l'Artiste* in Paris declared that his fame was a cause for national pride.[3]

Yet he did not leave Venice desolate and frustrated; in his breast-pocket, delightedly guarded, frequently re-read, was a note from Marie: 'As I touched your Venetian letter, saw your writing, my heart beat as loud as the bells of San Moisè; but when I read of your kisses, your embraces, I was utterly faint, *pauvre Marie*!

'. . . You were right to call me your true mistress. Yes, I love you madly, submissively, I leave you that I may feel the sharpness of absence and the voluptuous pleasure of return. I leave you that I may think about you clearly, far away from you, as I should seek the light to study a picture. . . .

'Happy are you, who have so many things to love: your name, your glory, and, even more precious than these, the dreams of your imagination, sweeter and dearer than all the caresses of women!'[4]

*　　　*　　　*

Gautier soon left Venice to realize another dream of his imagination: in a cocoon of overcoats and cloaks, on the imperial of a diligence, he

escended the slopes of the Apennines. Then 'villas began to appear by
the side of the road, the cypresses raised their black spires, the Italian
ines opened verdant parasols; the olive tree, unhesitant, ventured its
ad and glaucous foliage in the air; one grew aware of a movement of
pedestrians, horses, carriages, the approach of a great living city'. As
September night fell upon Florence, he arrived at the Porta San
allo.

His arrival, like his arrival in Venice, was melodramatic; he was
reeted by files of penitents, masked and clad in black, bearing smoking
orches, escorting a catafalque. Next morning brought a sudden change
f atmosphere: as he left the New York Hotel, near the Arno, two
ower-girls rushed upon him and bedecked him with roses and carna-
ons. Yet for all the flowers and a welcome meeting, a coruscating
onversation with Parisian friends, for all his admiration of architecture
ad the elegant cosmopolitan crowd in the Cascine, it is evident from
is brief chapter on Florence that Gautier's charmed existence had
een broken, that he was no longer living in a dream. Nor did Rome
eplace what he had left in Venice: the exultant mood had passed. 'I
eed your writing if I am to revive a little,' wrote Marie from Mar-
illes, 'for I am exhausted, and tomorrow is the fifteenth. You know,
t. Theresa's Day, our anniversary . . .'[5] Gautier relieved his feelings in
is letter to *la Présidente*, a prolonged Rabelaisian enormity that must
ave brought a blush even to Mme Sabatier's impervious cheeks. Then
e left Rome for Naples.

A document in the archives of the Neapolitan police sheds a curious
ght upon his visit:[6] 'On the 4th of this month [November 1850],
'eofilo Gottier, a very exalted Frenchman of the red party, left Naples.
Ie had stayed in Naples for ten or twelve days and was in continual
nd most intimate contact with don Vincenzo Capecelatoro, brother-in-
w of Ricciardi. He is a socialist writer, and we are quite convinced
at, inspired by the demagogic party in Naples, he will soon publish
me work or other and outrage the government.' A note from the
Ministry of the Interior on 20 November, and another from the
Neapolitan Prefecture of Police, dated 5 December, show that Gautier
as expelled from Naples. He embarked for Marseilles and the police
ade arrangements 'to prevent the return of this individual to the
apital of the Two Sicilies'.

It is a strange episode; for until the Franco-Prussian War revealed
is patriotism, Gautier's politics were passive in the extreme. He
elieved in his country, in the freedom of the individual; in France he
ccepted the Monarchy, the Empire and the Republic; he would never
ave been concerned with foreign politics, except as a spectator. The

Neapolitan episode finds no confirmation in Gautier's correspondenc
or his work; only one declaration of faith did he make in Naples: i
was, he recorded, in the ruins of Pompeii. 'To test the acoustics of th
ancient theatre we declaimed the monologue of Charles V, pacing th
Thymele with great strides, according to M. Ligier's tragic recipe:
A friend served us as prompter, orchestra and public, and took charg
of the applause and bouquets.'[7] It was a pleasant performance c
Hernani.

On 25 November Gautier burst into print in *la Presse* and announce
his return: 'Here we are back from our caravanserai, like Don Césa
de Bazan. One of our shoes is still in the ashes of Vesuvius. . . . The ba
weather brings us home; otherwise we should have left Naples fc
Palermo and Palermo for Tunis.' Perhaps the Neapolitan police coul
have made a comment; perhaps the demands of the Press brought hin
back to his attic rooms in the rue Rougemont, where his creditors an
family gave him little peace.[8] 'Louis looks like the shadow of himsel
he is wasting so from ennui,' wrote Gautier to Du Camp on 13 De
cember, 'and without the four months in Italy, we should have burs
with rage like dogs, or burst with spleen, like Englishmen.' When D
Camp met the travellers again, they were not even trying to struggl
against the tide of sadness and discouragement, and Gautier repeate
that 'the Fates had only wound black threads into the ball of h
existence.' He had no resources but his ill-paid work; and his wor
drove him unendingly: 'The insatiable monster that men call publicit
is ever demanding, ever devouring,' he wrote in *la Presse* on 30 De
cember: 'It will not be appeased by the honeycombs that tremblin
poets offer; it must have its daily fodder, papers, books, novels, drama
comedies, vaudevilles and revues. Frédéric Soulié and Balzac wer
crushed beneath the Press—and how many others have fallen un
recorded!'

12. *Un Ange Chez Moi . . .*

ON 15 JANUARY 1851, Gautier's new ballet, *Paquerette*, was first pe
formed and 'greeted by enthusiastic applause. . . . The story [explaine
the author] begins in French Flanders and ends in Hungary. Wh
Hungary? When you have seen this dance, as sparkling as a dragor
fly's waltz in a sunbeam, who can say we were wrong to follow Cerri
to a town that is hard to spell and perhaps no more exists than the s

coast of Bohemia mentioned in Shakespeare? If she had asked for
Lima or Timbuctoo we should have given it to her for her dance. . . .
The music, by M. Benoit, is clear, lively, rhythmical, and all the winter
we'll dance quadrilles to the tunes of *Paquerette*.'[1]

The spring, with other pleasures, was not far behind. In the last
days of March came a letter from Marie, who was returning to Paris and
asked Gautier's permission 'to dress in the latest fashion'. On 30 March
he wrote one of his happiest, most engaging poems: *Premier Sourire du
Printemps*. 'The weather is superb today,' he explained in *la Presse*,
soon afterwards, 'and were it not that our Sunday task must be done,
we should go and greet the spring in the Bois de Boulogne or on the
hills of Meudon. As we cannot show it this civility, we address it a
kind of hymn, a scrap of poetry rhymed the other week as we watched
the first buds bursting in the April showers. . . .'

> *Sous l'herbe, pour que tu la cueilles,*
> *Il met la fraise au teint vermeil,*
> *Et te tresse un chapeau de feuilles*
> *Pour te garantir du soleil . . .*[2]

Were the lines addressed to Marie, to suggest the pastoral pleasures
they would enjoy together?

*   *   *

On 15 April she was again in Paris, the Venetian fire still flaming
in her heart. But the meetings were not so simply arranged as they had
been in the Campo San Moisè: throughout the month Gautier was
harassed by visits to the *Salon*, by *Italia*, the record of last summer's
journey, by his unrelenting dramatic criticism; there was a concert to
organize at the end of June in aid of Algerian colonists: *le Sélam* would
be performed, and Ernesta would sing a cavatine from *l'Italienne à
Alger*.[3] And there, of course, lay the fundamental problem: Ernesta
remained in the rue Rougemont, with Estelle, and Ernesta must not
know that Marie existed. 'Will you be kind enough to tell my *true God*
that I expect him tomorrow, Wednesday, at four o'clock?' Marie
asked Louis de Cormenin, their messenger, in June. 'I should willingly
write to him; but I'm too afraid of spoiling things. So I must trouble
you yet again.' Could there be a sequel to Venice? They thought, that
spring, of escaping to the banks of the Rhine. And then, fickle as April
weather, they quarrelled. 'Gautier came at five o'clock yesterday,' wrote
Marie to de Cormenin. 'I told him, formally, and it's true, that if you
didn't come, I should give up the Rhine. . . . Come round, my dear.

I hardly ever see you, and I so enjoy our little informal chats. Gautier frightens me more and more; he isn't *gentle*, you know; that is the least of his faults; and then a friend is better ...'

And then the cloud passed. In Ernesta's absence she visited rue Rougemont, and rediscovered her passion. When, on 2 August, she left Paris, she took away 'happiness for the rest of her life'.[4] And even as, swallow-like, she sped away, there appeared in *la Presse* that most enchanting of all the tributes to her love, the poem that seems to capture Marie in her entirety, with all her coquetry, her Fragonard elegance, her piety and her Italian passion: *Coquetterie posthume*:[5]

> *Quand je mourrai, que l'on me mette,*
> *Avant de clouer mon cercueil,*
> *Un peu de rouge à la pommette,*
> *Un peu de noir au bord de l'oeil.*
>
> *Car je veux, dans ma bière close,*
> *Comme le soir de son aveu,*
> *Rester éternellement rose*
> *Avec du kh'ol sous mon oeil bleu.*
>
> *Pas de suaire en toile fine,*
> *Mais drapez-moi dans les plis blancs*
> *De ma robe de mousseline,*
> *De ma robe à treize volants.*
>
> *C'est ma parure préférée;*
> *Je la portais quand je lui plus.*
> *Son premier regard l'a sacrée,*
> *Et depuis je ne la mis plus.*
>
> *Posez-moi, sans jaune immortelle,*
> *Sans coussin de larmes brodé,*
> *Sur mon oreiller de dentelle*
> *De ma chevelure inondé.*
>
> *Cet oreiller, dans les nuits folles,*
> *A vu dormir nos fronts unis,*
> *Et sous le drap noir des gondoles*
> *Compté nos baisers infinis.*

Entre mes mains de cire pâle,
Que la prière réunit,
Tournez ce chapelet d'opale,
Par le pape à Rome bénit :

Je l'égrènerai dans la couche
D'où nul encor ne s'est levé;
Sa bouche en a dit sur ma bouche
Chaque Pater *et chaque* Ave.

13. Alarms and Excursions

THE VISIT to the Rhine had been abandoned, but Gautier still longed to lose himself in travel: still wanted to see the Crystal Palace that seemed to realize the dream of the *palais sous cloche* in *Fortunio*, that reverie of twenty years ago. Perhaps he needed to console himself for the absence of Marie.

On 11 August his wanderlust took possession: 'The moonlight was superb on Monday evening. The idea of going to see the blue and white rays on the damp leaves of a forest took hold of us in the middle of the boulevard de Gand; but instead of catching the train for Saint-Germain, we mistook the railway. ... It is very hard, when you find yourself at Dieppe, not to take the boat for Brighton; at Brighton an express train was ready to speed to London. And we who, until then, had virtuously resisted all the temptations of the Crystal Palace, resisted no longer, for we were very hungry at the thought of a fish supper in an oyster-bar in the Strand.'[1]

He stayed at the Hôtel Sablonnière in Leicester Square, that colony of foreign visitors: the hotel where Hans Andersen had stayed: the hotel where he himself had stayed so happily, two years earlier, with Alphonse and Régina Lhomme: 'I'm very near the room you had,' he told Régina, nostalgically, 'and I saw the little black horsehair sofa on which we had such long conversations and ate so many oranges. I lunch at the table where all four of us used to sit and I always feel I shall see you come down the stairs.'[2] With the energy that always seemed to distinguish him abroad, he hastened round the theatres: *l'Enfant prodigue*, he reported, was popular in London, particularly since they had introduced a camel from the Zoo. He sped to see Julia Grisi at Covent Garden, rushed on to the Adelphi, flew to the Royal

Olympic, where Helen Faucit (he had always thought her the pre-
destined daughter of Shakespeare) had returned for a brief triumph to
the stage.

His excursion, it seems, had been somewhat impulsive, and within a
fortnight he was short of money. He was (and his hesitation is hardly
surprising) too unsure of his reception to ask Emile de Girardin for an
advance; and he evaded the request by an invocation to that most
human of deities, Girardin's wife:

'Madame,
   'You have given me such a splendid description of the fairylands of
the Indian exhibition and have shown such a gracious desire to see your
impressions related by your completely devoted vassal that I departed
with the secrecy and speed of a Treilhet though I didn't carry off six
hundred thousand francs. I have seen Lahore, Calcutta, Kashmir,
Benares, Hyderabad under the crystal bell at Hyde Park and in three
hours I became as strong as several Hevas on matters concerning the
Ganges. I felt like an elephant among the bamboos and I recognized
my native country, for if I appear to have been born in Paris, it is pure
illusion: by Brahma, Vishnu and Shiva I swear that I now remember
sitting on a white ox with two humps. I am going to write this journey
of three thousand leagues and three thousand years in three articles
which I will send *la Presse* from London because I want to have the
things before my eyes—pacify your husband and tell him to send me
the money in London so that I can come home for I have little more
than 28 thousand francs on me [sic] and I am beginning to be afraid
that I shall have no money as Prince Soltikoff said at Allahabad.
            'Your elephant-in-ordinary,
                    THEOPHILE GAUTIER.'

   It was not the first time that Delphine de Girardin had helped to
smooth the path of her *éléphant*, but she responded with engaging
promptitude. In her largely illegible hand she dashed off a note to the
manager of *la Presse*, asking him to ransom his contributor, and Rouy
despatched the money next day (with a warning) to London. He was re-
paid by three lyrical accounts of the Indian exhibits at the Crystal Palace.
   And yet was the elephant really happy among his bamboos? Was
Gautier really lost in the marvels of London? It seems that neither the
Zoo nor all the wonders of India nor even '*la lady chinoise*' with her
two-and-a-half-inch shoes could wean him from his spiritual home. As
he left Gore House, after hearing the negro singers, the sound of a
Spanish song caught his ears and brought back that first elating,

Romantic pilgrimage of eleven years ago: the marble-pillared Court of
Lions, the jubilant oleander blazing into bloom in the gardens of the
Alhambra.

And the Court of Lions, the oleander, the sunlit, plashing fountains,
must have filled him with even sharper nostalgia when he returned to
Paris. One morning a startled Maxime du Camp heard a violent ring at
his bell, and Gautier, pale, hatless and dishevelled, burst into the study,
collapsed on a sofa and said: 'They want to put me in prison.' He had
refused again (he had refused consistently) to mount guard with the
garde nationale, and he had been sentenced to twenty-four hours'
imprisonment. That morning two of the *sûreté* had arrived with a
warrant, but he had escaped down the back stairs and run to safety.
Du Camp pointed out that Gautier might save himself much trouble
by complying with rules. 'I refuse to mar my appearance with a ridiculous costume,' answered that ardent apostle of Art for Art's Sake.
'I'm humiliated enough already, wearing a coat that would do for a
concierge, I won't demean myself with a tunic with epaulettes and a
shako with a pompom. . . . I shall only profess a religion in which they
believe in colour, I shall only serve in an army that respects the human
form.'

Whether the *sûreté* shared these aesthetic opinions, Du Camp does
not record; but on 29 September Gautier's readers were blandly informed: 'We confess in all humility that we did not watch the first
performance of *Mosquita la Sorcière*. . . . We were busy rotting on the
damp straw of the dungeons in the mausoleum of the *garde nationale*.'

14. The Flight of the Swallow

'*Eccomi alfine in Babilonia*,' wrote Marie Mattei to Gautier on 19
January. 'I arrived yesterday by the midnight train. I ask for a day to
recover my serenity, and tomorrow, Tuesday, if you like, you can come
to 16, rue de Sèze, mention my name, and come up to the first floor. I
shall be waiting for you at ten.'

So began a new chapter. Sometimes he called on her at rue de Sèze,
sometimes she came to the attic in rue Rougemont to smoke her cigarette, toy with her bouquet, and turn the four-poster bed with the
twisted columns into heaven. Ernesta, domestic, untidy Ernesta, who
wore her curlers at breakfast and her clothes awry was, for the moment,
readily forgotten: at least by her lover. They had always followed their

private paths, their own careers, and now she was a continent away, giving winter concerts in Constantinople. Free to express his passion for Marie, Gautier wrote *Trop modeste est ton vœu*, and, on 26 February, recalling their long journeys by coupé across Paris, the journeys on which they concealed their love in the smoke of his cigar and her papelito, he wrote her *la Fumée*. When, soon afterwards, she left him, it was to tell him, from Monticello: 'My idol, my life, it is no longer love I have for you, it is idolatry, dear beloved!' Her letter went into Gautier's lacquer coffer, in the drawer where he kept the letters of *les Italiennes*, Carlotta, Ernesta and Marie, 'some of those I have most loved and love the best'.[1]

He was soon to leave on a journey he had long planned: a journey he had discussed, in December, with Du Camp; he was going to follow Ernesta to Constantinople. If Marie could not go with him, he wanted her at least to meet him on his return, at Athens, or in Rome; there might, he thought, be a second Venetian dream.

Marie thought differently. The constant reminders of Ernesta in rue Rougemont: the sight of her bed, her serene Italian eyes observing, from Riesener's pastel, this lesser liaison: it had all touched Marie deeply, bitterly. She had always known she was trespassing in another's kingdom: had always seen about her the signs of established sovereignty. She knew that however many sonnets she received, however burningly he gazed towards *le petit lit aux colonnes torses*, however fiercely Gautier desired her, he did not need or even desire her alone.

And this was deplorably true: more true than she herself, in her most sombre moments, would have dared to imagine:

'My dear Ernesta [he had written on 17 February],[2]

'. . . My dear sweetheart, how happy I am to know you're admired, fêted, appreciated as you deserve! If anything could make me forget the sorrow of your absence, it would be your success. But let's banish the melancholy thoughts of absence and just think of our meeting. I'm making all my arrangements to join you; if you stay in Constantinople, I'll spend the summer there with you; if you come back we'll make the journey together. . . . It would be delightful to see a lovely country in your company. . . .

'How are your little financial affairs? . . . Give me all the details and reassure me. . . . Absent or present, your place is kept in my heart, the heart that you have entered for ever. Don't overtire yourself, and take care of your dear health. I'm very well myself, and I'm watching my beard grow: it's beginning to grow quite thick. . . . Du Camp's tailor has made me some good-looking clothes: a pair of black trousers, a air of grey, a coat and two waistcoats. They're really elegant and I'm sorry you can't see me like this because you would desire me. I shouldn't be difficult. . . . When I'm alone and I think about it, I desire you badly. . . .'

*   *   *

And now, in May, the thought of Ernesta in Constantinople brought Marie from her aerial castles to earth. It was not merely from sudden conscience: it was more probably from understandable jealousy of his permanent mistress, the woman to whom he had no legal ties but to whom, infallibly, fondly, passionately even, he would always return, that Marie grew cool. She had always known that Gautier, the hedonist, would not tie himself irrevocably by marriage; she understood now, sharply, that beside his other liaison, this one was secondary indeed. Her pride and heart were wounded, her bitterness was natural.

'I like Théo very much as a companion, he is a real friend [she wrote to Louis de Cormenin from Marseilles on 16 May]; but to follow him when he hastens to Ernesta, I should need to have a passion that I humbly admit does not exist. If, to settle his life and give him back an existence as you understand it, I had to sacrifice six months or a year, please believe I should not hesitate. But I can do nothing for him except efface myself in shadow and give him freedom to act. That is what I am doing. I have written to him to take the boat which leaves here on the first; I have told him that he will find me at the Hôtel d'Europe at Lyons on the 26th of this month, and that I will spend forty-eight hours with him. As for preaching to him, dear Louis, I have a horror of moralizing. . . . No, I think only Providence can draw him from this abyss; and I hope that God will not let him founder, for to tell the truth his trials are terrible, and he is bearing his cross heroically.'

The second fortnight of May was full of disagreements. Gautier would not leave by the boat on the first of June, he would sail on the eleventh. He wanted Marie to hasten to Paris. She could not bear the thought of rue Rougemont, and insisted that he met her in Lyons: 'Remember that this time three years ago we first spoke to one another in London, and the sky at Lyons is worth the sky in B. Street.' And to Cormenin she wrote, attempting to strengthen her hand: 'Try to make him leave on the second [of June], and he will find me at Lyons on the third. . . . *I want* to meet Gautier again, and I think I shall not see him again for a very long time. Indeed, when he comes back to Paris, where shall I be? In Rome, at least, if not in Calcutta.' In vain de Cormenin argued that after their meeting in Lyons Gautier would die of boredom,

waiting six days, alone, for the boat. Marie would not hear of Par
where she could not love, she said, 'without remorse'. Gautier, remen
bering the paradise of rue Rougemont, was disturbed by the phra
but Marie insisted: 'If the *sans remords* that I wrote without forethoug
so preoccupies Gautier,' she told de Cormenin, 'it is because he und€
stands it quite as well as I do, be sure of that, for he is extreme
sensitive. . . .' And then, in a torrent of explanation:

'Tell me, do you think it's nice not to take a walk or a drive witho
trembling in case one's recognized? And in Paris, I can't take Gautie
arm (that's reserved for Mlle Ozy or some other woman). And the
where am I to see him, in my rooms or his? . . . If Gautier spends t
night or merely the evening with me, I have to change hotels. . . . Sc
should go to him? That's what I thought you'd say. And unless one h
neither soul nor heart nor conscience nor skin, do you think one c
reach that little red bed without crossing the other room, or bru
against another woman's bed without being pricked by a myriad pin
I must tell you, now, that as I crossed that room . . . I could have di
of shame, and I understood the meaning of adultery. . . . Yes, thougl
stumbled over everything, I could no longer walk the length of that b
without closing my eyes, and last winter I suffered visibly. Gaut
knows all that as well as I do, better indeed than I; he saw how bitt
I felt when I had those breakfasts with him. I promise you they w
weigh upon my heart for the rest of my life.

'You see, then, it is a thousand times better to spend twenty-fo
hours *without remorse* no matter where, than to suffer in the past, t
present and the future. Does Lyons signify something? I said Lyo
as I might have said Avignon or Châlons, and I told him so. You s
to me: "What will he do from the 5th to the 11th?" I shall stay as lo
as he wishes, because for my part I love him simply and humbly, a
if something troubles me, it is that I cannot give him all my life, a
have given him all my heart.'[3]

She conquered her jealousy and came to Paris. Early in June, hi
up in rue Rougemont, in *le petit lit aux colonnes torses*, Gautier end
the last of his known liaisons. 'I have faith in you,' Marie had writt€
'I believe and hope you will love me all my life, and when I die y
will leave my place empty in the dear heart I have entered like a dagg
thrust—like the thrusts of many daggers. . . . You must love me becau
I will it with an irresistible will; and, when I have gone, your he;
will be so entirely dead that it could not love anyone with such a love

*   *   *

As the *Leonidas* made its way down the Mediterranean, Gautier struggled with melancholy. 'How strange it seems,' he wrote to Louis de Cormenin, 'to be on my way without you and without la Mattei: without my spirit and without my heart!' He tried to lose his dejection in poetry; he wrote the last nine stanzas of *Inès de las Sierras*, and from Syra, in the Cyclades, he sent the poem to Cormenin to end the anthology that would soon appear: *Emaux et Camées*. 'Without you, without Maxime, without la Mattei [he wrote], I feel that nothing really gives me pleasure. My solitude is overwhelming. I have left my heart in pieces and they drag me from every side. I have one lobe of my heart here; but the other! . . .'[5] Late in July he had received only one letter from Marie; on 17 August came the anniversary of the idyll in Venice. And it was on 5 September, almost exactly two years after the idyll had ended, that she wrote to him:

'. . . Alas! all is not joy in this life, and it is mad to seek consolation in creatures like ourselves. . . . My soul is sad, my health itself is suffering. I am writing to you in front of those trunks that always filled you with consternation when you came to see me and they barred the door. When shall I see you again, dear Gautier? I am leaving this evening for Marseilles, and on the 9th I am embarking there on the *Capri* for Naples, where I shall try to bathe and recover a little. I am exhausted, and I should be ashamed to show myself like this. It is purely spiritual. . . . But I am afraid I can no longer rediscover my *youth*, that is the word, and what am I to do? . . . You hardly seem happier than I, dear Théo, and, in fact, our lives, which appear so different, are more similar than you'd imagine. I notice that you are sad or gay as I am; and that our destinies take similar roads. Am I wrong? Perhaps you will say it is bad to go when you arrive, and that love . . .! Well, I believe you, and I am going so as not to show you the face of last winter.'

And then, abruptly, sadly, irrevocably, the liaison was broken:

'Do not forget me, Gautier, you have promised to love me for ever, little or much, it does not matter; keep a place for me in your affections, as I keep my heart for you, and when you arrive, send me, poste restante in Naples, a line of your handwriting. That will make me happy. Farewell.'[6]

*   *   *

Her melancholy gave place to indifference, increasing disenchantment. 'I have no desire for anything; I am no longer even bored,' she

wrote to Louis de Cormenin on 17 September. 'It is the life of an idiot,
the life I lead; in truth, there is only one thing in the world, to love the
Lord my God with all my heart, with all my strength and with all my
might, and to await the life eternal.'

She was moving nearer and nearer to religion; she went to Rome,
where Pius IX gave her his blessing: *Figlia mia, vi benedico.* 'You would
have come to Rome, you say,' she answered the anxious Gautier. 'But
I am not trying to escape you at all: and why should I try to escape?
My affection for you is so pure I can mention it without the slightest
scruple, although I am preparing myself to be completely devout and
since Naples I have been reconciled with God. But I can certainly love
you with all my heart and soul, as you say. And so I'm no longer sad
to be near you or far away. . . .'

And so her piety drew her, at last, from her lover; and in time, on
the manuscript of *Trop modeste est ton vœu*, she erased the words
'ton poète', as she tried to erase a memory from her life. Yet she did
not forget him: early in 1853 she asked de Cormenin if Gautier were
happy: 'I still love him and I shall love him for ever, so long as my
conscience allows me. Apart from my conscience (and it certainly rules
me) I do not like dragging a chain and staking my life to someone else's
ground. I was born to live alone. You know that I find it tiresome to be
subject to passion and to suffer demands, however mild, however
imperceptible they may be.'[8]

> *Je suis une hirondelle et non une colombe;*
> *Ma nature me force à voltiger toujours.*
> *Le nid où des ramiers s'abritent les amours,*
> *S'il y fallait couver, serait bientôt ma tombe.*
>
> *Pour quelques mois, j'habite un créneau qui surplombe,*
> *Et vole, quand l'automne a raccourci les jours,*
> *Pour les blancs minarets quittant les noires tours,*
> *Vers l'immuable azur d'où jamais pleur ne tombe.*
>
> *Aucun ciel ne m'arrête, aucun lieu ne me tient,*
> *Et dans tous les pays je demeure étrangère;*
> *Mais partout de l'absent mon âme se souvient.*
>
> *Mon amour est constant, si mon aile est légère,*
> *Et, sans craindre l'oubli, la folle passagère*
> *D'un bout du monde à l'autre au même cœur revient.*[9]

And so her love of religion, her love of independence drew Marie
Mattei back into the shadows. But not into darkness: for there remain
*Musée secret, Modes et Chiffons, l'Hirondelle, la Fumée, Coquetterie
posthume,* and a handful of other poems: 'That poor little anthology
which [as she had written] will survive my death, attesting that I, also,
have been loved.'[10]

15. A Turk of the Reform

Constantinople lacks the young fervour, the enthusiasm, the humour,
of *Voyage en Espagne,* and the Canaletto brilliance and happiness that
radiate from *Voyage en Italie.* As the *Leonidas* sails into the Mediterranean, one becomes aware of a traveller lethargic and dispirited.

Yet in the bold Spanish sunlight of Malta Gautier's dormant enthusiasm began to stir. He was not immune to the beauty of the night
when they sailed between two chasms of lapis lazuli powdered with
diamond stars; nor was he cold to the beauty of the day, when they
glided among the Cyclades, 'resting in a circle on the blue carpet of
sea, every island the birthplace of a hero or a poet'. Briefly the *Leonidas*
stopped at Syra, then left for Smyrna, where, for the first time, he set
foot upon 'the soil of Asia, the cradle of the world', and rode on an ass
towards the Bridge of Caravans: the bridge across the Meles where
Homer had bathed his feet. Then the *Leonidas* sailed east again,
towards the Sea of Marmara, past Gallipoli, its minarets vague in the
evening, past the Castle of Seven Towers, past the Seraglio, past
Leander's Tower, and into the Oriental fairyland of Constantinople.

Twelve and a half days ago Théophile Gautier had been in Paris;
now, with a fez and a six-months' beard, he 'looked sufficiently like a
Turk of the Reform not to attract attention in the streets', and set off to
absorb Constantinople. He stood on the Golden Horn, admiring 'a
view so strangely beautiful that one doubts its reality. . . . The palace of
Serai-Burnou, with its Chinese roofs, its crenelated white walls, its
trellised kiosks, its gardens of cypress, parasol pines, sycamores and
planes; the mosque of Sultan Achmet, rounding its cupola among its
six minarets like ivory masts; Saint Sophia, raising its Byzantine dome,
the mosque of Bayezid, the gusts of doves above it like a cloud . . .; the
Suleimanieh with its Arab elegance, its dome like a helmet of steel:
they stand out in strokes of light against a background of tints of blue,
mother-of-pearl and opaline, with inconceivable delicacy, in a picture
that seems to belong to the Fata Morgana'.

He sat in a café in Pera, watching the smoke spirals rising fro
chibouks and nargilehs, the cigarettes gleaming like glowworms in th
darkness. He watched the nocturnal illuminations during the feast o
Ramadan, when verses of the Koran shone in lamps between the mir
arets of Sultan Mahmud's mosque, and the streets of Constantinopl
usually unlit, were alive with light. Kebab was spluttering in the re
glow of brasiers, stall-owners encircled themselves with candles t
display their wares, and multicoloured lanterns burned in the nigh
Everyone, making amends for the daily fast, was devouring stuffe
vine-leaves, cucumbers, baklava, or white blackberries from the moun
on the fruiterers' stalls. And when Ramadan was ended, Gauti
plunged into the great bazaar, where they sold essence of bergamot an
jasmine, rose-water, Persian mirrors framed in delicate paintings, des
for reading the Koran, strange goldsmiths' work, and all the wardrol
of the *Arabian Nights*. Hungry for local colour, he watched the spinnin
dervishes gyrating until they fell from exhaustion and ecstasy, and th
howling dervishes, suffering torture with the impassibility of the er
tranced. He saw His Highness the Sultan, 'a supreme satiety upon h
pale countenance'. And he recorded it all in that kaleidoscopic trav
book which surely evokes the *saveur idéale* of Constantinople: a book s
accurate that the Maréchal de Saint-Arnaud, disembarking two yea
later for the Crimean campaign, wrote home to his brother: 'If yo
want to see Constantinople, read Théophile Gautier.'[1]

Only after two months was Gautier himself satiated with the etern
masked ball of the streets, weary of struggling against an unknow
language. When he left Turkey, it was not with the heartfelt sorrow h
had felt on leaving Spain, the 'incurable nostalgia' he had felt fo
Venice: indeed he felt but momentary sadness when he sailed on th
Imperatore for Athens: 'In my dreams I already saw the white colonnad
of the Parthenon, with its interstices of blue, shining upon the rock o
the Acropolis, and the minarets of Saint Sophia no longer gave m
pleasure.'

*   *   *

And so, in September 1852, with Ernesta and their younger daughte
Estelle, he arrived in Athens, where he met Edmond About, a studen
at the French School. 'In four days,' wrote About to Mlle Olga Pankra
tief, 'Gautier acquired the right to pass any judgment on Athens whic
might occur to him, and to substantiate it by the unanswerable words
I saw. I did him the honours of the Parthenon and the whole city. I eve
showed him the Duchess, who is not among the least curious of ou
antiquities. These two strong personalities saw one another and parte
on excellent terms.'[2]

The Duchesse de Plaisance was indeed a character to satisfy the most Bohemian taste. She was half American, she had long been separated from her husband, and she travelled with a vat of alcohol containing the body of her infant daughter. She astonished Athens by her fortune and her taste for adventures: in 1846 she had been captured by a brigand (an episode which was to give About the theme for *le Roi des Montagnes*). She usually lived alone, in conversation with God, Who sometimes deigned to send her messages, but her closest friend was an Englishwoman (mistress of a bandit). She received, with enthusiasm, all strangers passing through Athens.

About was less enthusiastic about his visitors. 'On the whole, the illustrious Théo seemed more anxious for paradoxes than truths,' was his characteristically acid comment: 'It's a bad spirit to travel in. He even asked me to write down the paradoxes I knew on the antiquities of Athens, which I was very careful not to do. For the rest, he talks much about himself and poses enormously. . . . A very good fellow, all the same, though a little temperamental; he talked nonsense in French to a mass of people who only understood Greek. He was accompanied [added About] by the decorative Mme Grisi, who has sung all the summer or rather all the winter in Constantinople. She has wrinkles the size of ruts, and she's balding, but she's a good housewife if ever there was one, and I don't believe there's so hard a worker in all the rue de Charonne. The first day, she made herself a hat and unpacked the trunks. The second, she saw the city and cut out a dress, the third, she sewed the dress and began a shirt, the fourth, she saw the Acropolis and packed.' They all set off for Corfu in an Austrian boat. Everyone was seasick except, according to About, Mme Grisi. 'On the boat she didn't stop sewing and looking after her daughter as well. . . . She made me a very pretty tobacco-pouch in cherry-coloured silk, which I shall piously preserve in memory of this *artiste couturière*. If her singing resembles her sewing, she is the prima prima donna in the world.'

This *artiste couturière* is not the seductive Ernesta of Riesener's portrait; but About's acidity may be explained. He left the Gautiers and returned to Athens to find a letter from Eugénie Fort. The mother of Théophile Gautier *fils* announced her coming visit to the *bassin méditerranéen*, she hoped to see About again, and she proposed a meeting at Corfu. She had already, so we are told, 'done many favours for young About. He even hoped that she would do him more'.[3]

* * *

On 17 July 1852, while its author was smoking a nargileh in Pera, *Emaux et Camées*, a diamond edition, a volume little larger than a cameo, containing only eighteen poems, was published by Eugène

H

Didier. 'Bernard de Palissy and Benvenuto Cellini would applaud these little marvels worthy of a great poet,' announced the *Revue de Paris.* Paul de Saint-Victor reviewed the book 'with pentecostal fire'; Xavier Aubryet, in *l'Artiste*, was moved to poetry:[6]

> *Chaque strophe dans sa richesse,*
> *Goutte diaphane ou jet de feu,*
> *Tombe, comme un pleur de déesse,*
> *Brille, comme un regard de Dieu . . .*

And Flaubert, in the pugnacious manner he usually assumed for Louise Colet, dismissed the book as 'pitiful,' worn-out, far-fetched, an anthology of poetic tricks.[7]

Emaux et Camées: the title is fair. The poems are chiselled and engraved by the most diligent craftsman. And, indeed, by the most conscious; for where another poet might have delighted in diversity of form, Gautier finds pleasure in writing nearly all the anthology in octosyllabic verse. And yet, if we persist in seeing the book as the triumph of a poetic jeweller, an inspired technician, we shall miss its significance, fail to understand how it took its place in nineteenth-century French poetry and in Gautier's life. For this restricted verse-form clothes widely different inspirations. There are—in the final edition of 1872, the edition best known—the seasonal poems: *Premier sourire du printemps, Lied, Fantaisies d'hiver, Ce que disent les Hirondelles, Noël*. There are the aesthetically significant poems: *Préface,* in which the poet maintains the independence of art; *Bûchers et Tombeaux* in which he finally disavows the Gothic and stresses his Classical sympathies; and *l'Art*, in which he proclaims the sovereign immortality of art and the artist. There are the philosophical poems: the pantheist *Affinités secrètes*, and *la Nue*, with its poignant idealism, *les Vieux de la Vieille*, that macabre, sublime Meissonier, and *le Merle*, with its sudden, transient moment of faith. *Symphonie en Blanc majeur* is a linguistic tour de force, *Variations sur le Carnaval de Venise* an imaginary journey, an echo of Sivori's violin. And Eugénie Fort, Victorine, Ernesta, Marie, Régina, la Présidente, la Païva, Princess Mathilde: all are discreetly or clearly reflected in this highly personal anthology. *Emaux et Camées* is often quoted as a technical masterpiece; but it is powerful and significant not only for its style, but because it enlightens many moments of Gautier's life, many aspects of his writing, discloses a man both sensual and sensitive, amusing and reflective, lyrical and philosophic. It shows the fervent pupil of Rioult, delighting in colour and texture, solidity and line; it shows the assured Court poet, the accepted and the rejected

ver, the frustrated journalist and the careful, brilliantly accomplished
chnician, the irrepressible Romantic and the evangelist of Art for
rt's Sake. And it does more, for it reflects not only Gautier but the
ohemian age, the Napoleonic cult, the *bourgeois* years of Louis-
ilippe, the licentious, iridescent, enchanting Second Empire. Even
the fashion for camellias and Parma violets, it recreates the Paris of
century ago. It may not do so with the ferocity and power of Baudelaire
les Fleurs du mal, but it does so quite as surely.

*   *   *

Emaux et Camées was not the only one of Gautier's works to recall
m in this summer and autumn of 1852. In August, after ten years of
iumph on all the stages of Europe, *Giselle* was revived at the Opéra;[8]
September, *la Péri* was danced again.[9] Louis de Cormenin, drowsing
rough a vaudeville, suddenly recognized a poem by Gautier, like some
r by Rossini in the midst of a Musard quadrille.[10] And a traveller
iling along the Algerian coast from Philippeville to Constantine, one
lm African night, heard a sailor singing: 'There was no sound
emembered the traveller] but that of the paddlewheels on the water,
id the phosphorescent waves were passing like string after string of
iamonds. . . . Then the song of the ship-boy echoed, pious, religious,
spired, through the quiet night, making us thrill in every fibre:[11]

> *Sur l'eau bleue et profonde*
> *Nous allons voyageant,*
> *Environnant le monde*
> *D'un sillage d'argent,*
> *Des îles de la Sonde,*
> *De l'Inde au ciel brûlé,*
> *Jusqu'au pôle gelé . . .*
>
> *Les petites étoiles*
> *Montrent de leur doigt d'or*
> *De quel côté les voiles*
> *Doivent prendre l'essor;*
> *Sur nos ailes de toiles,*
> *Comme de blancs oiseaux,*
> *Nous effleurons les eaux . . .*[12]

es, the ship-boy sang your thoughts, your poetry, all that your pen,
y dear Théophile, once coloured with your colours. He sang *les
atelots.'*
On 1 October *l'Artiste* predicted that Théophile Gautier 'was about

to return from regions loved by the sun, to tell us of some new no
talgia'. On 14 October, the readers of *la Presse* once again saw h
signature in the columns of their paper.

16. The Impenitent Romantic

THE NEW year opened with failure: Gautier asked for a post as I
specteur des Beaux-Arts, and asked (as he had asked three years ag
in vain. Sadly he returned to journalism; and the appearance of t
enlarged edition of *Emaux et Camées* in February only reminded hi
of his abandoned vocation, the vocation that no sinecure would he
him to pursue.

And his need of a sinecure became sadly evident when, on 22 Ju
the Tribunal de la Seine began to hear a lawsuit brought by Franç
Buloz, the director of the *Revue des Deux Mondes*, against Rouy, t
manager of *la Presse*. Buloz declared that Gautier owed him two tho
sand three hundred francs, an advance made three or four years earli
for *le Capitaine Fracasse*. The novel had not appeared, and Bul
(recalled his counsel) had already claimed his due, received a disdain
refusal, and on 2 December 1851 Gautier had been given six mont
in which to produce the work: after this period, if the novel remain
unfinished, he was to repay the advance and expenses. Six months h
expired, he had not produced a line for Buloz; he had, howeve
written for a rival, the *Revue de Paris*. Buloz now demanded payme
from *la Presse* for their contributor's failure to produce the novel.

Rouy's counsel argued that Gautier had no contract with *la Pre*
since he was paid cash for every article. However (continued counsel),
withhold this payment for six months to repay Buloz would have mea
renouncing Gautier, 'a sacrifice to which no one would readily resi
themselves.' *La Presse* had therefore continued to pay Gautier desp
opposition.

At this point the president adjourned the session and ordered Gaut
to appear within a fortnight before the tribunal. Next day, forestalli
his appearance, Gautier published his statement in *la Presse*: he h
owed Buloz only 1300 francs; his lawyer had paid Buloz' counsel
thousand, and had since offered him 300 in cash and a hundred
month until the debt was paid and the list of expenses received. Bul
added Gautier, had already quarrelled with Hugo, Balzac, Dum
George Sand, and 'all who have had the misfortune to write for him

The case was ended by an unexpected *deus ex machina*. Mirès the banker, Gautier's admirer, heard of the litigation: and from Marseilles he wrote to his cashier in Paris, 'a deed for which much will be forgiven him: "Get Gautier out of Buloz' claws." Which [recorded Monselet] was done.'[2]

> . . . *Salut, capacités bénies*
> *Qui pour Phébus sans capitaux*
> *Découvrez les Californies*
> *Et créez des Sacramentos.*
>
> *Chantons tous comme un chœur antique*
> *Dans un Poean encourageant :*
> *Vive la Banque poétique,*
> *Vive Plutus intelligent!*[3]

Four or five years later, Gautier wrote the first chapter of *le Capitaine Fracasse*. Ten years later, in 1863, the book was published.

*   *   *

Gautier rang in 1854 with *Lied*, a song in his happiest manner; he rang in February with *Fantaisies d'Hiver*. He called at Ingres' studio where the artist had just finished his *Apothéose de Napoléon Ier*: 'Théophile Gautier and princes, dukes, *bourgeois* and artists of every kind are all,' Mme Ingres informed her uncle, 'in admiring contemplation.'[4] The critic's appreciation of Ingres' ceiling appeared in the *Moniteur universel* on 4 February; next month, catholic as usual, he published his impressions of Delacroix' paintings at the Hôtel de Ville. Indeed, the name of Théophile Gautier, this ubiquitous, Protean author, this novelist, poet, critic, traveller, creator of diverse ballets, reverberated, bell-like, in the public mind: he welcomed April with his *Odelette anacréontique* in the *Revue de Paris*; he greeted May with *le Sélam* (performed in aid of the monuments to Soulié and Balzac).[5] And, on the last day of the month, at the Académie Impériale de Musique, made memorable by Cerrito, Taglioni and Petipa, came the first performance of his new ballet, *Gemma*.[6]

*   *   *

And yet, for all his activity, Gautier remained deep in Romantic melancholy: a prey to the ennui which so often, irresistibly, fell upon him; and he could not always turn to the strong and comforting maternal Ernesta, for she now departed with Estelle to the Château de Montlouis, near Tours, and left him alone in their new and spacious rooms in the rue Grange-Batelière, with Marianne, the Alsatian *femme-de-chambre*, to look after him:

'I'm wearing my overcoat buttoned up and I've kept the eiderdown [he told Ernesta in June]. The sparrow is flourishing; he stayed more than two hours on my shoulder as I scribbled my article for the *Moniteur* and he and Marianne understand each other very well. The house isn't very gay; if it weren't for the bird's *couic-couic* you would think you were in a tomb it is so peaceful. . . . I am rather languishing and piteous and dying more than ever of ennui. I haven't the courage to do anything to amuse myself, but perhaps there's nothing possible. . . .'

It was hardly possible to amuse oneself in Paris; the cold gave place to rain: 'A few white pantaloons have made their appearance and bravely faced the yellow sea of macadam. Mortals attired in nankin sit down at the green tables at Tortoni's and affect to eat ices as if it were warm; open barouches, turned into bathing machines by the sudden squalls, spin off to the Bois de Boulogne, taking young ladies as damp as if they were bathing at Trouville. . . . The Opéra is closed, the Odéon is closed, the Théâtre-Lyrique is closed. . . . There is hardly a critic left. . . .'[7] And Gautier himself soon departed. The director of the Theatre Royal at Munich had invited Parisian journalists to attend a dramatic festival, and on 11 July his farewell article appeared in *la Presse*.

*   *   *

'Munich, 10 July 1854

'My dear Ernesta,

'Here I am, arrived in Munich through torrents of rain, which stopped for a day or two just to start again all the harder. We are settled, the whole bunch of us, in a private house where we each pay 40 sous a day for our room, and we eat here and there.

'The city is very strange and will furnish us with a good deal of copy; I'll send you the article that I'm starting tomorrow for *la Presse*, and soon I'll send you one for the *Moniteur*. This letter doesn't count; it only shows I'm well and not minced up at all by the Railways. Tell me if *Monstre vert* [Estelle] has had her operation, if it has been successful, if you have sung well, if you're going to Le Havre with Alice, etc., . . . in fact tell me everything you're doing.

'As for me, my life here is simple: looking at pictures and churches and going to theatres in the evening. The director [of the Theatre Royal] received us most kindly. The theatre is very big, bigger than the Opéra, but rather dreary like the Odéon. I'm so sorry you haven't come; I miss you considerably. But one of these days we'll have enough money not to separate. I don't need to tell you we're getting on very well with the Saint-Victors. As for the Boissards, male and female, you know them and we're good friends.

'Write to me at this address at Munich: "Monsieur Théophile Gautier, c/o M. le Comte de Poninsky, Chamberlain to His Majesty the King of Bavaria."

'This address is a joke, they're hard-up Poles who let out rooms to earn a little pocket-money. . . .'[8]

*   *   *

'Munich, 16 July 1854

'Dear love,

'. . . I was very touched by the heroic manner in which our brave little *Monstre vert* bore her operation. Tell her I'm going to Nuremberg, a town which is just one big toy-factory, and that I'll bring her a very pretty village; I've bought a Black Forest cuckoo-clock, it's carved out of wood and represents a châlet, it's very nice.

'I'm tired out, seeing pictures, galleries, churches and entertainments and generally rushing round. . . . I'm very sorry I couldn't say good-bye to you more intimately, but I shall bid you good morning in all seriousness when I come home. . . .

'I am all yours, heart and body, kiss *Monstre vert* and go and see Judith, I'll bring back something for her too. . . .

'All good wishes to *la Présidente* and to [her sister] Bébé whom I adore.'[9]

*   *   *

Gautier's escape to happiness was all too brief. He returned to Paris in August. Late that month his father, proud, devoted, who had given him his first lessons, paid for his first book: his father, who considered his paternity a lasting title to glory, died at Montrouge. For all his bravado and cynicism, Gautier had been a dutiful and affectionate son, and he must have been much afflicted. 'What shall I say to you in the face of all you suffer [Chassériau asked, touchingly]?[10] What shall I say to you who have such strength of feeling, who know so much of life and the bitterness it brings? I grasp your hand, I embrace you tenderly, and I beg you to think a little of your friends, of those who, like myself, are deeply devoted to you.'

The journalist sadly returned to his task and acclaimed the return of Rachel to the Français for her final season: Rachel who, too, was stricken by bereavement. He watched the huge bulk of Mlle Georges struggling through *la Chambre ardente*: a pathetic wreck of Romanticism. He heard an opera by a composer 'almost unknown in France', Giuseppe Verdi: *Ernani*. *Ernani*. The name swept him back to that flamboyant night when he had fought his fight against classicists and *bourgeois*, fought

for the sacred cause of art. 'Today [he wrote] we can still recite whole
tirades from the play, and despite ourselves, against the music of Verdi,
we murmur the poetry of Victor Hugo.'[11]

17. Months of Moment

THE YEAR 1855 was to be sad and momentous. On 20 January, Gérard
de Nerval called on Gautier at the *Revue de Paris*.[1] He had, he said,
bought a rare curiosity, the girdle that Mme de Maintenon had worn
in performances of *Esther* at Saint-Cyr. He wandered off, half in life
and half in dream. On 26 January, the last pages of *Aurélia* in his
pocket, he was found hanging by the girdle from a grille in the rue
de la Vieille Lanterne. 'So charming and so winged [wrote Gautier],
so luminous, so tender, his spirit has gone for ever into air: has shuffled
off its mortal coil like rags no longer needed. It has entered into that
world of elohims, that world of sylphs and angels, into that paradise of
beloved shades and celestial visions with which it was already familiar.'[2]

The funeral service was held in Notre-Dame on 30 January and
attended by a congregation of three hundred. No one recorded, for
certain, whether it was the death of Gérard de Nerval that condemned
a disconsolate Lili Gautier to spinsterhood; Gautier and his sisters
kept the secret. Mysterious in death as he had been in life, Gérard was
buried at Père Lachaise. That day, in *la Presse*, Gautier paid his tribute;
and years later, in the *Salon*, seeing a picture of the rue de la Vieille
Lanterne, he recalled the scene and impact of his death:

'Yes, there indeed is the black cut between the tall scabby houses,
the gutter, sinister as a vent from Hell, the staircase with its unfeeling
steps, the rusty bar, a bit of cord still hanging from it. . . . So indeed
we saw it on a cold January morning, as we tramped through the dirty
snow: that abominable street, the witness of a lonely agony. At the
back of the narrow fissure, a pale ray caught the golden figure of Renown
on the fountain in the place du Châtelet, and made it gleam like some
vague symbol of glory. . . . A crow was fluttering at the top of the
steps. . . . Who knows if the bird's black plumage, its funereal cry, the
terrible aspect of the place, did not seem, to that spirit so long a prey
to dreams, to accord decisively, cabalistically: if, in the bitter breath of
the winter wind, he did not believe he heard a voice whispering: "It
is here!"'[3]

*   *   *

Gautier returned to the task which he and Gérard had so often done together: turned with sorrow and disappointment to record that the public, 'very indifferent to the *Freischutz*, had greeted the light opera *Robin des Bois* with transports of enthusiasm', to record that 'there will be a day when Parisians will like music for itself and forbid any tampering with masterpieces; but that day has not yet come.'[2] It was a pleasant relief to pay tribute to the play which earned a justified triumph at the Gymnase late in March: *le Demi-Monde*.

His happy improvisation on the triumph of Dumas *fils* was also one of his last dramatic criticisms in the paper for which he had written for so long. In the *Moniteur universel* of 29 March there appeared the first of his articles on the 1855 Exhibition: the fifty-two articles most of which re-appeared in the two volumes of *les Beaux-Arts en Europe*. It is true that Gautier had long found himself in financial trouble, it is true that the *Moniteur* paid him more than *la Presse*. But a series of articles of this importance should quite evidently have been given to the paper for which Gautier wrote his *Salons*, the paper to which he was virtually accredited. He had not even warned Girardin of his intention. And Girardin, hearing about it at second-hand, remembered the often exasperating behaviour of his contributor in the last nineteen years, behaviour he would no longer tolerate. On 2 April he wrote briefly and justifiably:

'My dear Gautier, it is indirectly and belatedly that I learn you have just deserted *la Presse* to join the ranks of *le Moniteur* and there describe the coming exhibition of painting and sculpture. I had been told about it, but I'd refused to believe it, not doubting that before you left *la Presse* you would come and warn me. If it is true that you have been promised a place as Inspecteur des Beaux-Arts, you will acquire a title the more to this position when the Government knows that your preferring *le Moniteur* to *la Presse* has cost you your dramatic criticism, and that the article which is due to appear tomorrow Tuesday will be the last that the readers of *la Presse* will see there.

'I sincerely hope you will find at the *Moniteur* nineteen years of such constantly devoted friendship.'[5]

And so Alice Ozy, desolate, was deprived of her place in Gautier's box on first nights, and, for two hundred francs an article, Théophile Gautier, the flamboyant partisan of *Hernani*, the author of *Mademoiselle de Maupin* and *la Comédie de la Mort*: Théophile Gautier, the Romantic of Romantics, became a critic on the government paper. Fortunio the critic became *l'aigle du Moniteur*.[6]

PART THREE

L'Aigle du Moniteur

18. *L'Aigle du Moniteur*

PARIS, IN this late spring of 1855, was all agog and aglow with preparations for the International Exhibition. Buildings were rising with the swiftness of a change of scene; and the Champs-Elysées was enhanced by elegant iron chairs, 'on which the nations might, at their ease, observe the march-past of civilization'.[1]

And, in due course, civilization came:

'Australians arrived by the last clipper with two or three barrels of gold-dust, Californians with a placer in their pockets, Baboos and nabobs boasting several lakhs of rupees, civilians from the East India Company on leave, blacks and half-castes from Haiti, Dukes of Marmalade and Marquesses of Marzipan, Chinese with almond eyes, hiding their rolled-up pigtails under opera hats, Turks and Egyptians in red fezzes, Yankees restraining themselves from stretching out their legs on the velvet edge of theatre balconies, descendants of Montezuma with blue hair and coppery skin, Englishmen of irreproachable mien, Spaniards leaving the theatre at every interval to wrap three shreds of yellow tobacco in *papel de hilo*, aesthetic and conscientious Germans come to decide for themselves if Molière is in fact just a fool without ideals, as Schlegel decrees; Venetians, Bergamasques, Milanese, Romagnols, Italians from all over Italy . . . more people than were dispersed at the ancient confusion of Babel. . . . But [finished Gautier breathlessly] you would find it difficult to discover a Parisian. The Parisian politely resigns his seat to his guests. For he understands that Paris, however vast it may be, is not designed to receive the whole universe at once.'[2]

Gautier himself was driven on every side: Delacroix asked him to dine,[3] the Ministre d'Etat appointed him to help award the prizes for the best dramatic works of 1854.[4] (Romantic survivors must have smiled to see that 'Monsieur Théophile Gautier, *homme de lettres*' sat on the commission with two Academicians, two *bêtes noires* of Romanticism: Désiré Nisard and Eugène Scribe.[5]) Journalism made more demands than ever. There was the historical pageant to watch in Orleans.[6] Rachel was giving her last performances before her departure for America: the last, though they might not know it, on the Parisian stage. La Ristori was appearing at the Salle Ventadour, earning the heavy applause of Rachel's enemies. There were all the foreign actors to assess, all the Parisian productions to describe, from the unpopular English production of *Hamlet* to the spectacular reconstruction of the Siege of Sebastopol at the Hippodrome, where every communiqué was translated with great fidelity to local colour. 'Let us hope [added Gautier] that the fall of Sebastopol will come to end the performance.'[7] On 18 August, from a balcony at the Gymnase, he watched Queen Victoria driving through Paris on her state visit to the Emperor. There were fifty articles to write on the immense exhibition of international art. In the crowded theatres, the densely filled galleries, the seething summer streets, he was constantly, unremittingly, at work; and the wanderlust which possessed him could not be satisfied. And, as so often, he was forced to write against inclination:

'My health isn't bad [he told Ernesta, who was giving concerts in London], but I have all the trouble in the world getting back to work. Turgan means well, but he's extremely fastidious, and it's hard to write a story in which there's no question of anything. He absolutely refuses to have the little actress at the Délassements Comiques. It isn't majestic enough. I've tried to set the thing in Spain, but then it would look like *Militona*. Now at last I've invented a certain Polish countess who will do the trick. . . .'[8]

And so the Countess Prascovie Labinska, a Lithuanian of illustrious birth, was conjured out of Théophile Gautier's brain; and *Avatar* was born. But Gautier had to fight more than editorial scruples and his own inertia. He had, yet again, to struggle against his intimate sadness: on 29 June there died the engaging, understanding woman who had so smoothed his journalism and so enhanced his leisure. Mme de Girardin died of cancer.

'It is with broken heart and tearful eyes we perform our weekly task. No loss could touch us more deeply: one of our claims to honour is the friendship that Mme de Girardin accorded us. How gentle she was, and proud, how generous and courteous, capable of great devotion and great sacrifice, indulgent to faults, implacable towards cowardice! No mean thought ever came near her, and he who was her friend for fifteen years has a right to be proud. How many long hours have we spent in conversation with her, beneath the portico with its Athenian columns, in this Greek temple of which she was the muse . . . enchanting hours that will not return again!'[9] Girardin, moved, sent Gautier a little casket: in it, touchingly, Mme de Girardin had kept the letters and poems of her *éléphant*.[10]

*   *   *

Much indeed had passed in Gautier's life since he had first entered

Delphine de Girardin's *salon*, sat beneath the Athenian portico for the first time. And yet had he really changed so profoundly? Were his old antipathies truly dead? One at least remained: on the last day of the year there appeared in the *Moniteur* a passage that the author of *les Jeunes-France* would surely have approved, a definition of that sitting target of Romanticism, that constant abomination of lovers of art, the *bourgeois*. 'If you pass a Raphael and admire your reflection in the casseroles of Drolling, you're a *bourgeois*. You prefer Paul de Kock to Lord Byron—*bourgeois*. You decorate your mantelpiece with spun glass dogs—*bourgeois*. Once upon a time, when the wild-haired, bearded students, wearing their velvet coats and felt hats *à la Diavolo*, flocked to the great Romantic performances, it was enough to have a florid face, a beardless chin, square collar and stovepipe hat to be apostrophized with this injurious epithet by the studio Mistigris and Holofernes. . . . Now it is quite understood that the *bourgeois* can possess every possible virtue, every conceivable qualification, and even have much talent in his trade. . . . But, for God's sake, don't let him mistake the shadow of a nose on a portrait for a tobacco-stain. . . . One would almost refuse him the title of man!'

*　　　*　　　*

'Let it vanish, then, this good year,' added Gautier, in the last days of December 1855. 'It has seen the capture of Sebastopol, the Universal Exhibition, the completion of the Louvre, three fine dates to inscribe upon its commemorative marble. We shall not forget it!'[11] And so the old year passed, and 1856 began with its balls and soirées, its concerts and private theatricals. The world of fashion flocked to the *hôtel* of the Marquise de Boissy (once the Comtesse Guiccioli, Byron's last attachment), to the *salon* of the Comtesse de Castellane, to Dumas' Greek tragedy, *l'Orestie*, at the Porte-Saint-Martin,[12] while the critic of the *Moniteur* plodded heavily round the theatres, though 'we are a dreamer, a poet, and we should have spent our life walking beneath the arcades composing sonnets for the beautiful eyes of Iris or Lucinda, if Peneia had not come to tug at the flap of our robe and counsel us to write a little prose.'[13] But in his prose the dreamer and the poet were often evident: 'As for myself, for whom Spain is almost a second motherland, the click of ivory castanettes has upon me the effect of the Ranz des Vaches on Swiss soldiers; and for all my domestic duties, it inspires me with irresistible longing to cross the Pyrenees, and to ride a mule by plain and by mountain along roads bordered with cactus and aloes, whence you perceive the azured sea pricked with white sails.'[14] In September 1856 he was on his way south for the bullfights at Saint-Esprit.

And, as usual, he escaped reality not only in place but in time: when he left Saint-Esprit for Paris, it was only to lose himself in ancient Egypt. It was characteristic of Gautier, who had paced the streets of Paris in Egyptian costume, that he described the land of Cleopatra long before he saw it: that his Egypt was, above all, the land of the poet's dream, the artist's imagination. Years ago, with his Egyptian stories *Une Nuit de Cléopâtre* and *le Pied de Momie*, he had established his poetic dreams. Now, in the autumn of 1856, with the practical if presumptuous encouragement of that literary climber, Ernest Feydeau, he set to work on a novel, *le Roman de la Momie*.

The nine-year-old Judith, rescued at last from her schooling at the Convent of Notre-Dame de la Miséricorde, installed herself admiringly at his feet, bandaging her dolls into miniature Tahosers and making Ernesta's workbox a sarcophagus. Sometimes she was permitted to hand books to her devoted and newly discovered father. And one evening she was rewarded by meeting Baudelaire. He seemed to her like a priest without a surplice; she seemed to him the epitome of beauty: 'You have fashioned her according to your dream', he said to Gautier: 'She is like a little Greek girl.'

Ernesta, leaving her lover to his Egyptian research, his diligent writing, the thousand demands of journalism, and the happy, energetic company of his daughters, departed for a concert season in Nice.

*   *   *

'Paris, 8 November 1856.

'My dear darling,

'I'm delighted that you have arrived safely, the tiredness will pass. You should have superb weather down there, good for people's voices. The autumn here is magnificent, there's fog till midnight, then the mists part and you see a radiant sky.

'Our little world is flourishing and all doing needlework; Estelle is making skirts for herself, and Judith is mending something or other. The white cat, Don Pierrot de Navarre, is getting on quite well with Gil Blas de Santillane, who has been brought to the house so he doesn't burst with spleen all by himself. . . .

'La Présidente had a *succès de ridicule* at the first night of Bouilhet's play. She'd donned a monstrous dome of a hat, a frightful washtub lid, chocolate-coloured, with feathers, ribbons and other extravaganzas. I think she'd managed to make herself ugly, difficult though that may be.

'*Madame de Montarcy*, Bouilhet's play, was most successful. "It's colossal," says Flaubert, butting into your navel and throwing back his great arms.

'I am passably well, even very well, except that I'm bursting with boredom. But that isn't new. I've profited from the fine weather to do a little walking and settle some business. I shall probably begin my work as editor of *l'Artiste* on 1 December, and Feydeau, Mario's friend, is collecting me documents for my *Roman de la Momie*, of which I've already produced four instalments, so all will be well.

'There's a quarrel between Paul de Saint-Victor and young About, aged twenty-seven. They've even sent witnesses to Villemessant, the editor of the *Figaro*, who hastened to declare that he simply adored Saint-Victor and hadn't read the article that slashed him. That's where things stand. The people who are always brave with other people's lives want a bit of a fight and cry "*xi, xi, xi*", as if provoking dogs. That's more or less the news. . . .

'I don't need to tell you I'd love to go away, like the late Lepeintre *jeune* in *les Cabinets particuliers*. Since you left, the house is soulless and I beg the children to make a bit of a din to enliven the solitude. . . .'[15]

My dear Nini [Gautier added, a few days later],

'Don't worry about the cats. The children aren't touching them. Gil Blas has chosen the top of the cupboard with the mirror as his habitation; he lives there, eight feet out of the children's reach, coming down just once a day to eat and attend to necessities. Don Pierrot de Navarre is gentle, as you know; I have forbidden the *monstres vert et jaune* to tease him, and they're obeying me. Estelle and Judith are really very good; they're beginning to understand that they must work. I am very pleased about it. As for me, I'm well, except for boredom: I don't know what to do with myself. Perhaps when I direct *l'Artiste* it will amuse me to be an editor. I shall begin on 1 December or 1 January.

'I have made the acquaintance of some wealthy *bourgeois*, relations of Tinant, the young man who did my medallion; they live magnificently at Neuilly, in a castle of a house, in the middle of a park. They asked me to dinner, there were thirty people at table, a Gamache wedding feast!! It seems it's always like that. . . . I went back to lunch: nine people, Ostend oysters, mutton cutlets, lobster, *pâté de foie gras*, roast partridge, poached eggs and truffles, Chester and Roquefort cheese, fresh and crystallized fruit, Sauternes, Bordeaux, Moët champagne, coffee, liqueurs, cigars. That's what they have every day, and you can go when you like. They bring you back in a brougham or a barouche, according to the weather. These prodigious and gigantic *bourgeois* are not called Gargantua and Gargamelle, but Monsieur and Madame Obert. . . .

'Take good care of yourself, my dear darling. . . . I shall send you two hundred francs, as soon as you've told me the surest way of sending it. . . .

I

If it isn't enough, let me know, you mustn't be poor on your travels
There is still some ink in the inkwell, and for your sake the pen will b
dipped in it. I hope your concert goes well, if it doesn't, you mustn'
fret. There is such terrible competition nowadays that nothing i
possible, even with talent. You need good luck, intrigue, and the *secre*
we do not know. . . .'[16]

                    *   *   *

November merged into December; Gautier dined with Flauber
they talked of Art for Art's Sake, and the astonished Gustave Claudi
recorded their imprecations against the *bourgeois*: imprecations s
violent that Gautier and Flaubert 'grew as red as cocks and had t
change their shirts'.[17] Through a dense cloud of tobacco-smoke, th
stormy discussions continued. The question of art was more than eve
in Gautier's mind, for on 1 December he became the editor of th
periodical which was to bring art to the public, art in every form, an
to offer him a fine chance of practising his principles.

L'Artiste had existed for over a quarter of a century, and in 185
Arsène Houssaye, the director, had combined it with the *Revue de Par*
and taken Gautier, Cormenin and Du Camp as partners. Since Gautie
could not afford to subsidise the venture financially, it had been agree
that he would subsidise it with unpaid articles: a proposition whic.
naturally proved impracticable. It was probably through the beneficenc
of his friends as much as his personal merits, that he now became
salaried editor, and that *l'Artiste* became an organ of Art for Art's Sake

19. The Artist as Critic

WHEN GAUTIER took over *l'Artiste* in December 1856 his ideas ha
matured, his prestige was established, and he was about midway in hi
career; it is a point from which to look back across his criticism of art
and forward across the art criticism to come.

If Gautier's appreciation of art was catholic, it was also that of a
artist. He did not approach art as a man of letters, a moralist or merel'
an amateur: he approached it as a practising artist who had learne
technique, learned the power of observation, developed his sense o
line and colour and dimension in a studio. Early in his career h
lamented that pictures were criticized as if they were books or dramas
he himself determined to judge painting as painting. In his *Salon d*
1763 Diderot had commented on *la Piété filiale*: 'Excellent, my dea

Greuze! Point a moral in painting, and always do it like that!'[1] Such an exhortation is the antithesis of Gautier's belief that the first condition of painting is to be painting. Diderot's comment would have been impossible to the critic who declared: 'When a fresco or picture does not give you pleasure independently of the idea and the subject it represents, the artist has failed in his purpose.'[2]

Gautier's conception of visual art (and, indeed, of art criticism) was not only that of a practising artist; it was, again, that of a fervent idealist: the conception of the apostle of Art for Art's Sake.[3] Gautier felt that visual art, like all the arts, was independent of passing circumstance; he felt, too, that the artist graced with the heavensent gift owed it to humankind to practise his art: that creation was his highest civic purpose.[4] Enjoyment of the universe, which, after all, was the work of the supreme artist, was to Gautier an act of devotion.[5] Indeed he considered that art itself was sacred; he never entered the *Musée ancien* without a religious emotion. Are we not in fact in one of the holiest and most venerable churches, in the temple of human genius?'[6] He considered that painting was the poetry and glorification of form,[7] that the artist's celebration of natural beauty and particularly of the human body, was the pantheist's duty to God.[8] Indeed, any artist who failed to fulfil himself, or even failed to exhibit, was guilty, in Gautier's mind, of a crime.[9] The true, the highest, the holiest purpose of sculptors was to write in marble the poem of the human body, the masterpiece of the Almighty;[10] and only the study of the human form could produce the complete artist. But art, as Gautier insisted, was not merely copying: 'Art should be idealized transcription, not photography';[11] and his belief in idealization remained. He insisted that painting was a means of expressing the secret ideal of the soul: 'Art is a desire! In the presence of the most beautiful women, the artist still dreams on.'[12] The Pygmalion who changed his statue into his mistress proved himself, in Gautier's eyes, not an artist but a philistine.[13] Artists should not merely gratify themselves, for they possessed a unique ability to suggest happiness and remind a forgetful humanity of ideal beauty.[14]

Gautier's criticism of art is constantly inspired by the religion of art[15] and by what he called the religion of beauty.[16] This conception of art as a religion (a conception expressed as early as 1835, in *Mademoiselle de Maupin*) sets his art criticism immediately on a higher plane than that of the Goncourts, who suggested that 'painting was a materialist art, animating form with colour, incapable of vivifying the soul, the moral and spiritual elements in man.'[17] Gautier believed with the Goncourts that art should be a visual pleasure; unlike the Goncourts, he believed, as Keats had believed in his *Ode on a Grecian Urn*, that beauty was visible truth with its own implicit message. He saw that visual pleasure was not only an end in itself, but a means of propagating the religion of art: that it could both please and ennoble the human spirit.

And so he believed, too, that though it might express a human ideal, art remained above human considerations. Just as Hugo had insisted, in 1831, in the Preface to *les Feuilles d'Automne*, that art was independent of politics, so Gautier repeated in a later time of disturbance: 'After all, it is art, and the word embraces everything born of the mind, the poem like the machine, it is art that so greatly matters. It is art that will resolve many problems beyond the comprehension of our vulgar statesmen.'[18] The same Hugolian fervour led Gautier to deplore the absence of leading artists at the *Salon*, and to insist that in times of political stress their duty to maintain aesthetic ideals was all the more urgent.[19] The politician moved in time, the artist moved in eternity; while the politician was disturbed by transient affairs, the artist kept his sovereign impartiality. The white stork winging its way across a painting of human torture symbolized, to Gautier, the lofty nature of the artist; and he believed that great artists were not only indifferent to human suffering but superior to human passion.[20]

This enduring belief in the sovereign independence of the artist, in the religion of art, in Art for Art's Sake, can be seen in Gautier's work from the time of *Mademoiselle de Maupin*. With it, however, goes an equally enduring practical sense for which he has not yet been given credit: an aspect of art criticism which Baudelaire and the Goncourt were not to discuss. It is true that in 1834, in the preface to *Maupin* Gautier had declared: 'Nothing is really beautiful unless it is useless' but the remark sounds like one of his favourite *boutades*. And whatever its sincerity he was soon preaching the need to apply the arts. As early as 1836 he insists that artists must be practical, that art must be applied to everyday things.[21] Again and again, in his criticism of art, one notices his strong practical sense: repeatedly the critic insists that art must be practical as well as ideal if it is to survive; and repeatedly he attacks the mistaken vanity which prevents the artist from propagating his work and improving public taste:

'There is nothing that art cannot enrich and enhance [he observes in 1836]. Nowadays Benvenuto Cellini would not refuse to make tops for Verdier's canes and paper-weights for Susse or Giroux. I know that certain artists, compelled to earn money, undertake such work, but they do it secretly, with a feeling of false shame that they would do well to lose. It is better to have made a beautiful clock, which serves a purpose, than a bad statue, which is good for nothing; indeed I should like

to know the use of sculptors and painters, if it is not to sculpt and paint
our canes and knives and silver, our furniture, portraits and houses.
Of course I should prefer a free and independent art, an art in love with
itself, like Narcissus; but, charming as he was, Narcissus died bent with
grief over the pale effigy he glimpsed in the fountain; and if art continues to stand apart in self-love like the sad adolescent, it is to be feared
it will meet with the same fate.'[22]

Statues (so Gautier suggested, in the same article) should be used in
exterior and interior decoration; frescoes should cover *salon* walls. He
affirmed that the discipline of a chosen subject, a restricted space, a
commission, would enhance the artist's abilities; and only if art became
widely appreciated would the climate be improved for creative work.
If the modern tendency towards small houses and small rooms made
art on the grand scale impractical, yet art must still be brought into the
home; if the purely decorative statue were out of date, the marble
nymph could turn caryatid and support a balcony. Perhaps it was because he himself had stood at an easel, had once considered painting as a
career, that Gautier was so concerned with the practical possibilities
of art; however that may be, the practical use of art remained a constant
theme in his criticism, and in 1870 he was still emphasizing, as he had
emphasized in the 1830's, that sculpture should be brought into the
home.[23]

One may do more than re-state Gautier's belief in Art for Art's Sake
and in the application of sculpture and painting; at the risk of paradox
one may suggest that this very insistence on applying art showed his
artist's idealism. He was not merely pointing out the home truth that
artists must earn a living; he was not advocating a profitable concession
to *bourgeois* tastes. He was already aware of the need to improve such
tastes: he was trying to educate the *bourgeois*, not attack him.

The spreading of artistic appreciation is indeed one of Gautier's most
constant themes. In an article which shows the technical knowledge of
a practising artist he teaches his readers how to distinguish original
paintings from copies.[24] He urges the Government to encourage artists
by awarding commissions rather than decorations,[25] he urges the public
to foster art by commission and purchase,[26] he concerns himself with
the design of locomotives as well as fashions,[27] and he blames the ugliness of civilization on the fact that artists abandon modern times to the
craftsmen and stubbornly seek their ideal in the past. It is significant
(for Gautier's sympathies so often attracted him to the classical ideal)
that he himself was far from trying to impose this ideal on modern
times: 'This world of azure and white marble that men call ancient art

may be balanced by a new world all resplendent with steel and gas, as
fine in its activity as the other in its peaceful dream.'[28]

*   *   *

Yet if he believed that the nineteenth century could become as beautiful as classical civilization, Gautier also deplored the existing ugliness
of his age. Just as he questioned the artistic value of frock-coated plays
and deplored realism on the stage, so his belief in beauty and idealization sometimes led him to wonder whether the artist could record
modern times.[29] If drama needed costume and poetry to remove it from
reality, painting and sculpture demanded idealization. Sometimes it
seemed that the very fact of modernity deprived modern times of the
perspective necessary to art; sometimes it seemed that the ugliness of
modernity made it difficult to interpret. At times it appeared to Gautier
that only in caricature could the nineteenth century be recorded: that
only the comic artist, laughing at the age, could present the contemporary scene.

To see the poetry in reality, to show, as Baudelaire urged in his
Salon of 1845, 'how great we are with our cravats and our patent-
leather boots', was indeed among the most exacting tasks of the artist
in an age when photography was favoured in art. Yet if Gautier were
sometimes sanguine about the artist's chance of success, he still maintained that the mission of poet and artist was to seek the strangeness in
truth. He admired Doré's illustrations to the *Inferno* because 'he possesses that visionary eye that can discover the secret and singular side
of nature.'[30] Indeed, he believed the discovery of a new aspect of life
to be the mark of genius; and he came, at least in his middle and later
years, to believe that if the artist could not discover the beauty of
modern life, it might be his own fault. The poetry of modern Paris is
enthusiastically emphasized in his essay *De la Mode*; and, watching
the casting of Pradier's statue of Sapho, he comes to feel that even in
industry the ideal, the poetic may be found: 'Industry, like art, has its
poetry.'[31]

But though Gautier perceived an artistic ideal in modern life, both
his philosophy and his natural preferences led him (as they led him in
his dramatic criticism) to those forms of art that were furthest in time or
spirit from nineteenth-century France. He felt, with his known predilection for ancient Greece, that a sculptor who followed the Greek
tradition was practising the religion of beauty; and so he admired
Pradier in what seemed to him a *bourgeois* century, for professing the
pagan, classical ideal: 'The pagan of 1846 protests against the reproba-
tion with which Christianity struck the flesh nineteen centuries ago.'[32]
The pagan of 1846: there is Pradier, and there is Gautier. There,

perhaps, is a key to Gautier's philosophy of art. Just as he declared that tragedy should be animated by modern emotions, so he believed that the classical religion of beauty should be inspired by the contemporary spirit: 'It would be fine to take up the work where the Greeks left it, and to continue the hymn to human beauty with modern feeling and the modern ideal.'[33]

Art, as Gautier wisely maintained, should be modern in spirit; but it should transcend reality. 'The supreme beauty of art is to be a creation within creation.'[34] Art was the work of God interpreted and enhanced by the human spirit. Gautier believed that the artist must express not only what he saw but what he would like to see; and he knew that even the greatest artist with the most fervent dreams might fail. And the true artist, as Gautier emphasized, did not only strive to find and express an ideal which, like all ideals, was unattainable: he naturally bore in mind a small world of his own, or, as the critic called it (following Goethe's example), his microcosm: he saw the outside world through an inward eye.[35]

*   *   *

Gautier's Greek standards, his pagan worship of beauty, rightly led him away from art which he believed to be the victim of cant; they led him, too, understandably but less wisely, away from Gothic art. He felt that the sense of beauty had vanished during the religious conflicts of the Middle Ages, that the Christian scorn of the flesh had prevented the artist's worship of physical loveliness, replaced the perfect figures of ancient Greece by the attenuated figures in Gothic cathedrals. It was the regret he expressed, as a poet, when he cried in *Bûchers et Tombeaux*:

> *Reviens, reviens, bel art antique,*
> *De ton paros étincelant*
> *Couvrir ce squelette gothique;*
> *Dévore-le, bûcher brûlant!*

Reviewing Cabat, 'the spiritualist of landscape', Gautier the critic likened him sadly to 'certain monks in the Middle Ages who exorcized the birds and the flowers of spring, seeing in them the temptations of the Devil'.[36] Such puritan spirit contradicted Gautier's wholehearted love of life: the unrestrained pleasure in living, in the works of God, that seemed (and surely remains) among the conditions of complete and vital art.

Gautier's lack of sympathy for Gothic art was richly compensated by his admiration of the Renaissance. To him the *Mona Lisa* was, quite simply, the most perfect of all paintings, by its abiding mystery, its fusion of reality and dream. His appreciation of Correggio was swift and poetic: Correggio, too, satisfied his passion for the ideal, could paint 'a crystallized dream of poetry', and to the critic it seemed that Correggio had discovered new powers in light and shade, that the man who failed to admire him had no soul. In the figures of Titian, Gautier rediscovered classical serenity, Greek equilibrium. Veronese exemplified his creed that 'the first end of painting is to be painting'; and in the *Marriage of Cana* he saw the pleasure of painting for painting's sake carried to its limit: recognized, glorified, his own love of splendour and display, his own theatrical and decorative tastes, his own affection for light and brilliance: a visible anthem to a bountiful God.

He admired not only the splendour and supremely graceful idealism of the Italians, but the powerful realism of Spanish art: the poetic depths that Murillo discovered in ugliness, misery and squalor. The lucid, mathematical spirit, the extraordinary honesty of Velasquez seemed to Gautier to show what realism could achieve when it did not degenerate into mannerist ugliness.

In the vigorous, abundantly sensual canvases of Rubens, Gautier found a genius after his own heart: recognized the unrestrained delight in the human form, in rich materials, the ebullient *joie de vivre* that he himself had shown since the days of *Mademoiselle de Maupin*. In Rembrandt's rough and powerful canvases he found an extraordinary and touching life: found, too, that world within world which was to him the creation of the true artist.

Gautier's appreciation of eighteenth-century English art was just and charming: witness his studies of Reynolds and Hogarth; and when English art was revealed to the Continent at the Exhibition of 1855, his impressions of contemporary English pictures were generally fair. It is true (one might expect it from the author of *Ménagerie intime*) that he shared the Victorian passion for the living sentimentalities of Landseer; and his comments on *The Order of Release* betray a rather strong affection for 'the supreme effort of English realism'.[37] But one cannot, in conscience, blame him for sharing some of the tastes of his time; and it is also evident that even in 1855 he recognized the pre-Raphaelites for what they were: diligent realists and accomplished narrative painters. Even in 1855 he predicted that they might suffer from their duel with reality.[38]

*   *   *

But however perceptive he was in his criticism of foreign painting, the largest, the most controversial and, practically, the most important part of Gautier's art criticism was devoted to the art of France. And among this criticism, some of the most significant is devoted to the art of the eighteenth century.

It was probably to Arsène Houssaye, whom he had known since the days of the Impasse du Doyenné, that Gautier owed some of his interest in the period. In 1838 Houssaye had begun to publish a series of eighteenth-century portraits in periodicals, and in 1842 these portraits were published in book form under the title *Galerie des Portraits du XVIIIe Siècle*.

When the tenth edition appeared in 1874, Houssaye claimed: 'Perhaps I was the first to return to that disdained and delightful world to which they all go today: those who discover America like Vespuccio.' But if Houssaye had expressed his enthusiasm for the fairy-tale world of Watteau, if he had shown both sympathy and discrimination, his appreciations sometimes betrayed a note of apology, and they remained those of an amateur, a man of letters rather than an artist. Houssaye gave far more space to the love-affairs of Greuze than he gave to his painting, and all his studies of the eighteenth-century artists were chiefly biographical. If Houssaye remained the first to publish substantial essays on the Age of Watteau, it was left to Gautier, the pupil of Rioult, the artist turned critic, to publish informed appreciation.

As early as 1838, Gautier had affirmed the importance of that eighteenth-century quality, *l'esprit*, and declared it to be unjustly disdained by his fellow-countrymen; he had vivaciously expressed his sympathy for the eighteenth-century theatre. His affection for the period extended, naturally, to its visual arts. This affection is reflected in his early poetry: in *Rococo* (later known as *Pastel*), in *Watteau*, both of them published in the eighteen-thirties; and there is a clear touch of the eighteenth century, of Watteau and Lancret, of the *déjeuner sur l'herbe*, about the ideal theatre in *Mademoiselle de Maupin*, the theatre which had taken from every country 'what was most graceful and typical'.

This affection for the visual art of the eighteenth century is distinctly seen in Gautier's criticism; and from his first years as a critic he declares: 'Grace, for me, is symbolized by the complicated shapes of the eighteenth century. Sofas with goats' feet, armchairs with medallions ... are charming and full of that smiling coquetry that touches the costumes and even the turn of the contemporary mind. The eighteenth century has a prettiness that recalls the little ways, the customary caresses of children. Is there truth behind it? There may be; but why analyse it?'[39]

In 1844 Gautier's review of Arsène Houssaye's comedy, *les Caprices de la Marquise*, already emphasizes, in a delicious verbal painting, his affection for Watteau; in 1849 his study of the *Musée ancien* includes a charmed and wholehearted appreciation of the same painter. And his appreciation of the eighteenth century extended not only to its artists but to its pre-eminent critic of art. If Houssaye had published his affectionate admiration of Diderot, Gautier was no less warm when, in 1854, he came to review a new edition of Houssaye's book: 'Voltaire is a cold, sceptical and mocking marquis, even in his bursts of philanthropy; Diderot is a corybant drunk with his god, foaming and raging in the sacred forest. . . . Diderot is more human, more living; he thinks with his heart as much as with his head; he feels love and admiration in his immortal *Salons* he founded the criticism of painting; he had the presentiment of drama, and alone, perhaps, in his time, he remains of our age. If he did not see God in a particular place in the heavens, he saw Him everywhere in the beauty of the universe, in the graces of woman, in the smile of the child, the flower and the bird, the lightning and the dew; he flattered himself that he was an atheist and he was only a pantheist like Goethe. . . .'[40]

The words that Gautier applied to Diderot might well be applied to himself: he, too, thought with his heart, as much as with his head; and there is a heartfelt warmth about his pleasure in the eighteenth century. In 1860, when the Louvre itself exhibited only one Watteau, one Fragonard and three Chardins, and refused to buy others, Gautier attacked his compatriots for scorning their national art. And he did more than accuse the public of negligence: he wrote a series of delicate, enthusiastic, beautifully visual appreciations of eighteenth-century masters; and in 1862, when the Goncourts published *l'Art du XVIIIe siècle*, he reviewed it eagerly, with a matching gaiety and grace, recognizing again an ideal art in the art of the eighteenth century. A few years later he again attacked the conservative French public for scorning the eighteenth century, and suggested the importance of the period:

'This eighteenth century, so maltreated by the pedants, has none the less produced a new style, an unknown form of art, adopted enthusiastically throughout Europe, a style that people have vainly tried to stigmatize by calling it *rococo*: an original, charming, flexible style, that lends itself to everything, a style of inexhaustible ideas and caprices, a style that has changed architecture, sculpture, painting, decoration, furniture, dress, and even the smallest accessories of life; there are not many of these complete renovations of style in the history of the world.'[41]

*   *   *

The high principles that informed Gautier's conception of art and the artist's purpose and guided, too, his appreciation of the masters of the past, may also be seen in his attitude to contemporary French art.

Although (as in his studies of English art) he sometimes shared the passing tastes of his age, his wide sympathies and his conviction that art comes before the artist' helped him nearly always to see his contemporaries in perspective.

Baudelaire's enthusiasm for Delacroix was indeed more than matched by the enduring (and, in its early stages, audacious) support of Gautier. Such support may be found as early as 1833;[42] and in 1837 Gautier points out that Delacroix, with Ingres, has revolutionized French painting in the last decade. Two years later he fiercely attacks the Jury for refusing the artist's work; and when, in 1845, two of four paintings are again rejected, Gautier opens his *Salon* criticism with a broadside. And if in 1851 he rebukes Delacroix for submitting paintings unworthy of his powers and of his status, he tempers his rebuke with the explanation: 'We have the right to be severe with him, we who have explained, discussed, revealed him, we who have preached about him to the public. Our long litany allows us to be demanding of our God. . . . Delacroix is still the unrivalled master, the most faithful representative of art in the first part of this century; he has wedded its every passion, anxiety and dream.'[43]

The Romanticism and the modernity of Delacroix were the qualities on which Baudelaire, too, insisted; they were the qualities the Goncourts had in mind when they assessed Delacroix as 'the imagination of nineteenth-century painting'. They remain the qualities that the twentieth century appreciates in his work. And Delacroix' acid comment on the critic's improvisations were surely more than compensated by visits to Gautier, requests for advice, invitations to previews of his paintings, and letters of gratitude for Gautier's 'poetic instinct'; and there is probably much truth in his admission to the critic: 'If it is true that intellectual struggle and activity make us live, we must also recognize that praise encourages and sustains us. . . . Your praise has had this effect: the smallest drop of this dew would be enough to sweeten many glasses of absinthe. . . .'[44]

It is, perhaps, only natural that Gautier should have appreciated the artist whose Romanticism is seen in every brush stroke: in his audacious colour, in his uncompromising use of paint, in his exotic and dramatic themes. But it is some measure of Gautier's broad sympathies that he not only enjoyed the coloured drama of Delacroix but the linear beauty of Ingres, whom the Goncourts dismissed, incredibly enough, as 'this miserly talent'. While the Goncourts criticized Ingres for coldness and lack of spiritual feeling, and declared: 'He draws nothing from himself . . . he extracts his works painfully from masterpieces,' Gautier, in his earliest criticism, acclaimed Ingres for his rare conviction:

'M. Ingres has a firmness of conviction that is, alas, too rare today [he
insisted in 1833]. When he saw, at the outset of his career, that his
drawing was good, he attached himself especially to drawing, and he has
gone straight forward . . . indifferent to success, and seeking to please
himself rather than others.'[45] Such indifference to popularity was, as
Gautier recognized, a sign of the true artist; and Ingres again proved
himself an artist by 'such holiness of lines, such religion of form'.[4]
The justice of this comment is amply confirmed by a study of *le
Baigneuse* or any of the impeccably suave, magisterially assured portraits in the Louvre.

Gautier's admiration for Ingres continued throughout his career:
more than once he is recorded in Ingres' studio, venerating the ageing
artist who, like himself, believed so persistently in Art for Art's Sake
That Gautier's admiration was reciprocated is shown by letters from
Ingres, praising his generosity and poetic insight: 'I venture to send
you these first attempts', the artist writes, offering him some sketches
for *le Bain turc*: 'They can only be appreciated by the few who, like
yourself, understand all the secrets of art.'[47]

If Gautier's recognition of Ingres may be quoted for its wisdom and
constancy, his recognition of Corot may be cited, in the first place, as an
example of divination. To Gautier, writes Everard Meynell, 'is due the
honour of first adding the name of the painter of the poetry of landscape
to the *Parnassus Directory*. In 1839 he wrote a poem to Corot's evening
landscape in the *Salon*.'[48] But Corot, who had helped to decorate the
room in the Impasse du Doyenné, had in fact been noticed considerably
earlier in Gautier's criticism. In 1836 he had already been quoted as one
of a trinity who had not received due justice.

Gautier was prompt to discover the poetry in Corot's landscape
discussing *Diane au bain*, he declares (and there is already a suggestion
of correspondence between the arts): 'Moschus would have sung of this
lovely place, Corot has painted it. For myself, I like this canvas as much
as an idyll by Theocritus.'[49] Gautier perceives the artist's manner as
well as his nature; and he records, most vividly, the early Corot, so
different from the painter of later years, the painter of solid shapes and
sunlit landscapes: 'Look at Corot,' he cries: 'Wouldn't you break your
bones on his stones?'[50] Gradually, however, the more familiar style
emerges; by 1849 the poetic element is well established, by 1857 Corot's
vagueness appears to be systematic, fixed and monotonous, and this
fixity and monotony Gautier suggests by repeating his own comment
and poetic correspondence: 'What can one say about M. Corot that
has not been said a hundred times [asks the critic sadly]? His landscapes are all alike, and yet no one dreams of reproaching him. . . . You

now how Corot treats these subjects: it is like La Fontaine translating
Anacreon with casual simplicity.'[51] The praise is there, but the reproach
s felt; and it is felt again in the gentle comment in 1866: 'M. Corot
as ended by only seeing nature through an ideal mist.'[52]

*   *   *

Millet, like Corot, was recognized as a master and sharply rebuked
or what Gautier considered a mistaken manner: in this case an exces-
ive use of paint: 'He trowels a masonry of colours on to the canvas
observed the critic in 1848]. M. Millet should not forego the solidarity
he gives his painting, but let him thin out his impasting by a few centi-
metres, and he will still be a warm and vigorous colourist, with the
addition of being intelligible.'[53]

It must not be thought that Gautier had, for a moment, indulged in
the acid criticism he generally deplored: he expressed his admiration of
e Semeur, and Millet himself admitted the justice of his comments.
And Gautier remained aware of the artist's powers: his poetic apprecia-
ion of les Glaneuses suggests that once again the spiritual identification
has occurred, and powerfully Gautier evokes Millet's spirit:

'We have already seen *The Gleaners* [he writes in 1860]. Three poor
women, bent towards the furrows that send back their burning rever-
berations, search for the forgotten ears of corn among the scratching
stubble with weatherbeaten, callous hands, deformed by toil. Millet
does not paint the ideal peasants one sees portrayed over looking-
glasses and doors; he seems to have the sombre, powerful description of
La Bruyère ever-present in his mind. His heavy, impassible figures
seem to slumber in the brutishness of misfortune, with the resignation
of the animal; they seem *telluric*, so to speak, hardly detached from the
original clay, and standing on the earth with feet that one might take
for roots; their clothes, which have no folds, stick to their rough-hewn
forms more like animals' hides than materials produced by human
industry. They accomplish their tasks in a clumsy, primitive way, in
hieratic poses, as if the mysteries of agriculture had just been revealed
to them. Their vague eyes have no thoughts; they express only a kind
of sad wonderment. The colour that clothes their bodies is deliberately
monotonous, earthy and grey. The artist, who was once a bold colourist,
seems deliberately to have impoverished his palette, and to have reduced
himself to the most extreme destitution to interpret rural misery. He
has simplified his drawing to summary indication, reduced his range of
colours almost to the cameo; but all these sacrifices have not harmed
him: his paintings have grandeur and style, their austere sobriety
charms the thought if it does not charm the sight, and over his

severe canvases there reigns a sad harmony which reveals a master.'[54]

It is one of Gautier's finest appreciations of art: it is, perhaps, an appreciation that could only have come from a practising artist, a practising poet. And yet, for all his admiration of Millet, for all his deep understanding, a critic who believed in the religion of beauty and main-tained that art was the interpretation of ideal loveliness would not accept what he thought systematic ugliness; and Millet's heavy figures and sombre colours are sometimes forbidding. This forbidding and occasionally Victorian nature was, almost inevitably, distasteful at times to Gautier: to the critic who, by his Romantic nature, admired the colour in Veronese and Delacroix; the critic who, by his love of grace, was drawn to ancient Greece and the eighteenth century. In 1861 Gautier declared that Millet had exaggerated his manner, producing not rough peasants but dull and brutish figures, impossible 'monstrous fantasies'; and though perhaps he was too vehement in his condemna-tions, Millet's figures were, if not 'monstrous', at least obtuse and plain. Again in 1862, in an article which showed a poetic appreciation of Millet's work, Gautier repeated his dislike of what he considered stylized and excessive ugliness; and again in 1864 he affirmed his opinion: 'When M. Millet wants to, and does not abandon himself to his systematic ugliness, he can express the beauty of the fields. But according to whether he listens to nature or his system, he produces entirely dissimilar works, some that deserve enthusiastic praise, others that one is forced to criticize, in spite of all possible good will.'[55]

Millet, it is recorded, 'was in awe of Gautier'; but he consoled him-self for his criticism with the reflection: 'Perhaps he could not say this much of everybody.'[56] He recognized that Gautier, if severe, was neither unkind nor unjust.

And the fearlessness and high principles that inspired Gautier's criticism of Millet inspired his comments on Courbet. He felt that while Courbet was powerfully gifted, he remained, like Millet, pretentiously brutal. Courbet, like Millet, seemed to Gautier to reject the search for beauty, to deny the artist's heavensent purpose: indeed, he appeared to the critic to ignore beauty altogether, and to carry realism beyond its limits, indulging deliberately in ugliness. And while Gautier grew increasingly aware of Courbet's powers, he could not bring himself to accept his principles. In a letter to Gautier, the artist asks for advice, and tells him: 'If I paint, or rather if I seek to paint, it is to deserve the criticism of a few men like you.'[57] In Gautier's praise of Courbet we see, once more, the recognition of a master; in Gautier's angry criticism of Courbet we see the concern he would have spared a mediocre artist. And throughout his comments we find him applying his belief that art is above the artist, that art is the search for beauty: we find him maintaining, with all the vigour of contemporary criticism, what he considered the highest purpose, the religion, of art.

These standards Gautier also applied to Manet: in Manet's work, again, he recognized a true artist and considered that realism was carried to excess. In the *Salon* of 1864 he paid vigorous attention to the terrible realist' in considering *les Anges au tombeau de Christ*. The following year he acknowledged Manet's influence but discussed him with some repugnance and disappointment. He felt that Manet had not developed his originality, not fulfilled his promise: that his *Olympia*, a paltry model stretched out on a sheet',[58] only showed determination to attract attention at any price. It is evident, from this excessively harsh judgment, that Gautier found it harder to overcome his disapproval of Manet than to sympathize with the other realists. And indeed by 1868 he wonders if middle-age has made him unable to understand the audacity of the younger generation, and in 1870 he dismisses Manet tersely:

'What can one say about *la Dame qui peint des fleurs* and *le Duo de solfège et de guitare*? Are they not painted in defiance of art, the public and the critics? Does M. Manet ignore or choose to violate the orthography of painting? Really, we cannot accept any more such mystifications. None of the early promises has been fulfilled, and every exhibition seems to prove that M. Manet has resolved to die in final impenitence, led astray by false doctrine and imprudent praise.'[59] The comments seem strangely violent to the twentieth century, which does not find Manet so much bolder than Delacroix, let alone consider him outrageous; and Gautier's misunderstanding of Manet is one of the disappointments in his criticism of art. And yet it is evident, again, that a Romantic of 1830, endowed with Romantic tastes and sympathies, would naturally find Manet unendearing; and if Gautier's violent disapproval has dated, his fierce devotion to his ideals still commands a certain respect.

*   *   *

If Gautier sometimes found it hard to appreciate the realists, he needed no effort, as his comments on Delacroix may have shown, to enjoy a Romantic artist. Admittedly, he did not display the enthusiasm for Decamps which the Goncourts expressed when they wrote of 'the modern master, the master of picturesque feeling'. He did, however, find in the painting of Decamps the microcosm that he felt true artists should possess, and he was (as one would expect from the follower of

Bugeaud, the would-be Algerian colonist, the author of *le Roman de l* *Momie*) entirely in sympathy with the Romantic Oriental world tha Decamps transferred spontaneously to canvas. And when he considere that Decamps was straying from his path, it was with fraternal solicitud that he advised him.

For Chassériau he showed enduring friendship and warm admiration and just as he welcomed Chassériau early in his career, so he encourage Regnault from the time of his first exhibit. Gérôme, again, was notice from the first: Gautier recognized his classical sympathies with pleasure Du Camp records how, walking round the *Salon* in 1847, the criti noticed a picture hung two or three rows up, *le Combat de coqs*: 'H considered the picture, then, turning to his companion, he said "There's a master." Gautier was right. . . . The leader of the *Pompéiste* was revealed.' Gérôme recorded his delight at the 'very fine article that Gautier accorded him.

The art of illustration, too, was readily admitted into the critic' pantheon; in her *Life of Doré*, Blanche Roosevelt points out tha 'Théophile Gautier was the godfather who baptised him with the nam of genius. . . . Théophile Gautier was so great a man that he recognize the boy Doré's talents and potentialities, the resources of which wer imperceptible to the outside world. . . . He was a very tower of strengt and protection.'[60] The Victorian extravagance of Miss Roosevelt' biography has become somewhat dated; but it is true that Gautie cordially welcomed an artist of such imaginative power: 'Imagination! he cried, in an appreciation of Doré: 'Imagination! A faculty that i refused to nearly everyone in our days of extreme civilization. How ca you invent, suppose, create, in short imagine, when everything i known?'[61] Doré showed that he could not only imagine, but discove new aspects of nature. His inspired illustrations to Rabelais and Per rault, the *Inferno*, the *Adventures of Baron Munchhausen*, were welcome throughout the 1850's and 1860's, in some of Gautier's most imagina tive and charming criticism; and a letter from Doré suggests the artist' debt, the critic's influence: 'You are the first of those whose opinions seek,' so Doré writes, inviting Gautier to his studio: 'I shall never b able to tell you, my dear Gautier, how much I shall appreciate your visi and how much I value sincere advice when it comes from you.'[62]

*   *   *

A study of Gautier's art criticism reveals, however, not only hi awareness of individual powers, but his consciousness of genera trends: the ability, essential to the critic, to take an eagle-eyed view o his subject and to relate it to the march of events.

Gautier recognizes the sudden, remarkable development of landscap

ainting in the 1830's, and by 1836 he can record that it is the most
mportant genre in the *Salon*. He sees the development of the genre as a
Romantic invention, and observes that nature was 'discovered' by
Rousseau: that nineteenth-century man, increasingly urban, increas-
ngly sceptical, has turned to nature for consolation; in 1853 he enlarges
on his theme, and, in a Romantic passage which betrays his own *mal du
iècle*, he suggests how the growth of pantheism has also encouraged
he development of landscape painting.

And Gautier sees the new pantheism not only in landscape painting
out, more happily, in the new cosmopolitan art. In the 1840's he recognizes that the railways are taking art beyond the known horizons, and,
with his usual poetic feeling and commonsense, he sees the railway
engine as the modern Pegasus and declares that science will give vast
new purpose to art. He repeats his delight that art is growing increas-
ngly international, and expresses the hope that a universal school of
art will transcend the national schools, rouse new dreams and desires,
oring a new poetry, and remind the public of their duty to read all the
book of creation.

And Gautier does more than observe and encourage the cosmopolitan
trends in contemporary art: he notices the new diversity of subjects.
In the reign of Louis XV, the republic, the empire, the restoration, the
first years of Louis-Philippe, French art had reflected clearly defined
interests; but the art of the mid-nineteenth century represented a multitude of subjects and techniques. Academic doctrines no longer
existed, at least among the younger generation of painters; and, inspect-
ing the *Salon* of 1849, Gautier finds to his pleasure that specialization,
which he has attacked in all his criticism, is ending. In 1864 he observes
happily that 'there are no longer clear-cut schools, or rival camps.
Individualities are more clearly defined than they have ever been'.[63]

The encouragement of the individual, of the characteristic: it has
always been one of the basic conditions of healthy art. This Gautier
understood; and wisely, constantly, he had urged the artist to develop
his originality, to have the courage of his talent, whatever sober warn-
ings he might be given, however audacious his originality might
appear. Just as he encouraged poets to write boldly for the theatre, so
again, wisely, in his criticism of art, he urged artists to paint audaciously.
And studying an exhibition of French paintings of the first half of the
century, he made the romantic, sound and profound reflection:

'From the study of these admirable works there emerges this conviction: that in art one never goes too far, and he who thinks himself
audacious is but timid; when you wrestle with nature like Jacob with
the angel, you must use all your muscles, all your sinews, all your

K

breath, your head, your heart—it is not too much. When you face
infinity, you cannot be excessive. Ingres, Delacroix, Decamps . .
always went to the end of their faculties, overexciting themselves, spur-
ring themselves on, trying to leap over the limit, and that is why they
attained it.'[64]

*   *   *

Gautier's art criticism, all-embracing as it is, records not only the
established arts of painting and sculpture, but the relatively new art of
photography. The friend of Nadar, who more than once sat for Nadar's
admirable camera, was not among those who believed that photography
would harm art. He saw it, instead, as the servant of art and as an art
in itself. As early as 1840 he and Eugène Piot had taken a primitive
camera with them to Spain; and eleven years later, in a review of *l'Italie
monumentale*, a book of Piot's photographs, Gautier discussed the scope
and purpose of photography with evident technical and artistic interest.

Gautier's considerations on architecture, like those on photography,
reflect the vicissitudes of contemporary work, and, if they do not show
a specialized technical knowledge of the subject, they reveal both practical and aesthetic sense. The Romanticism and foresight that inspired
his conception of Fortunio's *palais sous cloche*, that ancestor of the
Crystal Palace, the Jardin d'Hiver, and, indeed, of much modern architecture, were responsible for numerous architectural projects and
interests throughout his career. In 1838 he wants to see the Place de la
Concorde paved with marble mosaic; in 1850 he suggests (it is surely
the dream of an artist and a poet) that the decorations in the Place de la
Concorde might be used as models for a permanent decoration. With
such romantic projects went, however, a constant interest in modern
building, expressed with characteristic enthusiasm. In 1848 Gautier
suggests a solution to the traffic problem, an advanced, almost twentieth-
century plan for the new Paris: 'A modern street should consist of an
underground railway for waggons and commercial needs, with an open
road overhead for fast traffic, and two lateral galleries, covered in,
glassed in and heated, for pedestrians.' And then, an artistic touch,
'At the crossroads the galleries would be continued by arches like those
of the Rialto, and these might be decorated with flowers.'[65]

Gautier is indeed keenly and constantly interested in contemporary
developments. In 1851, as the tenant of a fifth-floor apartment in the
rue Rougemont, he pleads eloquently for more practical modern lodgings, designed to include a nursery, bathroom and study. And he is
interested in the grand as well as the domestic: the student of architecture may see in his articles, written, again, with the enthusiasm of an
artist, the rise and the completion of the new Louvre. It is evident that

the critic was in sympathy with the architectural tastes of his time; and his ideal theatre (suggested in 1856) is certainly conceived in a contemporary spirit. It has all the opulence of the mid-nineteenth century:

'As for the architecture of the building, it will be joyous and splendid in character. Polychrome architecture seems to us most suitable: marble columns with gold capitals, white bas-reliefs on backgrounds of minium or blue, plaques of brocatelli marble, of verdantique, bronze busts, shell-shaped niches, statues crowning the acroters; but it does not matter what style is chosen, provided that the aspect is gay, resplendent and rich.'[66]

The critic's vision recalls his aspirations for the 'sanctuary of the Idea'; and Gautier saw his theory realized within the decade, when he inspected the sumptuous and monumental work of his friend Charles Garnier: the new Opéra. In the *Moniteur universel* he published a valuable account of the building, and took the occasion to declare some architectural principles. Two points that he made should be emphasized: Gautier firmly believed (like Garnier himself and architects today) in functional design, and he insisted that honesty of purpose was essential to architecture. He emphatically repeated this belief when in 1871 he reviewed Garnier's book on the building of theatres. Garnier had discussed the importance of rational construction; Gautier comments: 'This is indeed a noble programme: the true enveloped by the beautiful; the useful supporting the form as the skeleton supports the human body. . . . It is an academic prejudice to sacrifice sincerity to a false symmetry obtained by superficial lies. Sincerity is always healthy, logical and vigorous.'[67]

The other point which demands emphasis is Gautier's interest in the architecture of the future: 'The use of cast iron [he writes in 1848] will permit audacities and airiness that will leave us nothing to envy Gothic architecture: railway stations will be the cathedrals of the future.'[68] Just as Gautier had seen the railway engine as the modern Pegasus, widening the horizons of sculptor and artist, so he perceived that the railways would have a powerful new influence on architecture. The observation he made in 1848 recurred to him when he watched the inauguration of railway lines across France; and in 1868 he enlarged on it, suggesting how the railways would dictate new forms of building, how they might bring different forms of art together, and combine use and beauty:

'Life is decidedly changing shape, and travelling, which used to be so distasteful to the Parisian, is now among his habits. . . . We already thought so when we inaugurated some or other railway line as a newspaper reporter, and, foreseeing the future, we found that the stations, vast though they might be, were too small. We said . . . that the stations would soon be the cathedrals of humanity, the focal point, the meeting-place of nations, the centre where all would converge. . . . We added that it would be the railway station that would produce this new type of architecture so vainly sought, because this kind of building did not exist before and should adapt itself to unknown needs.'[69]

We are far indeed, here, from the preface to *Mademoiselle de Maupin*. And with an artist's enthusiasm, an artist's vision and commonsense, Gautier continues: 'Architecture, which derived from the temple in antiquity, from the church in the Middle Ages, will derive from the station in modern times. Look at its colossal vaults with pillars and framework of cast iron . . . these vast halls where the travellers wait: is there not a new indication there from which an architect of genius can deduce marvels? Necessity has produced this kind of building. Art has only to clothe it in splendid and pleasant forms. The beautiful is wedded to the useful more easily than one thinks. These enormous gates demand to be framed in sculptures; these large expanses of wall call for the fresco. . . . Stations are the ante-chambers and halls of the nations when they visit one another, and they cannot be too sump-tuously decorated.'[70]

*   *   *

In these passages on the architecture of the future we find the main characteristics of Gautier's art criticism: practical, progressive and idealistic. Only an artist could have shown such constant interest in the application and propagation of the arts, could have criticized technique and welcomed experiment with such understanding and fervour. Only an artist who was also a poet could have identified himself with so many forms of art and transposed them as vividly, as lovingly as Gautier transposed the worlds of Watteau and of Millet, into literature.

20. The Little Mark Upon Our Heart

FOR ALL the aesthetic satisfaction that *l'Artiste* must have given Gautier, for all the social pleasures it brought in its train, he remained unsettled, profoundly despondent when he became its editor in De-cember 1856. And the letter he wrote Ernesta, still in Nice, as the year came to its end, reflects a life that many might have called successful, a life that he himself considered wretched and ill-starred:

'Dear darling,

'Here is the year about to change government and I cannot kiss you on the stroke of midnight. Separately we shall begin this new phase in our life. It saddens me a little, I admit, and I need all my respect for your freedom to leave you like this, far away from home. But you, too, have your artist's ideal and I know you want to use your talent. Now my affairs are arranged to make your existence easy and pleasant, without these ugly financial worries that spoil everything. You will be happy in your nest, as soon as you want to come back to me and our dear children. I approve of your idea of going to Milan and I'll help you to get there; meanwhile, as your New Year's present, let me give you this poor little hundred-franc note, I could have wished it were double or triple, but you know what a burden the house is, and besides it's only a fortnight since I joined *l'Artiste* and started to draw the money from two accounts. New Year's Day is an occasion for pillage under the name of gratuities for a heap of ragamuffins, and the time is drawing near. . . . But don't worry at all, there'll be enough for everything.

'I am well, except from time to time, when there comes this feeling of anguish and sadness. It is a stupid feeling, entirely unjustified, but I cannot guard against it, all the same. But it's in my very nature, so you mustn't pay attention.

'I'm so busy with my two papers and my novel (I continue it through everything) that I haven't a minute to myself. My existence, as a person, is suppressed; I am nothing now but a pen with three nibs. People say that not only do I not decline, but that I'm increasingly good, and my articles are most successful. *L'Artiste* is going very well and the circulation is growing every day. When you receive it you'll see that I'm scribbling and therefore that I am not dead. That makes up a little for the rarity of my letters; but believe that no hour of the day goes by without my thinking of you, and you ought to feel my thoughts hovering about you.

'The children are very well. They're good and very sweet; you should have had letters from them quite recently. As I write to you, they are both at their catechism with Mlle Huet; she is taking great care of them and hasn't been out of the house twice since you left. So your little angels are looked after as if they were little devils and you needn't worry about them. Your friend the white cat grows as you look at him, he'll soon be the size of a sheep. He is so gentle, so endearing, so clean, that I often come downstairs just to look at him. Gil Blas has grown fond of him, and, like an old cat who knows his business, he licks him, washes his face and spruces him up. It's the oddest thing in the world.

'Cormenin has come back, he's collected Estelle to be measured for a dress. There's the news. I have dined with Prince Napoléon at *le Lion*, lunched with Camille Doucet, dined with Arago, Nieuwerkerke and all the beaux-arts people. I notice that I am much more esteemed since I have a periodical of my own. Oh wretched humanity!'

He was sombre indeed. On 3 January 1857 the Goncourts met him: heavy-faced, expressionless. He told them how he was woken each morning by the vision of food: how, at half-past seven, the thought of meat got him out of bed: how, when he had breakfasted and smoked, he set out pen and ink and paper, the rack for his torture: 'It bores me, it's always bored me, writing, and then it's so useless! . . . I don't go fast, but I keep on going because, you see, I don't try to improve things. An article, a page, is something instantaneous: it's like a child. Either it works or it doesn't. I never think what I'm going to write. I take my pen and write. I am a man of letters, I should know my job. There I am in front of the paper, like a clown on the springboard. . . . And then, I have a very orderly syntax in my head. I throw my phrases into the air like cats, I know they will always fall on their paws. It's very simple, you only need good syntax.'[1] His cynicism was probably momentary, his boredom was sincere.

And he was all the more despondent since Ernesta was protracting her absence: sadly he wrote to approve her decision:

'I am brave and I know how to do without those I love in their own interest. . . . I'm sure you have in you an artist who has not yet shown herself and may still appear. You have the voice, the knowledge and, perhaps (forgive me this fatuity), in living with me you have acquired an understanding you lacked when you were younger. I shall make every possible sacrifice for your triumph. I am making the greatest, that of not seeing you. . . .

'I'm horribly bored, but it's nothing new and I am made that way. . . . The children are being good and were very upset when your letter came and I told them you weren't coming back yet. . . . I want you and love you with all my heart, and the proverb "out of sight, out of mind" isn't true for me. When lives have been fused like ours, two hundred leagues do not divide us. . . .'[2]

He wrote on, wearily, in the *Moniteur*: reviewing performances he knew to be ephemeral. And round him frolicked the careless Paris of the Second Empire, the Paris of the Carnival, with 'all the turmoil and forced gaiety, all the excitement and eating, and drinking, and dressing, and dancing, and parading, and [added a Victorian] the tomfoolery, got up for the occasion.'[3] At the last grand ball at the Tuileries the Duke of Brunswick had worn a tunic 'so covered with embroidery that the colour thereof was hardly to be discovered, and fourteen orders in brilliants, seven at the right side, and as many at the left'; an Imperial Guardsman, waltzing, had dropped his partner on the Emperor's lap. At Mme Walewska's the Comtesse Castiglione created a furore in a 'robe and corsage of cloth of silver, the latter [observed a reporter] perfectly tight and considerably *décolleté*'.

It seemed a frivolous, tinsel time, no time for serious literature; and yet, in these weeks, a book was being finished that would outshine, that would eclipse it all. On 7 March Baudelaire wrote to Poulet-Malassis[4]: 'Tomorrow, Sunday, Théophile is coming to the *Moniteur*; I want to show him the dedication before I send it to you.' On 9 March he sent his publisher the dedication 'discussed and sanctioned and approved by the magician', the dedication he entrusted to Poulet-Malassis 'with infinite love', the dedication of *les Fleurs du mal* which remains the most resplendent tribute Gautier received:

AU POÈTE IMPECCABLE
au parfait magicien ès lettres françaises
à mon très-cher et très-vénéré maître et ami
THÉOPHILE GAUTIER
avec les sentiments de la plus profonde
humilité
je dédie ces fleurs maladives
C. B.

*   *   *

And Gautier needed such encouragement. Even now, when *le Roman de la Momie* was being serialized in the *Moniteur*, he was receiving blunt comments from Julien Turgan, the editor: 'You're looking at so many engravings, paintings and granite monuments, that in spite of yourself you're producing frescoes, not a living picture. . . . You haven't set out to produce an Egyptian necropolis, you wanted to produce a living Egypt; your superhuman work has given you such a monomania that if you're not careful you'll be left with a sacred scarab in the brain.'[5]

There is a certain truth in Turgan's bluntness. The characters in *le Roman de la Momie* are lifeless: Tahoser, Poeri and Pharaoh are as unconvincing as Lord Evandale and his German scholar. They have no individuality, they speak with a verbosity that only recalls the financial needs of the serial-writer; and they do not, naturally, touch the reader's emotions. What is most significant in the novel is, again, the Romantic theme of an ideal passion: the passion of a nineteenth-century English peer for an Egyptian girl of 3500 B.C. And what is most evidently remarkable is (as Gautier knew) the highly detailed reconstruction of ancient Egypt with its monuments and palaces, its people and ceremonies. 'The history is yours, the novel mine; I have only had to cement the precious stones you brought me.' Perhaps, in the dedication to Ernest Feydeau, there is more truth than Gautier understood. But if *le Roman de la Momie* was too evidently written with reference books at hand, it remains a loving recreation of an age. It is drawn by the vigilant pupil of Rioult, the lover of form and colour, contour and shade. It is modelled by the d'Albert of *Mademoiselle de Maupin*, who 'liked to follow the curves of contours into their most hidden folds'. And Gautier recognized the nature of his distinction. 'People damn me or praise me,' so he told the Goncourts, 'without understanding the first thing about my talent. My whole importance, and they've never mentioned it, is that *I am a man for whom the visible world exists*.'[6]

*   *   *

Late in July 1857, the dramatic critic of *le Moniteur universel* went to Dieppe for the fêtes; a municipal luncheon given to the French and English journalists, and a firework display raining gold and silver on the sea persuaded him that 'no bathing season had ever been more brilliantly inaugurated'.[7] And his happy mood continued with better reason. The traveller and the critic in him were both delighted. He had signed a contract for 30,000 francs to spend two months in Russia and write *les Trésors d'Art de la Russie ancienne et moderne*.

This lavish publication, to be illustrated by two hundred Richebourg photographs, published under the patronage of Alexander II, and dedicated to the Czarina Marie Alexandrovna, was a project sufficiently exotic to rouse Gautier's appetites; and the prospect enthralled him. Crossing the Tuileries gardens with Eugénie Fort, one summer afternoon, he explained it with enthusiasm; and Eugénie (who still doted on him, who willingly accepted a Platonic friendship twenty years after the end of their liaison), confided in her diary: 'How I forget everything when I am with him! I feel younger, the past is forgotten with him for he is always in the future.'[8]

But to posterity the Russian project was not the most significant literary event in Gautier's year. On 13 September there appeared in *l'Artiste* his answer to an *Odelette* from Théodore de Banville. The poem was entitled *A Monsieur Théodore de Banville: réponse à son Odelette*. It is better known as *l'Art*.

It was in fact more than an answer, for Banville had precipitated the poetic formulation of ideas that Gautier had expressed, in prose, for the last twenty years. He had only crystallized Gautier's conception of the poet's task, his literary creed. The first ten verses of *l'Art* express the persistence and care that art demands of its practitioners; in the last four verses Gautier insists upon the eternity of art, the immortality that sets art above earthly potentates and the gods themselves:

> *Tout passe. —L'art robuste*
> *Seul a l'éternité,*
> > *Le buste*
> *Survit à la cité.*
>
> *Et la médaille austère*
> *Que trouve un laboureur*
> > *Sous terre*
> *Révèle un empereur.*
>
> *Les dieux eux-mêmes meurent,*
> *Mais les vers souverains*
> > *Demeurent*
> *Plus forts que les airains.*
>
> *Sculpte, lime, ciselle;*
> *Que ton rêve flottant*
> > *Se scelle*
> *Dans le bloc résistant!*

The longing to give permanence to transient arts, to passing beauty, is one of the basic themes of Gautier's criticism. 'The actor needs the critic more than any poet, composer or artist,' so he had written as a critic of the theatre.

'Without the critic the actor, so to speak, does not exist.... The actor is both the artist and the canvas: he sketches with a gesture and instead of a lasting touch, he has but a passing intention. . . .

'There is, we doubt not, though we know not where, somewhere, high above and very far away, a boundless region, a sort of place of refuge where goes what leaves neither ghost nor body, that which is nothing, having been, like sound, like gesture, like the beauty of women grown ugly and good intentions that have not been fulfilled. . . .

'A well written article might be that place of refuge for the fugitive and impalpable inspirations of the dramatic artist. . . .'[9]

·　　·　　·　　·　　·

Dramatic criticism, in Gautier's eyes, was not, then, merely analysis, praise and condemnation; it was also a daguerreotype of the theatre, a transposition of a passing art into lasting prose. This idea of the critic's purpose was inspired by the wish to immortalize that would inspire the poet of *l'Art*; and this three-dimensional reconstruction of the nineteenth-century theatre gives Gautier's criticism a richness, a lasting use and a permanent importance that in Janin or Sarcey are conspicuously lacking.

Gautier the music critic tries to catch and preserve another transient art, by translating music into visual terms. Here again he transposes an art; and in his music criticism at its best he uses correspondences with vigour and brilliance, discovers the plastic means of describing sound, of expressing the emotions that evaded definition.

And to Princess Mathilde he was explicit: 'I've regretted all my life I gave up my first occupation. . . . Since then I've done nothing but make transpositions of art.'[10] Gautier the critic of art is moved by the same desire as Gautier the critic of drama and music: here again he tries to perpetuate transient beauty. For he sees that painting, too, is a fugitive art: he reflects that the loveliest canvases will fade in time, and 'if there is a melancholy thought in existence, it is that two or three centuries hence there will be nothing left of Raphael, Titian, Paul Veronese and the great masters of art. Every day their paintings pale like dim shadows. . . . There is nothing imperishable on earth but poetry and sculpture.'[11] Here again is the theme of *l'Art*. Just as the poet's task was to immortalize beauty in verse, so the art critic's purpose was to understand and enjoy, to absorb and transpose, and by his transposition not only to bring beauty within the reach of the public, but to give it permanence and ensure its lasting appreciation. And this plastic criticism, this transposition of art is more than a *tour de force*, a descriptive artist's exploitation of intellectual weakness. It is the realization of Diderot's dream; for Diderot had defined the ideal critic of art as the one who could identify himself with every school. Gautier's transpositions of art were brilliant proofs of such versatile identification, of such catholic enthusiasm; and the critic that Diderot considered ideal was the kind of critic that Gautier himself set out to be and, indeed, the kind of critic which his generous, enthusiastic nature best fitted him to become. And if transposition remains an unconventional method of criticism, yet the transposition of theatre, music and pictures into prose, if made with visual power and discernment, may do more to encourage the appreciation of art than the most expert technical assessment. As Chevillard wrote, perceptively: 'The work of art worthy of the name is material poetry. . . . It must be described poetically, and that is why the fine

d loving phrases of Théophile Gautier, drunk with art, raising our
ul and setting it face to face with beauty, are admirable criticism
though, strictly speaking, they are not criticism at all. At the heart of
l our aesthetic emotions one discovers love.'[12]

This belief in the permanence of art, this constant attempt to give it
sting form, is one of the main themes of Gautier the critic and artist:
What in fact is the artist's purpose? To express his dreams in plastic
shion and to give immortality to passing forms. Who would wish to
ake a woman of the Vénus de Milo, whose beauty, caressed by the
morous centuries, survives civilizations?'[13] It is naturally the theme of
e theorist and poet. And when, in l'Art, he urges all poets to per-
tuate their dreams in lasting marble, he is only giving more durable
rm to the creed which he always professed. For art and love, as he
cognized, were inspired by the same longing to perpetuate and to
cape from nothingness:

'Art, like love, is but an effort of the soul that longs to escape from
ath. Of poet, painter, sculptor, there disappears only the envelope of
ay, the thought remains entire; in love, though you are unaware of it,
ur secret motive is to escape from nothingness and to hand on the
rch of life to another before the cold blast blows it out in your hands.
very man who is worthy of the name seeks to assure himself the immor-
lity of body or soul, and that is why there is nothing real in the world
it art and love, for they alone create.'[14] It is an explanation of Gautier's
astic criticism, of one of his chief purposes as a critic and a poet: the
rpetuation of beauty. It enlightens his character and his philosophy.

   *   *   *

It was Banville who finally precipitated l'Art. And it was Banville,
is October of 1857, who inspired (albeit indirectly) Gautier's letter to
ainte-Beuve, another splendid profession of faith:

My dear master,
 'I am re-reading for the third time . . . your admirable article on
'héodore de Banville, in which you raise so firmly and so high the
anner of Romanticism, the banner under which we fought together,
ou a general, myself a private soldier.
 'I thank you in the name of all that remains of the School. Perhaps, if
omeone proposed a bronze medal for the survivors of the great literary
rmy of 1830, as they did for the Grande Armée of Napoleon, they would
nd more veterans than they expected. . . .
 'Yes, we believed, we loved, we admired, we were drunk with beauty,
e had the magnificent mania of art! As you so well express it, after
nacreon, we have the little mark upon our heart, and by it we shall

recognize each other, in whatever oblivion the age may leave the fir
things which so rightly impassioned us. We must not blush for ou
youth. . . . The lyrical genius hovers above our decimated battalio:
shaking its golden wings. And we alone, in France, still know ho
poetry is written!

'For myself, if I had possessed the least personal fortune, I shou
have devoted myself entirely to *the love of the green laurel*; but in tl
prose into which I have fallen I have always defended the interests
art, and proclaimed the names of the sacred masters with all my hea
and soul.'[15]

Sainte-Beuve replied:

'My dear poet,
'Your letter is very precious, it touches my heart. It is a warrant
noble brotherhood. I too have deserted Art more than I should ha
wished: necessity has compelled me. But we are of the tribe of Israe
though we make bricks and carry stones for the Pharaohs; and ou
happiness, our legitimate pride and our consolation is, from time
time, to feel it.'[16]

* * *

The day that Sainte-Beuve wrote his letter, Eugénie Fort dined wi
the veteran of the *Grande armée romantique*, and (did he ever tire of it
he recalled the Romantic past. He was very affable, he wore a Turkis
robe and a fez: 'he was superb, he looked like a real Turk, he stayed a
the evening crouching on the corner of a big Divan.' The year 18
vanished in a haze of tobacco smoke, with Gautier discussing hashis
dreams and a plan for an Indian ballet.

21. The Seal of Respectability

BY THE early months of 1858, an important change had been made i
his life. The editor of *le Moniteur universel*, determined to make his co
tributor a conventional success, had suggested he moved from that B
hemian street, the rue Grange-Batelière, to the conventional suburb
Neuilly: the rose-coloured doublet, he said, would fade in the mists
the Seine and become a white waistcoat, the insignia of respectabilit
And at Turgan's instigation Gautier moved with his mistress, servant
daughters and *ménagerie intime* to the house with which he wou

always be associated: the house in which some of his finest work would be written: 32, rue de Longchamps.[1]

And naturally, despite the orthodox address, the unpretentious house with the large suburban garden, respectability refused to come. The day after Gautier's arrival, two dozen friends appeared, to arrange his books and pictures, eat risotto and dance on the terrace. They were only the first of a ceaseless and remarkable caravan: Prince Poniatowski was soon invited to 'laugh and drink quantities of Rhenish wine and a little brandy in the intervals of not infrequent cigars'.[2] One midnight the placid street was brusquely woken by a gigantic figure shouting up, with the vigour of Lablache, at Gautier's window: Dumas *père* was home from Naples and could not wait to see him.

And neighbours who ventured to cross the threshold would soon be disconcerted by Gautier's *ménagerie intime*. Don Pierrot de Navarre, that white grandee among cats, would interrupt their conversation as if he wanted to express his own literary opinions; he was, said Gautier, 'an aesthetic cat like Hoffmann's Murr; and we strongly suspect him of having scribbled his memoirs by night in some gutter or other, by the light of his phosphorescent eyes.' Séraphita, Pierrot's companion, named after the Balzac novel, posed coyly on the most becoming cushion and sniffed scented handkerchiefs. A cageful of white Norwegian rats devoured the nuts and raisins at dessert, or swarmed up the banisters at their master's whistle and hid themselves in his warm pockets. And when the white dynasty ended, the black dynasty began, for Pierrot and Séraphita left their offspring, named after characters in *les Misérables*. There was Enjolras, who was shaved all but a mane and a fur tip on his tail, and looked less like a cat than a Japanese chimera. There was Gavroche, the kindly, who invited starving cats from the streets to share his meals. And there was Eponine, with her slightly slanting eyes 'of a green like the eyes of Pallas Athene', Eponine, whose velvety black nose had 'the texture of a fine Périgord truffle': Eponine, the dearest of all the menagerie, whose place was laid beside Gautier at table. Eponine would arrive at the first tinkle of the bell, settle herself on her chair, put her forepaws on the table, and eat her way through dinner dish by dish.

Turgan must soon have learned that if Gautier were a success, convention remained out of the question.

*　　　*　　　*

But however Turgan's hopes were thwarted, Gautier himself was happy in this summer of 1858. On Bastille Day, *Sacountala*, his Indian ballet (the ballet, no doubt, he had mentioned to Eugénie), was performed at the Opéra; and now, at last, after sixteen years of waiting, he was granted the scarlet seal of eminence, a little of the official recognition he deserved. By an Imperial Decree of 30 July he wa promoted Officier de la Légion d'honneur.[3]

'Théophile Gautier, Officier de la Légion d'honneur' cried Viel Castel (a Chevalier).[4] 'Théophile Gautier! The journalist who wrote *Mademoiselle de Maupin* and published the phrase "blessed cuckold like St Joseph"! Well, let us hope all the staff of the *Moniteur* will soon be decorated.' Flaubert preferred not to send direct congratulations and asked Feydeau to deputize.[5] Charles Garnier (soon to design the new Opéra) wrote with affection: 'It is almost a feeling of egoism which makes me rejoice, it seems to me that the honour they do you reflects a little on me: I promoted you Commandeur long ago.'[6]

And however Bohemian he might remain, however impassive the outside world might think him, however sincerely he believed in Art for Art's Sake, Gautier himself was delighted: for 'it is the same with the Académie and the Institut as it is with the Légion d'honneur. You make a joke of them, you profess superb indifference; but when the Institut opens its doors and you acknowledge receipt of the brevet, you are in your heart of hearts completely enchanted, and you stroll about the town all the week, with your bit of red ribbon, brand-new, in your buttonhole.'

On 13 September Eugénie Fort recorded in her diary: 'TG leaves on Wednesday for St Petersburg.' And briefly, as he sets out, he poses for the camera: Théophile Gautier, Officier de la Légion d'honneur, wearing his Russian fur cap, his Russian pelisse, and tossing back his superb and leonine head. He gazes into the future with tired, disillusioned eyes but his hands are clasped together with a certain sense of achievement. One might even call it contentment.

*   *   *

'On the horizon, slowly, it emerged, between the sea of milk and the sky of mother-of-pearl, girt with its mural crown crenelated with turrets, the magnificent silhouette of St Petersburg, its tones of amethyst a line of demarcation between two pale immensities. The gold sparkled in spangles and needles on this diadem, the richest, the most beautiful that ever the brow of a city has worn. Soon, between its four bell-towers, St Isaac's raised its cupola, gilt like a tiara; the Admiralty darted its glittering spire, the church of St Michael the Archangel rounded its Muscovite domes, and the church of the Horse Guards pointed its pyramids, their spires decorated with crosses, and a multitude of more distant towers gleamed with metallic light.

'Nothing was more splendid than this golden city on this silver horizon, where the evening had the whiteness of the dawn.'

·   ·   ·   ·   ·

This radiant city of St Petersburg was peopled by figures as brilliant
as those in medieval missals: Guards officers, their tunics starred with
decorations, *tchinoviks* or functionaries, in their long pleated coats,
moujiks in scarlet tunics, Alexander II, regally simple in white and gold,
dancing a polonaise at the Winter Palace. Down the Nevski Prospekt
bowled the *drojkys*, delicately built as Queen Mab's carriage, drawn by
horses *tout pralinés* with frost. And in Moscow rose the Kremlin, its
walls as white as silver, 'an architectural crystallization of the *Arabian
Nights*'.

And yet, for all its coloured moments, *Voyage en Russie* is not the most
distinguished of Gautier's travel books. Though it remains a feat of
descriptive writing, though he conjures up costumes and buildings,
landscape and art, with remarkable range of expression and visual
power: yet the book remains, like *Constantinople*, strangely impersonal.
It may be, partly, that too much space is devoted to pure art; it may be,
also, that much of the book was written from recollection in Paris; it is
very probably because no human beings, not even Théophile Gautier,
emerge from the pages. *Voyage en Russie* is not written by an eager
Romantic still fresh from the Impasse du Doyenné; it is not written by
an impassioned lover. For all its splendour it is the work of a journalist
who is sometimes forced to spin out his copy.

*   *   *

And in the letters that Gautier sent back to Paris one is again aware
of the weary and despondent journalist, the writer saddened and disillusioned by twenty years of unremitting work:

My dear sisters [he wrote to the ageing Lili and Zoé, now living out
their lives at Montrouge],

'All my regret is that I'm not richer and that I give you so little. I
am responsible for you to our dear father and mother, now dead, and
while I am alive you will always have what I've not needed to promise
you. . . .

'The work is getting on well, but it all takes a long time when you
are far from home and have to keep up a house eight hundred leagues
away: when, on pain of dying of cold, you have to buy a pelisse for four
hundred francs, and live, the three of you, in a city two or three times
as expensive as Paris.

'. . . Imagine having to write copy when your mind is racked by all
these anxieties; imagine having to be gracious, entertaining and gay
with a crowd of people, and you can judge if I spend my time pleasantly!
You know how disgusted and bored I am with men and things; I live
only for those I love, for, personally, I have no pleasure left on earth.

Art, pictures, books, even travels, amuse me no longer; for me they a
only reasons for weariness and never-ending toil. Don't add to all the
griefs with phrases like those at the end of one of your letters, or I sha
lie on the ground and let myself die and stir no more.

'I am glad you visted the graves of our dear ones, and put flowers o
Mme de Girardin's marble tomb. She loved me well, and I still lame
her loss. I was very sad, on 2 November, thinking of all those who a
no more. It was almost night at noon; the sky was yellow, the ear
was covered with snow, and I was so far from my country, all alone, in
room at an inn, trying to write an article on which, most bitterly, th
bread for so many mouths, both large and small, depended. I goad
myself on, stuck the spurs in my flanks; but my mind was like a wea
horse that would rather be kicked and die in harness than try to sta
up again. Yet I wrote that article, and it was very good. I wrote one o
the Sunday our mother died, and it paid for her funeral.

'Forgive me for writing of such sad things, but your letter hurt me.
tell you the truth so that you can really understand and never doubt m
whether I'm far or near. To others I must disguise things. But, like m
own, your hearts have been tried by adversity, and you know how
suffer without dishonourable and useless laments. As for me, I am li
the savage tied to the stake: everyone goads him to wrest a cry or
shudder from him; but he does not move. No one has the satisfacti
of hearing him groan.

'So be of good courage; I have tried to arrange things and I shall s
that you're given your little allowance. Alas! it is meagre indee
Within a few days, there will be a solution; it will either fail or succee
In either case the problems will be over; I shall have money and se
you some, or I shall come home, and, within a week, all will be settle
Real presence will have its effect.'[7]

'My dear Nini [he added to Ernesta, in February],
'... I'm slogging like a galley-slave to set up the first instalment [
Trésors d'Art de la Russie], and to get away, for despite the welcome th
give me, I'm yearning to be in Paris, to see you and kiss you, and th
children, too; in fact to get out of my fur and get back into my ski
It is a long while since I left, but when I think of what we have done a
obtained, I don't think it would have been possible to stay an hour le
and get away faster. I'm sending my literature to Feydeau who is unde
taking to have it printed and post it back to us. They are building hu
here for Richebourg, hewing and hammering. Everyone's going at
hell for leather. I think that my article on St Isaac's will be as good
my article on St Mark's of Venice.

Ernesta Grisi in old age. From a photograph in the possession of Mme Alice Théo Bergerat

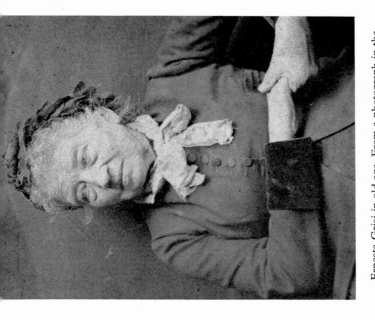

Ernesta Grisi in 1850. From the pastel by Léon Riesener in the possession of Mme Alice Théo Bergerat

Théophile Gautier with Ernesta Grisi and their daughters,
probably at Neuilly, 1857. (*Gernsheim Collection: Photo:
Richebourg*)

'Dear Nini, I hope that this time you'll understand the money is for
you. I'll send you more before long. . . . I'm not fixing a day for my
arrival, but it will be soon. I'm scribbling like mad to finish the work
and be able to leave decently when the first instalment's appeared. . . .
Please believe, poor darling, that your absence is as sad for me as
mine may be for you. I who am so melancholy, even when I possess
you, think how gay I must be eight hundred leagues away, all alone,
for the pleasantness of my companions doesn't replace you and you
are the only being I love in the world. . . .

'I look twenty times a day at the smiling, delightful portrait that
Richebourg has brought me, and the little picture which gathers the
whole nest together. But I prefer your face on the other, your sweet
full mouth seems to ask for a kiss, why can't I send it to you by telegram!'[8]

*　　　*　　　*

On Sunday, 27 March 1859, at about six in the evening, as Mme
Sabatier's guests in rue Frochot were beginning an excellent *consommé
au macaroni*, there came an unexpected ring at the door. And then, so
Feydeau remembered, a singular figure entered the dining-room. 'He
wore a fur cap which came down to his eyes, fur-lined boots, a long fur
pelisse, and he stood before us, silent, motionless, his hands crossed in
his sleeves. It was Théo. . . . We were so enchanted to see him again
that when we all left la Présidente's house together, we shouted for joy
in the street and woke the whole *quartier*.'[9]

22. The Tethered Poet

THE CELEBRATIONS were brief. Gautier's Russian visit had been so
prolonged that he had naturally lost the editorship of *l'Artiste*, and
Arsène Houssaye had again become editor-in-chief.[1] It was with relief
that Gautier signed his contract with Amyot for *Saint-Pétersbourg* and
received an advance of five hundred francs (the book, better known as
Voyage en Russie, appeared only eight years later). 'I'm working hard
enough to fall dead over my paper,' he declared in July, 'for my seven
months' absence have cracked the house, I must stop up the holes and
shore up the leaning walls.'[2] He wrote twenty-six articles on the *Salon*,
reviewed the usual host of indifferent vaudevilles. But, as Baudelaire
had recognized, his work was not generally appreciated. And if Hetzel

L

published six volumes of Gautier's dramatic criticism, if he introduced
them with a trumpet-blast of praise, he also informed the author
frankly enough, that Hachette had refused to entertain the project, that
Michel Lévy had only accepted on stiff conditions, and that he alone
had shown the inclination and courage to exhume Théophile Gautier's
journalistic past.[3] It was probably with Hetzel's letter ringing in his ears
that the critic wrote dejectedly to a friend, a few weeks later: 'It would
be very nice of you to come and dine Wednesday at Neuilly, it's 31
August, my birthday. On that unfortunate date I entered the world
where I was to write so much ill-paid and useless copy.'[4]

And something of the same despondency and weariness enters the
letter he wrote on 10 September to Ernesta, who was staying near
Hamburg:

'. . . It's always the same thing: writing copy, going in search of
money; my life doesn't change. The house has been cleaned from top
to bottom, and when you come back you will find it all as bright as a
new pin. The new maid is sweet, slow, rather dirty and a little dishonest
over the shopping. As for the children, they do their two hours' piano
and are passably well-behaved. They are quite good, for them. I read
them your letter which seemed to please them. You can trust Lili
with your animals; they have never been better looked after. Pierrot is a
little better, his heart doesn't beat so hard. The hens are squawking
and laying eggs. The canaries are putting on weight. The rest of us are
flourishing. Since you're no longer here to growl in your fine contralto,
the house is silent as the tomb. You could hear a silk handkerchief
rustle. . . . The sad time is at meals. It seems quite strange not to see
you in your place, with your piles of plates, distributing the food to
your menagerie; but I console myself with the thought that you are
enjoying the peace you needed so much . . . I'm very sorry not to have
come with you; but where the goat is tethered, it must browse.'[5]

And where the bird was captive, it must stay; yet listening to the
song of the gathering swallows, Gautier longed constantly to depart.
And *Ce que disent les Hirondelles*, which appeared in the *Moniteur
universel* a few days later, continues his letter to Ernesta and expresses
the useless longing for freedom which would not leave him:

> . . . *Je comprends tout ce qu'elles disent,*
> *Car le poëte est un oiseau;*
> *Mais, captif, ses élans se brisent*
> *Contre un invisible réseau!*

Des ailes! des ailes! des ailes!
Comme dans le chant de Ruckert,
Pour voler, là-bas avec elles
Au soleil d'or, au printemps vert![6]

*   *   *

'The *Jour de l'An* in Paris,' declared *The Illustrated London News* in
1860, 'the *Jour de l'An* in Paris is a social institution, consisting chiefly
in a flying visit, of which an embrace, some sweetmeats, and a present
are the usual characteristics.'[7] The boulevards, from the Madeleine
to the Bastille, were converted into 'a double line of tastefully arranged
bazaars', pilgrims were returning home with their loads of *étrennes*:
Punches or *Polichinelles* protruded from their pockets, drums hung cor-
pulently from their waists,' while 'the little denizens of the nursery'
eagerly, impatiently, awaited their return.

In *le Monde illustré* Gautier recalled another January custom: the
benediction of the Neva which he had watched, a year ago, from a window of the Winter Palace. It was still his delight to escape from contemporary Paris, in distance or in time; it was with pleasure that he
wrote *la Femme de Diomède* for the inauguration of Prince Napoleon's
maison pompéïenne, or lost himself in fantasy, dreaming 'of the violets
of the spring, of crickets drunk with sun, of the white and virginal berry
of the myrtle'.[8]

In the summer, with Toto, his son, now a youth of twenty-four, a
youth with business acumen and literary pretensions, he added some
final touches to the early instalments of *Trésors d'art de la Russie*. It
seems, indeed, that there were only final touches to write. The harassed
and indolent journalist had long understood the value of ghost-writing;
Noël Parfait, Louis de Cormenin, Maxime du Camp, Arsène Houssaye,
Ernest Reyer, Adolphe Bazin (and even, so Gautier asserted, his
Abyssinian servant, Abdallah Pergialla): all had probably been, or
were to be, his *critiques blonds*. Now his son had become his anonymous and ill-requited assistant. Gautier, like all egoists, could be
deplorably selfish; the vast project he had discussed so ardently with
Eugénie had long grown tedious, and after he had returned from
Russia, Toto had spent nine months in St Petersburg and Tsarskoë-
Selo, coercing a difficult photographer into action, visiting buildings,
consulting architects, delving into libraries, meticulously writing notes
which needed small alteration.[9]

Now, depending almost entirely on his son, the veritable author of the
work, Gautier cast his tired eyes over the wearisome guide-book description that would, inaccurately, bear his name alone: the grandiose
project that would not be finished. He was reminded constantly of his

escape to Russia, his imprisonment in Paris. Ernesta was in London and as usual (for he needed her Italian vitality, abundant vitality that filled the house) he felt lonely without her:

'My dear Nini,
   'I hope your next letter will announce a definite date for your return You will be received with open arms by everyone and especially by me your *petit ami*. Don't worry, don't tire yourself. We're getting on well the Russian affair is making progress and there will be a year or two o security before us. I shall end by getting something and then all will b for the best; I shall have a little rest and recover my strength and gaiety If you can arrange an engagement, your personal satisfaction will give me pleasure. If it can't be arranged, don't worry. You can busy yoursel with the house and we shall soon have finished paying for Villiers thanks to father Gide. Everything I receive from that quarter will be put at your disposal. Then I'll get the Crédit Foncier to advance me enough to build a nice little house and a good hen-run. Are your hun dred francs enough? You mustn't be hard up through excessive thrif and cut a bad figure. The weather's appalling; it's cold, it's pouring torrents and we're swmming in mud up to the belly. . . . I'm off now to write an article on a Ponsard play that was stopped by authority at the fourth performance. There's something enjoyable for you! But we are not in this world to be happy. There's nothing new in Paris: books plays or music. There are still the same pictures in the printseller's windows; the same old codgers are smoking cigars in the identica places, the buses go on being full, they're demolishing houses to buil equally ugly ones, and when you come back you'll think you've never been away. As for me, you'll still find me loving you with all my heart and devoted to you till death. The children are pretty good and are practising pieces by Acher that I bought them. They ask me to kiss you which is a pleasant errand. The sisters have performed their office of duennas most diligently. Toto grasps your hand and the cats send a friendly purr. . . .[10]

It was a lame attempt to cheer Ernesta; Gautier (was it the imminence of another birthday, the approach of his half-century?) was utterly de-jected. Early in August Maxime du Camp met him in the Tuileries gardens. He was foundering. All the difficulties of his life seemed to crowd together before him. He talked of his sorrows, his struggles, his existence of thorns and snares; he wondered what was the use of celebrity and talent or his faculty for work. 'They make me write dramatic criticism,' he said, 'because I can write it; it's lucky I can' saw logs, or they'd make me saw wood. I'm a racehorse, and they've harnessed me to a cartload of rubble. They haven't a poet of their own, not a single poet, and it doesn't even occur to them to ask me for poetry. They think I'm their debtor, and the odious task they impose on me hardly stops me from dying of hunger!' And he added, fervently: 'Oh! if only I had twelve hundred francs a year, I should leave it all. I'd escape, I'd go to the Latin Quarter, somewhere round the Luxembourg; I should lead a student's life, write poetry, a book of sonnets, and never, never, never should I set foot in a theatre!' And then: 'How lucky they are, the people who follow that fanatic Garibaldi!' Du Camp replied he was leaving in five days to join Garibaldi's army; he asked Gautier to come as the chronicler of the expedition. Gautier refused: 'I am the animal tied to the post of journalism; I must browse among the bitter herbs of the Press. . . . Oh Max! three times fortunate Max! . . . Oh Max, you don't realize your good fortune!' They said good-bye. Then Gautier turned back and opened his arms. 'Oh Max! embrace *le pauvre Théo*!' They were both moved to tears.[11]

*　　*　　*

Du Camp departed and Gautier turned once more to his grey existence, to try once more to forget reality: this time in a brilliant series of articles on eighteenth-century art, in the world of Watteau, a world that was 'like an Elysium where the spirit consoled itself for the brutalities of realism, a dream of amorous leisure and intelligent badinage. None of the miseries of life invades this enchanted world, and, beneath the white wig of Truffaldin or Pandolphe, old age itself is but a comic mask.'[12]

And none so devoutly wished old age were but a mask as the author of *la Comédie de la Mort*: as the man now approaching fifty who still could not believe in immortality. 'You see,' he explained to the Goncourts, 'the immortality of the soul, free will, it's all amusing till you are twenty-two; but afterwards you should have a mistress who respects your nerves. You should arrange your home comfortably, and possess adequate pictures; and, above all, you should write well.'[13]

23. Return to Russia

THE FIRST of these precepts Gautier put into practice. If Eugénie Fort had long ceased to be his mistress, he was still drawn to her by the existence of Toto. Eugénie was always soothing, admiring, ready to commiserate; and just as he needed the physical love and domestic security that Ernesta gave him, just as he needed the ideal inspiration of Carlotta, so he relied on Eugénie's constant practical sympathy. And if Eugénie had not been entirely faithful to him, she gave him lifelong devotion, and, in middle age, accepted every crumb of affection he cast her. She must have hoped that one day some benevolent deity would reward her patience.

On 1 February 1861 Gautier called on her, 'very affectionate. He wanted me to go out with him, but I refused'. Back in her rooms in the rue de Condé she wondered if she had been wise; a few days later she called on Gautier at the *Moniteur*, and they walked along the *quais* in the sharp sun, talking 'of what? One would hardly believe it. Of regret we had been unable to live together, of the good and beautiful life we should have led, how he would have grown rich and I should have been very happy. I say this today [added Eugénie], but the conversation often recurs. Poor Théo! Whose fault was it?' Whose fault, indeed? The poor spinster hardly knew, so constantly, for twenty-five years, had she revolved the problem in her unhappy mind; at moments her diary implies that she had rejected Gautier, at others that he himself had deserted her. Now they were both disappointed and middle-aged; she was living soberly, frustrated in her affections; he, in the eyes of many, had earned the world's respect, but he was disappointed in his career, increasingly disappointed in his household, long disappointed by his passions.

Gautier's despondency passed with March. He had many preoccupations: he signed his contract with Gervais Charpentier for *le Capitaine Fracasse*, undertook to finish the novel within two years. Eugénie and Toto urged him, energetically, to stand for the Académie. He dined with Eugénie, spent an evening with Sandeau, another with Princess Mathilde; and for the Princess, in May, he wrote *la Fellah*, and she answered by painting him a watercolour with her own imperial hand.[1] On 2 May there appeared the first of the twenty-five articles to be collected in his *Abécédaire du Salon de 1861*; at the end of the month, at the Tuileries, he presented the Emperor with the early part of the sumptuous *Trésors d'Art de la Russie*. 'The Emperor,' records Eugénie, 'received him pleasantly.' In July came a tribute of better worth in the eyes of posterity: a sequel to the dedication of *les Fleurs du mal*. Baudelaire published an eager appreciation of Gautier in the *Revue fantaisiste*:

'Imagine that the French language has become a dead tongue: that in the schools of new nations they teach the language of a people who were once great, of the people of France. If, in those epochs, perhaps less distant than modern pride conceives, the poetry of Théophile

Gautier is rediscovered by some scholar who loves beauty, I can imagine, understand, perceive his joy. There is the true French language! There is the language of great minds and civilized men! . . .'[2]

It was this poet, so endowed, so entitled to remembrance, who wrote a fortnight later to the publisher of his *Abécédaire du Salon* and asked him urgently for his five hundred livres as he was about to return to Russia.[3] On 3 August he gave Eugénie a copy of the book (it was possibly, like the *Trésors d'Art*, largely written by their son); and at nine o'clock that evening Eugénie noted: 'I have just left them. Father and son are off to Moscow for three months.' 'M. Théophile Gautier is returning to Moscow to finish his great work on the arts in Russia,' added *le Moniteur universel* with unconscious irony. 'Our readers may rest assured that his absence will not last long; besides, some more of his travel impressions will soon come to console them.'[4]

*   *   *

The readers of the *Moniteur* were soon enjoying Gautier's account of the coronation of Alexander II, and his description of the Russian summer. 'We are beginning to live among princes, generals, and counsellors of state,' Toto informed his mother. 'It would all be perfect if it weren't for the slowness and laziness of Gide who has so far sent only one incomplete copy of the book. . . . Father is fairly well, though at moments he's desperate and furious about Gide, and so longs to come home that I have all the trouble in the world to make him stay.' 'Unless I have copies of the book,' wrote Gautier to his publisher, 'my journey is useless, and the affair which began so excellently will dissolve like the mists of the Neva.'[5] But to Ernesta, who was staying with their daughters at Saint-Jean, he was careful not to mention his concern; he drew instead a gay and pleasant background to both his Russian projects:

'Dear darling,

'I have still had nothing from you except your nice letter of 6 August from Geneva, which gave me very lively pleasure. I saw from it that you had been warmly welcomed, and that the children were good. We are at Moscow, ready to leave for Nijni-Novgorod, where there's a very strange fair. It brings all the costumes of Russia together in a single place. It's as if you were making a long journey, but everything is gathered before your eyes. After Nijni-Novgorod we'll come back to Moscow and thence to Saint Petersburg, then, eagerly, to France; the year is hardly favourable for artistic enterprises. It's very warm here and very fine. It's only sixteen days since we left and it feels to me like a year. It isn't exactly that I'm bored, but my heart is no longer free enough to run gaily about the world. Too many threads bind me to the dear house, to you, the children and the *sacrée boutique*. I would have had to bring the whole lot and I'm not rich enough for that; but it would have been charming. I vexes me to leave without recent news from you; but if I waited I should miss the Volga boat, the convenient and untiring way of going to Nijni I hope, when I come back, to find a big bundle of letters from you and the children. I've told them in St. Petersburg to forward anything that comes for me.

'Good-bye, dear love, although nine hundred leagues divide me from you, there is no hour when I do not think of you and the dear angels, and I ask myself why I left. And yet I have two very nice travelling companions. You know the kindness of Olivier, there is no kinder creature on earth. As for Toto, it is superfluous to praise him. He looks after me, dresses me, arranges my life for me with the most affectionate devotion. He has been very useful to us. His stay has profited him; he knows enough Russian to get on and act as interpreter. . . . Without him, we should certainly be at a loss.

'I feel about Moscow what you feel about Geneva: without the snow it seems much less beautiful. As for my companions, they're in ecstasy, and with good reason. As I write to you, Olivier is playing the *Prière de Moïse* on the *salon* piano, and this Italian memory, in the midst of Russia, charms me more than I can say. It only needs your dear and tender contralto. A thousand kisses.

'Judith, you promised to write to me; Estelle, you said the same Where is your literature, you adorable little wretches?'[6]

The literature was waiting for him at Moscow on his return; and devotedly he answered his favourite daughter:

'My dear Judith,

'I give you back the title of "my last hope", that I'd taken away from you, for I know, from your mother's letters, that you are quite faithfully keeping your word of honour to be good and obedient.

'You could not imagine, dear child, the profound satisfaction you give me, and the tranquillity you give my mind, which is stirred by so many cares of every kind. Continue so, since you love me, and find in your affection the strength to bear all the little miseries that life is made of, wherever one may be. Your good behaviour shall be rewarded at once: I shan't add a word of moralizing. And that is considerate for a father.

'You haven't, you say, had the same impressions as I have of Lake Geneva, and you attribute this difference of effect to the fact that I was "far from my family, with money in my pocket". That is true, but not as you think; the interior disposition is everything; the landscape is within ourselves as much as outside, and it is our thought that colours it, sad or gay, kindly or hateful. If you had stifled a certain little rebellious or rancorous thought, you would thoroughly have enjoyed this beautiful landscape, so calm, so gentle and so serene. A drop of gall is enough to turn all the azure of Lake Geneva green, and cover the sun with bigger and blacker spots than the ones you see through your telescope on the terrace at Neuilly. Be happy with yourself and you will be happy with the horizon.

'But here I am playing the preacher again and beginning to moralize. I promised you a moment ago I wouldn't. I hope you'll soon understand the truth of what I'm telling you.

'The mountains didn't give you the effect of novelty you expected. You felt you had seen them already, like the sea; they seemed to you "small and mean". That is because reality rarely fulfils the promises of the imagination, and also, perhaps, because you haven't really seen the mountains. These cabbage-patches and vineyards you describe are only found on the lowest slopes of all; but when you are at the foot of these kitchen-garden hills, they hide the snowy summits, the glaciers, the pine forests and torrents; just as, in life, the fools prevent you from seeing a man of talent. I think I'll be able to come back soon enough to make you see Alpine nature in all its grandiose and virginal beauty. Be careful not to be too quick to apply the critical faculty to things that are genuinely beautiful: for the sake of a witticism you would deprive yourself, in the long run, of the faculty of enjoying them. Do not kill admiration in yourself. Enthusiasm goes well with youth. You will have time enough later on to find that what had seemed sublime to you at fifteen or sixteen is stupid and ridiculous. Don't follow my example. Alas, I shall soon have reached my half-century, and the need to analyse everything has made me fatally and incurably sad. But, at your age, I shouldn't have joked about the Alps.

'Read Walter Scott; I permit it and even recommend it; it's an excellent and instructive occupation. I learn from your good mother that it would be easy enough to divert you, that you have a very pure and accurate soprano voice. You know how flattering this is from an Italian and a Grisi. I'm delighted; but what has given me special pleasure is the entire good grace with which you yourself have asked to sing, and the docile attention you give to your lessons. . . .

'Good-bye, dear child of my soul; continue well disposed, and you will see everything smooth out before you as if by enchantment.'[7]

·   ·   ·   ·   ·

There was no more loving father than the poet who was so often
called impassible, no gentler man than the Eagle of *le Moniteur universel*.
Nor did many husbands show their wives more lasting affection than
Gautier showed Ernesta. And having answered his daughter, he turned
to his mistress:

'We have had a very strange journey from Tver to Nijni-Novgorod
on the Volga in a steamer. Three hundred leagues there and as many
back. It was a rest for me. My sweating has gone. And yet it was a
singular rest, this journey on which we went a fortnight without un-
dressing and going to bed. There is no need to tell you that there were
no Chinese at Nijni, since it was to see the Chinese that I had gone
there. It appears that one arrived three years ago. They expected one
this year, but the Chinese War has frightened him and he didn't care to
venture among the European savages, doubtless for fear that they cut
off his pigtail. . . .

'My health is fine, especially since the excursion on the Volga. . . .
This forced inaction has done me a lot of good. I'm very pleased with
the nice things you tell me about the children. I'd made a little speech
to them before I left and they promised to behave. I see they're keeping
their promises. I shan't tell you to be nice to them, because you are, but
show a little grace and tenderness. Coddle them and show that you
notice their new behaviour. You know we like to be spoilt in our family.
It's a fault, but it shows a proud and tender heart; if people snap at us,
they get nothing except invincible, mulish resistance.

'I see you made an excursion on Lake Geneva. As you say, it's not
worth the Gulf of Lepanto and the coast of Greece, but it's very fine
all the same. . . .

'In the packet of letters there were a few words from my sisters and
all is well at Neuilly. A letter from Gide tells me the Empress of Russia
has deigned to be very pleased with the latest instalment [of *Trésors d'Art
de la Russie*], arrived at last! and has sent him, Gide, vile publisher, a
very fine diamond ring. (Why not send it to me? I'd have given it to
you at once.) So things are beginning to look good. The Emperor will
return to St Petersburg about 15 September, and I shall be able to see
him and my mission will be finished. And you can imagine how fast I
shall speed to Geneva, if you're still there, for it seems to me an eternity
since I left and I'm in great haste to find myself once more in your dear
little arms.'[8]

The longing was genuine; it was the vital, dominant Ernesta of whom
Gautier thought after nearly twenty years' liaison. It was not that sad,

ell-meaning spinster, the mother of his son. It was, perhaps, at Toto's
suggestion that he added a line or two of postscript to the filial letter;
and his gallantry to Eugénie was, by now, automatic:

My dear love,
'You are as sparing with your copy as a weary old journalist.—Six
weeks, and a single letter! At least we have only received one. . . . From
far as from near I love you unchangeably—you know it and don't doubt
but it is a repetition you will readily forgive me. I kiss you in the least
academic fashion possible although I have just been elected an Academi-
an. Toto is a dear and very sensible. Chastity and economy reign in
the household.'[9]

*　　　*　　　*

Théophile Gautier, associate member of the Imperial Academy of
Arts of Russia[10] (an honour which gave him, he said, the rank of Russian
general and entitled him to a division at his funeral), returned to Paris,
by way of Geneva, late in October. And from Geneva, where rheumatism conveniently detained him, where he delighted in the ministrations
of Giselle, he brought himself to send Eugénie another few lines: 'My
poor darling I've been stupidly seized by the foot and nailed to a sofa
for a week which could have been better spent but I'm recovering and
hope to embrace you at the beginning of next week. I long to see you
in your new nest judiciously chosen near the *moniteur*. . . .'[11] Was it
pure coincidence that Eugénie had chosen to move to the rue de Beaune,
a few yards from his office? Was her decision diplomatic? Perhaps she
was aware, like her former lover, that the new rooms might have their
use.

Any joy that Gautier felt on returning to Paris soon dissolved like the
Neva mists. He was unwell, but he laboured on; there is a tradition that
he used different coloured inks to relieve the monotony of journalism,
and 'went through all the colours of the rainbow'. Every Sunday, in the
offices of *le Moniteur universel*, Gustave Claudin watched him at work
on his Monday article, covering square after square of paper with
microscopic writing; after every sheet he rose mechanically, went to
the printer, gave in the sheet, and (an unconscious habit) picked up a
letter of print, examined it, replaced it in its box. The habit of working
in a printer's office, among the clatter of presses, the chugging of
machines, the slamming of doors, the clamour of conversation, had
become so fixed that he told Du Camp: 'I think I can only write now
when I'm smelling printer's ink.' He always waited till the last moment
to write his articles, for 'you never have yourself guillotined before
time'; and when they brought him the proofs, he marked the errors

with his finger-nail and 'went away, taking deep breaths of air, like
miner coming up from his underground passages when his day is don
As usual, after his travels, depression overwhelmed him. On 2 Decemb
he called on Eugénie and spoke 'most touchingly of his regrets that I
had not lived with me. He would have done such fine things! He wou
have become rich! He read me the poem he has written these last fe
days: *Après le Feuilleton*':

> *Mes colonnes sont alignées*
> *Au portique du feuilleton;*
> *Elles supportent résignées*
> *Du journal le pesant fronton.*

> *Jusqu'à lundi je suis mon maître.*
> *Au diable chefs-d'oeuvre mort-nés!*
> *Pour huit jours je puis me permettre*
> *De vous fermer la porte au nez.*

> *Les ficelles des mélodrames*
> *N'ont plus le droit de se glisser*
> *Parmi les fils soyeux des trames*
> *Que mon caprice aime à tisser.*

> *Voix de l'âme et de la nature,*
> *J'écouterai vos purs sanglots,*
> *Sans que les couplets de facture*
> *M'étourdissent de leurs grelots.*

> *Et portant, dans mon verre à côtes,*
> *La santé du temps disparu,*
> *Avec mes vieux rêves pour hôtes*
> *Je boirai le vin de mon cru:*

> *Le vin de ma propre pensée,*
> *Vierge de toute autre liqueur,*
> *Et que, par la vie écrasée,*
> *Répand la grappe de mon cœur!*[12]

24. The Displaced Contemporary

IN THE bright, frosty weather of January 1862 the Court was often skating at its favourite rendezvous on the Lac de Madrid. 'Emperor and Empress mingle familiarly with the general throng,' observed the Paris correspondent of the *Guardian*; adding, somewhat tactlessly: 'In her pretty costume, and with the abundant colour produced by exercise in her cheeks, Her Majesty is scarcely recognizable.'[1] Haussmann continued his urban improvements; Mignet, at the Institut de France, enthralled his audience with his appreciation of Henry Hallam. And in *le Moniteur universel* Théophile Gautier explained the triumphs of the pedestrian Ponsard.[2]

Twenty-seven years of dramatic criticism had brought him to dislike and even despise the large majority of theatrical performances; and, meeting one of the Goncourts in an interval of *Rothomago*, he took his arm and walked a little way down the boulevard. Puffing at his cigar, he muttered: 'That's how I like the theatre: from the outside. I've three women in my box to tell me about the performance. Fournier, a man of genius! Never a new piece with him. . . . It's such a clumsy, abject art, the theatre. Don't you find the times are killing?'[3] Two days later, when they called at Neuilly to present him with *l'Art du dix-huitième siècle*, he again lamented the age in which they lived. He no longer felt himself contemporary.

Now it was Millet whom he appreciated in the *Moniteur*, Manet who recorded him in *la Musique aux Tuileries*. But it was Delacroix to whom his sympathies still inclined him: Delacroix who, like himself, had never lost his instinctive Romanticism. Gautier lived still, in spirit, in the Romantic age, escaping from the world of the Second Empire, from the harsh journalistic pedestrian world that did not seem to understand either art or literature and still, even now, rejected his writing. In mid March he called on Eugénie for his usual consolation: the *Moniteur* had refused an article on Baudry. Eugénie told him to send in his resignation; but how could he resign, he who depended on these constant sums of 200 francs for the livelihood of so many? To Gautier it seemed that the *écu* was the ruling force of the time, that Balzac had introduced into literature the religion of money. And money entered the theatre itself, the theatre that should have been the sanctuary of poetry and beauty. 'As the religion of money is the only one today without an unbeliever, it is generally a question of a large sum that someone can

keep or return. This alternative is as interesting as, once upon a time
were the struggles of Chimène, debating between her love and he
revenge. To give money away, when the tribunals would not summon
you for keeping it, is the ultimate effort of modern heroism.'[4]

Gautier had been right to tell the Goncourts that he was no longer
contemporary; and while he moved in the world of 1862, often and
often he returned to the past in thought. No doubt that was one of th
reasons why, nowadays, he so frequently went back to Eugénie, trying
to recapture, in her presence, his own Romantic years. No doubt tha
was one of the reasons why he called on her, on the eve of his visit to
London, and 'repeated time and time again that I could not leave Paris
that I was a centre of happiness for him, the only one he possessed'
He spoke 'at length of himself, of his unhappy life, of his duties toward
his sisters, his daughters and his son, and he ended: "Rest assured tha
you have the better part of me: down there they have my house and
my money, but you yourself possess me".' She did indeed possess par
of him: he wanted her constant admiration, her quiet, undemanding
devotion, her unfailing, soothing sympathy. And yet, however truly h
spoke to her, he constantly needed, still depended on Ernesta; and it wa
Ernesta, with their daughters, who now followed him to London.

*   *   *

On 30 April Gautier left to report on the second International
Exhibition. He arrived at an august and cosmopolitan city. 'The grea
hotels,' recorded a gratified observer, 'are in the full swing of a roya
and illustrious patronage. . . . Now it is the Crown Prince of Prussia
now the Dowager Queen Christina of Spain, now Prince Oscar o
Sweden né Bernadotte; the staircases of Long's, of Mivart's, of Clar
idge's, are worn by regal and princely footsteps.'[5] The imagination wa
caught indeed by the international throng, and it soon became necessary
to contradict 'absurd stories of the Japanese living principally on raw
fish and asphyxiating half the waiters at Claridge's with the fumes o
opium'.[6] Gautier, less spectacular, settled in Panton Street; and on
1 May, at dawn, wearing his white cravat, he set out for the opening.

The 'great international edifice' that met his eyes in Hyde Park wa
no second Crystal Palace, but a domed building in yellowish brick which
reminded him of an Oriental bazaar and suggested (understandably) a
station, a covered market and a greenhouse all in one. The opening wa
to take place at one o'clock; it was now hardly eight, and 'everywher
hammers were echoing, crates were being opened, fragile exhibits wer
being unwrapped, carpets being laid; and conversations were going on
as polyglot as those in the Tower of Babel, where answer misunderstood
question, and vice versa. But this difference of tongue, which onc

rought the dispersal of nations, will [he wrote, optimistically] have a different effect to-day.'[7] In this 'outsize cathedral' he sat for seven hours, noting the architecture in conscientious detail while, one by one, the delegates arrived: among them that astounding personage in full Albanian costume who 'looked like Lord Byron's Corsair but turned out to be Mr Drummond Wolff, the commissioner for the Ionian Islands'; and the Japanese delegates, whose appearance contrasted sadly with their reputations: 'The spectacle of half a dozen middle-aged parties with half-shaven heads, brown holland inexpressibles, and paper boots did not,' remarked *The Illustrated London News*, 'come up to our notions of the magnificent.' 'A kind and gigantic gentleman' identified the illustrious who were passing in procession: 'His Royal Highness the Duke of Cambridge, Knight of the Garter, His Grace the Archbishop of Canterbury, the Right Honourable Viscount Palmerston. . . . We shall not record Lord Granville's speech nor the Duke of Cambridge's reply,' added Gautier (who knew no English). 'The silence of twenty thousand people is enough to drown an orator's voice, had he the lungs of Stentor.' Then a choir of women dressed in white sang 'exquisite verses' by Mr Tennyson, and the Court procession made its way from the building. The Exhibition was open.

For a month and more the delegate of *le Moniteur universel* remained in London, regaling himself and his readers with a study of English art. Yet not the least pleasant event of his stay was his dinner with Thackeray.[8] The author of *Vanity Fair* much admired the author of *Mademoiselle de Maupin*; and Alcide de Fonteyrand surely warmed Gautier's heart when he told him of a champagne party attended by the chief contributors to *Punch*, where 'they drank a toast to M. Théophile Gautier, requesting me to convey to him the appreciation and homage of the assembly. In the first rank of these lovers of *Mademoiselle de Maupin* was Mr Thackeray'.

*   *   *

Gautier returned to France about 10 June, and was soon in the familiar shabby room, confiding to Eugénie the opinions he would certainly not have published: 'He gave me, at some length, his opinion of *les Misérables*—and he is not satisfied with it.'

At the end of June, he and Delacroix were the witnesses at the second marriage of Arsène Houssaye: it was indeed a splendid Romantic congregation that midnight in the church of Saint-Louis d'Antin, a congregation that included Sainte-Beuve and Janin, Girardin and Nadar, and that irrepressible poetess and ex-mistress of Flaubert, Mme Louise Colet.[9] And perhaps the wedding recalled a misspent past and gave fresh impetus to Gautier's lamentations; for again and again, in July,

he called on Eugénie, again and again he repeated his jeremiad. 'I don
always record our conversations,' she confessed, 'for they generall
concern the same subjects: Toto, his reticence, his work, well done bu
inadequate, regrets that we cannot live together, how difficult it is fo
Gautier to change his present position, how little happiness it give
him.' Yet were their conversations merely duplicates? It seems no
that a new element had entered them, that she herself had had a chang
of heart. Perhaps, at last, she realized his incurable selfishness, saw th
futility of her own life in Paris. 'It all concerns me little,' she added, '
don't want to alter my life of solitude except to make it more solitary
At the end of the month she told him she would leave rue de Beaune.

He was, of course, shaken, said she was 'cruel to abandon him', tha
she must wait. Again and again he returned: coming, one feels, mor
frequently than ever to dissuade her from leaving. The rue de Beaun
became his home; while Eugénie sat at her sewing, he relaxed and rea
until it was time to return to the turmoil of Neuilly. And of course h
unhappiness, his constant visits, his apparent need of her, had th
desired effect. Eugénie's profession of independence gradually weak
ened: 'Poor dear!' she wrote in her diary. 'Poor dear! what can I do t
make him happy? . . . I shall stay in Paris as long as I can.'

On 2 August he spent the afternoon with her, and 'we spoke muc
about himself, about his work and the little interest the public seeme
to take in it. I told him, and it's the truth, how often Toto and I ha
deplored this indifference. And yet he is so loved; but it is a genera
disease—the indifference of everyone to everything. Many details abou
Neuilly. "What would you have me do?" he said to me. "We'll conso
one another. I'll give them enough to live on and tell them that they ca
live in their own fashion, I'm determined to live in mine."'

A few days later he left for Algiers to attend the opening of th
Blidah railway. Yet was it Eugénie's company he wanted? 'There is
palm tree under my window, a mosque a few yards away,' he told th
ever-engaging Régina Lhomme. 'It's charming—but how delightful
would have been to see this splendid panorama together. . . .'

*   *   *

Now he stayed there alone, a middle-aged Romantic, seeing agai
'white Algiers, resting on its mountain, its head and feet bathed i
eternal blue'. There again, among the orange-trees of Blidah, he recap
tured a little of the spirit of eighteen years ago; there, in Algiers, h
found the realization of a constant reverie:

'The flute of the dervish is sighing, the rebeb playing arpeggios, th
tarbouka is marking time. . . . The indolent dancers rise as in a dream
little by little they grow animated, raise their henna-tinted hands an

Gustave Flaubert, from a photograph, probably by Carjat

Princess Mathilde, from the bust by J.-B. Carpeaux now
in the Louvre

Carlotta Grisi, after a drawing by Théophile Gautier

The Villa Grisi-sur-Saint-Jean, about 1868. Carlotta and
Gautier may be seen on the balcony (*Collection Bergerat*)

wave their embroidered handkerchiefs; shivers of gold and silver tremble on their brilliant costumes; the rings on their feet are tinkling and marking the beats. . . . The graceful silhouettes stand out against a background of white walls, and, on the tops of the terraces, the veiled women applaud, while the bats, awakened, circle above the courtyard in their flight.'[10]

*   *   *

On 22 August he returned to Paris. Next day, when the weight of existence had fallen back on his shoulders, when he had woken roughly from his dream, the Goncourts met him at dinner. He was raging against civilization, the engineers who destroyed the landscapes with their railways, the municipal-minded; and turning to Claudin he said there were moments when he wanted to kill M. Prudhomme, the *sergents de ville*, everyone in existence. 'Some of us aren't French,' he added, to the Goncourts, 'we belong to different races. We are filled with nostalgias. And when one feels not only nostalgia for a country, but nostalgia for an age . . . such as you, for example, feel for the eighteenth century, such as I feel for the Venice of Casanova, oh! then the nostalgia is complete. Come and see me, one evening. We'll talk about it all. . . . The three of us will take turns to be Job on his dung-hill.'[11]

The Goncourts arrived at Neuilly on 31 August: not for this lamentation, but for *Pierrot posthume*, the family entertainment given to celebrate Gautier's fifty-first birthday.[12] Next day, another melancholy sign of the passing of time, Gautier attended the funeral of Bocage: Bocage, who had been Didier in *Marion Delorme*, who had been Buridan in *la Tour de Nesle*, who had competed in his time with the genius of Frédéric Lemaître, the passion of Mme Dorval, the epic majesty of Mlle Georges. Yet another link with Romanticism was severed.[13]

And in the ever-ready diary of Eugénie one meets the Gautier of this autumn: a Gautier weary, disturbed, distracted, bored by his work, needing all the sympathy she could give him to write the endless instalments of *le Capitaine Fracasse* for the *Revue Nationale et Etrangère*. 'We went over all the beginning of *le Capitaine*,' she wrote on 2 November. '"Pay me compliments," Gautier said, "tell me it's good, that will help me to get to the end."'

Ernesta's mother had died, and Ernesta was in Geneva. Readily, in her absence, he demanded Eugénie's sympathy. Readily Eugénie sympathized. And readily, when he left the rue de Beaune, the ageing Don Juan returned to Neuilly, settled down by the fire, lit his fifteenth cigar that day, and scribbled off to Ernesta: 'And when are you coming back to us, my darling? It's a very long time already since you left.'

M

Within a few hours, no doubt, he was climbing Eugénie's stairs to tell her how he regretted they lived apart. On 20 December he came for a moment and read her *le Château du Souvenir*, the poem he had written a year ago: recalled herself and Victorine, himself in his rose-coloured doublet, Petrus Borel, Napoléon Tom, Joseph Bouchardy: the whole Romantic procession of the past. Its aura only intensified with the years.

> *Encore une autre fois décembre*
> *Va retourner le sablier.*
> *Le présent entre dans ma chambre*
> *Et me dit en vain d'oublier.*[14]

25. The Widening Rift

'IT IS held a point of orthodoxy in Lutetia,' remarked *The Illustrated London News*, 'to be jovial on the *jour de l'an*; and accordingly the inhabitants of this delicious capital, from the ineffable *Gandins* of the Jockey Club and the mysterious association termed *les Moutards*, who are held to be the cream of creams of all whipped creams, down to the humblest wearers of blouses, are all as gay as any number of larks.'[1] All, it seems, except Théophile Gautier, who spent the first day of 1863 at his unending work. He was probably glad to lose himself in journalism, for the bickering and shouting, the unpredictable temperament of Ernesta, constantly oppressed him, and he called on the ever-ready Eugénie to complain of his household, and to argue, with callous humour, that women should enter the world at fifteen and quit it at forty.

He was happy, nowadays, to escape from the rue de Longchamps. Readily, on Sundays, he lunched with the Houssayes on his way to the *Moniteur*. 'Very often his article was written in the avenue Friedland, on the table still spread with flowers and fruit. Théo sipped his coffee or champagne as he chattered and scribbled. . . .'[2] Eagerly he attended the luncheon given in honour of Dickens, the luncheon 'distinguished by a pheasant shot at the last imperial shoot at Versailles': the luncheon when wit 'flew over the château Margaux and champagne', and Dickens not only expressed himself 'in the most academic French', but was moved to tears by Mme Trebelli's singing at dessert.[3] Readily Gautier attended Princess Mathilde's receptions, and often he returned to the long-suffering Eugénie to tell her of his vexation with Neuilly and, with stonishing want of tact, to repeat yet again that he wished they had ived together. 'How often the phrase has reappeared in our conversations!' she wrote on 23 January. 'He explained to me how he is dominated by a feeling of false pride that has often prevented him from realizing good intentions and satisfying eager desires.' 'He is still complaining of the arrangement of his life,' she added, a few days later. 'He wants to change and improve it, but how? He does not know himself.' One evening he called for supper and told her how he regretted not being the master of his own existence. She answered bitterly that in a year's time she would enter a convent unless she felt she was needed; he ignored the remark and again complained of Neuilly and said the situation could not last. She returned to Versailles. When she came back to Paris early in April, she found him 'anxious, he wanted to see for himself how I looked, how I was installed, what my financial situation might be'; he wanted, also, to make his eternal complaint. 'Always this Neuilly,' she added, exasperated. 'He agrees with me it's becoming a mania, an illness with him. I told him to chase the thought away and devote himself to some pleasant work.'

What pleasant work could there be? It was only embittering to turn to Des Essart's poem, *les Hirondelles*, which urged the journalist to return to poetry.[4] It was only frustrating to come across Houssaye's tribute to 'the fine poet who finds a luminous palette in his inkwell';[5] and when *Giselle* was revived in May at the Odéon, and drew record audiences in the stifling summer heat, it was, after all, the revival of an old success.[6]

Yet the first months of 1863 were not entirely spent in vexation and the preparation of *le Capitaine Fracasse*: April brought a new element into Gautier's social life. On 27 April, by the unanimous votes of Gavarni, Sainte-Beuve, Turgenev, Taine, the Goncourts and the other members of that new and exclusive dining club, he was elected to Magny's: to the company who met every other Monday at Magny's restaurant for epicurean dishes and superlative conversation. 'You will be admitted on Monday 11 May, at half-past six,' wrote Jules de Goncourt. 'A speech is not essential.'

But live conversation was vital; and Gautier's maiden speech was a spirited defence of Balzac against Sainte-Beuve. He talked of language in a way to commend them all; he returned to condemn the *bourgeois*, discuss the nature of poetry, to discourse upon la Païva, Hugo, George Sand, to shock, amuse, instruct, enchant them with daring and paradox. The prince of conversationalists was rarely more felicitous than he was among his intellectual peers, at these dinners which suggest no parallel.[7] 'It was a feast to be with him!' said Arsène Houssaye. 'What abundance

of ideas! What felicity of expression! What an art of conversation! You
were always aware that he was the great artist in words. No question
ever found him silent. When he argued with Renan and Berthelot
philosopher and scholar confessed they were defeated by the poet.
And the Goncourts, revelling in his conversation, called at Neuilly for
more, found him at table, eating crayfish with his daughters, 'those
pretty, mutinous Parisian Orientals', and heard him criticize Renan and
outline the violent, unorthodox book that should be written on Christ.

Yet though the Goncourts' host announced himself revolutionary
and the critic on the *Moniteur* conventionally described the celebration
of the Emperor's birthday,[9] neither host not critic revealed Gautier
completely, and it was left to Eugénie Fort to finish the portrait: 'He
had done his first *Salon* article [she wrote in May], including three
columns on Chavannes, in his fine, majestic style, he explained to me
how he wants to reach that limit of beauty where the human hand is
effaced. He wants it to seem not done. He wants people to say "He
creates" and not "he writes". He calls that transforming himself. The
man, the poet of 1830 ended in 1850. Today he is grand, simple, solemn
as he used to be strange and paradoxical. That is his will and he has
achieved it. Just as his personality dominated all his work in his youth
so he is trying now in maturity to efface himself completely. Beauty
nothing but beauty.'

And it is, again, the diary of Eugénie that reflects the Gautier of these
months: tired, unwell, disillusioned. 'As for his theme, it is always
How painful life is in many ways, how ill he is understood at home, and
then (and often) how he regrets the past. . . . We talked a lot about
ways of understanding and feeling love, of the good side of what he
calls the pathetic. He would like to live alone for several months. He
thinks he would write something beautiful.' They walked slowly along
the banks of the Seine one torrid day in July: 'TG was sombre and
silent, and I did not feel gay. . . . He is resigning himself to this mono
tonous life. He believes that it must be so. To do his work regularly
conscientiously, receive his money and return to the house where not
a soul understand him. I am the only person with whom he is himself.'
But Gautier was not resigned to his condition: late in August he still
spoke of Neuilly in the same terms, and he was 'far from happy'.

About this time he departed for a brief holiday at George Sand's; he
found Nohant (so he said at the Magny dinner, over a mixture of rum
and curaçao judiciously mixed by Sainte-Beuve) as entertaining as a
Moravian monastery. He had arrived at night, by way of the farm
scared by a pack of dogs. He had suffered from a surfeit of game and
chicken. Breakfast had been at ten; on the last stroke of ten, the guest

sat down and Mme Sand arrived like a somnambulist and slept throughout the meal. After breakfast they played bowls, which revived her
enough to talk; but sex was a topic strictly forbidden. From three to six,
Mme Sand retired to write, at six they dined, after dinner she played
patience till midnight. By the second day he could stand the silence no
longer and declared that Rousseau was the worst writer in the language.
The discussion had lasted till one in the morning. George Sand, he
added, could not sit down without conjuring up a supply of pens and
ink, cigarette paper, Turkish tobacco and ruled notepaper; one day
she finished a novel at one in the morning, and promptly began another.
Her writing had become an organic function.[10]

*   *   *

October began unhappily enough; the diary records tempestuous
scenes in the rue de Longchamps. On 3 October Eugénie and Gautier
dined at *la belle Gabrielle* and talked about women, and 'I was forced
to agree that they were real monsters! For some years he has been seeking pure truth [burst out the diarist] and this is what he discovers!'
When she met him the following week his dissatisfaction with Neuilly
was taking clearer shape: 'He told me again he would like to settle
his daughters, send their mother to the country and live in rue de
Beaune. We took measurements and mapped out the apartment. He was
anxious to know if I should be happy with two thousand francs a year.
He thought I was growing more placid. I explained that after ripe and
solitary reflection I had come to terms with myself, and was more at
peace. He said he would soon own a house and land some miles from
Paris. "With my pension of three thousand francs, and a haven, I
could retire if need be. But I don't want to yet, I can and will work and
live in Paris another twenty years. Only after seventy do I agree to be
old and unemployed." He is right [added Eugénie], he is made to work
all the time. Then he said (and no doubt without considering the person
on his arm): "We shall be very happy, you'll see." Alas! no doubt I
shall see, but I shall count for nothing.'

26. *Le Capitaine Fracasse*

THÉOPHILE GAUTIER had often regretted (so his daughter Judith
tells us) that he had too little leisure to write *le Capitaine Fracasse*. He
needed at least a year of independence to do the research and finish the
two volumes, but he could not shake off his weekly journalism. And

perhaps (despite the lawsuit with Buloz) *Fracasse* might have stayed in its chrysalis had not Charpentier wisely offered to pay for the manuscript page by page. One morning, at a large table invisible for paper, Ernest Feydeau found Gautier. His shirtsleeves were up to his elbows and he wore an unusual air of concentration. 'What a pile of copy!' Feydeau exclaimed. 'You look as if you're enjoying yourself.' 'I'm writing *le Capitaine Fracasse*,' said Gautier, 'and in fact I *am* enjoying it.'[1] One by one the impeccable, microscopic pages received the blue stamp of approval from Charpentier's cashier; and on Christmas Day 1861, when almost a volume was written, the first instalment appeared in Charpentier's journal, the *Revue Nationale et Etrangère*.

Yet even now, after twenty-five years of waiting, as it flowed from Gautier's quill, *le Capitaine Fracasse* brought its problems. One day, when it was nearly finished, he returned from Paris and summoned the family to confer on a matter of moment. He had just told Charpentier the end of *Fracasse* and Charpentier was 'stricken, desperate, distraught': he said that the future of the book was lost, the sale and success were compromised, the public would be deceived in its hopes and legitimate foresight; in short he begged the author to reverse his decision and abandon an ending which would 'desolate people of feeling'. In his final chapter, Gautier had brought Sigognac to sit in the ruined chapel of le Château de la Misère and await his death; Charpentier begged for the reward of virtue and 'the final apotheosis in the Temple of Hymen'. The younger members of Gautier's family supported Charpentier; Gautier refused to make this *bourgeois* concession, and the debate at Neuilly proved indecisive. Charpentier bided his time; a few days later he attacked again and won. The last instalment of the novel appeared on 10 June 1863, and on 14 October *le Moniteur universel* announced the imminent publication of the book.

Next day Eugénie Fort and Gautier lingered along the Left Bank, among the windswept burnished leaves, and talked of his writing. 'He said he was attaining perfection, becoming immaterial, that the labour was disappearing in his art. He has long been seeking perfection in everything. They're very busy with *le Capitaine Fracasse* which is about to appear.' On the 18th he told her Doré was doing a drawing, they were getting posters ready. 'Gautier is letting himself be gently guided [she noticed], he seems indifferent but really he is pleased.' She wanted to leave Paris but *Fracasse* restrained her. On the 23rd Gautier brought her a proof of his foreword; and as they took their gentle customary stroll, she read it, and found it 'charming and full of poetry':

'Here is a novel advertised, some thirty years ago, by Renduel. . . .
Why rescue this almost forgotten work from the past when it would

have been so simple to write a work more in harmony with today? . . . From time to time, amid the thousand cares of life, the incessant demands of journalism, remorse would come upon us and we thought, with a certain shame, of this promise unfulfilled. . . . The Orientals believe that the figures in painting and sculpture come on Judgment Day to beg their creators for a soul. We were afraid that *le Capitaine Fracasse* might appear to beg that of us. The baptism of the title gave him a sort of existence which had to be completed. . . . We had at least to build a home for the wandering ghost. . . .' And so, on 26 October 1863, *le Capitaine Fracasse* was published. Gautier finally paid 'this letter of credit that his youth had drawn on his maturity'.

*   *   *

Le Capitaine Fracasse is not a great novel. It has an unmistakable air of Romantic melodrama: indeed a Hugolian *naïveté*. The captain himself is a *jeune premier* to delight the heart of Hugo or Dumas *père*. The heroine is the illegitimate daughter of a prince, the villain is Byronically seductive, the father grey-haired and noble, the comic characters evince Gargantuan thirsts and appetites. In this romance of a troupe of strolling players, every décor from the Porte-Saint-Martin reappears: the ruined castle, the brigand's lair, the panorama of old Paris, the dungeon and the scaffold. Every melodramatic platitude that Gautier smiled at on stage is remembered in *Fracasse*, from the near-rape of innocence to the recognition of the long-lost daughter, from the conversion of the villain to the finding of buried treasure in the penultimate paragraph. Duel, ambush, capture, disguise, an execution: no constituent is missing. The vices are painted in good broad telling colours, and the shrieks may be heard a mile off. The plot, meandering through three hundred pages, is no more plausible than the characters.

Yet if *le Capitaine Fracasse* is not a great novel, it remains a *tour de force*, an example of the descriptive art: it is, as Gautier intended, a purely picturesque work, and though the fire and lyricism of *Mademoiselle de Maupin* have long since died, paragraph after paragraph quietly glows: the candlelight portraits of the actors, vivid and sharply distinctive, round Sigognac's table; the likenesses of the animals, which would enrich *Ménagerie intime*; Zerbine's conquest of the Marquis de Bruyères and Léandre's visit to the Marquise; the discovery and burial of le Matamore. The visual descriptions are marked by pathos, humour, cynicism, by beautifully detailed perception, by language that has some of the untrammelled spirit of Rabelais and a plastic quality found in Gautier alone. If the characters are pale and the plot is thin, the language, effervescent, prodigal, precise, commands admiration.

*   *   *

And admiration greeted *le Capitaine Fracasse* in the autumn of 1863. 'At last it's appeared,' cried *l'Artiste*, 'this *Capitaine Fracasse* of which we have heard so much for a quarter of a century. Théophile Gautier has just written *le Capitaine Fracasse* as he wrote *Mademoiselle de Maupin*. The same pen, the same power, the same relief.'[2] 'It is the true novel of the age of Louis XIII,' wrote *le Moniteur universel*, 'the posthumous masterpiece of the seventeenth-century poem of adventures.'[3] Edmond Texier declared it the masterpiece 'of a terrible master who makes the French language give more than it can give, the Eugène Delacroix of style. After the man who makes the language of his time, isn't the greatest man [asked Texier] the one who unmakes it?'[4] 'M. Théophile Gautier is not unmaking the language,' answered *l'Artiste*, 'he is remaking it.' 'I know no living author,' said Louis de Cormenin, 'capable of a more masculine, more frank, more masterly style, of analysing the characters with more penetration or sketching them with such intensity of life. It is not too much to hope that this fine book will at last give Théophile Gautier the entry of the Académie-Française. . . . It will be both an act of justice and an act of reparation.'[5] Flaubert told Gautier he had never shown a greater gift.[6] Gratified and astonished, Gautier hastened to the rue de Beaune: 'I told him the triumph was much more for the author than the book,' Eugénie recorded candidly. 'He has rarely written books which could interest the public.'

The public, however, were interested now: two editions of *Fracasse* were exhausted within ten days, on 9 November the third edition appeared, and on 14 November Charpentier was rushing through the fourth edition for the following week. And if Eugénie told Gautier, with amusement, that *Fracasse* had popularized him, she could also witness his triumph among the elect. November brought a series of glowing appreciations from Sainte-Beuve, 'a debt to one of my most distinguished contemporaries in art and poetry. . . . He is and he will remain among the most distinctive, the most complex and most brilliant products of this age of art which has given so much'.[7]

On 30 November, when Sainte-Beuve published a fine article on Gautier's criticism, Gautier himself sent his news to Ernesta in Geneva. It was a strange letter, considering his comments to Eugénie; it was also sadly revealing. He was maddened by Ernesta's temper, her slovenly habits, her lack of intelligence and understanding, her domineering nature; and yet, after nearly twenty years, she still gave him physical pleasure, and without her practical help, her constant guiding presence, without (it must be said) her mothering domination, he felt, as he had always felt, entirely lost:

My dear Nini,

'Thank you most cordially for the knitted socks and cravat, which have arrived safely. I put them on at once, to the delectation of my feet and neck, for this morning it was three degrees below freezing point. . . .

'I have been elected a member of the *Conseil supérieur d'enseignement pour les Beaux-Arts*: a purely honorary function, but it puts you in a good position for other things. *Le Capitaine Fracasse* is more successful than *les Misérables*, and the success grows daily. Sainte-Beuve has just written his third article on me; it is admirable, and no one was ever praised more intelligently. Next year there will be an illustrated edition [of *Fracasse*] and Charpentier thinks they will sell 60,000 copies without raising a finger. In fact it's going very well. The house is quiet; we're a little moribund, but resigned to it. . . . I don't mind lending you for a bit to your charming Carlotta, but I don't want her to keep you. She must renounce you at the latest by——, that is the strict limit, or I shall come in search of you with gendarmes, and take her off, too.

'All the animals are as well looked after as if you were here. Myrza is bathed, and given forcemeat-balls, and taken on people's laps. The cats receive their caresses and the pittance due to them. They're warming themselves as they wait for their good mistress.

'Good-bye, dear Nini. I'll see you soon. A thousand kisses for you and a dozen for the *sorella* and the *ragazza*.'[8]

It might well be a letter from husband to wife after a long and happy marriage; it is certainly sincere. The truth was that, for all his criticism, Gautier needed both Ernesta and Eugénie, and vacillated constantly and selfishly between them. A fortnight later he called on the fading, frustrated woman in rue de Beaune. 'We spoke of the past,' wrote Eugénie, 'of our long affection, we thought we still got on well for people who had known one another for over thirty years! What a fine life we should have led if we had lived together!' And then, an eloquent summary of the situation: 'I dined at home.'

27. The Quest for Happiness

'A LONG time ago,' said *la Petite Revue* on 2 January, 'M. Théophile Gautier cried abomination on our top hat. We met him yesterday, however, crossing the Pont des Saints-Pères and wearing the unspeakable stove-pipe on an easy head. He was doubtless on his way to the *Moniteur*. . . .'

The ponderous Olympian bound for the Quai Voltaire appeared
indeed, increasingly conventional. He was a Government critic, a
member of the *Conseil supérieur d'enseignement pour les Beaux-Arts*, the
president of the *Société nationale des Beaux-Arts*, a member of the Jury
for the *Salon*;[1] and when he told Eugénie of his projects, he mentioned
not only a novel for next year but 'the hope of having a place that brings
him in eight or ten thousand francs'. He was frequently in the Imperial
circle; at Princess Mathilde's he was observed deep in conversation
with her cousin, the Emperor.[2] And the pugnacious supporter of *Hernani* had come, in his frock-coated fifties, to encourage the production
of classical tragedies.

And yet, in this prince of poets, the past perpetually struggled with
the present, the Romantic always wrestled with officialdom, the *mal du
siècle* was not hidden by the Olympian mask. As Gautier told the Goncourts, there were two men within him, two ever-contrasting characters.
He enjoyed material pleasures, but he informed Eugénie: 'I feel myself
becoming a pure spirit. Everything material in me is vanishing. My
imagination seems more real than reality.' He was mature in judgment,
sober in appearance (even to the discreet red rosette in his buttonhole),
but he could not believe that he was middle-aged, and he boyishly
interrupted a religious discussion to boast of an achievement of twenty
years earlier: 'As for me, I'm strong, I register 357 on the punchball.'
He developed the theory, at the Magny dinner, that a man should not
show sensibility, that to do so was degrading, that he himself had suppressed his heart in his books; but he continued to confide, unceasingly,
in Eugénie, and express himself faithfully, week by week, in *le Moniteur
universel*.

And, sadly enough, the genial man who boasted of physical prowess
was also unhappy and ailing. Eugénie noticed he was unwell in the early
months of the year, and advised him to spend next winter in the south,
in Cairo or Monaco: 'What a description of Monaco he could write!'
Gautier only needed her suggestion to plunge into Romantic dreams of
travel, and when she next saw him he talked of living in Algiers and
even described his house and his slaves. But his dreams had all the
nebulousness, all the heartrending solubility, of dreams; they dissolved
as rapidly as his lacquer dream of China when the Minister refused to let
him join the China Expedition, even on the terms of a private soldier
and chronicle the land of *le Pavillon sur l'Eau*. Now, in this spring of
1864, he remained in Paris, ill and troubled. March brought the *Salon*
and he was tired by his sessions on the Jury, his prolific reviews for
the *Moniteur*. In April came another problem: he and Eugénie discussed the question of her allowance. He suggested that he had enough

ligations already and that she should depend on her son. Eugénie
d not know whether to be astonished, revolted or desolated by his
mbarrassment. She was certainly upset, and refused to see him for
fortnight. 'Toto came,' she recorded on 26 April, 'and we talked
out Gautier. We're afraid he is more than ever lost to us. And yet it is
he loves, or so he says!'

His love was his old Romantic passion, the usual passion he felt in
e spring, the passion that the mirage of Cairo, Monaco, Algiers had
rred within him: 'What! just because we are paid to discuss the theatre,
ve we lost the right to watch the spectacle of the great globe itself?
ust the chandelier replace the sun for ever? No, a thousand times no!
ll the week, dreamy-eyed, like a plain poet master of his time, we
llowed the earliest swallow in its flight, and contemplated in ecstasy,
ke a Chinese man of letters, "*la fleur du pêcher et la fleur du prunier*".'[3]
ut the dramatic critic of *le Moniteur universel* was not his own master:
urnalism still tethered him, Neuilly oppressed him unceasingly:
Everything bores him, everyone displeases him,' wrote Eugénie, late
May. 'I reminded him that about 1830 he was saying the same thing.'
nd soon his depression deepened: Fiorentino, the music critic of the
Moniteur, died suddenly; and on 4 June, at Fiorentino's grave, Gautier
ronounced his only known funeral oration. It was more than a valedic-
on to a colleague and a friend; it became, abruptly, his own afflicting
mment on his own exhausting, ever exacting, constantly frustrating
areer:

'Oh! it is heavy indeed, the task that men think so light! The strong-
t fall beneath it. You need the body of an athlete, a spirit winged,
ntiring, never sleeping. To be amusing on a given day, never account-
g for the sorrows, failings and unease of life, to be amusing about
verything, about nothing, to be oneself through others, to improvise
n the chance theme thrown out by the theatre, to have an ever-ready,
niversal erudition; to keep nothing for oneself of life or time or leisure,
run to the end of the town at the summons of an idea, to be concerned
ways with another's glory, never with one's own; to be the trumpet
hen one might be the lyre; to join the activity of the man of the world
the work of the man in the study; to cast upon the winds, uncounted,
he pages that would be the glory of a book: all the public know it is a
rivolous trade, to be practised carelessly; but many earnest people
ould find it hard to do.'[4]

Such a burden Fiorentino had at last laid down; such a burden
emained on Gautier's shoulders. And Eugénie, still hurt, engaged him

in long discussions about her hardships, while he repeated he found
difficult to give her money. 'He earns a lot, it is true, but he has eno
mous expenses to cover and sacred obligations to fulfil!' remarke
Eugénie sharply. 'All this is said without any bitterness, any dire
reproach, but it is good for me to understand that I am an expens
which should only concern Toto; that twenty-five years ago I shoul
have accepted the offers Gautier made me. Nothing is more true; bu
the present is there in all its truth and one can't forget it.' And th
present was unrelenting. The lover who had once proposed to her no
advised her to settle in rue de Beaune: it would, he explained, inspir
Toto to work more and support her better. Was he unaware how suc
conversations hurt her, did he callously try to intensify her regret
Eugénie could not decide; but she offered to live abroad if work wei
found for her. But Gautier and Toto quarrelled over her future, ar
the sad conversations continued: early in July she confessed herself
the end of her resources and asked Gautier for a louis a week. H
agreed, and she left for her rooms at Versailles.

She returned to Paris late that month and saw him again. He rea
her part of *Pierrot posthume*, then left her, as usual, to her lonelines
'This evening I had to walk through the city,' she wrote in her diar
'and at the sight of Notre-Dame I stopped once more, admiring ar
doting upon it! How often I went there with TG in 1830! And ho
many eloquent, poetic speeches I heard him make with the fervour
artist and poet. . . !'

> *Pour me refaire au grand et me rélargir l'âme,*
> *Ton livre dans ma poche, aux tours de Notre-Dame,*
>   *Je suis allé souvent, Victor,*
> *A huit heures, l'été, quand le soleil se couche,*
> *Et que son disque fauve, au bord des toits qu'il touche,*
>   *Flotte comme un gros ballon d'or. . . .*
>
> *Comme pour son bonsoir, d'une plus riche teinte*
> *Le jour qui fuit revêt la cathédrale sainte,*
> *Ebauchée à grands traits à l'horizon de feu;*
> *Et les jumelles tours, ces cantiques de pierre,*
> *Semblent les deux grands bras que la ville en prière,*
> *Avant de s'endormir, élève vers son Dieu. . . .*[5]

So he appeared, the Gautier of 1830: responsive, ardent, poetic; no
he seemed 'only an intellect, a brain, a spirit. Do not ask him for feelin
for his family or his friends, they are lacking in him, he can do nothir

about it. And without any doubt,' reflected Eugénie, 'he suffers from it, though he does not know it'.

* * *

Soon afterwards the author of *Voyage en Espagne* set out for the opening of yet another railway: the railway from Paris to Madrid, and crossed his beloved frontier again at la Bidassoa. 'Must we admit it? . . . As we sat on the springy cushions of a large and comfortable carriage, we rather regretted the old *correo* with its ten mules harnessed two by two, its *delantero* who stayed in the saddle from Bayonne to Madrid, its perpetual carillon of bells, its rattle of ironwork and musketry of whips. Let us hope these retrograde emotions will be forgiven in an old Romantic of 1830, a Romantic madly in love with local colour, who saw Spain when the civil war was hardly over and there was perhaps a certain danger in verifying the exactitude of *Hernani* with ones own eyes.' Now, in middle age, the old Romantic saw the fading of the fairy-lands: nearly twenty-five years ago, when he had crossed the Sierra de Guadarrama, he had been drunk with exaltation. 'The first journey is like first love,' he wrote sadly, now, in *le Moniteur universel*:[6] 'It brings emotions which do not return again. Who would have thought then that a railway would cross the proud crest of the mountain, that the eagles would hear the whistle of steam in their domain?' Who would have thought that pleasure excursions would be run to the Escurial? And how could the partisan of *Hernani* have given credence to those who told him an omnibus would meet his train at Toledo? 'Oh civilization, such are the blows that you inflict upon us! To the Romantic, swearing by his Toledo dagger and sword, you answer "Omnibus!"—and Romanticism, all abashed, climbs sullenly into the dreadful vehicle, pays two *reals* for himself and a *real* for his trunk.'

* * *

Gautier returned to Paris to see the new version of *Pierrot posthume* at the Vaudeville on 30 August. Then he departed to embrace another cloud in Switzerland. Here, at Saint-Jean, near Geneva, in a white eighteenth-century château in a green world of chestnut trees, a château whose windows looked upon the saw-teeth of the Alps, the foaming meeting of the Rhône and Arve, a château that had been given her by Prince Radziwill, her protector, Giselle had come to earth.

To many of those who saw her, Carlotta Grisi resembled a benevolent *bourgeoise* rather than a fairy, a retired haberdasher rather than Giselle.[7] Though the château at Saint-Jean was filled with the relics of her career, though at sixty she could still (she said later) perform the *saut du rêve* from *la Péri*, though her walk was enchanting, her complexion like a camellia and her eyes intense as eidelweiss, Carlotta had changed. She had renounced the entrancing clothes of her past for sombre woollen dresses, enlivened, timidly, by ribbon and lace collars. She had renounced the admiration of Europe for the affection of her daughter Ernestine. She had settled down into prosperous, motherly and, perhaps, rather ordinary middle-age.

But the figure clearly seen by the outside world (seen, even, as 'a little Balzacian *bourgeoise* of the *maison du chat-qui-pelote*') was radiant, still, to the author of *Giselle*. The violent green embroidery she sent him from Geneva was sacred in the *salon* in the rue de Longchamps; he kept a plaster statuette of Carlotta (was it Thomas' statuette of Carlotta as Giselle?) in a glass bell, as a concierge might keep a bridal wreath in her lodge; and, showing it to Maurice Dreyfous, he cried: 'Look how charming she was!' And seeing another Giselle at the Opéra, he remembered how, years earlier, Carlotta had sprung, enchanted, from obscurity:

'I took Estelle to see *Giselle* danced by Mlle Granzow [he wrote to her]. She who has not seen the only, real, incomparable Giselle, the Giselle with golden hair and violet eyes, was very satisfied with this one, despite her black eyes and hair. For myself, no one will dance Giselle again . . . the Giselle you made so charming and so tender, so touching, so poetic, so impossible to posterity. The ballet recalls so many memories that it always disturbs me profoundly. I think of the fine years that are gone . . . and I return in thought to those performances when I leant against your canvas cottage or your canvas tomb, waiting to catch a little smile as you passed, a friendly word, holding your cloak to put it round your shoulders when you came into the wings. It was I who took you back, after the curtain fell, after the applause, to the door of your room. Yesterday, more than once, I felt the tears come to my eyes at certain phrases in the music which brought back little forgotten things to mind; and these came to life again so tenderly, so sadly, that my heart swelled in my breast and stifled me. It seemed to me that as I went from the auditorium to the stage I was going to find you with Mamina and Annette, behind the folding screen where you put on your powder and re-arranged your hair in the looking-glass. At last, to master my emotion, I said to myself: "Your memory is still living; maturity still dreams the dream of your youth, and if you can no longer visit Giselle in her painted canvas cottage, you can find Giselle in her villa at Saint-Jean, and she will receive you there with the same gracious smile that welcomed you behind the scenes on the left of the stage, that happy stage where she had her home as the Queen of the Vintage-gathering and as a Wili."'[8]

Voilà longtemps que je vous aime :
—L'aveu remonte à dix-huit ans !—
Vous êtes rose, je suis blême ;
J'ai les hivers, vous les printemps.

Des lilas blancs de cimetière
Près de mes tempes ont fleuri ;
J'aurai bientôt la touffe entière
Pour ombrager mon front flétri.

Mon soleil pâli qui décline
Va disparaître à l'horizon,
Et sur la funèbre colline
Je vois ma dernière maison.

Oh! que de votre lèvre il tombe
Sur ma lèvre un tardif baiser,
Pour que je puisse dans ma tombe,
Le cœur tranquille, reposer ![9]

*   *   *

On 18 October 1864, at six in the morning, Gautier returned from Geneva to be met by Toto at the Gare de Lyon. That afternoon he called on Eugénie and informed her he was sorry to be home. A few days later he looked in, briefly, 'speaking much good of Geneva and much ill of everything else'; and his indifference continued well into November, for on the 10th Eugénie still found him 'ill disposed towards all his circle, including us'. He remained cold towards Toto, and on the news that Toto might depart for Beirut to become attaché to a pasha, he 'refused to comment'.

Gautier's apparent coldness hid depths of despondency. His dissatisfaction with Neuilly had only been intensified by his visit to Geneva, and he longed to burst his domestic bonds. Ernesta's slovenly appearance was the least of her faults. She had never been especially intelligent, and twenty years of living with an impractical lover had naturally made her domineering. Though Gautier needed her, he resented the fact that she made domestic decisions; he was tired by her temperament. And in the lotus-land of Saint-Jean her sister Carlotta reminded him of the abyss between dream and reality. It was not surprising that he called again on Eugénie, discussed their son's departure, and told her that he, too, often thought of departing, of living alone. Is it fair [he asked] that a man should give people twenty years of his life, his talent and

independence if he does not make them happy? I've counted it up: s
much for duty, so much for affection, so much for happiness, and so or
so much for gratitude, and I find the balance very light on one side.
have 3,500 francs assured without any work, I can share it between m
sisters and the others. I think that after that I can regain my freedom
Eugénie reflected that he would be wise to regain his independence
'but do these things ever happen', she asked, 'without some grea
event?' Often he called on her in these final weeks of 1864: spoke of hi
article on Moscow, wrote out a poem he had composed that mornin
on the omnibus, and again and again deplored his unhappiness. On th
last day of the year he complained of Neuilly 'in a way to make on
believe it would all break up. I urged him to make the house at Villier
habitable. "I have had enough," he said, "I shall go mad. . . ."'

*   *   *

And the new year, 1865, began with the usual jeremiad: on
January Gautier brought his *étrennes* of regrets; within forty-eigh
hours he returned, 'still in search of happiness. He would like to enjo
himself: experience a new sensation. He says it is I who gave him th
idea that fidelity in true love was the strongest and deepest emotion on
could feel. I'm afraid [wrote Eugénie] it may be too late for him, but
new idea will take the place of today's'. Eugénie was mistaken: Gautie
called again, called yet again, 'still dominated by his search for happi
ness. And I must admit that his face suggested utter depression
Encouraged by her endless sympathy (it was, indeed, all he demande
of her), he lamented his state: 'I feel weak, I'm dropping from inani
tion, I'm the raft of the *Medusa*, I'm devouring myself. I shall neve
renounce a pleasure due to me.' Eugénie was silent; she felt inclined t
tell him he had ill-arranged his life, that he wasted his money, did no
love his children enough. But resolution was lost in doting affection
'He himself is so good, so good and sweet!' she ended. 'And perhap
he's right. I admit I don't understand why everyone round him doesn'
combine to make life pleasant for him.'

The outer world needed no encouragement: Mallarmé acknowledge
his influence in *l'Artiste*,[10] Parisian society welcomed him as a lior
Emile Montégut acclaimed him in *le Moniteur universel*.[11] But Gautie
remained restive. 'He has changed his theme,' reported Eugénie on
March. 'The search for happiness, the desire to experience passior
have turned into the wish to seem young. He curls his moustache up a
the ends, stands hand on hip, and throws back his head. All with tha
mixture of gravity and jest that never fails to charm.' Together the
read Montégut's latest article, examined every point and considered i
very true. 'The great event in Gautier's existence,' Montégut ha

eclared, 'is not his participation in Romanticism, it is this journalist's
areer which one day opened before him, the race in which he has ever
nce run without respite. Alas, poor Gautier!'

28. *Poète mathildien*

T G TOLD me he'd been to Princess Mathilde's,' noted Eugénie Fort
ne day in 1865. 'He is only at his ease with princesses. They are very
appy, they have no wants, they are splendidly dressed, which pleases
im. The rest of women disgust him.' Eugénie's indignation is easy to
nderstand, and there is a certain truth in her comment. For though
Gautier had always been at ease in her own presence, though he had
ved for years with the *bourgeoise* Ernesta, though he felt happily free
with *demi-mondaines* like Alice Ozy and Aglaé Sabatier and the flirta-
ious, engaging Régina Lhomme, he found, in his *amitié voluptueuse* with
Princess Mathilde, a particular and lasting pleasure.

The conservatory of her *hôtel* in the rue de Courcelles, 'that radiant
onservatory which made one believe in eternal spring',[1] recalled the
alais sous cloche of Fortunio; and in her drawing-room the bust of her
ncle, Napoleon, stood out against a background of purple velvet and
wept the visitor's thoughts from banal existence into an imperial,
nvigorating world. While the Court at the Tuileries pursued its inces-
ant frivolities, Princess Mathilde gathered artists and writers round her
nd heartened them with frank affection and practical interest. 'Her
uests are not announced,' explained *l'Artiste*.[2] 'What need is there to
nnounce Emile Augier and his friend Meissonier, Dominique Ingres
nd Emile de Girardin, the blond beard of Houssaye, the high life of
M. de Morny and M. de Nieuwerkerke? Who does not recognize M.
Chaix-d'Est-Ange, alternately *procureur impérial* and amateur of art?
Who does not recognize Viollet-le-Duc, Vernet, Gounod, the majestic
Théophile Gautier draped in his hair?' The Emperor himself would call
o talk literature with Dumas *fils*;[3] Flaubert and the Goncourts returned
gain and again, Sainte-Beuve was charmed to be a friend and coun-
ellor, Banville had plays performed. Even Viel-Castel, incurably
mbittered, recorded Princess Mathilde in his diaries with affection.
And *la bonne princesse*, unfortunate in love, found a certain compensa-
ion in encouraging, receiving and returning devoted friendships.

At 24, rue de Courcelles, in the eighteenth-century château at Saint-
Gratien where her closer friends would stay, the harassed journalist

N

from the *Moniteur*, the frustrated *père de famille* from the rue de Longchamps found himself, as if by magic, at his ease. With rare tact
Princess Mathilde understood and encouraged the relationship he
demanded: a relationship profoundly respectful yet gently loving, ack-
nowledging the Princess yet constantly remembering the woman: the
relationship he so charmingly defined as *amitié voluptueuse*. Other
women gave Gautier physical satisfaction, inspired his sensual or ideal
passion; but none accorded him the same delicate, intimate and endearing understanding. Once he found himself in the presence of Princess
Mathilde, he blossomed imperially, like the orchids in her winter
garden. When he presented himself unexpectedly and an officious servant enquired if she would receive him: 'What?' she cried: 'Do you
ask if I wish to receive my poet?' To her he remained (as he longed to
be, all his life) a poet, not a journalist. She adapted herself to his exotic
tastes, his continual nostalgia for distant time and place, encouraged
his coruscating conversation, made him improvise with his graceful
gaiety and childlike good humour. And, at Sainte-Beuve's suggestion
she drew his portrait: 'He was a man of middle height with a broad
long torso and short legs; he had the head of a southerner, a monocle
to correct his short sight; he wore his hair long, curling on his neck, a
relic of the Romantic of 1830. His expression was kind, though a little
sleepy, his glance calm, without vivacity, like his gestures and his whole
manner. In private he often sat on the floor, cross-legged, a cigar
between his lips: you might have taken him for an oriental.'[4] And so it
was that Count Joseph Primoli recalled him at Saint-Gratien: saw him
again, at the feet of the Princess, 'gathering up the lines of poetry that
seemed to be born under her magic glance, and making them into
sonnets'. And Princess Mathilde delighted in her poet's fertile invention: 'Come back quickly,' she wrote, when he was away: 'My Wednesdays are dull and colourless without you.'[5]

                    *   *   *

One may linger for a moment at Saint-Gratien: it is one of the
brightest facets of the Second Empire, and it shows us Gautier in his
most facile, most engaging moods. There were always a few lines making
love in his mind, records Primoli: you only needed to give him four
rhymes to receive a quatrain, and in fifteen minutes, on given rhymes
he would compose a sonnet.

One morning in August 1867, the young Primoli, on holiday from
school, waited for Gautier to take his daily constitutional in the park at
Saint-Gratien.[6] At the turn of a path the *poète mathildien* made his
appearance, wearing a hat that might have belonged to Fracasse: a
broad-brimmed grey felt enhanced by a swan's feather which he had

doubtless found by the lake. Slowly, gravely, he approached, leaning on a gold-handled cane: he might have been Jupiter down from his pedestal. With ineffable majesty the god invited his worshipper to walk with him 'and deigned to talk to him as to an equal'. As usual, he was maturing a sonnet; and, naturally enough, it was addressed to his hostess. He recited the first four lines with boyish enthusiasm:

> Hôte pour quelques jours de votre beau domaine,
> Voyant le gai soleil qui dore le matin,
> Et perce d'un rayon les feuilles de satin,
> Je descends dans le parc et tout seul m'y promène.[7]

New images, he said, would present themselves when he thought about them least; at the edge of the wood he caught a rhyme that had escaped him. 'He always went from rhyme to idea,' observed Primoli: 'From time to time one of those rare, familiar rhymes sang in his memory and recalled him to his task without interrupting the conversation. . . . At last the noonday sun pierced the clouds and, in its rays, like some marvellous flower, the sonnet half opened its petals and soon blossomed.' They continued their silent walk, without the poet's seeming to dream of the sonnet that he sculpted; by the time they returned to the point of departure, the second quatrain was finished:

> On pense aller bien loin, mais tout sentier ramène,
> —Quand il vous a montré le village lointain,—
> A travers prés et bois, par un sentier certain,
> Au portique où César a mis l'aigle romaine. . . .[7]

The luncheon bell interrupted their walk; and in the distance they saw the Princess coming to meet them. As they walked towards her, Gautier improvised the final tercets; and, kissing her hand, he greeted her with enchanting facility:

> A la blanche villa, votre temple d'été,
> Où, lasse du fardeau de la divinité,
> Vous daignez n'être plus que la bonne princesse.
>
> Ainsi fait mon esprit trompé dans ses détours:
> Il croit poursuivre un rêve interrompu sans cesse
> Et devant votre image il se trouve toujours.[7]

*   *   *

Her Junoesque image was indeed often before him. Soon afterwards he returned from some provincial expedition to find another imperial invitation:

'Princess [he answered],

'. . . Your dear note crowns all my hopes. I longed to return beneath your roof, which shelters its guests so pleasantly, but I did not dare. Paradise is charming, but that is no reason why mortals should pester the divinity according to their good pleasure. I shall come, then, to provide myself for the winter with a sunbeam and a ray of sunlight from your eyes. While I await this felicity, let me, on paper, kiss the twenty-second centimetre of your adorable foot.

'Your devoted and paradoxical servant,

THÉOPHILE GAUTIER.'[8]

29. *Spirite*

IT WAS a less gallant Gautier who called at the rue de Beaune on 24 April 1865, and sprawled, in shirtsleeves and slippers, 'all over the cushions. We talked about himself,' recorded Eugénie, 'but now his preoccupation is to forget his weariness and discover pure serenity. He is concerned with his appearance and health. He takes an hour to dress every day, morning and evening. That keeps him busy and makes him less nervous. He is certainly better groomed and better turned out.' The news that Janin had failed to be elected to the Académie, that Sainte-Beuve had been made a Senator, must have stirred Gautier's ambitions. He was trying to change his way of life.

Yet however impeccably groomed this stately Officier de la Légion d'honneur, he must have smiled when, in May, the Mayor of Tarbes demanded his complete works for a local library and declared that the name of Théophile Gautier, 'attached to the *lycée* like a coat of arms, was passed down as a model from generation to generation'.[1] It was not merely that the *lycée* prided itself on a pupil who, in fact, had not attended its classes; it was that, fundamentally, Gautier remained as Romantic as he had been in the days of the Impasse du Doyenné. The society who tried to establish the seaside resort of Yport in Normandy and offered building sites to men of eminence could not persuade Fortunio to consider a *bourgeois* retreat; 'the oriental Théo' could not bring himself 'to sling his hammock on the north winds'.[2] And it was surely evident to the Goncourts, when they dined with him at Neuilly early in May, that he was still Bohemian at heart.[3] Round the succulent *risotto* sat Flaubert, with the blue eyes and long moustache of a Viking warrior; Eponine the cat; a Hungarian violinist with the face of Satan;

ın exotic painter, jaguar-eyed; Gautier himself, bearded like the pard; ınd, not least remarkable, Tin Tun Ling, professor of Chinese to Gautier's daughters: Tin Tun Ling, who had been discovered wandering, one spring morning, round the distant purlieus of the Odéon, wearing his pigtail down his back, a parasol in his hand, and a robe embellished with flowers and chimeras. He had been looking for some ˈanciful address, been rescued by the orientalist Clermont-Ganneau, ınd adopted by Gautier who had made him, for a moment in time, part ›f his décor. And the vagabond Chinaman recorded his gratitude: One day, ten thousand times blessed, I encountered Théophile Gautier. His heart was vast and benevolent: he opened his house to me, and I ˈntered. He was to me a celestial host and a kindly light.'[4]

And when, about now, the correspondent of *la Petite Revue* rang the ›ell in rue de Longchamps, the door was opened by the gratified Tin Tun Ling. The correspondent looked into the *salon* crammed with pictures, bronzes and curios, Cordier statuettes and Turkish sabres, a ˈdivan, a number of cats and a Pleyel piano; then he went down into the ˈgarden, a garden very green and very countrified, stretching far away, ˈdown to the banks of the Seine, the garden where Gautier's daughters ˈwere strolling, 'both charming, tall and distinguished, with the most ˈintelligent and engaging smiles in the world'; and there in the garden ˈhe found the same Bohemian atmosphere. 'When Gautier comes down ˈhe crosses his legs Turkish fashion, and talks or dreams. He is casually ˈdressed: in shirtsleeves in the summer, a jersey in the winter, his head-ˈgear whatever comes to hand, usually a beret or a Turkish fez; and he ˈknows the art of conversation like no one else. Sometimes he sits on a ˈswing between two poplar trees at the bottom of the garden, and indo-ˈlently swings backwards and forwards, chatting all the while. At home, ˈthe author of *Fortunio* is the best of men; he is genial, affable, funda-ˈmentally sceptical, and all the more charming for that. He has the ˈexpression of a child, his eyes are kind and gentle, his laugh is highly ˈsympathetic and infectious. His leonine head seems a very symbol of ˈstrength.'[5]

And Sainte-Beuve, in *le Constitutionnel*, finished the portrait: 'When I read modern poetry, I say to myself almost immediately: "This is the ˈschool of Gautier, Banville, Leconte de Lisle or even Baudelaire." They ˈare the leaders of today and impose themselves on new poets.'[6]

*　　　*　　　*

And yet, for all the laughter, the apparent strength, the influence, ˈGautier remained unsettled and oppressed. On 6 June he told Eugénie ˈof his latest plans for the rue de Beaune: 'A library there, the divans

here, a dressing-room there. Carpets everywhere. He dreams of living
there in complete freedom.' On 19 June he talked at her for more than
three hours, and ended: '"Ah, my dear, if you'd listened to me, how
rich we should be today, and what a fine life we'd have led!" I came
back to my little corner of Versailles [Eugénie added] with my ears
ringing with his words. I have heard them so often.'

On 17 July, in a Parisian heatwave, he arrived 'exhausted, covered
in sweat, and spoke much of Neuilly, of Geneva'. He was deeply
troubled about Judith, who had received a proposal from a Persian
general. Mohsin Khan was already married in Persia, but his temporary
marriage would soon expire, and he assured Judith that she was born
to be a Persian princess. She herself was hardly tempted; but Gautier,
bitterly afraid, drew deterrent pictures of Persian life and ordered the
general to restrict his visits. Mohsin Khan (he was later Ambassador
in London) bade farewell in tears.[7] The rue de Longchamps was more
disturbed than ever.

Yet if Neuilly were turbulent, Saint-Jean was soothing, and Carlotta
sent Gautier an affectionate invitation. On 23 July he left for Geneva,
and on the last day of the month, taking over the criticism in *le Moniteur
universel*, Toto wrote his valediction: 'M. Théophile Gautier is roaming
about the Alpine scenery: he has gone to pay a short visit to Nature,
that dear ancestor from whom our feverish existence too often divides
us. . . . To celebrate the thirty-fifth year of his literary life, Théophile
Gautier wanted the innocent pleasure of missing a week's dramatic
criticism.'

The thirty-fifth anniversary of his *Poésies*, his first book of poetry,
fell on 28 July. That day, from the Hôtel du Cygne, at Bernex, near
Vevay, Gautier sent Ernesta a letter which already showed signs of
gaiety. It described the vinegrowers' festival at Vevay, a festival that
inspired two articles in the *Moniteur*, later a chapter in *les Vacances du
Lundi*. And the *Moniteur* had already announced the work that would
occupy his summer in Switzerland, in advertising the imminent appearance of his novel *Spirite*.[8]

*   *   *

This serial, for which he was paid two hundred francs an instalment,
this serial, of which Eugénie admiringly, all unknowingly, read the
proofs in Paris, recalls the theme of *Giselle*, of *la Péri*, of *Arria Marcella*:
the theme of the love of mortal and immortal, the love of present and
past, of impossible passion. It is the story of a man in love with an ideal.
It is also the most personal reflection; for the image of Spirite in the
mirror of Guy de Malivert is the portrait that Gautier gazed upon, so
often, in his imagination, in the Venetian mirror at Neuilly:

'A roseate pallor slightly coloured the countenance in which the lights and shadows were scarcely seen, a countenance which, unlike terrestrial figures, had no need of this contrast to assume a shape, not being subject to the light which illuminates us. Her hair, the colour of an aureole, like golden smoke, blurred the contour of her brow. In her half downcast eyes swam pupils of nocturnal blue, of an infinite sweetness, recalling those parts of the heavens tinged at twilight with the violets of evening. Her exquisite nose was of ideal delicacy; her smile, in the manner of Leonardo da Vinci, yet more tender, less ironic, gave an adorable line to her lips; her neck, bent forward, was lost in a silver half-tint that might have served as light to another face.

'This poor sketch, drawn of necessity with words created to render the things of our world, could give but a very vague idea of the apparition that Guy de Malivert contemplated in the Venetian mirror. Did he see it with the eyes of the body or the eyes of the soul? Did the image exist in reality?'[9]

On 17 November 1865, when the first instalment of *Spirite* appeared in *le Moniteur universel*,[10] Gautier answered the question in a letter to Carlotta: 'Read, or rather read again, for you know it already, this poor novel whose only merit is to reflect a graceful image, to have been dreamed beneath your great chestnut trees and written, it may be, with a pen touched by your hand. . . . The idea that your charming eyes will rest awhile on these lines where, beneath the veil of fiction, breathes the true, the only love of my heart, will be the sweetest recompense for my work.'[11]

*   *   *

'Saint-Jean, August 1865.
'My dear Nini,
'Forgive me for not answering your nice letter at once, but I was tired from rushing through the poem *A l'Impératrice*, which Dalloz had asked for. These are delicate and trying things that one could well dispense with, but cannot refuse. . . .

'I've written to tell them to give you money, have you received it? I hope that no new whims of this madman Dalloz will stop my finishing *Spirite* and *Moscou* for Charpentier. They're important. I am only beginning to recover a little, my fury over the Persian affair, my cold, the poem, have all disturbed me more than I can say and the calm of Saint-Jean can only just soothe me in my anxious, nervous, acutely sensitive state. . . . I don't feel very brilliant, spiritually or physically. . . .'[12]

'Saint-Jean, 29 August 1865

'My dear Nini,

'You told me in your last letter you wanted to give me a surprise and
meet me at Saint-Jean, but that you couldn't do so for want of money.
It can all be arranged, and I shall be surprised just the same, or I'll
pretend to be, which will be the same thing. *Spirite* is launched and is
going well. A few days hence it'll make a little pile of money with which
you can catch the train about the 15th, so that I've time to finish or at
least progress with my novel. You'll stay till the end of the month and
a few days more if the weather's good, and we'll come back together.
I have with great difficulty persuaded Carlotta to share the cost of the
food while the family's staying with her: that will make us more at ease.
One guest is all very well, but four's too many; and whether I give you
your mouthful here or there is all the same to Don Pagaras de Pénaçul.
Be economical this fortnight and only pay what's essential.

'Here I am more tranquil and serene. I'm drinking Evian water, and
I find it suits me. The salutary action of Saint-Jean is beginning to make
itself felt, and the weather, which until now has been just a perpetual
storm, is turning fine again and restoring peace to the heavens and to
one's mind. Tomorrow or the day after is my birthday; it's been celebrated with a pomp that marked the fatal date all too clearly. In two
days my fifty-four years will have well and truly struck! Alas, my poor
Nini, what would you have me do? It isn't my fault. I'd rather be
twenty-five. I am twenty-five twice over, and a bit more! Oh Heavens!
I resist as hard as I can and I'd very much like not to be an old dod-
derer!'[13]

'Saint-Jean, 31 August 1865.

'My dear Nini,

'. . . Everyone's waiting for you and sends you their warmest love.
As for me I hold you with all my might to my old heart, which is 54
today. Here they have joyfully celebrated my birthday, but, inside
myself, I was rather melancholy. Yet after all, it is better to grow old
than to die, and, as Auber says, it's the only way of reaching a
great age.

'A thousand kisses; and this time I shall really see you soon.'[14]

*   *   *

Ernesta, Judith and Estelle were still at Saint-Jean at the end of
October,[15] for cholera had broken out in Paris. And amid the excited
Italian French of the Grisi sisters, the chatter of his daughters and
Carlotta's Ernestine, Gautier resolutely continued his novel. But the
novelist who drove himself, page by page, instalment by instalment, to

rite *Spirite*, was far from the magnificently virile author who, thirty
ears ago, had tossed off *Mademoiselle de Maupin*. Already the flaccid
ce, lank hair and ponderous figure of the photographs suggest heart
ouble and general lassitude. Rheumatism, haemorrhoids, excessive
weating, frequent colds, depression, lethargy: his letters emphasize
hat he had degenerated far from the Leander who had aspired to the
leçon rouge, from the Hercules who had registered the phenomenal
unch on the punchball, from the Nimrod who had superbly driven his
air of dapple-greys across the place de la Concorde.

The place de la Concorde. Gautier often recalled it. He had been away
om Paris for three months. And now, inevitably, as it does upon all
who have lingered along the Quai Voltaire, the Quai de Conti, as it
oes upon all who have seen the radiant bridges, the Ile de la Cité
white on the Seine in sunlight: as it had done on Gautier, years ago,
ven during the days when he had lived in the fabled Court of Lions in
he fabled Alhambra at Granada, Paris began to exercise its fascination:
During my holidays (somewhat long it is true) I shall have written a
ook, that's what you call resting [wrote the critic of *le Moniteur univer-*
el in October]. Winter is coming, with its squalls and blasts, to sweep
way the last miasmas, and I am going to see great Paris once again:
'aris, who does without me at least as well as I do without her, though
have a core of old affection for her. For it is there that life and spirit
parkle, that the great punchbowl of intelligence blazes away, it is
here that one can chat and jest and banter, use the rhetorical figure
nown as irony; it is there that friendly travellers return from all four
orners of the horizon, it is there that one has one's wigwam as a civilized
avage. . . .'[16]

And it was there he returned in mid November, to his usual seat
t the Opéra and the Gymnase, to review the revival of *Robert-le-*
Diable, and *le Passé de M. Jouanne*.

30. The Great Punchbowl

T WAS a luxurious, licentious, magic world, the Paris of the Second
Empire in which Gautier moved. There were the Saturdays of Mme le
Hon, the Duc de Morny's mistress: at her *hôtel* in the Champs-Elysées
everything had to be admired because everything was admirable: the
Hobbemas and the Watteaux, the Teniers and the Ostades'; and Mme
e Hon herself was so elegant, so fascinating that, like Scarron's wife,

she made her guests forget their very food.¹ Further along the Champs
Elysées, Mlle Marie Garcia would perform the feat of setting Sainte
Beuve and Scribe, Ponsard and Gautier at a single table (she had eve
invited Rachel with a rival actress, Mlle Brohan). In the *salon* of Jeann
de Tourbey, later Comtesse de Loynes, *la dame aux violettes, la dam*
aux yeux gris who, it is said, inspired the description of Salammbô
Gautier met Flaubert and the Goncourts, and Girardin, fierce an
lugubrious, with his death's-head and his lock of hair like a kiss-cur
on a skull. At Mme du Deffand's Fridays, with other intimates who ha
'withstood the tests of fire and water and Rhenish wine,' he revelle
in conversation which recalled the verbal duels of the Renaissance; an
at the actors' ball at the Salle Favard, at three o'clock in the morning, h
caught a superlative glimpse of Mme Sabatier when, 'to revive th
flagging admirations, the one and only statue by Clésinger made he
entrance in a flood of lace enough to damn the virgins of Cologne. He
head, so marvellously fine and graceful, was wreathed with silve
gladioli, whose long leaves hung down to her arms (the ones that wer
missing from the Venus de Milo).'³ Not the least of the *demi-mondaine*
was Mme Musard, who had been given a fortune by William III o
the Netherlands; people spoke wonders of her table, of her clothes: o
the dress with three thousand pearls she had worn at her dinner for th
Prince de Chimay. One needed a ticket to visit her stables, and sports
men coveted the favour of lunching with her twenty famous horses
while men of letters who dined more formally were impressed by he
three black and three white servants wearing silk stockings, buckle
shoes and seventeenth-century *perruques*. Yet even Mme Musard pale
beside the courtesan of courtesans, la Païva, who, on the strength of he
liaison with Count von Donnersmark, held regal court in a littl
Parisian palace: 'At Plato's banquet (I dare not say Aspasia's) there ar
only intelligent people,' wrote Gautier. 'One has to be scintillatin
from the soup onwards.'⁴ It was at this dazzling table that Napoleon II
inviting himself to dinner, asked the name of the Merovingian king wh
sat opposite; and, being told it was Théophile Gautier: 'He charme
my imprisonment at Ham,' said the Emperor, 'like Sainte-Beuve an
Arsène Houssaye. When I read them I was no longer a captive.' 'I hope,
replied la Païva, 'that Théo will be a senator under Napoleon III.' H
answered with imperial and empty charm: 'All your friends, marquise
shall be senators until I make them princes.'⁵

There were, too, the more official receptions. At the Minister o
Agriculture's dinner, Gautier was impressed by the huge electric ligh
revolving like a magic lantern and variegating the colours of the garden.
At the Friday soirées of the Comte de Nieuwerkerke, Director-Genera

f the Imperial Museums and careerist lover of Princess Mathilde, he
net Baron de Rothschild, Alfred de Vigny, Berlioz, and Eugène Giraud,
caricaturist-in-ordinary to the household, who ended every reception by
caricaturing a guest.[7] Life was an inextinguishable firmament of dinners
nd concerts, balls and receptions. Indeed, 'the month of March, like
he month of February, has been starred with festivities,' recorded a
lazed observer in 1868. 'The Tuileries concerts, the Sundays of Prin-
ess Mathilde, the Thursdays of the Princess de Metternich, the Fridays
f the Comte de Nieuwerkerke and General Fleury, the Tuesdays of the
Ministre des Beaux-Arts, the Ministre de l'Intérieur and the Ministre
le la Justice, the Wednesdays of M. Duruy, the dinners of Mme de
'aïva, the balls of the Duchesses of Sainte-Clotilde and Saint-Philippe
lu Roule, not to mention the concerts of M. Garfounkell. . . . I was
bout to forget the Saturdays of the Préfet de la Seine and the Préfet de
Police, the dinners of Maréchal Canrobert. . . . The artists and men of
etters one most often sees are Alexandre Dumas, Flaubert, Gau-
ier. . . .'[8]

One saw them, too, at literary assemblies. In his famous long gallery,
nhanced by the sketches of Hugo and Gautier as well as Watteau and
Greuze, Arsène Houssaye, the former director of the Français, enter-
ained with dramatic magnificence; in his gallery, as he pointed out,
ou might have founded and published a periodical, elected an Aca-
lemician, negotiated a treaty or even discovered a planet.[9] It was
Houssaye who, years ago, had celebrated his directorship with an
mmortal dinner, where 'Mme Arsène Houssaye had M. de Lamartine
n her right, M. Victor Hugo on her left. Mlle Rachel, who sat opposite,
iad M. Alfred de Musset on her right, M. Eugène Delacroix on her left.
The other celebrities were Pradier, Ponsard, Sainte-Beuve, the Comte
le Morny, Alexandre Dumas, Emile Augier, Théophile Gautier and
Scribe.'[10] A list of Houssaye's guests in 1868 reads, again, like the index
o the national biography: Auber, Banville, Coppée, Flammarion,
Flaubert, Gautier, Girardin, Leconte de Lisle, Villiers de l'Isle-Adam
and all the Parnassians'.[11] Some of them met again at the *dîner des
Spartiates*, held every Tuesday at the Moulin Rouge, where the guests
vere chosen by a secret committee '*composé de quatre gourmands* [sic]',
r at the *Figaro* dinners at Véfour's.[12] At the Café Foy, under the gentle
egis of Vernet's painted swallow on the ceiling, the Académie de
'Hirondelle, Gautier among them, held their sessions: they only cost a
undred sous, recorded Arsène Houssaye, 'but people spent very much
nore wit and gaiety than money'.[13] Even more engaging were Doré's
Sunday dinners in the rue St. Dominique, where Mme Doré always
vore her turban and 'always looked like an accomplished gipsy', and

the guests delighted in 'rich viands, fine wines, unlimited fun and
abundance of celebrities'. For every party Doré contrived a new diver
sion. One evening the wine was decanted in carafes which were reall
musical-boxes and they played enchanting waltzes and polkas through
out the dinner. On grand occasions Chevet called up an army of chef
and assistants, and the guests 'were treated to dishes invented in honou
of Gustave's latest illustrations'.[14]

Yet for all the splendour of such dinners, some of the most coveted
best remembered evenings were Gautier's own Thursdays at Neuilly
Doré spent every Thursday evening, when he was in Paris, at the rue d
Longchamps, with his inseparable foil, Arthur Kratz, an Alsatian baro:
who (so Gautier claimed) was entitled to an escort of four halberdiers
Mme Sabatier, that endearing *vivandière de faunes*, announced he
entrance with her usual soprano trill and Doré promptly dragge
her to the piano to improvise Tyrolean duets. Préault arrive
to toss off Cyprian wine.[15] Régina Lhomme, of Spanish mien
posed coyly in a mantilla. Dalloz and Turgan drove over from th
Moniteur: Dalloz young, elegant, suave and pale, Turgan squat an
gauche, brusque and kindly. There came (among Gautier's mos
intimate friends) Alphonsine Lafitte and her husband Alexandre, com
poser, and organist at Saint-Nicholas-des-Champs. The Dumas strod
in, *père et fils*; the Goncourts sat at table, disconcertingly observant
Baudelaire followed, impeccably groomed, monacal yet satanic in ex
pression. Every actor, singer, or artist, every composer and poet witl
aspirations or friendship arrived for entertainment. One admirer mad
his way across Paris preparing an address. He rang the bell violently, an
'the door opened and disclosed Gautier himself—Gautier, with hi
enormous, stately figure, his impassive, strongly-marked face lit up b
majestic eyes, the whole head crowned by a profusion of curling locks
The visitor was struck speechless with pleasure. The two men stared a
each other until the situation became unbearable. . . . Looking com
passionately at his dumb caller, the poet finally said: "*Articulez seule
ment quelques sons.*"' Other visitors showed more initiative: 'We coul
bring you an unheard-of word, force our way up your stairs, recite you
works under your windows from the first line of *une Larme du Diable*...
We have thought, sir, of every expedient to reach you. . . . Some tim
after two o'clock tomorrow, innocent of all manuscripts, we shall mak
a pious pilgrimage to Neuilly; and were you to barricade yourself behin
crates of Kandjars, we should still get a word or a glance from you.'

And then, one evening, Flaubert and the Goncourts found Gautie
still at table, singing the praises of '*un petit vin de Pouilly*'. Flauber
borrowed one of Gautier's suits, took off his collar, transformed himsel

to a formidable caricature of stupidity, and danced his famous dance, *Idiot des Salons*; Gautier, not to be outdone, removed his coat and danced *le Pas du Créancier*, and the evening ended with Bohemian songs.

Was it Flaubert whom Gautier loved to welcome best of all? One may, for a moment, linger on their friendship: the friendship of man and man, of master and master, strengthened by a common abhorrence of the *bourgeois*, a common entire devotion to art. It was probably in Gautier that Flaubert discovered his pessimism, his descriptive vocation, his passion for colour, his doctrine of Art for Art's Sake, his exclusive cult of form, his hatred of the *bourgeois*. It was Gautier, it is said, who inspired *Salammbô*. No one could be the friend of Gautier without becoming the friend of Flaubert, too. 'He was,' wrote Flaubert to Feydeau, after Gautier's death, 'a great man of letters and a great poet.' And one evening, at a dinner where the food was poor, the conversation trivial, Gautier's neighbour had asked, without preamble, after the author of *Madame Bovary*. 'Then the man I had hardly seen in profile turned round to face me and said, softened at last: "Do you know Flaubert?" I leant forward a little; he put both his elbows on the table, toyed with the end of his knife, and said, before I could answer: "What a charming man! There's someone I love. I detest relationships with men. I couldn't live with any man. But Flaubert is different. He has the delicacy of a primitive, he isn't afraid of words, and he respects things. If I were a woman, I should want him to love me."'[17]

31. The Marriage of Judith

THE YEAR 1866 opened brilliantly in Paris with 'grand masked balls that far excelled anything heretofore attempted'. At the Tuileries the Emperor appeared 'in a Venetian mantle, the Empress *à la* Marie Antoinette, the Prince Imperial as a juvenile Masaniello; and a young lady, name unknown, as Noah's Ark'.[1] At the Magny dinners Théophile Gautier dazzled George Sand and the Goncourts with paradox,[2] and then, going round to the humdrum little street behind the offices of the *Moniteur*, he inflicted accounts of his soirées on Mme Fort.

On 26 February he arrived in a far different mood, 'very vexed by a project of marriage for Judith'. Judith had not been tempted by Mohsin Khan, but she was now determined to marry Catulle Mendès, and was merely awaiting her majority to do so. Judith, only twenty, had the air of a langorous Juno and a profile acknowledged as perfect even by

Leconte de Lisle; Hugo himself would write sonnets for her, Baudelai
would admire her criticism. She was Gautier's daughter threefold, b
her birth, her beauty and her intelligence, and she could hardly fail
be his best-loved child. 'We who are outwardly insensitive are seriou
about the serious things,' he wrote to her, with truth, 'and we fe
them more acutely than expansive people. You know that you are th
last hope of my wretched life: a life of sorrow, weariness and tormen
The slightest equivocal word about you puts me in a rage which
cannot always control. Remember how much you're worth. . . .'[3]

The suggested son-in-law who caused Gautier infinite disquietud
was the twenty-two-year-old son of a Jewish father and a Cathol
mother: 'fair-haired, bright-eyed, with a slight coldness in his glanc
Mendès seemed in his youth a Northern Christ, but a Christ who wa
not born for the Cross.' His conversation was sparkling, his writin
distinguished, he had already founded the *Revue fantaisiste*, whic
included Baudelaire and Gautier among its contributors. But if Gauti
admired Mendès as a writer, as a son-in-law he could not consider hin
Mendès was homosexual and entirely amoral.[4]

Three years ago Mendès' engagement to Judith had been announce
(no doubt as a *canard*) in the Press, and Gautier had issued a categorica
denial.[5] Now, as Judith approached her majority, he could only dis
suade; and he was both enraged and terrified: terrified because he knev
her seriousness of purpose, perhaps foresaw the disasters which th
marriage must bring, the divorce in which it would end; enrage
because Ernesta, stubborn, stupid and passionate, persistently encour
aged both Mendès and her daughter. Gautier asked Turgan to act a
intermediary and forbade Mendès meanwhile to enter his house. O
26 February he left the turbulence of Neuilly for the soothing atmo
sphere of Saint-Jean.

And there (how strong the magic of Giselle, how strange the powe
of places!) the infallible enchantment drew about him. On 12 March h
wrote *le Merle*: vivacious and vernal. And on the night of 15 March
in the train that brought him back from the perpetual spring of Switzer
land to the domestic thunder of Paris, he wrote *la Nue*: the poem tha
was to enter the fifth edition of *Emaux et Camées*, the poem that holds
in its final verse, the idealism and happiness he had expressed long ago
in *Mademoiselle de Maupin*: the best, indeed the heart, of his philosophy

A l'horizon monte une nue,
Sculptant sa forme dans l'azur :
On dirait une vierge nue
Emergeant d'un lac au flot pur.

Debout dans sa conque nacrée,
Elle vogue sur le bleu clair,
Comme une Aphrodite éthérée,
Faite de l'écume de l'air;

On voit onder en molles poses
Son torse au contour incertain,
Et l'aurore répand des roses
Sur son épaule de satin.

Ses blancheurs de marbre et de neige
Se fondent amoureusement
Comme, au clair-obscur du Corrège,
Le corps d'Antiope dormant.

Elle plane dans la lumière
Plus haut que l'Alpe ou l'Apennin;
Reflet de la beauté première,
Sœur de 'l'éternel féminin'.

A son corps, en vain retenue,
Sur l'aile de la passion,
Mon âme vole à cette nue
Et l'embrasse comme Ixion.

La raison dit : 'Vague fumée,
Où l'on croit voir ce qu'on rêva,
Ombre au gré du vent déformée,
Bulle qui crève et qui s'en va!'

Le sentiment répond : 'Qu'importe!
Qu'est-ce après tout que la beauté,
Spectre charmant qu'un souffle emporte
Et qui n'est rien, ayant été!

A l'Idéal ouvre ton âme;
Mets dans ton coeur beaucoup de ciel,
Aime une nue, aime une femme,
Mais aime!—C'est l'essentiel!'[6]

* * *

Next morning, 16 March 1866, at eight o'clock, Gautier appeared on Eugénie's doorstep. 'He has quite decided not to return to Neuilly. I am not persuaded that he will keep to this wise resolution but we shall see. He had breakfast and left at eleven. This is the plan for the moment: Gautier is going to live at 58 rue Jacob. I shall stay in rue de Beaune.

We shall wait for 2 April, the time fixed for the final decision about the marriage. He is more than ever determined not to return to Neuilly. At five he came to spend two hours with me, and of course we only talked of this momentous affair. In the evening I went to rue Jacob and came back very weary.' The following afternoon he returned to the rue de Beaune. Toto was with him, looking after him, and he was already better; he told Eugénie he was glad to be free, but she was unconvinced. On the nineteenth he appeared for another long conversation, next day he returned yet again. 'Matters are still the same. Gautier has seen his sisters, who naturally agree with him about everything. They are waiting for the return of Turgan who is acting as intermediary. In the evening I went to rue Jacob for a moment.' Next day he came once more for consolation. 'He is still determined. But when action is necessary we shall see. He's comfortable in rue Jacob but he's thinking of settling down. Where and how?'

Eugénie's questions were answered that day in *la Fleur qui fait le Printemps*, the poem which, it seems, had come to him a week and more ago, under the senatorial trees at Saint-Jean:

> . . . *Il me faut retourner encore*
> *Au cercle d'enfer où je vis;*
> *Marronniers, pressez-vous d'éclore*
> *Et d'éblouir mes yeux ravis.*
>
> *Vous pouvez sortir pour la fête*
> *Vos girandoles sans péril,*
> *Un ciel bleu luit sur votre faîte*
> *Et déjà mai talonne avril.*
>
> *Par pitié donnez cette joie*
> *Au poète dans ses douleurs,*
> *Qu'avant de s'en aller il voie*
> *Vos feux d'artifice de fleurs.* . . .
>
> *   *   *
>
> *Adieu, je pars lassé d'attendre;*
> *Gardez vos bouquets éclatants!*
> *Une autre fleur suave et tendre,*
> *Seule à mes yeux fait le printemps.*
>
> *Que mai remporte sa corbeille!*
> *Il me suffit de cette fleur;*
> *Toujours pour l'âme et pour l'abeille*
> *Elle a du miel pur dans le cœur.*

Par le ciel d'azur ou de brume,
Par la chaude ou froide saison,
Elle sourit, charme et parfume,
Violette de la maison![7]

t was neither Eugénie nor the tardy trees that could bring him con-
olation: it was, as the poet recognized, Giselle, whose statuette pre-
ded over the riven household at Neuilly.

And Giselle herself, from Saint-Jean, presided now over the rue
acob. To and fro sped the letters of explanation, of consolation: 'I am
stonished [she wrote on 25 March] that my sister hasn't yet learned of
our return, God grant she doesn't until Turgan comes back. . . .
Whatever happens don't lose your serenity or your temper, and remember that this child's ingratitude is not worth the loss of your
ealth. Do please let me know what happens. . . .'[8]

Carlotta was understanding, but she was far away; for want of her
resence, in the disturbing days of March, Gautier still depended on
ugénie. Every day, precisely at four o'clock, preceded by Toto, he
rrived for sympathy. He was still determined to break with Neuilly;
nd poor Eugénie, in her heart of hearts, must have seen herself assum-
ng the place she had always secretly, for the last three long decades,
vanted to fill. Farther and farther Gautier moved from the rue de
Longchamps. On 27 March they sent for his clothes, on the 28th she
ustled round to rue Jacob to help him dress: he had always been
tterly impractical and could not even choose a hat or pack a trunk.
Nor could he tie his cravat; and tonight he was dining at the rue de
Courcelles. Poor Eugénie! Never, since their son was born, had
Gautier seemed so near; and never, had she known it, had he been so
ar. In his pocket was an anxious, devoted letter from Carlotta;[9] and
hat night, as Eugénie lay in bed in her shabby room, and struggled
hrough *les Travailleurs de la Mer*, he left Purgatory, briefly, for his
ther heaven: found himself at the feet of his loved Princess.

He chose, next day, not to visit his ex-mistress; and when he did
rrive, it was to recount his social victories in the rue de Courcelles.
He described his triumph at the Princess's,' she noted bitterly: 'A
riumph of eloquence. Sainte-Beuve, the Goncourts and Taine told
im everything he said was beautiful, was Plato.' But Gautier's exhilara-
ion was short-lived; he was soon ill again with rage and anxiety about
udith's marriage. 'This family disaster greatly disturbs him,' she
vrote on 31 March. 'He is stricken, furious, humiliated. At ten o'clock
Toto and I took him home and put him to bed.' The first days of April
assed as she might have expected: she waited, maternally, every day,

o

to soothe both father and son. Gautier (he was, this year, vice-president of the Jury) came to her after a *Salon* meeting, weary and distraught, burst into a torrent of insults and threats of revenge. 'I quite understand how you feel,' wrote Giselle, from Geneva, 'and we know how lonely you must be: you who are so made for domestic and family life. I hope that once this wretched child is settled you will find the calm you need so much with Estelle; whatever happens, my dear, you know we are always delighted to see you at Saint-Jean, and if we cannot give you all you are losing, at least you can be sure that we will do all we can to give you as much happiness as possible. So come when you like, we are always ready for you. . . .'[10]

It was Eugénie Fort, who lived so near his office, who received his visit. On the evening of 7 April he arrived more tired than ever, slept before supper, ate his supper half asleep and slept again; on the ninth he arrived 'absorbed, tormented by this marriage. The contract was to be signed that day.' He showed Eugénie a letter from Judith; then departed to drown his sorrow in a flood of paradox at Magny's. And there Taine spoke of depriving oneself of love, and Gautier, abruptly recalling Ernesta and Giselle, burst in fiercely: woman, taken as a physical purge, did not rid man of aspirations for the ideal.[11] Next day Eugénie went to rue Jacob for a conference with father, son, and Gautier's two sisters. On the eleventh she dined with Gautier: he intended, he said, to write a short story, *l'Ange gardien*. He had still not decided what to do with his life. 'Come when you like,' wrote Carlotta, 'your room is ready.' Gautier left that evening for Geneva. On the fourteenth Toto and Turgan went to Neuilly. The marriage was postponed until the Tuesday. On 16 April Gautier returned from Geneva and went to visit Turgan at Auteuil. Next day Eugénie noted: 'Judith is married. Everything went off in perfect order.'

The marriage (which was to end in justified divorce) had not, in fact, been orthodox. The wedding breakfast had been held at the house of one of Hugo's friends; Gautier had refused to attend it, and Judith's witnesses, Flaubert and Turgan, had stayed away out of consideration for him. At the table sat only Mendès' witnesses, Villiers de l'Isle-Adam and Leconte de Lisle, Marras and Tin Tun Ling, Mendès' parents, Estelle, and Ernesta.[12] And Ernesta, who had encouraged Mendès actively, persistently, Ernesta, who had so often ignored Gautier's authority, Ernesta, who had brought him such anxiety and frustration, such prolonged unhappiness, was now no longer the mistress at Neuilly. Gautier the indolent had at last been moved to action. The liaison of some twenty years was broken.

32. The Sanctuary of Saint-Jean

AND SO Ernesta retired to the little house at Villiers-sur-Marne which Garnier had designed, which Gautier had hoped to acquire with the profits from *Trésors d'Art de la Russie*; and there, sadly enough, she was to spend many of the years that remained to her, breeding silk-worms with the devotion she had shown the *ménagerie intime* in the rue le Longchamps.

On 18 April, tired and unwell, Gautier went with Estelle to his sisters' house at Montrouge to recuperate and read *Bleak House*;[1] he soothed himself, too, in the world of poetry. Three days later he sent Carlotta *Fleur qui fait le Printemps*: 'Oh God! how bored I am, how hurt and how disgusted, how intensely I long to bathe in the azure of Saint-Jean!'[2]

My dear devoted friend [she answered],
   'Don't imagine I could forget you, my dear Théophile. . . .
   'How sad that you cannot be here at this moment! If only you knew how enchanting it is at Saint-Jean! Everything is in flower; the life of youth is in everything. The birds are twittering charming things that I'd like to repeat to you; but I dare not, for fear I'd give you too much regret. Meanwhile rest assured, my dear, that I am with you in all you do, and follow you in thought in your work and in your vagabond journeys in the great City.
   'I embrace you tenderly and with all my heart.'[3]

One April morning Gautier called on Eugénie, and told her, comfortably, what memories of youth he had rediscovered among the old familiar furniture, in the intimate life with Lili and Zoé, his sisters. He had almost decided to return to the rue de Longchamps; he regretted Eugénie's hardship and declared he wanted a carriage. He was always sure of her devotion; and so, while he treated her deplorably, he continued to make demands. On 28 April he called three times to see her, and found her at last at midnight, when she patiently made up his bed on the divan; next morning she had to suffer a long romantic tirade about revenge and hate, and hear the news that he would have his carriage in a fortnight. And now that he was in every way free to marry her, now that he could have realized the dreams they had so often

spun together, he let her cloud castles, so long, so lovingly built, mel
into air. He insisted he must be free.

He was, of course, as Eugénie must have known, far too impractical
far too dependent, to regain (or even want) his freedom. He was in fac
exchanging the rule of Ernesta for the rule of Lili and Zoé: strong-willed
unintelligent spinsters absorbed by lasting hatred of the Grisis an
possessive devotion to their famous brother. On 14 May he announce
that his sisters were already installed at Neuilly to keep house. He urge
the middle-aged Eugénie to stay in rue de Beaune for the sake of he
son: 'He will grow used to seeing you every day,' added Gautier, 'an
in the end you will live together.'

Ten days later came the inevitable footsteps. He was anxious an
depressed. 'He cannot have the workmen to do the repairs at Neuilly
And then there are difficulties from Villiers, too, letters to solicitors, etc
Then the *Salon* articles are being refused at the *Moniteur*.' Harasse
by his home, by Ernesta, by his editors, he left to soothe himself a
Princess Mathilde's. But the rue de Courcelles gave him only passin
consolation. 'He is in a state of nerves which is painful to see [wrot
Eugénie late in May]. He talks very bitterly.'

All through June he vacillated between pleasure and depression. On
evening he came in tired from the *Salon*, another he came in happy wit
his new domestic arrangements and told her 'confidentially' he wa
having a bathroom installed. A few days later the balance was upset, an
he arrived furious. He had seen Judith at the Français, and Ernest
had visited rue de Longchamps. Eugénie was sometimes angered, an
naturally, by his moods, by his inability to admit that perhaps he migh
be wrong. 'He finds it very difficult,' she noted, crisply, 'to admit he i
not perfection itself.'

*   *   *

However acidly she made the observation, Eugénie might have mad
one comment in his favour: Gautier was productive. On 5 July sh
reported: 'He has written a sonnet on red'; it was doubtless *le Rose*
On 9 July she noted he was spending a few days 'at Chamarand
again', at the Duc de Persigny's, and on the sixteenth he called t
describe the American woman at Chamarande. '*Le Sonnet*,' adde
Eugénie in her diary; it was surely *l'Impassible*, this gently Baudelairean
magnificently grandiose compliment:

> La Satiété dort au fond de vos grands yeux;
> En eux, plus de désirs, plus d'amour, plus d'envie;
> Ils ont bu la lumière, ils ont tari la vie,
> Comme une mer profonde où s'absorbent les cieux.

Sous leur bleu sombre on lit le vaste ennui des Dieux,
Pour qui toute chimère est d'avance assouvie,
Et qui, sachant l'effet dont la cause est suivie,
Mélangent au présent l'avenir déjà vieux.

L'infini s'est fondu dans vos larges prunelles,
Et devant ce miroir qui ne réfléchit rien
L'Amour découragé s'assoit, fermant ses ailes.

Vous, cependant, avec un calme olympien,
Comme la Mnémosyne à son socle accoudée,
Vous poursuivez, rêveuse, une impossible idée.[4]

It is this sonnet that Primoli admired perhaps most of all Gautier's poetry. And it is Primoli who records more of the Mrs Moulton for whom it was written. A quarter of a century later, meeting her in Rome, he recited the sonnet to her. She did not recognize it. 'I seem to hear the lines for the first time. . . . I'll look for the page; if it hasn't been torn up, it should be in my plush box with my menus and invitations.' And she asked Primoli to copy the sonnet in her album. Never, he reflected, had she better justified Gautier's portrait; but he should have called her *l'Indifférente*, not *l'Impassible*. She was a woman, not a divinity.[5]

A few days after Gautier had recited *l'Impassible* to Eugénie, she recorded that he was still writing sonnets, and on 30 July he told her some lines he had written for Princess Mathilde. On 6 August he was already contemplating a story about Renaissance Venice, and within a few weeks the *Revue du XIXe Siècle* announced the imminent appearance of another novel, *le Dénouement turc*. The *Revue* continued to advertise, but in vain; for 'Art, like Hell,' as Gautier wrote, 'is paved with good intentions'.

*   *   *

On 2 October, after a three-week holiday at Saint-Jean, with his usual regret and strange relief, the vagabond journalist returned to Paris. 'It is certainly sad to leave the Lake of Geneva, this lake that is bluer, purer, more ideally translucent than the waters of the Elysian landscapes painted by Breughel. . . . And yet, leaning over the rails of the steamer, as the paddle-wheels stir up pearls and diamonds and emeralds, you sometimes find yourself wondering what they are doing in Paris. The theatre which you abandoned with such pleasure now disturbs you. You say to yourself: But supposing they suddenly performed some masterpiece to be compared with Aeschylus, Shakespeare or Molière!

How lamentable to miss a first night like that! Nature is fine, no doubt, but art is even finer, for art is man added to nature, with the feeling of infinity. And you pack your trunk and hasten back to Paris to write the somewhat belated analysis of *les Parisiens à Londres* or *la Confession d'un Enfant du Siècle*, a vaudeville in one act, for that is all the modern Athenians have produced in your absence.'[6]

*   *   *

The last chapter of *Voyage en Russie* appeared in the *Revue Nationale et Etrangère* on 1 October; in mid October, hesitant, uninspired, Gautier began his *Guide de l'Amateur au Musée du Louvre*: 'a work,' reported the diarist, 'that gives him little pleasure.' By the end of the month he was again in Geneva, for Carlotta's saint's day; on 16 November he returned to Paris, where the yoke of criticism immediately descended on his shoulders. And a yet heavier burden soon fell upon him. On 20 November, prematurely, Louis de Cormenin died.

His death was a sharp break with the past, with the Algerian journey of 1845, with the Venetian idyll of sixteen years ago, with the paradise of the rue de Sèze. It meant the loss of a gifted writer, an intimate, endearing companion. Gautier was much moved; and Du Camp never met him after de Cormenin's death without his saying: 'I am glad to see you; we can talk about poor Louis.'[7] One can understand Gautier's intense depression at the end of the year which had taken from him his brilliant and favourite daughter, destroyed the liaison of twenty years with Ernesta, and deprived him of an old and intimate friend. And for once Eugénie seems unduly harsh when she comments, on 3 December: 'Gautier wants me to pity him. And why? "I need affection, my children don't give me and never have given me the feeling of fatherly love. I need a companion, man or woman, to go out with me, someone to talk to as I go around. With you I talk, you're the only person I visit, the only one with whom I'm completely sincere. I tell you everything I do. But I'm not with you often enough." What he also needs [snapped Eugénie] is a beautiful slave to get him out of the bath.' A week later, Gautier returned to complain again of sadness and tedium: 'I am like a man who is waiting. Waiting for what? I don't know, but I feel an imperious need for a new element in my life.' Eugénie's comment was blistering: 'I'm afraid he regrets the *element* that disappeared last April.' She referred to the money he had given her.

What he needed, ageing and disappointed, was more probably an element of romance. He found it in his dinners with the devoted Princess, the imperial, intimate dinners he so often described to Eugénie; he knew he would always find it on the shores of Lake Geneva. 'The blue sky and the sun stay in Geneva, in your enchanting eyes,' he told Carlotta. 'You have kept all the sunlight.'[8] And on 23 December, having despatched a few copies of the new edition of *Fracasse*, an edition embellished by Doré's illustrations, he abandoned Eugénie to her diary-filling and left Paris to spend Christmas at Saint-Jean.

* * *

'My dear Estelle [this on 28 December],

Though I should be back in Paris on Tuesday morning for New Year's Day, I'm writing you this little scrap of a letter to show you I think of you from far and near and don't forget my home and its dear denizens. When I arrived Rose had just had measles and had given it to Ernestine who was still confined to her room so that they put off Christmas Day until next Sunday. As they're postponing Christmas and advancing New Year's Day because of my imminent departure, the two ceremonies will be held together, and the exhibition of New Year gifts will take place in the drawing-room with the display of presents from the tree. It will be splendid. Carlotta's working like a galley-slave, she's gilded and silvered four dozen nuts, and in the gleam of a pile of rosy candles they'll make the Swiss fir-tree like an orange-tree from the Garden of the Hesperides. . . . As for me, I've given myself the pleasure of going four whole days without writing copy. That is my own New Year gift to myself, but to-day I'm beginning the stuff for the Monday article.'

On 1 January he arrived in Paris to plunge into the white vortex of the New Year.

'When I open my window [he wrote, next day, to Carlotta], when I open my window—for as usual I've risen long before dawn and I'm writing to you in daylight—I can see the falling snow and the trees in the garden powdered with rime like marquesses in the days of Louis XV. There's nothing so lovely as this white forest stretching from house to river. The great ivy, near Estelle's window, might be a green velvet cloak embroidered and spangled with silver. . . . If the snow stretches as far as you, how fine Saint-Jean must be with its floury panorama of mountains! For want of the Jura . . . and other Alpine giants, I look at a row of poplars and trees like Genoese filigree. One must learn to content oneself with one's possessions. And I take my leave of you, most regretfully, to get dressed and snatch some breakfast, climb into père Girault's suburban brougham (he's my hirer of carriages for state occasions), and go off to see Maréchal Vaillant, *Ministre des Beaux-Arts et de la maison de l'Empereur*, to which etiquette obliges me as a member of the *Conseil supérieur de l'enseignement* and vice-president of the Jury.

That will make you laugh, you wicked republicans and radicals of
Geneva, who believe not in God, nor devil, nor emperor, nor even in
etiquette.'[9]

Gautier's flippancy was soon to vanish. Within the week came another
grave event in the family. Villiers de l'Isle-Adam, audacious, pleasant,
diverting (and sharply defined by Mendès as '*un magnifique incomplet*'),
had fallen in love with Estelle at Judith's wedding, had become engaged
to her; he wrote now to say that his family would not support him, he
could not assure her future and must renounce his claims. His renuncia-
tion brought certain sorrow to the lonely, sisterless girl in the rue de
Longchamps, for she was not to marry for five years. Yet it brought a
certain relief to her father, for in the house at Neuilly she moved with
grace and charm, this figure caught in her check gingham dress by the
camera of Nadar. Less brilliant than Judith, she was perhaps a more
endearing companion: 'my dear little bird, the last in the nest and the
only one that remains to me.'[10]

*   *   *

Deep in Romantic melancholy, a melancholy that the past few months
had but intensified, Gautier resigned himself to the continuing round
of distasteful work, the continuing monotony of existence:

'Contrary to my habits I only work at home now and I send my
literature to the printers [this to Carlotta]. Snow, frost, ice and fog don't
make the perpetual journey from Neuilly to Paris, from Paris back to
Neuilly very pleasant. The thaw has plunged us into an ocean of mud,
and unless a carriage calls for you at the door, you arrive with mud up
to the ears. But the weather seems to be improving and the worst of the
winter is over. I hardly leave my red room and I write near the fire, on a
little white wooden table easier to manage than the great oak table with
twisted legs encumbered with a quintal or two of books. My Bouillet
dictionary serves as a desk, and my black cat Eponine, my constant
companion, sleeps on my left arm, while my right hand scrawls on the
little sheets of paper that you remember. Sometimes she sits on the
corner of the table and looks at me for hours, presenting me with two
miniatures in the depths of her yellow eyes: two portraits even more
lifelike than Crosnier's enamels. You would think she wanted to com-
municate a thought that she cannot express and describe things that to
me are invisible. And so the hours pass by, oh! very slowly, to the
sound of her little purr and the crackling of the wood in the hearth.
I may also tell you I've considerably reduced the number of cigars I
used to consume, I only smoke five or six a day instead of twelve or

fteen. As you see, it's a great reduction. Am I better in health for it?
don't know yet, but it seems to me that this privation vaguely troubles
ae and makes me more melancholy. Cigars are the baubles of boredom;
ut I shall persevere, for it's stupid to spend one's life making smoke.
Vhile I'm writing in the red room, Estelle is painting in the chintz
om, Henriette is sewing in the dining-room, and the two sisters come
nd go, busy with the housework. So life flows on, and so they pass
way, these futile days when I do not see you. . . .'[11]

*   *   *

Poor Eugénie Fort! Her part, after all, could only be the part of con-
dante. Eagerly she called on her former lover, eagerly she received his
ndless visits; patiently she bore his tirades, his lamentations and
nsults, his callousness and his deplorable selfishness. Did it occur to
er that he often came because the rue de Beaune was only a few
ninutes' walk from the *Moniteur*, because he wanted to sprawl on a
ivan, linger over wine, after the noise and bustle of the office? Did she
ver suspect that he cared nothing for her criticism, that he only
ccepted her sympathy and praise? Did she ever delude herself, when
e sat serenely on her bed and read to her, that he would, in time,
esume his old relations: that, if marriage were out of the question, the
iaison might be renewed? She cannot have seen him so often without
spirations; she must surely have thought that habit would at last make
er indispensable.

Meanwhile, not unmindful of posterity, she recorded him. 'TG
roposes to write a tragedy to force the Académie,' she noted on 11
ebruary; and, a few days later: 'He wants to write a tragedy, a pre-
ccupation that stops him from doing anything else.' A few days later
he found him busy with officialdom: 'all sorts of meetings, the Jury,
he Conservatoire, etc.' He had been elected, with Banville, Berlioz and
Verdi, to the music committee for the 1867 Exhibition.[12] And Eugénie
roudly welcomed him every Monday and on many days besides, and
ontinued to record his achievements and projects in her spidery hand.
TG is very busy [she noted on 2 May], he doesn't stay long. He is
rying hard to enter the Académie. He is making the applications con-
cientiously.' It was in fact election day; but the chairs of Barante and
Cousin were won by Gratry and Jules Favre.[13] It was another defeat for
Gautier, the only candidate who had purely literary claims.[14]

*   *   *

May continued more pleasantly with a visit to la Païva, when Gautier
resented the Goncourts to the highly coloured courtesan, and they all
rank tea in the wildly ostentatious mock-Renaissance drawing-room in
he Champs-Elysées.[15] And then one night, late that month, he wandered

with the two brothers round the Great Exhibition,[16] in a Champ-de
Mars so transformed, so glowing, so exotic, that at times they seeme
to walk in a Japanese painting, among the cosmopolitan flags of the
Middle Empire. And June, too, brought its pleasures: a glittering
international throng invaded Paris, and the second act of *Giselle* wa
performed before a veritable audience of emperors.[17] And among the
same imperial multitude, with Napoleon III and Alexander II of Al
the Russias, moved the author of *Giselle*: one of the few writers asked
to the Tuileries when 'no one was allowed to mingle with the sovereign
unless he were something of a sovereign himself'.[18]

And yet the Jupiter who walked with royalty in the blue moonligh
of the Tuileries gardens, at a fête to delight the Almanach de Gotha
to enchant the brush of Watteau, was wretched. 'He has been ill, he
complains a great deal. His life is so sad he cannot bear his isolation
What can he do?' The question remained unanswered in July; with
Ernesta and Judith gone, Estelle regretful, his sisters, dominant, obtuse
ruling his life, Gautier was more miserable than ever. Again he planned
to live alone in the rue de Beaune. Late that month he visited Eugénie
at Versailles and father, mother and son paced about the park for two
dismal hours. 'We feel we aren't really together,' wrote Eugénie sadly
'Our thoughts are solitary, we aren't content with each other.'

Some, at least, of Gautier's solitary thoughts may be surmised. His
friends were concerned about his precarious finances, and on the death
of Ponsard, who had held the sinecure of librarian at the Elysée, Alfred
Arago had suggested Gautier as his successor. It was evident that
Princess Mathilde should plead the cause of the *poète mathildien*, but
Gautier (who showed his Princess an understanding not shown to
Eugénie) did not dare visit her for fear of looking interested.

'My dear Alfred [this on 20 July],
   'When I came home I found a telegram from Saint-Gratien which
has thrown me into great perplexity. It's an invitation to dine with the
Princess on Sunday. There's nothing terrible in that, you'll say, but
I'm full of anxiety, have you mentioned anything? Since your ingenious
friendship suggested this idea to you and the death of poor Ponsard
made a possibility of what had been only a dream, I haven't dared to
see the Princess, feeling I was guilty of an interested thought. Until
now I have found it sweet to see her, hear her, admire her quite freely,
with no other end than, at times, to bring a slight smile to the corners
of her charming lips, when I let off a little firework display of paradox
to amuse her. Now I am embarrassed, ashamed; it seems unworthy to
use the benevolence she has deigned to show me and if you don't

xplain the thing frankly yourself, I shall certainly never breathe a
ord about it. I'd rather die. So deliver me quickly from this anxiety:
s it's your idea, I'm afraid you had better execute it. For me it would
iean security of life, rest in time of exhaustion, and, above all, freedom
i my choice of work. I should still keep my articles on the Theatre and
ie Fine Arts but apart from that I should do nothing but verse plays,
icreasing the poetry and lessening the prose. I should rhyme sonnets as
 strolled beneath the trees and I'd finish the tragedy of *Electra* I
romised the good Princess. In short, I should be very happy. As for
iy titles, you know them better than I do and you'll know how to
resent them. I put my hope in your hands, then, and I hope to gain
ioral support by meeting you on Sunday among the guests at Saint-
iratien.'[19]

'he Mathildian answer probably sped to Neuilly before Gautier took
ie Sunday train to Sannois: it was the most endearing imperial
eprimand:

'I might well be a little angry: you say you're a friend of mine and
ou refuse to tell me a wish you would love fulfilled! You must agree
hat it's paradoxical.
'But don't worry: the request is made, sent, warmly supported. I'm
emanding an act of justice, and I have complete confidence in my
idge.
    'I take your hand in affection.
                    MATHILDE.'[20]

Alas, the imperial judge did less than justice; the Emperor who, at
ie Opéra, had applauded *Giselle* with an audience of emperors, would
ot now support its author; the host who had invited Gautier to the
'uileries, a few weeks earlier, would not now accord him a corner in his
alace.

My dear cousin [was his explanation to Princess Mathilde],
'I should have been delighted to do something to please you by
aming M. Théophile Gautier librarian at the Elysée, but I've done
way with the post which was only a pretext for giving Ponsard a
ension.'[21]

Princess and poet had to bide their time. And, while they waited, she
sked him repeatedly to Saint-Gratien. He spent the last week-end in
uly sitting under her princely cedar of Lebanon, lazing on her veranda

where (though she detested the smell of tobacco) she lit his constant
cigars with engaging resolution. 'Do you remember,' asked one of her
guests,[22] 'do you remember the charm and wit with which he sang of
your endearing grace? When an ingenious thought, a witticism fell from
your lips, he gathered them up at once like so many jewels. . . . And if
he praised your sweet relationship, that bond he described so charmingly as *amitié voluptueuse*, if he extolled the particular elegance of your
dress, you said at once, delighted by his perfect cadenced prose: "Come,
Gautier, a sonnet!" The poet who proclaimed himself your own, the
old lion who became a Newfoundland dog at your feet, did not keep
you waiting.'

> *A table, l'autre jour, un réseau de guipure,*
> *Comme un filet d'argent sur un marbre jeté,*
> *De votre sein, voilant à demi la beauté,*
> *Montrait, sous sa blancheur, une blancheur plus pure.*
>
> *Vous trôniez parmi nous, radieuse figure,*
> *Et le baiser du soir, d'un faible azur teinté,*
> *Comme au contour d'un fruit la fleur du velouté,*
> *Glissait sur votre épaule en mince découpure.*
>
> *Mais la lampe allumée et se mêlant au jeu*
> *Posait un baiser rose auprès du baiser bleu;*
> *Tel brille au clair de lune un feu dans de l'albâtre.*
>
> *A ce charmant tableau, je me disais, rêveur,*
> *Jaloux du reflet rose et du reflet bleuâtre:*
> *'O trop heureux reflets, s'ils savaient leur bonheur!'*[23]

And surely Princess Mathilde must have been as gratified as her own
Court poet, as the author of *Baiser rose, Baiser bleu*, if she knew of the
tribute paid to him that summer. One of her household sent an autograph album to Bismarck, who had visited the Paris Exhibition; and in
the train that bore him back to Prussia, Bismarck turned the pages of
the book and came across the microscopic handwriting of the author
of *Emaux et Camées*, the autograph of *Vieux de la Vieille*. He read it.
Then, in a corner of the page, he added, bluntly: 'Pregnies Station,
14 June 1867. Von Bismarck regretted he had not written this poem.'

*   *   *

'Gautier is spending a few days with me,' wrote Princess Mathilde,
somewhat anxiously, to Sainte-Beuve, on 26 September. 'I'm afraid he

may be bored. He has come back from Switzerland where he attended Garibaldi's reception at Geneva.' 'Gautier will not be bored,' replied Sainte-Beuve. 'He has a sensitive and fertile spirit. . . . What he finds, what he sees and what he paints are unimaginable. . . . Théo has more sensibility than the general public supposes, and his heart is moved as much as his soul in the presence of true beauty.'[25] Sainte-Beuve spoke fairly, but he presented only one facet of the diamond; almost as he wrote, the Goncourts were observing the enormous audacity of Gautier's conversation.[26] He still delighted in exasperating the *bourgeois*, and it was with undoubted pleasure, if a blank expression, that now, a government critic of fifty-six, he questioned a Minister about his relations with his wife.

And in Gautier's own letters and the constant diary we find the final pictures of this kaleidoscopic year: Gautier visiting Toto, now *sous-préfet* at Ambert; Gautier coming home to greet Estelle, 'to see your little face like the face of a Chinese princess growing bored behind her lattice'. And last, inevitably, Gautier leaving Paris to spend Christmas with Giselle, in the fairyland, the abiding sanctuary of Saint-Jean to which, so often, instinctively, he returned.

33. Librarian to Her Highness

'I MUST GO to Paris tomorrow to see TG,' scribbled Eugénie Fort on 1 January. 'He should be back from Geneva.' He returned as dreamers return from a gold and silver dream to the cold, uncompromising light of every day; and one seems to catch an undertone of autobiography in *le Moniteur universel*, a few days later: 'If life has not kept its promises, art, at least, has never deceived us.'[1]

But he was soon too busy to be depressed: an invitation arrived from the Tuileries and he had to enquire about dress; Court dress, came the answer, for an intimate of the household.[2] And he was concerned again about the Académie. 'Now at last,' declared *l'Artiste*, 'it is the turn of Théophile Gautier and Jules Janin!'[3] He was to give a sitting to Hippolyte Lazerges for *l'entr'acte de première représentation au théâtre de l'Odéon*. There was Bizet to be assessed at the Théâtre-Lyrique, an adaptation of Balzac to be seen at the Gaieté, a study of Baudelaire (who had died in August) to write for *l'Univers illustré*. When Eugénie returned to Paris on 13 January, Gautier soon arrived; he stayed talking optimistically for hours. 'He wants to do something very beautiful,' she noted. 'I urged him to choose some other form than the newspaper article, where such fine passages are wasted. He's doing Baudelaire's biography and he's very pleased with it. He thinks that 1868 should be favourable for him in many ways, but I don't know which. He avoided mentioning the Académie.' Poor Eugénie! Having poured out his soul to her, he sent Régina Lhomme two earnest invitations to Neuilly. And, as usual, he took his pleasures elsewhere but continued to visit Eugénie for consolation. It was to Eugénie, not Régina, that he observed that 'life is only interesting for the first twenty-five years when everything is new, after that it is just a tedious repetition complicated by obligations'. And Eugénie found him selfish, temperamental, insensitive and still endearing, observed him with sad devotion and tried to concentrate her interest in their son. 'As for my thoughts, they are all for my son. Except for one or two financial preoccupations, they are all and always for Toto. Perhaps I should make some attempt to bind my existence closer to Gautier's. Yet I cannot expose myself to a refusal. And so often he laments about his life. He knows he would be happy if I were in the house, if he had me always near him. He finds it strange to give me a very modest allowance while he has a house where one person more would cost nothing. But as he always ends "It's impossible", I have nothing more to say. What does he want? Does he want something? Or is it only conversation?'[4]

What he wanted—what he had wanted since the days of *Mademoiselle de Maupin*—was some unattainable Utopia. On 14 February, dining with la Païva, having enchanted the Goncourts with paradox, with the loftiness, the originality, the fantasy of his thoughts, with a conversation even more coruscating than his prose, he turned to boredom, to the boredom that gnawed at him. 'If I told you,' he wrote to Carlotta, 'if I told you I often get up at three in the morning, the days when I haven't gone to bed at three, to begin or finish the work that is indispensable. . . . I don't know what to do with myself. . . . I'm as bored as a trunk left behind on a railway station. . . . How I long for a little cobalt blue in these fog-bound skies!'[5] To Eugénie he complained of his solitude at Neuilly, his financial commitments; and strangely, touchingly, the outrageous Romantic who had worn the rose-coloured doublet at *Hernani* told her now that Toto was the fortunate member of the family: Toto, safely established as *sous-préfet* at Ambert.[6] His health was rapidly worsening. Towards the end of March he had a heart attack, which left its effect upon him; it was followed by another early in April. Eugénie was deeply disturbed, and the *Figaro* published so alarming a statement that Sainte-Beuve and Dumas *fils* sent enquiries, the Emperor despatched a courier to Neuilly, and even the Goncourts

ere shaken out of their egoism and would have driven to see him if
rincess Mathilde had not reassured them.[7] Eugénie, on a visit to Paris,
und Gautier alone in the rue de Longchamps: still tired from his
test attack. They read a little and he showed her round the house,
hich she considered charming. And whatever her indignation, her
acillation, whatever self-deception she had attempted, she under-
tood now the depth, the inalterability of her feelings. 'What can I say
bout it all?' she wondered when she was home. 'I can say little. I
annot be surprised that I was well received. The aunts have always
een the same with me and I with them. Estelle is a nice child and no
oubt it's indifferent to her whether I'm there or not. As for Gautier,
e attaches small importance to any move. As for me, he was there and
 could not see him anywhere else—and I want, whatever the price,
nd always, to see him. I belong to him.' 'My life has been a failure,'
he added, later. 'I should go to his family and live with him as he used
 ask me. Today he is right, so I have nothing to say.'[8]

But she had doubtless much to regret. On 18 May he took her,
riefly, to dine at the Café d'Orsay; then the luggage 'and all the
omenfolk of Neuilly' arrived in a carriage, and at eight o'clock, with
is sister Emilie and Estelle, he left for Geneva.

*   *   *

On 15 June a fit and happy Gautier strode down the rue de Beaune.
Ie had been 'given cod-liver oil like a young English consumptive';
nd the cod-liver oil, the candle-lit chestnuts of Saint-Jean, the moun-
ain air of Mont Blanc, the presence of Carlotta, had soothed, revived,
spired him. 'He is quite decided to do everything that pleases him.
Ie is going to work hard, fulfil all his obligations, all his engagements,
e will keep his old affections, for the Bible says: "Cleave to the woman
f thy youth." But he wants a calm and peaceful life.' And he wanted
ow, it appears, a strikingly conventional existence. 'Never a woman
 the house unless she is married,' he told Eugénie. 'A good house, well
ept, good living and hard work. The Académie and then the Sénat.'
n le Moniteur universel he wrote in praise of classical tragedy; while
he latest book to be set on the shelves at Neuilly was the book he had
elped to write for the Minister of Public Instruction, a survey which
ombined Romantic enthusiasm with official purpose: the Rapport sur
 progrès des lettres depuis vingt-cinq ans.[9] And the author of this scie
atriotique, as he called it, established himself yet more securely in
mperial and official circles: on 21 July, he left to spend a week at Saint-
Gratien.

And yet, for all his outward orthodoxy, his apparent serenity,
Gautier still belonged to 1830. He insisted that he believed in nothing,

admitted no social laws, that civilization hampered him, that he was a
savage. He regaled the Goncourts and Princess Mathilde with eloquen
audacity, enormous compliments, astonishing conversation in whicl
Rabelais and Diderot seemed to meet. And to the Goncourts he showec
yet again that he was no marble-souled impassible. Lying one summe
afternoon in a boat on the Lake of Enghien, he asked them why it wa
that a gifted man, a man with many friends, a man without enemies
should not be a Senator or Academician or even be granted a museum
sinecure. Perhaps, he reflected, it was only the need to earn his daily
bread that had prevented his being one of the four names of the century
If he were ill for a fortnight, his household would just survive; if he
were ill for six weeks, he would have to enter a poorhouse.[10]

On 27 July he left to refresh himself at Geneva, to write *les Vacance*
du Lundi, his impressions of the mountains, for *le Moniteur universel*.[1]
It was some time in September that he returned to Paris.

*   *   *

He returned to a world of imperial diplomacy. There was a change of
administration at *le Moniteur universel*, and Gautier was apprehensiv
about his future:

'I take up my pen unable to tell you anything of the future situation
[this to Carlotta], because I have absolutely no idea what it will be
Dalloz wants to continue the big and the *Petit Moniteur* and just remove
the word *officiel*. Will he be allowed to? And will the papers, deprivec
of their government character, keep their subscribers? These are ques
tions that cannot yet be settled. What is certain is that these revolution
are very tiresome for me, vex me more than I can say and put me in a
delicate position. I felt so settled at the good old *Moniteur universel*,
had so long been accustomed to the paper that the change throws my
whole existence into confusion. Financially, of course, I shall lose
nothing by it, for my little scrawled-over pages are worth banknotes
and I shall place as many as I can write. But if I stay with Dalloz and
reject the offers that the minister, so they say, will make me for the new
paper, I become openly hostile and cancel out all the goodwill tha
people claim to have for me—though this goodwill has never producec
a thing.'[12]

The Government was to publish its *Journal officiel* from the beginning
of the new year, and Gautier was, in fact, to contribute to it. But in
October 1868 this lay in the future; he remained anxious about his
career. So, too, did Princess Mathilde; and, determined to ensure her
poet's happiness, she set to work with her usual vitality: 'It's so difficul

to put one's purse at the disposition of those one would like to help, if they are in Gautier's situation [she wrote to her counsellor, Sainte-Beuve, in October]: I want your advice on how to set about it. I'd thought of giving him the title of my librarian so that I could attach 6,000 francs to the post. But wouldn't that be ridiculous? Tell me honestly. And would he accept it?'[13] Sainte-Beuve answered promptly and wisely:

'Dear Princess,

'Théo could certainly make a very pretty and somewhat fanciful library. . . . If Your Highness really entrusted this to him, offered him two or three small rooms, so that he could select some books and arrange them for convenience and elegance, if in fact Your Highness would accord your books a quarter or half a quarter of the care and importance you accord your pictures, I don't see why Théo shouldn't be your *reader* and *librarian* with privileges and emoluments.'[14]

Sainte-Beuve's advice was taken, and Princess Mathilde dashed off a note to the Emperor, asking, as a point of etiquette, for his sanction; he replied, from Biarritz, with the familiar suavity: 'I am charmed you should make M. Théophile Gautier your librarian: I'd have been happy to assure him such a place if I had had a vacancy myself.'[15]

It only remained for the Princess to ask Gautier to Saint-Gratien and tell him of her project. She scribbled off her letter:

'If I haven't answered sooner [came the reply] it's because I hoped to bring you my news in person. I have a little trouble with my ankle which stops me from putting on shoes; it will give in after a few days of bedroom and slippers. I've tried hard and ingeniously to prove to myself that it isn't gout, but it looks very like it. Everyone has his weak points, and not everyone is sculpted in Carrara or Paros marble, like Your Imperial Highness. If goddesses are never ill, poor human beings, their worshippers, do not enjoy this serene inalterability. In any case, cured or not, with slippers or buskins, I shall come to Saint-Gratien on Wednesday. "Who looks at your feet?" you once remarked on a similar occasion. Just like the peacock I'm very concerned with my legs. But I shall spread my tail and in your august bounty Your Highness will only look at my feathers.'[16]

But the so-called gout did not surrender to bedroom and slippers. Wednesday found Gautier in the rue de Longchamps: 'How can one appear before an Imperial Highness in slippers and white cravat? It's

P

as contrary to elegance as to etiquette.' And in the Princess's mind a
new difficulty arose: perhaps Gautier would be too proud to accept the
sinecure. Off sped another letter to her counsellor:

'I had a nice reply from the Emperor about my request to make Théo
Gautier my librarian. If I had only listened to my instinct, I should have
written to Gautier at once to tell him what I'd done without his knowledge. But Hébert seemed to me to imply that the proposition would not
suit him, that he would be very touched by my intention, but . . .

'What do you think? Should I still wait or should I write to him?
If you see him, couldn't you touch upon it? I have to make out the
decree in the Emperor's name, but for that I must be sure of Gautier's
acceptance.

'I should have thought it needed less diplomacy to give people
pleasure.'[17]

It took one more diplomatic move, which was made by Sainte-Beuve.
Within the next few days, Gautier came to see him, and l'oncle Beuve
took the initiative. He wrote to the Princess:

'Gautier had no inkling of the affair. . . . I told him everything; there
wasn't a moment's hesitation, but an outburst of natural gratitude both
for the benefit and for the delicacy with which you bestowed it.

'All the imperial government's debt to Théo has now been paid,
thanks be to you, Princess; it remains for the Académie to acquit the
debt of literature to one of the most charming of our writers.'[18]

On 1 November l'Artiste announced that 'M. Théophile Gautier has
been made librarian to Princess Mathilde: a true librarian and a true
reader.' Her Imperial Highness, in her flourishing, largely illegible
hand, triumphantly sent an invitation to 'Monsieur Théophile Gautier,
bibliothécaire de S. A. I. la Princesse Mathilde.'[19]

The following evening, one of the Goncourts encountered the
librarian on the stairs in the rue de Courcelles.[20] 'Tell me honestly,'
asked that functionary: 'Does the Princess have a library?' 'A word of
advice, my dear Gautier,' said de Goncourt: 'Behave as if she had
none.'

34. The Vagabond Librarian

'MY DEAR FRIEND,' wrote Viollet-le-Duc to Mérimée on 5 January, 'Sainte-Beuve is not enormously concerned with what is happening or will happen at the Académie. He certainly thinks that Gautier will be elected, and Gautier flatters himself that he will pass.'[1] Sainte-Beuve indeed seemed sure: he declared that Gautier had an excellent chance of election 'if he did not alarm the great with his beard and his smell of cigars.'[2] Princess Mathilde determined the immortals should not be alarmed, and set to work to charm and convert all she met. She even organized a dinner at Sainte-Beuve's, to which Pongerville, the dour translator of Lucretius, was expressly invited; and the whole evening was spent in persuading him to tell his two stories: his interviews with Louis XVIII and Millevoye.

While these diplomatic overtures continued, the candidate was forcing himself to make the obligatory calls:

'I'm going on conscientiously with my academic visits as I promised you [he reported to Carlotta]. But alas! there no longer sits beside me, in Girault's brougham, the sweet, encouraging companion who made a pleasure of my tedious journeys. I don't just leave my card: I ask if people are in, I ask when I might see them if they're out, and I come back and make them speeches to suit their characters. I must say everyone has received me in the nicest possible manner, and though one mustn't pin one's faith on these old baboons, my election seems to be in a fair way. Whatever the papers say, there are only two serious candidates for Empis' chair: Auguste Barbier and myself. In both camps our chances are considered equal. So it's a question of making sure of one or two doubtful votes to weigh the balance one side or the other. They say that M. de Falloux (a clerical!) is quite well disposed towards me. I must find the beatific, apostolic, Roman style of the conversation with His Grace the Bishop of Geneva that so amused you. Perhaps, if he approved of me, he might bring another vote or two on this side.— All of which is hardly amusing, but I am persisting with the mulish stubbornness which you say you find in me, the stubbornness which suffices instead of will. For my real ambition would be to go to Saint Jean and not the Académie. But we are here below to do the opposite of what pleases us. I've made the conquest of Pingard, the usher of the Académie, a most influential person despite the apparent humility of

his functions. He adores me and keeps me up to date with everything
Whatever happens, a telegram will leave Paris for Geneva ten minute
after the election to tell you the result. God grant that it is favourable
for I don't know anything more tedious than these overtures for an
genius with a little pride. If I lack genius, at least I have pride. . .
How adorable the wakening of spring must be round the pink and blu
lake, the lake that the mountains hold in their cup of silver!

'The other day I was at the Opéra. Mlle Fiocre was performin
Fenella. I didn't see well from where I was and I went on stage—I hadn
set foot on it for several years. By an old instinct, I found the place wher
I used to stand against a ladder when you were dancing. To and fr
they moved before me, all sorts of unknown faces, and my thought
most melancholy, returned to the time when you sprang forth from th
cottage that, laughingly, we used to call your domain: fresh as a flowe
light as a butterfly, gay as youth, and luminous as fame! How I love
you then, in my timidity and silence! You passed and threw me a quic
smile and I felt weak with emotion. You were there no longer, and
found you again, after twenty years, in the same place, with the sam
ardour and—who knows?—perhaps I was closer to your heart than
used to be in those fine days when I knew such misery!'[3]

On 25 April Carlotta's worshipper visited Eugénie Fort at Versaille
'He isn't very well,' she noted, 'not ill, but a little depressed, he ha
palpitations.' Princess Mathilde had in fact sent her doctor to him som
months ago, and Elloco had diagnosed heart trouble. 'You're done fo
as soon as you start looking after yourself,' Gautier had told the Goi
courts. 'Here am I taking cures. Well, you see, it's no good any more.
To Carlotta, however, he spoke differently:

'I'm determined that you'll have a letter from me before the gre
day of judgment. . . . Mérimée, whose funeral orations had been deli
ered, has come back from Cannes quite fit. They've cured him
galloping bronchitis by giving him hourly glasses of brandy alternatir
with cups of soup. Thanks to this treatment, his pulse, which was 13
has come down to 75 and the invalid is well; it's one voice that's certai
for me; I've actually seen him today. I've also seen Sainte-Beuv
who has made arrangements to go to the Académie in three stages. Fir
he will have his hair cut at a hairdresser's quite near him, then he wi
have a bath a little further on; and finally he will lunch at Magny's, anc
accompanied by Troubat, his secretary, will appear at the Institut
two o'clock. As for me, I shall be with Pingard, the usher of th
Académie, who will transmit the votes to me as the nominations com

n. Oh! what a plague it is, and how much simpler it would be to live with the people one loves! But once you are caught in the rigging, you must try to get out the other end, not too flattened if possible. If I so bestir myself, it isn't that I'm ambitious, it is that I want to be free and finish my life as I please. Oh! what a glorious day when I am unharnessed from my cart! Will that day ever dawn for me?'[5]

To Eugénie he did not mention the Académie: he told her that he had written two sonnets and a dedication in verse for the book that he was offering the Princess. He recited it all as they walked from her rooms in the Avenue de Saint-Cloud to Versailles station. And he was to write more poetry for Princess Mathilde: at her suggestion he versified part of the Emperor's essay on the return of Napoleon's ashes from Saint Helena: a poem to be declaimed to Napoleon III when he visited his cousin on 29 April. On the evening before the visit, the evening before the election to the Académie, the Goncourts met Gautier in the Princess's winter garden. They did not know whether to think him audacious, indifferent or mad. They found him telling de Sacy, who might have voted for him next day, that one of the women he had most loved had been a panther woman with mottled skin, an exhibit at a fair.[6]

Next morning, a ciphered carriage sped purposefully from the rue de Courcelles to the Quai de Conti. Princess Mathilde, ignoring all conventions, had come to the Institut to await the result of her long election campaign. Gautier received fourteen votes instead of sixteen. Auguste Barbier was elected. 'She was so furious that she wept with rage and called the Academicians "pigs!"' Not very imperial, perhaps, but very feminine.'[7] Then she sped to Neuilly to console her candidate.

Her exasperation was boundless: Gautier learned of his fourth defeat with imperturbable calm, welcomed her with a grateful smile and tried to appease her. He had only presented himself to be agreeable to her. 'But they might at least have chosen one of our friends!' she insisted. 'How could they prefer an unknown writer whose only claim to glory is his infamous tirade against my uncle?' 'Forgive me, Princess,' her candidate answered serenely: 'Auguste Barbier was wrong to attack the Emperor; but he is a poet, and the Académie did itself honour by its choice.' Princess Mathilde could only answer: 'If you think so, you have your deserts.'[8]

That evening, at the rue de Courcelles, the Goncourts offered their condolences to Gautier. He was, he said, consoled for his failure: the Emperor had wept at his poetry. ('I should have preferred him to have the Académie, not the Imperial tear,' one of the brothers remarked in the *Journal*.)[9] Poor Princess Mathilde! To Carlotta, as to the Goncourts, he professed his indifference: 'Believe me, my Academic mishap doesn't trouble me in the slightest; my only real ambition is to gain your friendship; if your heart votes for me, what do I care for the votes of these *vieilles perruques*?'[10]

And yet, for all his serenity, for all his protestations, one suspects that Gautier's indifference was a pose: that the desire was hidden now, but remained. He may have been more touched than he cared to admit when Hébert wrote to him: 'I find the Académie-Française unworthy of its name; it should represent the country by welcoming those of her children who do her honour.'[11]

*   *   *

A few days later, Eugénie Fort met Gautier in Paris. She recorded no remarks about the Académie, only his delight with his Imperial poem, *les Mânes de l'Empereur*: he had written it, he said, in a day: in the Bois de Boulogne, then in a carriage and finally at the Jardin des Plantes. The effect had been superb. Then they walked together, the doting, fading woman, the ageing Olympian, towards the city boundary at Neuilly, talking of the past. 'He had been thinking for three consecutive months how he could get me to live at Neuilly. He had thought of nothing better than a regular position, and he would agree to it readily if he were not afraid of a very wicked woman who, so he thinks, has her rights!' The exclamation mark is eloquent: Ernesta had no legal claims upon Gautier. Nothing prevented his marriage to Eugénie.

Nothing, unless, perhaps, it was the eternal dream of Giselle. And having poured out his soul to Eugénie, and presented Princess Mathilde with the sonnets he had written her, exquisitely bound in green with imperial violet end-papers, he left, on 12 May, to visit his sacred Saint-Jean and bask in the sunlight of Switzerland for the rest of the month.

*   *   *

On 2 June he was again in Paris, well and happy, visiting the Princess and writing the rest of his fifteen articles on the *Salon*, a *Salon* in which his own bust, by Megret, looked down upon the throngs of visitors.[12] He called at the rue de Beaune, and again revealed his mind, though by now Eugénie did not take his pronouncements too seriously: 'Something strange is happening inside me,' he informed her. 'Work does not tire me, food does not sustain me, pleasure does not weary me.' 'He thinks [continued Eugénie] that if we hadn't left one another in our youth he would never have had any other woman but me! I note these things simply for record, I don't attach too much belief or too much doubt to them.'

And Eugénie was surely wise; for while she remained unable to afford a servant, while she darned and mended to fill her solitude, Gautier,

rning fifteen hundred francs a week, admitting he gave her little,
ntinued to improve the house at Neuilly with ornamental plates and
her amenities. 'When he has finished arranging his house [she noted]
e will give me a little more.' Late in June, when he had finished his
rticles on the *Salon*, he arrived on her doorstep, his pockets stuffed
ith banknotes. But again there was nothing for his former mistress.
Ie called to talk yet again of money, to disparage all women. Then
eling, perhaps, that he had gone too far, he returned to lament the
neliness of his existence. 'He'd like a house in which he could find
ien to talk with him and women to divert him. But it could not be in
is own house, it could not be one of the women in his household, not
is sisters, not his daughter. . . . What then? These conversations always
ad us to memories and the past! To the same reflexions which always
em to tell me: there is regret but no hope. This I know; and Gautier
ust certainly see that no word of mine gives the faintest hint for the
iture. I shall never expose myself to a refusal.' The patient woman in
ie shabby lodgings had indeed much to bear. One is tempted to say
iat Gautier was insufferable. A few days later, he called for further
ympathy and told Eugénie that 'he was bored at home, no one spoke
) him, he went home as late as possible. He was sorry he hadn't
rranged his household so that he could live happily with his family and
few friends'. She must have been relieved when he left, soon after-
ards, to spend a month in Geneva and in Italy.

*   *   *

Princess,
'Where do you suppose your vagabond librarian is at this moment?
Astride the Pegasus which dominates the terraces of the *Isola Bella*? In
ontemplation before *The Last Supper* of Leonardo da Vinci, that still
dorable shadow of a fading masterpiece? Or at the Brera museum? Or
1 Venice, in a gondola less sumptuous, to be sure, than the barge of
Cleopatra, in which you deigned to take me to the harbour of Enghien?
No, none of all these. I am at Crema. . . .
'If I told you that on the shores of Lake Maggiore I regretted the
ake at Enghien, you would no doubt believe me, for you don't like
ravelling, but I have the excuse that I've taken *nearly* all my heart away
rith me. Our little party leaves this evening for Venice, whence we shall
o to Parma to see the Correggios. If Your Highness has the gracious
ffability to answer, send your golden bee to Villa Grisi-sur-Saint-Jean,
Geneva, where we shall be in a few days' time.'[13]

But the imperial bee did not wing its way to Geneva; and on his return
o Saint-Jean a disappointed librarian wrote again:

'Princess,

'I dare not hope that my letter, sent from some uncivilized countr
called Crema, has reached you. The loss would not be great for You
Highness, but it deprives me of a hieroglyph in your charming hand, th
deciphering of which would have filled the tedium of absence, for yo
would perhaps have answered me and so proved that you have not com
pletely forgotten your librarian. . . . I shall be back in Paris on 1 October
which means that Saint-Gratien will see me the same evening.

'It seems I shall have to go to Egypt for the opening of the canal tha
joins the blue sea to the Red. Well! without flattery, I'm grieved t
think that the honour of being watched from the top of the Pyramids b
forty centuries and a half will cost me eight Wednesdays with You
Imperial Highness. It's really very expensive. The pleasure of lookin
from a window-seat at that fine nape of living marble is very superior t
the pleasure of studying all the old granite adorned with ducks, comb
and napkin-rings. . . .

'If my prose is stupid, forgive me, Princess, I will write you sonnet
to make amends; but, as you have advised me to write *large*, I am lik
a painter in letters, I think only of my figures and not of my phrases.'[1]

The vagabond librarian returned to Paris in September, earlier tha
he had expected, to acknowledge two Sèvres vases sent by the Empero
in return for the poem of the rue de Courcelles. The gift must hav
recalled Marie-Antoinette's injunction to give cake to those withou
bread, and Gautier cannot have failed to notice that the imperial han
that addressed the envelope even now mis-spelt his name.[15] On
October he left Neuilly for the land of *le Roman de la Momie*.

* * *

He sailed in the *Moeris* from Marseilles on Friday, 8 October: leavin
with some apprehension of misfortune, feeling, with his profound
ineradicable, Romantic superstition, that a journey which began on
Friday boded ill. And for once his presentiments were justified: as h
explored the ship, he fell and broke his arm. His Egyptian journey wa
spoiled from the beginning.

'The papers are so indiscreet nowadays that you will certainly rea
there about my accident [so he told Carlotta]. I fell on the stairs between
decks and dislocated my left shoulder and slightly fractured th
humerus. I want to avoid you undue anxiety. M. Broca, a most distin
guished doctor (the good Duchosal should know him), patched me u
very nicely . . . [and my right hand remains] free to write and tell yo
how much I think of you. You see what it is to leave on a Friday

The one occasion I wanted to be a sceptic, you must admit it wasn't a success; they won't catch me at it again. Apart from the accident (which has no painful consequences) my health is excellent: I haven't been seasick. If my writing isn't as formed as usual, it's because I'm writing at sea so that I can put this letter in the post at Messina, where we touch this evening. The three doctors on the ship have decided that I could continue the journey without inconvenience and that it was wiser than returning to Paris alone. . . . If I had been sure of the discretion of the journalists on board, I shouldn't have said a thing and you'd only have seen me cured. . . .'[16]

*   *   *

In Cairo they rode on asses to Shepheard's Hotel, 'a singular hostelry' like a huge dim convent. 'Here I am in Cairo at last,' he wrote dismally to his Princess. 'I have the arrant presumption to count you among the three or four people who are interested in me and may be sad or anxious about my misfortunes. That is why I keep you informed of every stage in this journey which began so ill. . . . I am not in pain; I am only very thwarted by my sling and the forced inertia of my left hand. You don't know, unless you've had experience, how useless the right hand is without her humble sister: the sister who's never mentioned, but does at least half the work like the unknown collaborator of a famous dramatist. . . . But let me not lessen the merit of the right hand, since it serves to remind Your Highness of my profound gratitude and absolute devotion. . . . I am staying at Shepheard's Hotel, Esbekieh Place, Cairo, Egypt, and I need not tell Your Highness what I hope by giving you this very detailed, largely written and perfectly legible address.'[17]

Princess Mathilde answered by return; but there was sad news to give: the news of the death of Sainte-Beuve. He had been among the most intimate, most admired guests at Saint-Gratien, but, always impulsive, she had quarrelled with him, and it was only a little before his death that he had sent her a note of reconciliation:

'Poor Sainte-Beuve died without my being able to see him [she wrote to Gautier]. I went there, but he was so ill I didn't go in; there were a lot of people round him. I had often sent for news of him; he had thanked me and dictated a brief word to me. I have mourned him sincerely, and I remember nothing now but his good friendship, the charm of his mind and conversation. . . .

'I grasp your hand—the good one—remember me to the friends around you and believe in my constant, loyal and devoted friendship.'[18]

.   .   .   .   .

'Princess [answered Gautier],

'Your letter, ornamented with an address, a model of imperial calligraphy, has reached me safely in Cairo and I need not tell Your Highness what joy it has given me.

'I will admit, Princess, that for all the local colour, there are many nostalgic hours when I think of France, of Paris, the homes of those I love, and if my desire were enough to bear me home, I should not be long.

'It was in the middle of an Almehs' dance arranged by the Minister of Finance that I learned of the death of Sainte-Beuve, and I was sorely moved by the news, and by regret that I had not called to see him before I left. See how negligence may become an occasion for remorse! I was touched by the grief Your Highness showed for the loss of his great and charming spirit, by the way in which you forgot his wrongs to remember only his virtues. It is not in vain that everywhere you are known as the good princess. . . . Unfortunately for me, you are set too high for me ever to repay you. I can only offer you barren devotion, sincere and humble friendship.

'The other day I was in my room, rather miserable, finding that time was long as one often does on one's travels, when the door opened and there appeared a charming young man, fresh and rosy, wearing a blue veil like a young Englishwoman, who smiled and called me by name. It was the poet of Saint-Gratien, the charming Primoli in person. This meeting in Cairo has given me the liveliest pleasure. We see one another several times a day and we make excursions together. He will tell you better than I can of our visit to the Virgin's Tree, and our visit to the ruins of Heliopolis which were remarkable for their complete absence. The fortnight that remains before the opening of the isthmus would have been long, but it will seem short in this pleasant company. . . .'[19]

He was depressed by ill-health, he was lonely, the weariness of late middle-age was upon him. And now the death of Sainte-Beuve recalled the golden vanished days of Romanticism: 'Make haste and love each other [so he exhorted Giselle], life is so short! I learned some sad news yesterday: the death of our dear Sainte-Beuve. . . . So there's that bright and lively spirit extinguished, that star of intelligence disappeared for ever. He was fond of me and I certainly returned his affection. Our old guard grows smaller every day and there are not many veterans of *Hernani* now. Happily our emperor Hugo still stands upon his rock; but to-day he is a great captain without an army. . . .'[20]

He sat despondently in Shepheard's Hotel, indulging in his old hypochondria: exercising his 'poor left hand, immobilised for so long',

hand now 'like one of those wooden hands displayed in glovers'
indows'.[21] He visited bazaars and mosques and palaces, and looked for
a quite authentic royal scarab, going back to at least 2000 B.C.', to make
little trinket for Carlotta. 'It would not,' he wrote, 'become the author
f *le Roman de la Momie* to send you, from the feet of the Pyramids, a
ounterfeit scarab, made in London. . . . That's what I'm thinking about
a the city of the old caliphs as I vaguely watch the points of minarets
sing tall in the bright sky, and the fellahs, Arabs, Copts, veiled
omen, naked children, asses, horses and camels led in files. . . .'[22]
nd with the thought of Carlotta's scarab remained the thought of
arlotta: 'My heart,' he wrote, 'is very tender, very vibrant at the least
motion, full of the memory of those I love and the longing to see them
gain. All the time one doesn't spend with one's friends is wasted time:
al presence is everything. . . .'[23] Had the inveterate traveller, after
airty years of travel, finally satisfied his appetite for wandering? 'I hope
he wrote to Princess Mathilde] I shall soon find myself once more in
our Highness' presence, in that wonderful conservatory in the rue de
Courcelles where the temperature is so mild it makes Cairo look like
iberia. I have never felt such a longing to return to France. Until I
:turn, which I shall do as promptly as possible, I kiss (with the most
oluptuous respect) your beautiful imperial hand.'[24]

*　　　*　　　*

And so, as he awaited this great pilgrimage of civilization, when the
rhole boulevard des Italiens seemed to meet in the desert, when Zola
vas present as a reporter and Ibsen reached a turning-point in his
areer, when De Lesseps saw the triumph of a long-negotiated enter-
rise, Théophile Gautier restricted himself to writing downcast letters
nd a few brief chapters on Alexandria and Cairo. It was, happily, in a
ifferent tone, in a letter to Carlotta, that he described the opening:

'Our expedition to the Isthmus of Suez was very picturesque and
ery entertaining. To avoid the long way round by Alexandria and Port
aid, I went from Cairo to Ismailia, and there we camped under canvas
ke Arabs, as the town wasn't big enough to lodge all the guests. I was
odged, with my friends, in tent 3, facing M. de Lesseps' chalet, on the
ank of the sweetwater canal encumbered with *cangs* and *dahabiehs*,
ocal vessels very like the boats on Lake Geneva with their great scissor-
ails. We had a square ante-room and an octagonal *salon*, all in canvas
tretched out on stakes and held up by an ingenious system of rigging.
'here were five of us in it, and we got on as well as could be. We had
ur meals in huge tents at the expense of the Khedive or the Suez Canal
Company. The assault on the table was comic and human voracity

appeared in a quite bestial light. There were three services of dinne
and at the last there was hardly anything but radishes, ham bones an
Chester cheese. We went to meet the Empress on Lake Timsah, at th
place where the maritime canal coming from Port Said, that's to sa
from the Mediterranean, flows into it. We went with a few Frenchme
on one of the company's steamers. When we arrived at the mouth of th
canal, below the Viceroy's chalet, the cannon thundered and the im
perial yacht, *l'Aigle*, made her majestic entrance into the lake. Th
Empress, in white with a blue veil, was standing on deck with D
Lesseps at her side. At the same moment, at the other end of the lak
two big packet-boats of the Messageries, coming from Indo-China, an
a Dutch vessel coming from the Red Sea through the Suez Canal, mad
their appearance. The effect was magic, irresistible, and so fine th
there were tears in everybody's eyes; the Empress, extremely move
had an attack of nerves and withdrew into her cabin where she relieve
her emotions in abundant tears. She soon re-appeared wiping her ey
amid the acclamations of all the boats which (in spite of protocol) ha
closed about her. The Emperor of Austria followed on his ship, the
the Crown Prince of Prussia. It was magnificent. In the evening ther
were illuminations, an Arab fantasia, performances by howling, groar
ing and spinning dervishes, pantomimes, a reception of the sheiks of th
desert installed in picturesque striped and lit-up tents. The celebration
entirely European in Cairo, were entirely Egyptian in Ismailia. It wa
the Viceroy's idea and did credit to his good taste. The Empress di
embarked from her yacht and rode on a dromedary, which she did wit
consummate grace; it isn't easy, considering the animal's extreme
brusque reactions. Next day we embarked on *la Péluse*, the biggest bo
of the Messageries impériales, which is 105 yards long, 24 wide, weigh
2,500 tons and draws $19\frac{1}{2}$ feet. In spite of a few mishaps, next mornin
found us in the roads of Suez, when the sun rose on some fifty vessel
fifteen or twenty of which had been in the Mediterranean the nigh
before. And so this ancient barrier is overcome, and when they have cu
through the Isthmus of Panama, we shall sail in a matter of weel
around the world.'[25]

It is a lively chronicle. Yet it is, perhaps, from the poet of Sain
Gratien, the young and charming Primoli with the blue veil and read
pen, that we have the happiest account of Gautier in Egypt. When th
Empress arrived on *l'Aigle* to open the Canal, and he boarded th
imperial yacht to pay homage, 'what should the august traveller b
reading but *le Roman de la Momie*, which seemed to her the most perfe
of itineraries. "You must have stayed a long while in this country," sh

aid to him, "to have been so impregnated by its atmosphere, and shown
s its people with such exactitude." "I had never been to Egypt, but I
ad seen it!" he answered, with such assurance that the Empress did not
nsist: she knew that she was talking to a visionary and a poet.'[26]

        *   *   *

Two routes were offered to the Khedive's guests on their return to
Europe: they could sail home by way of Marseilles or Brindisi. Gautier
hose to see Italy again. At Naples (had he forgotten the police restric-
ions?) it was raining so persistently that he had barely two hours' lull
n which to visit Pompeii. In Rome he spent a few sunlit days with
Ernest Hébert 'in that charming palace of Art called the Villa Medici'.
Hébert was working on the picture that was to be shown at the *Salon*
of 1870, the picture that Gautier considered his possible masterpiece:
e Matin et le Soir de la Vie. In the garden of the Villa Medici the
director of the Ecole de Rome had a little studio half hidden by laurel-
rees; and in that mild December Gautier watched him at work in the
ure, bold Roman light, followed his painting stroke by stroke 'and little
oy little saw the ideal mingle with reality. . . . In art as in religion, merit
s not enough, there is also need for grace. Hébert has received it.'[27]

This was Gautier's last recorded glimpse of Italy. By Christmas Eve
he was dining with an eager Eugénie Fort in the familiar décor of Neuilly.

35. The Royalty of Literature

THE NEW YEAR began with excitement: on 2 January Eugénie called
on Gautier to discuss their prospective daughter-in-law, Elise Portal.
Gautier met Elise within the week and pronounced her charming. On
11 January he formally asked for her hand for his son, and a few days
later Eugénie recorded happily: 'It's a question of cashmere, velvet
dress and engagement ring,' while Gautier even felt disposed to give a
dinner. 'You know how little all this humbug touches me,' he said,
with a lame attempt at self-defence, 'but we must let them know that
Toto belongs to a family.'

And yet, despite the convention, the old loyalties remained. In February, when *Lucrèce Borgia*, that epitome of Romantic drama, was
revived at the Porte-Saint-Martin, the critic of *le Journal officiel* burst
out with uncompromising praise, and Hugo answered, delightedly, from
his exile: 'How can I describe my emotion? I read you, I seem to see
you. We are young again as we used to be. . . . Your hand has not left

my hand. You are still a great poet and a great friend.'[1] Those who read
the *Officiel* a few days later were again reminded of Gautier's sympathies by *Une Galerie romantique*: 'If one of those strokes of fortune
which hardly ever befall men of letters had suddenly enriched us, we
should have made up a sort of Romantic *salon carré* capable of holding
its own beside the finest old masters.'[2] And his public must have seen
his Romanticism, too, as he discussed the brief returns of Frédérick
Lemaître to the stage,[3] recalled the genius of Mlle Mars and Mme
Dorval, or wrote his impassioned article on the most Romantic of
Romantic composers, Berlioz.[4]

On 24 March his thoughts must certainly have returned to the days
of *Mademoiselle de Maupin*, the days when he and Gérard de Nerval
had lived in the Impasse du Doyenné, when Eugénie had given birth
to 'le petit Fortunio'; on 24 March Théophile Gautier *fils*, now *sous-
préfet* at Pontoise, was married. 'I left alone at ten o'clock for the Mairie
at Passy,' recorded the bridegroom's mother. 'I was the first to arrive.
A moment later came TG. I left my carriage and got into his. He too
was alone and we had half an hour to wait. We went into the wood, and
came back at eleven. I must admit I was anxious. How would the
ceremony go off? Houssaye arrived, then Gourjault, then M. Portal,
Elise, Toto. It all went off perfectly. TG played his part in everything
with his usual amenity. We dined and spent the evening at the Frères
Provençaux.' Two days later came the religious ceremony, and 'nothing,
nothing, can describe my utter joy, my happiness and pride when I took
my son's arm, climbed the steps and walked towards the choir. I sat
down at his right with TG the other side. . . . It was a beautiful
ceremony'.

'Does the thrush I once wrote a poem about still walk in yellow
slippers down the sanded paths, and has he resumed his song?' So
Gautier asked Carlotta. 'I saw one this morning in the garden at
Neuilly. From a distance I took it for a crow or a rook, and the omen
hardly pleased me. And then it began to whistle gaily as if to show me
it wasn't one of those funereal birds, but instead a pleasant messenger
of April.'

*   *   *

For all the pleasant messengers, Théophile Gautier was in many
ways unhappy in these final Imperial days: disappointed in the vocation
he felt he had abandoned, disappointed, too, in the career he had had
to choose. Journalism, he wrote in May, when he spoke of Berlioz, was
'a torment forgotten by Dante and reserved for the Hell of art'. For
every review he contributed to *le Journal officiel*, for every 250 livres
that he received,[5] he felt he was moving further from poetry. And when

May, Dinah Félix, Rachel's sister, was made a sociétaire of the
médie-Française, his comment was eloquent: 'The sociétariat is, for
tors, what the Académie is for men of letters: it is a distinction and a
compense. It is everyone's secret ambition, an ambition that remains
ough aspirations are often deceived.'[6] His own aspirations had been
ceived frequently; there were few critics now whose judgment mat-
red to him, and writing brought him little but despondency: 'I was
ry touched by your praise of *la Nature chez elle* [so he told Carlotta];
wrote it largely at Saint-Jean and a little of your charm and scent
ould linger about the book; no-one has mentioned it. . . . But your
ffrage is enough for me and contents my heart. As for self-esteem,
have not known it for years; I work without great appetite, rather by
ill than by inspiration, distracted in spite of myself, and thinking of a
ture that does not seem roseate, I must admit. The days continue,
ill and monotonous. I shall not say I am bored, you've forbidden me
do so, but, truth to tell, I am not much amused.'[7]

Talking with Maxime du Camp, Gautier recalled the *miserere* of his
istence. He had, he said, only two memories that were truly sweet,
emories of freedom, expansion and release: his memories of Spain in
40 and of Venice ten years later. 'These recollections apart, he found
othing but sadness; even in the hours of folly and passion in which
e claimed to have forced the gates of Mahomet's paradise, he found
oments of bitterness which disturbed his peace. . . . For all his extra-
rdinary strength and the fulness of his desires, he was a dreamer
rayed into the midst of a troubled, an implacable civilization, a civiliza-
on that passed him by, treading him underfoot without even noticing,
ithout his complaining. He felt himself not misunderstood, but abso-
itely outside the world into which chance had thrown him; and so,
ith a sort of fierce modesty, he did not lament. What was the use?
one would have heard him. Sometimes he cried: "Poor Théo" and
e who knew him were not unaware how much grief was concentrated
i the exclamation.'[8]

*　　*　　*

Yet Gautier, the stray, unhappy dreamer, stood now, in 1870, as poet,
critic of art and literature and drama, as novelist and traveller and
eator of ballets, among the royalty of literature. Charles Yriarte found
im

'. . . slow and calm, with an infinite sweetness almost like resignation.
ou feel a perfect balance between the tranquil spirit and the majestic
ody. No agitation troubles him, no emotion rouses him, no fear dis-
irbs him. . . . In this unchangeable sweetness, this conscious benignity,

this absence of pride and fatuity, there is something of ancient strengt
and the invulnerability of marble.

   'As he has aged, the poet has become majestic; the long hair falling t
his shoulders, the classical brow, the features calm and reposed, exemp
from traces of modern agitation, give him the countenance of anothe
age; as you look at him you think of cameo and onyx, of Albert Düre
and the Renaissance, of great eras and great artists, of everythin
foreign to a prosaic century and a generation which resists conceptio
of the ideal.

   'You will find the poet of *Emaux et Camées*, in his entirety, concen
trated in this vague glance which moves but does not rest; he seems t
be sunk in an eternal somnolence, a somnolence betrayed in his eye
which are themselves a poem; his eyes are covered by a transparer
bluish film, and the thick brows which overshadow them add yet mor
to the mystery of his glance.

   'He is a wonderful conversationalist, he holds you in the spell of h
sweet and prodigal words. . . . His conversation cradles you, seduce
you, enchants you, makes you its own, and leads you to the land whe
all things are forgotten, nearly always to the land of the sun, the land d
dream, to the happy banks where you gather the red fruit of th
lotus. . . .

   'It seems to me that the poet already wings above us, and that h
posterity has begun. . . . He will never be popular, for to the multitud
he is unapproachable, and he isolates himself among his shining peer
But his public is artistic Europe in its entirety.'[9]

   And, among his shining peers, one may take a final look at the Gautie
of the Second Empire: he stands, an ageing Olympian, with Napoleo
III, conversing (so Houssaye tells us) on ideas and emotions.[10] It is lat
in March 1870, the scene is Princess Mathilde's winter garden in th
rue de Courcelles. Coppée's brief play, *les Deux Douleurs*, has just bee
performed, and *tout le Paris du tout Paris* is there: princes, ambassador
ministers; ministers of yesterday and ministers of to-morrow. Th
Emperor, we are told, was very gay, and 'talked a little with everyone i
the splendid *salons*—those wonderful conservatories where you believe
in the spring.'[11]

PART FOUR

La Comédie de la Mort

36. A Descent into the Maelstrom

EARLY IN June 1870 Théophile Gautier sat under the massive trees at Saint-Jean. The literary world was paling about him; the companions he had known in the Impasse du Doyenné, the rue de Longchamps, were fading and would fall as inevitably as the chestnut leaves overhead. Bouchardy, whose wild melodramas had been among the pleasures of his Romantic years, had just died before his time;[1] and on 20 June the final spark of Jules de Goncourt was extinguished. Gautier returned to Paris for the funeral.

'Yesterday [he wrote back to Carlotta] was certainly one of the saddest days in my life. The moment I arrived, I snatched some food, put on my black and went to the Goncourts' house at Auteuil. It was a wonderful day which seemed ironic for our mourning. When Edmond caught sight of me he threw himself into my arms and burst into floods of tears, and soon I was weeping with him. It was heartrending. The poor man, completely gone to pieces, looked like a ghost; he had turned quite grey, he who had been dark-haired last time we met. It was most horrible! As the funeral went on, his hair whitened visibly, and when we came out of the cemetery it was quite white! His face was emaciated, his neck, grown suddenly thin, showed dewlaps and tendons like the neck of a man of seventy. The sight so affected me that I was overcome by convulsive and quite uncontrollable sobs. Mass was said in the little church at Auteuil. . . . I was near the catafalque, and on the black velvet hatchment shone a silver G—it was my initial—so that I had the vision of my own burial; besides, the friends who were there for Goncourt will come for me, if any remain when my turn comes. When we left the church, we had to set Edmond's feet one before the other, with our hands, otherwise he would have fallen. From there we went to Montmartre, where Jules was laid in a family vault with three places, beside his mother. The third place will not be empty for long—I consider Edmond as a dead man. He has received the death-blow, as they call it; life will never return to this broken heart. A distant relation took Edmond away, where, I do not know, and we dispersed. I went from the cemetery to *le Journal officiel* and thence to Saint-Gratien, for at home I found a note from the Princess asking me to dine if I'd returned. We talked about Goncourt all the evening, and I came back at one in the morning.'[2]

It was not only the world of letters that was to fade about the ageing
critic of le *Journal officiel*: there was a régime to fall, an era soon to
end.

*   *   *

'I am rusticating at Saint-Gratien [so Gautier told Carlotta on Bastille
Day]. In the morning, after I've drunk my soup, I go and row on the
lake until *déjeuner*, which makes my arm strong and supple and my
breathing easier. After *déjeuner* we smoke and chat and stroll a bit in the
park, then the princess goes into her studio and begins to paint as if
her life depended on it. I go up to my room again and produce some
copy, for my rest is always mixed with a quantity of writing. . . . At six
o'clock the guests from Paris arrive with news from the city, where there
is now considerable agitation. Will there or will there not be war with
Prussia? I know absolutely nothing about it, though Mme Benedetti,
wife of the French ambassador in Berlin, is staying here, and I'm dining
every day with the cousin of Augustus. They are both as silent as
sphinxes. All the same, the princess seems to believe that peace will not
be disturbed. . . . I hope it will all end like the Shakespearean comedy
Much Ado About Nothing. . . .'[3]

Next day, Friday, 15 July 1870, the Franco-Prussian War began.

*   *   *

'This declaration of war seems to have sent everybody mad [Gautier
wrote to Carlotta twelve days later]. There's delirious enthusiasm, universal joy. If necessary, everyone would set off, even the women. People
are marching up and down and yelling the *Marseillaise*. They sing it at
the Opéra and the whole audience rises and repeats the refrain with the
cast. The troops were escorted to the railway stations by the whole
population, who carried their knapsacks, rifles and accoutrements;
they're given money, wine, cigars and brandy, and at every station
from Paris to the frontier they find public-houses put at their disposal—
free, of course—by the towns through which they pass; women and girls
embrace them and toss them flowers. The very mothers, which is more
remarkable, tell their children to go, and put rifles in their hands. The
fund for the wounded and the war receives enormous subscriptions:
100 thousand, 20 thousand, 10 thousand, a thousand francs; 100 francs
is a very ordinary gift. The *Crédit foncier* has offered 500 million and
some other financial establishment has offered the same. People send
quantities of wine and brandy, cigars, mattresses, blankets, medical
supplies, horses, yachts to save the wounded sailors, everything you can
possibly imagine. The other day they smashed the grilles of the courtyard where the volunteers were enlisting, the crowd was so great. The

militia demand to be sent to the front: everyone wants to eat Prussians. The old rancour of 1814 is not dead. So don't believe that people here regret this deplorable conflict. On the contrary, they are enchanted and I have never seen such a bubbling over of happiness; all the medical students are enlisting as male nurses, and soon there will be no one at home but the sick and lame, and even they insist at the boards of appeal that they are fit to campaign. If anyone spoke in favour of peace he would be killed on the spot. A legion of 500 Hanoverians paraded in Paris, headed by a banner, asking to march with us against the King of Prussia and Bismarck; I'm telling this because you can't receive many papers at Morgins and because it's the exact truth. Like you, I have a horror of war, but you must reflect that this one was indispensable, to judge by the thirst for battle it excites even in the mildest. If the Emperor wanted to make peace he could no longer control the fury unleashed to-day. For all the fine speeches on fraternity made by the sages and philosophers, one must believe in racial antipathy. I agree with you: since they absolutely have to massacre each other, let them make haste and come back to reasonable life as soon as possible. As a Frenchman, I want victory, but I could well have done without the war. But we must undergo what we cannot prevent. Who knows what measureless conflagration will devour Europe? Will it be limited to a duel between France and Prussia? I'm very much afraid it may end in a general massacre. . . . To leave Paris in this hour of trouble, uncertainty and fervour, when the fate of the nation depends on a throw of the dice, is impossible. We want to go to Berlin, the Prussians want to come to Paris; I hope they will not come, and I shall not be forced myself to defend the Pont de Neuilly.'[4]

The early fervour, the frenzied singing in the streets soon died away. On 4 August came Wissembourg; on 6 August came Woerth. The sudden turn of events brought anxiety, depression, suspense. Gautier passed his time between a troubled Neuilly, an anxious Quai Voltaire, and a Saint-Gratien whose high imperial walls could no longer shut out the world. There indeed, beneath the great summer cedar of Lebanon, or in the studio where the brushes lay unused, the canvas white, the agony of waiting was most intense: for it was there, with the Emperor's cousin, the best-loved of the Bonapartes, that he saw the Second Empire irretrievably falling:

'I have waited a little to answer you [he wrote to Carlotta, from Saint-Gratien, on 12 August]; I did not want to write while I was still overwhelmed by such disasters, but the good news for which I waited hasn't

come, there isn't any and we live in absolute ignorance of the move-
ments of our own troops and the enemy's. It has to be secret for the sake
of operations, but you could not imagine a more anxious, more exhausting time. One is enervated, unable to think of anything, to work at
anything. Someone comes in; you ask feverishly: "Any news?" And the
answer is invariably: "None." For want of real news, the most absurd
rumours, coming from God knows where, are spreading through the
city and causing inconceivable panic and madness. I should never have
thought such demoralization possible. All political parties are agitating,
hoping to triumph in the disorder, and they're arguing as if the
Prussians were not marching on Paris. I hope they won't reach it and
that this shame will be spared to France. For the rest, the country is
rising to a man, but how can you arm, enregiment and train nearly a
million men in so short a time, and then how can you feed them? What
vast resources it supposes! And then there are the Prussians at home:
the reds, the democrats, the Rochefort and Flourens followers, who,
through hate of the Emperor, would give the country over to Bismarck,
and we have to keep 30 or 40 thousand soldiers in Paris to control these
wild beasts. There perhaps is the greater danger. While these monsters
have their hideous wrangles, the poor soldiers go to be killed at the
front and fall in silent heroism. It seems that the little virtue that
remains to France has taken refuge in the army; it is only there that one
still finds courage, devotion, sacrifice and obedience. They wash away
the mud of politics with their blood. What a wretched epoch! What a
lamentable age! . . . I am rooted here,—any absence would look like
flight,—waiting for events that no-one can foresee. What does the future
hold? At the very moment of writing, perhaps they're fighting and our
destiny's being decided. Defeat would deliver us up to the horrors of
invasion. But I cannot believe that France will not be victorious now
that a setback must have taught her vigilance. Whatever happens, the
clash will be terrible and there will never have been a more fearful
massacre on earth.'[5]

On the broad terrace at Saint-Jean where the only clash was the distant clash of meeting rivers, Carlotta read his letters, read her papers,
and grew anxious:

'Don't grow alarmed prematurely [he reassured her, with a lame
attempt at optimism]. No doubt things are very bad and the situation is
serious, but nothing is desperate yet. The campaign has hardly begun.
. . . A great victory can make amends for the early failures. Under new
leaders, our heroic soldiers, no longer exposed in small numbers to

countless masses, may take their revenge and throw the enemy back beyond the Rhine. The struggle they prepare so silently will be terrible, a veritable battle of giants. Everyone has left: there are no more men at home. There are only children and aged invalids. Even if the first army were retreating, one doesn't walk over two million Frenchmen with rifles, and Paris will not suffer the dishonour of seeing the Prussians again. They have sworn to spend the last man and the last écu rather than accept invasion, and that vow will be kept. Cold rage and silent energy have followed the bravado and hysteria of the first days. They are doing now what they should have done before: let us hope it will not be too late. We must, then, wait in patience for the result of the supreme struggle. If it can be delayed for several days, our chances will increase and the enemy's will diminish. Regiments of militia are leaving every moment and, what is better, old soldiers recalled to the colours. All the blood that France possesses she will give; it will not flow in vain. That is why I remain. And then I belong to the household of the Emperor, and to leave at the moment when wretches and madmen are yelling for his fall, would be a shabby deed. You would not love me if I were capable of doing it. . . . But I am none the less grateful for your offer and for the warmth of heart that inspires it. If all were lost, the Emperor driven out, the Republic proclaimed, only then (if I were not crushed, with my family, beneath it) would I try to emerge from beneath the pile of ruins, and then I should profit from your hospitality until I could make my life again. But our eagle will end by plucking this miserable Prussian eagle that looks like a vulture! How horrible is war![6]'

It was the Prussian vulture that plucked the eagle of France. In Paris the tension grew enervating.

'The theatres, courageous in their fashion, continue to give performances,' wrote Gautier late in August. 'We cannot say that they have their usual number of spectators, yet they are not utterly deserted. After the febrile anxieties of the day, after you have devoured, to the last edition, every broadsheet that appears, looked at the bulletins, done your amateur strategy, listened in turn and sometimes simultaneously to pessimists and optimists, tried to read or work, you feel a millwheel spinning in your head. And then, if you are too young or too old, too myopic or too weak to serve your country, you feel a certain repose in allowing your thoughts a momentary rest, in surrendering without resistance to the fantasy that takes you for an hour far from painful reality. . . . You must not repent this innocent distraction. At moments of greatest grief, the works of the spirit bring calm and consolation, and give the soul the pasture that it needs.'[7]

The only distractions in Paris were but momentary; the war news grew increasingly serious, Eugénie recorded that at Neuilly they wanted to settle in the rue de Beaune. On 22 August Edmond de Goncourt called on Gautier, and together they mourned for the little house in the rue de Longchamps where Gautier had hoped to spend his undisturbed old age.[8] On the boulevards everyone looked enquiringly at the passer-by, listened intently to snatches of speech, uneasy, anxious, afraid Gautier decided to take Estelle to Switzerland.

And it was there, in Switzerland, where he was to leave her with Carlotta, that he learned the news by telegram: the Emperor had surrendered to Bismarck at Sedan.

*   *   *

'I am numb, overwhelmed [he wrote to his secretary, Adolphe Bazin, from Montreux on 5 September]. At my age it is terrible indeed to see France invaded, Paris perhaps bombarded, my life, so laboriously built up, instantaneously destroyed.

'Poor Emperor! What a lamentable end to a dazzling dream! And my dear Princess! What dreadful sorrow! What inconsolable grief! There it is, destroyed for ever, the Abbey of Thélème of Saint-Gratien! Shut like a tomb, the gracious Decameron where so many sparkling conversations were held! Where is she now, the good and beautiful creature, so beloved and so understanding? . . .

'I confess that I believe physically but not spiritually in what has happened. That will never enter my head. The clearest thing is that even if we are thrifty, we've hardly enough to live on for a month. . . . But the curtain is down on the theatre. When will he appear, the real polichinelle, *il vero Pulcinella*? No-one knows.'[9]

'There is no more Saint-Gratien for me, no more calm, no more rest [wrote Princess Mathilde from Mons on 8 September]; a black crêpe covers everything, present and future. The agony of August has ended in the death of all I loved, of all that charmed my life.

'I am on foreign soil, still trembling to hear of fresh disasters; every day adds another grief to my grief. You know me well enough, I am sure, to know that I do not regret the position, that I only regret what touches my very heart: my country and my dear friends. None of my friends has failed me, and my heart is more than moved. My sorrow is extreme. I shall wait here. I am near Paris, in a peaceful country, but sad unto death. Everything is black, silent and desolate. You go on living, that's all, with death in your heart and tears in your eyes. . . .

'I congratulate myself that I begged you to go away. It is one care less for me to know you are in a safe place that you love.'[10]

But Gautier, ailing and prematurely old, had already left for France. He would not evade responsibility; an irresistible patriotism drew him home. In the first days of September he had said good-bye to Estelle and Carlotta on the quayside at Chillon.

37. Ugolino's Tower

'Paris, 9 September 1870.

'My dear Estelle,

'. . . I arrived this morning with a train of militia; we were afraid the train might be intercepted at any moment, but we passed through without any trouble. At Geneva station, a few minutes before we left, Rosine arrived out of breath with a telegram from London. I opened it and read this enigmatic message: "Am in London with Elise since yesterday Meley Hotel. Théophile Gautier *fils*." I couldn't explain the journey to myself at such a moment and I inferred after a minute's reflection that poor Toto must be destitute. . . . Paris is very strange just now. All along the route there are soldiers, front-line troops, militia and others, sleeping in tents and cooking in the open air. It is pouring torrents, which will delay the Prussians a little; they will be in Paris at the beginning of next week. I have still been unable to find out if the good Princess was arrested or not. I shall go to the rue de Courcelles to enquire myself. . . . They're demolishing the houses and felling the trees in the outer zone and the ruins look lugubrious in the rain. . . . We haven't yet left Neuilly where I found the aunts better and more settled. Have no worries about our fate. We have enough money to live on for at least two months even if they did not print a single line of copy. The affair of the *Officiel* may perhaps be arranged. . . .'

But to Edmond de Goncourt Gautier spoke differently. He said the revolution would be his own end. And then, recalling the fate of the *Poésies* of 1830, the financial disaster of 1848, he added: 'I am a victim of revolutions. And now I cannot begin to shape my life again.'[1]

On 9 September Eugénie called at Neuilly; Gautier urged her to live with him and his sisters in rue de Beaune. But the thought of the coming siege filled her with understandable panic. 'I should like to be with him, but rue de Beaune! That so terrified me that I instantly said no.' Gautier pointed out that unless she came he could give her no money. She had 150 francs: enough, she calculated, for two months; and she went to Versailles. Turgan, blunt as always, told Gautier to put his pictures in storage: the drawings of Sophocles, Aeschylus and Euripides that Ingres had given him, the *Lady Macbeth* that came from Delacroix, Appert's great bouquet of peonies and poppies that might have burst from their marble vase at some Veronese banquet.[2] The day that Haro's removal cart rumbled down rue de Longchamps, to take away the *décor* in which he had dreamed his life and lived his dreams, he understood even more surely that his life would topple over, that he himself would stay beneath the wreckage. He followed the cart as if it had been a hearse, his sisters, unkempt, uncouth, on either side, and Eponine, faithful and understanding, in his arms.

*   *   *

'Dear Princess,

'I was moved to tears by your kind letter. To think that in such a disaster you could remember your most humble servant, your obscure friend, since you are willing to give me the title which will always be the greatest of my glories: I am moved to the most secret depths of my soul. I had gone to Montreux, to take Estelle to her aunt Carlotta, who is spending the summer by the lake. And there a telegram of twenty words told me the whole catastrophe of Sedan. At first I couldn't believe it and thought it a Prussian invention. I rushed to Geneva, where the terrible truth was confirmed. There I read in a paper that you were arrested and held a prisoner in the Hôtel d'Angleterre at Dieppe, and I left immediately for Paris, in the hope of reaching you, of being in some way useful to you or showing you, at least, that there was someone who belonged to you. I did not believe a word, as you can imagine, of the stupid story of the thirty-six cases and the fifty-one millions. At the rue de Courcelles they told me Your Highness was safe and well. . . . Although I cannot contribute anything to the defence, I shall share the danger with the others. Children should not abandon their mother when she is dying, on the pretext that the air is unhealthy.

'Your letter was forwarded from Switzerland with a word from Estelle, after many détours, and I do not know if my answer will reach you; nearly all the railways are cut. In two or three days they will all be cut, and we shall be isolated from all the world. For how long? Only God can tell! The city is seething like a kicked anthill. . . . The life we lead is terrible. . . . You read and re-read the papers twenty times: they're full of absurdities, lies and tirades. You ask everyone you see:

Is there any news?" and they answer: "None." "The Prussians are
t Noisy or Joinville." "Someone has seen four uhlans." And through
ll this tumult one can feel no sense of direction. One is silently dragged
o the bottom of the gulf by the vortex of fate. Have you read a story by
.dgar Poe, *A Descent into the Maelstrom*? It gives exactly the impression
veryone feels today. Round and round you slip on the walls of the vast
unnel of the abyss, describing, like the bark engulfed, ever-narrowing
ircles until you reach the black hole at the bottom, the hole you look
t with unspeakable horror. Sometimes a cross-current throws you to
ne side like wreckage from the ship. That is the only hope that we can
eep. If the Prussians were defeated, the battle would still not be won.

'The necessities of defence have driven us from Neuilly. They have
rdered us to "evacuate the premises" as soon as possible. The little
ouse where you deigned to visit your poor lame poet will probably soon
e only a heap of cinders, and I have taken refuge in Paris with my two
isters at 12, rue de Beaune, where we have settled ourselves as well as
e can. But I am ashamed to speak of my little personal ruin in the
resence of a misfortune like your own! If I do so, it is because I know
he interest Your Highness deigns to feel for me. That I should see you
o longer, I who had formed so sweet a habit of living near you, almost
t your feet! I whom you allowed to kiss your beautiful imperial hands!
ince your radiant smile no longer shines upon me, the sun seems black.
nd as soon as I can leave this circle of Hell, the first visit you will
eceive will be mine.

'Your Highness's most devoted servant,
'THÉOPHILE GAUTIER.'[3]

*   *   *

It was not Princess Mathilde of whom he dreamed, most often, in the
iege. It was the symbol of his Romantic past, the talisman for his
uture: it was the ideal figure of Giselle. Lovable, unattainable as Spirite
ad seemed to Guy de Malivert, the vision of Giselle seemed to Gautier
ow. In these stricken days, when even Eugénie was not there to sem-
athize, his only escape, an unbearable and enchanted escape from the
iege, was the unfading mirage of Saint-Jean. Often and often he wrote
o Giselle; somehow it seemed like conversation. His privations were
ss if he could confide them; and even as he spoke of the rigours of the
iege, he seemed to see her looking up from her endless embroidery
nd patiently, affectionately, consoling him:

'Paris, 4th letter by balloon. 31 October 1870.
'I write to you none too hopeful that my letter will reach you. The
veather is appalling, very much against the departure of balloons:

furious wind, and unceasing rain. All the same I shall try to write, an
perhaps this scrap of paper will get through to you. The situation is a
grievous as it can be. We heard tonight of the surrender of Metz whic
had been left unaided. Bazaine is a prisoner with sixty thousand men
and the Prussian army he held in check before Metz is now free an
will fall on us again. We captured Le Bourget the day before yesterday
the enemy recaptured it this morning. . . . I don't think we shall b
freed between now and 4 November. My health, and my sisters' health
is good, despite the fantastic food in which we indulge. We are eatin
horse, donkey, macaroni without butter or cheese; we shall soon b
down to rats and mice. The horse is excellent, but the donkey is a rea
delicacy. There is nothing less true than the phrase: "Tough as a
donkey." The plan seems to be to get us through famine, for there ha
been no serious attack. The Prussians do not even answer the fire fror
our forts, and it's all limited to skirmishes in the suburbs with peopl
going in search of potatoes. I am writing some articles called *Voyage*
dans Paris for the *Officiel*; they are having a great success and they wi
make a strange enough book after the siege. There is nothing mor
melancholy than Paris at this moment. The cafés shut at half past ten
the shops don't even open during the day. We're rationed for gas as w
are for meat. We only light one jet in four and the sight of these blac
streets, where a rare passer-by brushes against the walls and we do no
hear the sound of a single carriage, is really not calculated to enliven us
But either we bury ourselves beneath the ruins of Paris or we die o
hunger if we cannot fight our way out. The resolution is very firmly
made.'[4]

Gradually, as the Siege wore on, he counted the days, dated his letter
by a new revolutionary calendar. He attempted, still, to be gay; but th
attempt was weaker. The illusion of conversation with Giselle ha
vanished; his letters might be sent, perhaps they might even reach her
but her answers (if she answered) did not come.

'Letter No. 7 (74th day of siege, 30 November 1870
'I am writing to you to the sound of a terrible cannonade. They ar
making a sortie with a great many soldiers and artillery. The match i
being decided at this moment and my thoughts naturally go toward
you and my poor little Estelle, whom I haven't seen for so long. I hop
you are all very well over there, and dear Ernestine, too. I am well, an
indeed much better than before the siege. To say we are living pros
perously would be a lie: this morning I regaled myself with a rat *pât*
which wasn't bad at all. You will understand the sadness of our life

The rest of the world no longer exists for us. For nearly three months,
now, we have been without news of those we love. It was time to make a
violent effort to get out of such a situation; it is being made. Will it
succeed? God grant it will! But they are going about it with desperate
resolution and heroic fury. Everyone feels that he must conquer or
perish. Ah! my poor Carlotta, it is a most lamentable year, the year
1870. What events, what catastrophes! And that without all the solace,
all the sweetness of your friendship! I cannot now forget all these
sinister things at the sight of you, cannot even have the resource of
seeing your dear writing. I know you are thinking of me in that haven of
Saint-Jean where I have spent so many charming hours; but, though
you know correspondence is impossible, you feel utterly sad and con-
jure up a thousand dreams. You imagine your dear ones ill, unhappy,
or, what would be worse, forgetful. A balloon is leaving tonight: will it
be more fortunate than the earlier ones that were taken by the Prussians,
and carried two of my letters which you therefore can't have received?
I am writing to you in all haste. The news of the expedition is good; the
affair is going well and perhaps the victory that has so long deserted us
will return! . . . Be well assured that if I do not come and see you, it is
the fault of 300,000 Prussians: it would not take less than that to stop me
from bringing you my good wishes on your saint's day.'[5]

The Feast of St Charles had passed, and Christmas would soon come:
the Christmas he loved to spend among her gold and silver Christmas
trees, in the resplendent Garden of the Hesperides that she created.
And soon it would be New Year's Day: only celebrated by the cannonade: 'Dear darling,' he wrote to Estelle, more sadly, in December:
'Don't forget your poor father, shut up in Ugolino's tower with two
million starving people.'[6]

*   *   *

Meanwhile the tower was besieged, the Siege went on. In Gautier's
Tableaux de Siège it has been described painfully, sharply, and for all
time. Over the book hangs a pall of claustrophobia: a heavy feeling of
suffocation which no desperate walks within the walls, no voyages along
the Seine, no train journeys round the city borders, no dismal pacing
about the ramparts can dispel. In the Théâtre-Français (where, by
some strange irony, they are playing *le Médecin malgré lui*), the foyer
is filled with hospital beds; and Basile, coming off stage during *le
Mariage de Figaro*, passes a sister of charity going her rounds. The very
animals of Paris seem to recognize that the hands which stroke them are
no longer the hands of friends, but the hands of the hungry, and the
sparrows are trapped for food or fly to safer climates. And the poet

crosses a nightmare Bois de Boulogne, a landscape of felled trees as
desolate as the cemetery at Scutari, to catch a momentary glimpse of the
little house at Neuilly, *la maison abandonnée*: a volume of Alfred de
Musset still lies open upon the mantelpiece, and a scent-bottle, loosing
its pale aroma, seems like the perfume of some evaporating age.

Tableaux de Siège. The visual pictures remain, and yet perhaps the
poet is more evident than the artist: a poet weary, indignant, roused,
determined, a Gautier who keeps his lifelong concern with art but has,
it seems, more deeply than before, understood the other values in life
as well.

Gautier had always considered politics as a mere change in outward
form. 'After all,' he had written, thirty years ago, 'nothing remains of
an age but its literature and its arts; political discussions and even the
gravest events are all swept into oblivion, but a fine verse never dies, a
lovely statue outlives a dynasty and a religion.'[7] To the apostle of Art
for Art's Sake, the poet of *l'Art*, politics had always been transient, art
(and he took the word in its widest sense) was permanent and remained
significant. Politics had played a small part in his writing; the friend of
the Duc d'Orléans had become the devoted friend of Princess Mathilde.
It was not that Gautier lacked interest in politics. It was only that his
political opinions were as catholic as his critical judgments: 'You can
have your personal rule and principle,' he remarked to Maxime du
Camp, 'but it is stupid to want to impose them on other people.'
Théodore de Banville records more precisely: 'To tell the truth, his
ideal was self-government. The only existence which seemed desirable
to him was that of a gentleman living in the forests and prairies of some
vast country, far from civilization, riding his horse across the great
plains, armed with a carbine and good revolvers, protecting himself and
if need be protecting others, in the manner of Theseus and Hercules. . . .'[9]

It was a poetic conception, no doubt, but Gautier's conception of
politics remained that of a poet and artist until 1870. Then the Franco-
Prussian War moved him to distress and fury. The longing for foreign
countries, for distant time and place, which he had so often felt, so often
described, was now abruptly forgotten; he recognized himself as a
Frenchman and, more, as a Frenchman of 1870. And his emotions,
patriotic, it may be, rather than political, touched a new depth in him,
gave a new direction to his journalism, informed the most moving and
some of the most vivid, best written of his articles: the articles reprinted
in *Tableaux de Siège*.

*   *   *

The year 1871 began with the hundred and fifth day of siege and the russian bombardment of Paris. Sentries were posted at the craters to keep away the public, and street urchins picked up shell splinters 'and sold them to the *bourgeois* from one to five francs apiece'. Gautier was recovering slowly from illness: to Estelle he described it as a heavy cold; but writing to an official at the end of the month about his bread and meat cards, he admitted that he had suffered from pneumonia, that it was dangerous for him to leave the rue de Beaune. In his fifth-floor labourer's garret, barely furnished, where he was sometimes forced to live on a sparrow killed by chance on the rooftops,[10] where he slept in his Russian *pelisse* to save himself from cold[11] (it was the fur *pelisse* in which, twelve years ago, he had returned so gladly from St Petersburg to enchant *la Présidente* in the rue Frochot): in this fifth-floor garret in the rue de Beaune Théodore de Banville found him, ill and frail, whiling away the Siege with *la Legénde des Siècles*. And here it was that Edmond de Goncourt found him, one February Sunday, a fortnight after the Armistice, with his famished cats and his two unkempt, ageing sisters. He sat in a haze of cigar smoke, in a Venetian cap, like a doge in distress, like some melancholy Marino Faliero, relieving his emotions in Rabelaisian conversation.[12]

Dear child [wrote Gautier that same day to Estelle],

'I was at the *Officiel* on 7 February, very depressed, as for five months I hadn't received any news from those I love, not knowing if my family were alive or dead, when someone brought me a telegram. You know what effect a telegram has upon me in ordinary times; this one nearly made me ill. My hands shook as I opened it. A quick glance reassured me. All was well, and I savoured every word, read it twenty times over. . . . Two hours later they brought me two letters, one from you enclosing one from Ernestine, another from Carlotta. What joy! What felicity! I was no longer used to such happiness! One thing intrigued me. It was the address *quai du Mont-blanc No. 3*, Carlotta's letter explained it. She has acted wisely, and though she must regret Saint-Jean the sacrifice had to be made in the disastrous circumstances in which we find ourselves. . . . Anyway, let's hope I shall soon be able to come and kiss you in Geneva, but the journey is still very difficult, very encumbered with annoying obstacles and formalities; and the times are very hard for a convalescent who has suffered two months of utter famine as part of his cure. . . . Food is beginning to appear again but everything is horribly dear. A leg of mutton is five francs a pound and everything's going up, all the horses have been eaten. There are no more carriages in the city, or rather there are only carriages but no animals to draw them. You have to lug your own case to the station. It

isn't convenient but all these inconveniences wouldn't stop an intrepid
traveller like me particularly when you, Carlotta and Ernestine stood
at the end of the road.'[13]

Carlotta! The vision of Giselle was real again. The conversation
might be renewed; and heartworn, careworn, he poured out his feelings.

'After five months in a dungeon they half open our prison door; they
lift the lid off our coffin and we can at last renew our relations with th
living world. Telegrams are beginning to arrive with one or two months
delay. . . . How joyfully I recognized the little blue monogram announc
ing a missive from Geneva I need not say: you can well imagine it. It'
no good knowing that reply is impossible, you grow sad at writing
letters which seem to be lost in space and you end up by believing tha
people forget you; it isn't the famine or the rain of shells that has been
most painful in Paris, it has been this sequestration, this horrible isola
tion that kept you apart from your friendships and family affections
from all that touched your heart, that left you ignorant of what wa
happening a mile beyond the city. We were absolutely cut off from th
world, not knowing what they did in the provinces, whether or not they
were coming to our aid, abandoned by the universe, deprived of al
spiritual consolation, reduced to the most fearful extremities. All tha
was nothing beside this anguish, this waiting ever deceived. A pigeon
came back with half its feathers gone. Still no letter! One no longe
dared to say: It will come next time. On your saint's day, at Christmas
on New Year's Day, at the happy times when I used to go and see you
I felt dull with melancholy, exhausted with grief. I yearned for tha
Saint-Jean which, alas, you no longer inhabit! that Saint-Jean which
framed your beloved image so well in my memory. How I have thirsted
since the armistice to leave Paris and see you again, to live a norma
life for a little while by your side!

'From the day when I bade you farewell on the Montreux boat, my
existence has only been a long nightmare, a reversal of reality, a serie
of catastrophes so wildly impossible that my soul, despite the evidence
still refuses to believe them.'[14]

38. The Ruins of Sodom

N 18 FEBRUARY Flaubert wrote to Princess Mathilde: Edmond de
ncourt had sent him good news of the rue de Beaune. Edmond de
ncourt must have glossed reality. Gautier was so low in health that
e sight of normal food at Maurice Dreyfous' dinner had reduced him
tears.

'I have been very tired by this illness [he told Carlotta]: the con-
escence was longer than it would have been in any other circum-
nces. But it is not easy to recover during a siege the last weeks of
ich have recalled the raft of the *Medusa* of famishing memory. An
nce of horse a day and 200 grams of bread which looked like turf-dust
e not a diet to restore your strength. We held on beyond the limits of
ssibility and many people died of hunger under the less alarming
le of anaemia. As for myself, I don't know if I should have held out
other fortnight. The moment was approaching when one would have
d to toss for who should be eaten. We were so concerned about
ding some or other broken meat, were it a dead rat, that we paid no
tention to the shells. We had come down to cutting old hides into
rips, soaking them in water and making them into forcemeat-balls
hich passed for a delicacy. Old cabbage leaves were being sold for
 sous each; we bore it all in the hope that the provinces would come
our aid. Paris can say like François I: "All is lost save honour."
owever crushed we may be, there is no shame in being French. . . .'[1]

There was no shame, but there was agony. Gautier had joked with
reyfous about the Prussians' arrival in Paris: had declared that he
ould greet them with his diploma as Member of the Imperial Academy
Arts of Russia. It conferred on him, so he said, the rank of Russian
neral, and the Prussians would present arms.[2] But on 1 March, when
e heavy-helmeted invaders entered Paris, Dreyfous had walked with
autier through the Tuileries gardens, as far as the place de la Concorde,
here a few French cavalry were waiting in case of demonstration.
autier, with his extreme short sight, mistook them for Prussians.
ad Dreyfous not supported him, he would have fallen.

'I am recovering slowly [he told Estelle], though I had a slight relapse
hich set back my convalescence. I'm still coughing a great deal and

R

I'm not very strong. Still I think that a few days hence I'll be in a sta
to take the train to Geneva, to come and kiss you after so long a
absence, to hold you to my heart. How many terrible things have hap
pened since the day I left you on the quayside at Chillon! It seems
me that ten years have passed. I've emerged all bruised from the rubb
of events and I'm trying to piece the fragments of my broken li
together. It isn't amusing, towards the end of one's career, after so muc
work and trouble—but it was written, as the Mussulman fatalists sa
They're gradually taking the furniture back to the little house
Neuilly. . . .'³

Then fate again intervened. On 18 March, incensed by the capitula
tion of Thiers' government, the Commune seized power in Paris, an
the national troops were forced to begin a second and more bitter sieg
of the city. The day after Gautier returned to the rue de Longchamp
he was forced to move. It was from Versailles that he wrote at the en
of March to his daughter:

'Man proposes and the revolution disposes and that is why the tru
packed for Geneva took the road to Versailles. . . . You have seen in th
papers the details of this inexplicable insurrection: it would have bee
so easy to stop it at the beginning and they gave it time to develop, g
organized, and overwhelm the city without a struggle. The Assembl
Nationale wastes its time in vague discussions instead of makir
energetic resolutions and gives no support to the sane part of Par
which is terrorized by a few ruffians. . . . What will become of us n
one knows. . . . If this goes on for a month we shall all die of hunger. .
Five months of siege, misery and famine were enough as it was. Stran
to say I am feeling better, and despite all these catastrophes I a
gradually coming back to life: this life which I very nearly quitted on
and for all. . . .'⁴

While Lili stubbornly lived in the cellar in the rue de Longchamp
Gautier and Zoé tried to settle with Eugénie at Versailles, at 3, avenu
de Saint Cloud; but they could not rest:

'Here we are engaged in civil war [wrote Gautier to his daughter c
6 April] and we are going to lay siege to Paris. . . . In the meanwhile li
could not be more intolerable. All day long you are on the alert, listenir
to the cannon, the shooting nearer or farther away, discussing the occa
sional news that arrives from Paris and crosses the lines. You snatch t
papers from the vendors' hands, and walk up and down in front of t

Hôtel des Réservoirs and the Assemblée Nationale to watch for the coming and going of deputies to pick up some odd scraps of information. Nothing is more enervating. The posts to Paris and the suburbs are no longer running, and we know nothing of the destiny of friends who could not escape or didn't believe such disorders were possible. . . . They've been fighting at Courbevoie and the Pont de Neuilly. . . . Our house was untouched. We were all three of us at Versailles and Lili, who'd walked from Neuilly, had crossed the bridge an hour before-hand with no idea that in a few minutes it would become a battlefield. We are regretting the time of the siege when at least there was hope. . . . Such, my poor darling, is the life your poor father leads so far away from you. I'm always held back as I'm about to leave and I'm bursting with spleen and rage. Yet I hope that one of these days I shall come to occupy the little room at 40 francs a month that you've found for me, and spend three or four weeks with you. I need it after the hardships I have suffered. You asked me in your last letter what illness I'd had. . . . It was severe pneumonia, complicated by famine, and I nearly died of it without noticing, I was so weak. But I am better now. . . .'[5]

As spring advanced to summer, the fratricidal warfare grew more intense. Lili was trapped in her cellar: indeed, the whole population of Neuilly was living underground. All communications with Neuilly and Paris were severed, and in Paris, heard Gautier, there reigned a Communard terror to be compared with the Terror of 1793. Princess Mathilde, in the peace of Brussels, heard of his tribulations and asked him to come to her;[6] but he remained at Versailles with Eugénie and Zoé. 'All the people I love are scattered in the four corners of the world,' he wrote to Régina Lhomme. 'Some are in Brussels, some in Geneva, Paris, Nice (since you are there, you who are so dear to my heart, so truly understanding). As you say so rightly, at our time of life —or rather, mine, for you dear Régina are always young and beautiful— we need a peaceful existence among old friendships and young affections, in a world of ease and well-being that we have well deserved after so many years of work and troubles. We have a right to a fine autumn and a splendid sunset, and it is annoying to find oneself in the midst of a tempest, in the rain, hail and thunder, without a hope of seeing the fine weather again, for the clouds are piling up on the horizon, darker and darker. And yet the other day at Versailles there was a double rainbow, which signifies, according to the Bible, that there will be no more Flood. Let us accept the omen. . . .'[7]

*   *   *

Yet the double rainbow that hung above the avenue de Saint-Cloud

brought little hope to him. One day, towards the end of April, as the
crossed the great courtyard at the Palace of Versailles, Anatole Franc
and Fernand Calmettes saw a pathetic figure standing by the statue o
le Roi Soleil: 'With his stained and dusty coat, his weary countenanc
and his absent gaze, he seemed like the wreck of a human being.' Th
cannon thundered in the distance in the direction of Mont Valérien
and Gautier stared towards the horizon, to Paris. With a few words c
veneration Anatole France drew him from his dream. Gautier graspe
the hands held out to him; then, gazing still towards Paris, he sai
simply: 'It is the stupidity of the *bourgeois*.' They had the impressio
that he felt less wretched if he could blame the chimerical enemy o
his generation, the Philistines of his age.[8]

*   *   *

'One would like to write something pleasant and reassuring [he wrot
now, to Carlotta], and the days pass without tomorrow realizing th
hope of today. So one has to take up one's pen all the same. I canno
even return to Paris, where I am condemned to death as a corresponden
of the Government paper, nor to Neuilly, where poor Lili had th
unfortunate idea of returning in a moment of deceptive calm. She i
living there in the cellar, under a perpetual rain of shells, and she stil
finds means, by soldiers, of sending us letters to prove that at least sh
is not dead; the last was on the 20th. You can easily imagine the fearfu
anxiety in which we live. It is impossible to get help to her and extricat
her; so we have to wait. In a few days it will be over, so they say, but i
is very long, especially when someone you love is in the midst of th
fire. . . . The cashier of the *Officiel*, driven out of his country house a
Meudon by the bombs and grape-shot, has taken refuge with us wit
his wife, cousin and child. Besides we have to put up two soldiers o
the Garde Républicaine. The whole lot of them sleep on the floor, o
bits of carpet and sofas; for there are only two mattresses, the greate
part of the furniture having been hidden no one knows where becaus
of the Prussians. It is the most curious Noah's Ark. We should laugh a
it if we were all together, but at heart we are dreadfully troubled; per
haps we shall only find a pile of rubble in place of our house. What doe
it matter provided that poor Lili, so gentle and so good, comes out o
it safe and sound! . . . But it cannot go on like this; the end is coming
The clash will be terrible, for the obstinacy is equal on both sides an
no one will give in. What a calamity for our poor Paris, besieged by th
Prussians, besieged by the French with perhaps more fervour! Th
claw of the devil is verily upon France. There is something diabolica
about it all.'[9]

.   .   .   .   .

Princess Mathilde had urged him, in vain, to come to Brussels; Carlotta suggested he lectured in Switzerland. Ailing and distraught, he refused her suggestion.

'We were besieged, and here we are besieging [he wrote to her on 5 May]. And perhaps it is sadder, for we're firing on our own city. Tonight there was a terrible attack and we still don't know the result. The gunfire has been unceasing. Lili is still in her cellar; it's impossible to cross the Seine, the Armistice would only allow us to return to Paris; we must wait another few days, we're always waiting! The great attack will soon be made; perhaps it is being made at this moment. But, for God's sake, let it finish one way or another, such a life is intolerable! We are beginning to settle down in our disaster and adopt the habits of *émigrés* of the first revolution. . . . Your lecture plan would be quite nice for me, but I couldn't speak in public, I have no voice left and I grow hoarse after three or four sentences; no doubt that will pass with the warm weather. . . .'[10]

With the slow coming of summer it seemed indeed as if the protracted nightmare would end. On 10 May the Treaty of Frankfurt was signed; the Franco-Prussian War was over. On 17 May there came a visitor from the outside world: Claudius Popelin, the enameller, arrived from Brussels, bringing good news of Toto, Elise and their children, now in Belgium; and bearing news, too, of the exiled Princess. It seemed now that the two worlds would meet, that the end of hostilities was approaching. And 'really mankind is mad', wrote Lili to Zoé. 'How could it create such havoc in such a lovely countryside? The roses are more beautiful than ever, the spring is so fine, it isn't much fun to have to stay in a cellar like a bottle of vintage wine. . . . Take as much care of yourselves as possible, and don't worry about me, I'm guarding myself like a precious stone for you. . . .'[11]

'The entry into Paris cannot be delayed,' wrote Gautier next day to Estelle, 'and in two or three days we'll be able to go and rescue poor Lili from her cellar and see what remains of our house at Neuilly. There was a fire (started by a shell), but Lili bravely put it out with water from the reservoir, otherwise everything would have been burned. . . . The kitchen and dining-room have been pock-marked by bullets. There's no damage in your room or mine. Just a few bullets in the studio ceiling. . . . They've pulled down the Vendôme Column, razed and pillaged Thiers' house, they're going to take a hammer to the Sainte Chapelle (monumental fanaticism) and violate the Emperor's tomb, they're going to bury his august remains at Clamart in the cemetery of the tortured beside the carcass of Troppmann. . . . The Savages, tattooed with red and wearing rings in their noses, are dancing the scalp dance on the smoking ruins of Society. . . . I am going to seek some peaceful corner of the earth where I can earn my daily bread and that of my family among rational beings.'[12]

He was weak with worry, ill with privation; and Eugénie confided in her diary the sadness of life at Versailles. On 23 May the Treaty of Frankfurt was ratified. Early next morning Gautier, Eugénie and Zoé set off for Neuilly, where they found Lili well 'and the house still habitable'. They returned home that night to hear that Paris was burning.

It was in this nightmare, at Versailles, which more than any other place must have recalled the radiant greatness and the fall of France, that the *poète mathildien* remembered the birthday of his princess and wrote her his yearly greeting:

'Princess,

'When you receive this letter it will be 27 May, your birthday. I have not forgotten this sacred day, this happy anniversary we used to celebrate with such joy and love in the celestial paradise you created round you. From that paradise we were driven without eating any apple, without any disobedience to the divinity. She herself is banished from the enchanting place that she filled with happiness, with life and light.'[13]

> *Paris brûle, la flamme à l'horizon s'élève;*
> *Cependant mai revient, mai rose et parfumé,*
> *Ramenant avec lui l'anniversaire aimé,*
> *Date chère où revit incessament mon rêve.*
>
> *Le sang coule! . . . aux bourgeons monte la jeune sève*
> *Et l'azur luit au ciel par la poudre enfumé;*
> *Les oiseaux ont repris leur chant accoutumé,*
> *Comme si le canon ne tonnait pas sans trêve.*
>
> *Et moi je pense à vous à travers ma douleur;*
> *Saint-Gratien m'apparaît aux bosquets de Versailles:*
> *Du souvenir sacré rien ne distrait mon coeur.*
>
> *Mais mon humble jardin, dont croulent les murailles,*
> *N'a rien à vous offrir, tout criblé de mitrailles,*
> *Dans un éclat d'obus que cette pauvre fleur.*[14]

On 28 May, the day after Princess Mathilde's birthday, the Commune was overthrown. Paris was free.

*   *   *

But whether Gautier lived in Eden or in Hell, his unremitting journalism was with him. 'My government has sent me to Paris,' he wrote bitterly in June, 'to sit upon the charred ruins of this Sodom and contemplate them like Volnay to get *copy* from them. I have profited from the occasion to meditate on my own ruins.'[15]

He was indeed the ruin of himself: Maxime du Camp, who met him among the blackened rubble of the rue de Lille, was horrified by the change in him. Dragging his steps, leaning heavily on his companion's arm, Gautier approached him. His cheeks were flaccid, his eyelids swollen, his pallor even whiter than usual. His lips were half open as if he would utter a cry of indignation, and, raising his arms, he cried: 'And this gang of ruffians, tikes, incendiaries, murderers, calls itself the sovereign people!' He lumbered to the palace of the Conseil d'Etat, dragged himself up stairs that were still encumbered by débris, and searched among the remains of Chassériau's painting for a favourite picture. He found it intact, as if by miracle, and for a long while remained in contemplation, as if he had recalled his youth in the midst of destruction and it were speaking to him of former times. 'I am saturated with horror,' he said. 'I want only one thing: to sleep. But I must produce *copy* so that I don't die of hunger.' And then, with his old longing for the Orient: 'If I knew some kindly Turk who liked French poetry, I should go and settle with him in Constantinople; and I should exchange a few sonnets to the glory of the Prophet for a plate of *pilaf* to eat, a *chibouk* to smoke and a carpet to lie on, and try to forget I belonged to Western civilization. I don't want to die,' he added, 'I want to be dead.'[16]

It was the ghost of Théophile Gautier, sick in body and sad at heart, who returned at last, at the end of June, after nine months of privations, to seek the peace that was denied to him in Paris, to live in humble proximity to his dream: to find the soothing devotion of his daughter and the unfailing magic of Giselle on the untroubled shores of Lake Geneva.

39. Fine Autumn

SLOWLY THE world tried to right itself. In the cooling ruins of Paris men debated the coming elections at the Académie-Française. Villemain, Prévost-Paradol and Mérimée were dead, and among the candidates most likely to be chosen were (according to *l'Artiste*) Dumas *fils* and Gautier.[1] 'And yet,' remarked the critic, 'they are men of letters!' From Brussels Princess Mathilde returned to her sanctuary; and Flaubert urged Gautier to join them early at Saint-Gratien.[2] They had not seen one another for eighteen months.

On 17 August, in the loved château on the shores of the Lake of Enghien, Edmond de Goncourt met Gautier for the first time since the Siege.[3] Under the familiar benevolence of Princess Mathilde a little of his sparkle returned: 'Théo comically complains that he no longer enjoys the privileges of youth with women,' noted de Goncourt on 22 October, 'and at the same time he sees himself refused the privileges of the old. He asks to be declared, officially, a person of no consequence, and to enjoy all the immunities attached to the position.'[4] But whatever Gautier's jesting, he could only briefly warm his body and soul before the hearth at Saint-Gratien. And time and time again he returned there in the autumn and winter of 1871, as if he could not be soothed and compensated enough for the days of anguish in the rue de Beaune, the days of apprehension in the avenue de Saint-Cloud, the days of enforced absence. Eugénie Fort noted sadly that he and Estelle were frequently at Saint-Gratien: 'He has been very ill, but he's often been to Saint-Gratien all the same. . . . Gautier has been very ill again. . . .'

He was indeed ill. The Princess was alarmed by the progress of his heart trouble. He walked with difficulty, slept little, was often breathless. Physical strength abandoned him. Yet he went nearly every week to spend a few days with her: grew dearer to her in his suffering, touched her by his unchangeable serenity.[5] And at Saint-Gratien Edmond de Goncourt spent long hours with him:

'Poor dear Théo! Already he showed the affection of those who are going to die. Forgiveness and indulgence had come to him. He had cast off the truculence, the pose of insensibility, all the unnatural affectations of the man of 1830, which had sometimes brought harsh judgments from those who did not know him. His natural generosity was suffused, now, with tenderness: a tenderness which had—what can I say?—a kind of elegance. . . . Every night at Saint-Gratien, every autumn night, at eleven o'clock, when the château was asleep, we went up to Théo's room, and the conversation began; through the windows, in the mother-of-pearl mist risen from the Lake of Enghien, the moonlight turned the distances into German ballads. And then we talked, or rather he talked, in his flowing gandoura-like robe, sitting on the hearthrug like a son of Islam, cross-legged, his slippers adrift on the floor, talking into the night, slowly, gravely, peacefully, on and on, while none of us dreamed of sleeping. Oh! the lofty ratiocinations, the triumphant aesthetics, the irreverent doubts of all the catechisms, the astonishing sophisms ending

n one of those delicate *tours de force*, like a huge elephant gathering
tiny flower. . . . Oh, the sweet words of those mild nights!'[6]

*   *   *

They were courageous performances. Gautier himself remarked in
mid December: 'I am dead but not forgetful.'[7] He lingered on in Paris:
t was little to him, now, but a dim solitude. More dead than alive, he
continued his reviewing; but he lacked the courage to write poetry.
He was stricken by premature old age and the sight of what he called
his decrepitude. He had been one of the handsomest men of his time
and he could not resign himself to losing his looks. Often he stood in
front of his mirror, contemplating his ageing reflection: watching the
unbearable sight of human dissolution.[8] Long ago, when Maxime du
Camp had asked him what gift he would have liked to possess, Gautier
had answered: 'Beauty.' And death, to him, seemed the epitome of
ugliness.

Nor was it only that the artist dreaded the hideousness of death.
The poet of *la Comédie de la Mort* feared the uncertainty:

> Peut-être le tombeau n'est-il pas un asile
> Où, sur son chevet dur, on puisse enfin tranquille
> Dormir l'éternité,
> Dans un oubli profond de toute chose humaine,
> Sans aucun sentiment de plaisir ou de peine
> D'être ou d'avoir été.
>
> Peut-être n'a-t-on pas sommeil; et quand la pluie
> Filtre jusques à vous, l'on a froid, l'on s'ennuie
> Dans sa fosse tout seul.
> Oh! que l'on doit rêver tristement dans ce gîte
> Ou pas un mouvement, pas une onde n'agite
> Les plis droits du linceul!
>
> Peut-être aux passions qui nous brûlaient, émue,
> La cendre de nos coeurs vibre encore et remue
> Par delà le tombeau,
> Et qu'un ressouvenir de ce monde dans l'autre,
> D'une vie autrefois enlacée à la nôtre,
> Traîne quelque lambeau. . . .[9]

The thought of approaching death had haunted Théophile Gautier
throughout his career; the thought of the aftermath filled him with

anxiety. And perhaps, in these months, he sharply recalled that night
some thirty years ago, by the fountain of the Abencerrages in th
moonlit Court of Lions in the Alhambra, when he had reflected: 'Th
hour will come when you will be lying down as you are tonight and yo
will rise no more.'

*   *   *

It was about now, at a wedding at Hurepoix at which Gautier was
witness, that Emile Bergerat met him for the first time.[10] The fac
renowned for Parnassian serenity, the face which had something o
ancient strength and the invulnerability of marble, was strained b
illness, and Gautier, stretching out his hand, asked: 'May I introduc
my ruin?' Dining at Flaubert's on 2 March he said in desolation: '
feel already as if I were dead,' and Flaubert wrote anxiously to Georg
Sand that Gautier had grown strangely old and had not long to live.
'Théophile Gautier did not dine with the Princess yesterday,' Edmon
de Goncourt observed on the fourteenth. 'He is due to see Ricor
today. I don't like to hear of Ricord at any sick-bed. Nowadays he is th
official undertaker.'[12] Gautier was dragging himself from event t
event: to a dinner-party that Bergerat gave in his honour,[13] to th
grateful warmth, the mild evenings of Saint-Gratien. 'All my friends ar
dead,' wrote Flaubert to George Sand on 16 April,[14] 'and I am afrai
that the last of them, poor Théo, is not for this world much longer.' 'H
is dying of ennui and misery,' he told her a fortnight later.[15] 'Nobod
speaks his language any more. We are like fossils that have strayed t
survive in a new world.' And Gautier himself, writing to Maxime d
Camp, ended his letter with the words *delenda spes*.

In the first days of May, Princess Mathilde told Flaubert tha
Gautier was gravely ill. She sent her librarian and poet, when he coul
no longer bear shoes on his swollen feet, the softest of Persian carpets
and day after day, in those summer afternoons, her imperial carriag
made its way down the narrow suburban street as she came to sit wit
him, to charm and console him until evening fell. And more: on th
familiar paper embossed with imperial crown and golden bee, she wrote
when he could not come to Saint-Gratien: 'No, I do not forget you
No one has taken your place. . . . I love you with all my heart and m
heart has not yet grown old.'[16]

He himself had grown old suddenly, suddenly heard the three bris
knocks that no actor might ignore. There was, as he had often said,
death more terrible than the death of the body: it was the death of th
spirit. 'If there is something sad in the world,' he had written, once
'it is the decadence of genius. Nothing is so afflicting as the sight of a
artist who has outlived himself and walks about the streets, soul absen

ɔhial empty, perfume gone; real death is nothing in comparison. . . .
The true, the incurable sorrow, is to know one has lost the *gift*.'[17]
'Death,' he had written in his youth, 'is not only the closing of the eyes,
t is to have no more genius.'[18] Such sorrow, such a death, was the death
ɪe had dreaded, nearly four decades ago, in *la Comédie de la Mort*:

> . . .*L'invisible néant, la mort intérieure*
> *Que personne ne sait, que personne ne pleure,*
> *Même votre plus cher* . . .[19]

Such a death, premature, frostlike, seemed to come upon him now. It
was not yet the fading of intelligence, it was a torpor of the mind.
'Almost invisibly,' observed de Goncourt, 'all-enveloping, touching his
attitudes, his speech and gestures, though one cannot well define it in
words, it descends upon him.'[20] It was now that the Government
decided to help him; on 14 May, Charles Blanc, of the Ministère des
Beaux-Arts, sent him a thousand francs in the guise of an advance for
a ballet.[21] The following month, on Hugo's recommendation, Jules
Simon accorded him a pension of three thousand francs.

The gift from Charles Blanc (for gift it evidently was) arrived on the
eve of Estelle's wedding. Consoled at last for the loss of Villiers de
'Isle-Adam, she was to marry Emile Bergerat: a fervent admirer of
Gautier, a young dramatist and man of letters who would earn his own
celebrity. Gautier, in his loneliness, knowing that now he had not long
o live, had agreed to the marriage on condition that Estelle's portrait
emained in his studio and that Estelle and Bergerat came to live with
ᴉim.

'Isn't it today that Estelle is married?' Flaubert asked Princess
Mathilde on 15 May. 'Poor, poor Théo! . . . I'm afraid the event may
ɔe disastrous for him.' The wedding brought a momentary peace, for
Gautier's family were reconciled to each other. A few days before the
ceremony, there had been a family lunch at Neuilly. Mendès had come
o play indifferent battledore and shuttlecock on the terrace, to take
ᴉis place at last, with Judith, among the family. Zoé and Lili, Toto and
Elise, Bergerat and Estelle had assembled, apprehensively, round the
able. And on either side of Gautier sat Ernesta, her tempestuous nature
amed, and Eugénie, reflective. Now, in the church at Neuilly, they
ɪssembled again; and at the *Dominus vobiscum* Gautier rose, and
ɪnswered the *curé* with a gesture like the blessing of a high priest of
ʃupiter. Yet in the church where Faure himself came to sing, the church
hat still bore the marks of splinters from Communard shells, one
ensed an artificial happiness; a black pall with its silver G, awaiting
ome imminent funeral, seemed (as it had seemed at Jules de

Goncourt's funeral) like a premonition. And at the wedding breakfast
Edmond de Goncourt felt the forced gaiety, the general anxiety at
Gautier's condition. His legs and feet were so swollen that he had to
wear slippers; he sat in a dream. And when Estelle left with her husband
in *le carrosse du père Girault*, in the old hired carriage that had so
often taken her, with the critic, to first nights, Gautier embraced
them in silence, then took Eponine on his knees and continued to
dream.

Late in May Eugénie found him working: 'He is a little better, but
he has no strength.' On 3 June she felt he had improved, he was talking
slightly more. On 13 June: 'He is not worse, but he is weak and sad
above all things.' Flaubert saw him and left in distress. And like some
abandoned, stricken Jupiter, Gautier sat on in his red Voltaire chair
at Neuilly, gazing into the Venetian mirror, lost in a constant reverie.
'How sweet it would have been to ease his latter days!' said Alice Ozy,
long years afterwards. 'I should have loved him poor, infirm, so that I
could care for him, regale him with everything, fill his house with books
and flowers. . . .' But Gautier was not thinking now of Alice. More
often, as he held her onyx paperweight in his hands, as he gazed into
his mirror, his thoughts were with Spirite under the great trees at
Saint-Jean; 'and the family, finding him sunk in thought, would tiptoe
away, whispering: "Don't wake father, he is in Switzerland." And so
indeed he was, as if in Paradise.'[22]

And he followed Carlotta not only along the broad terrace of chestnut
trees overlooking the meeting rivers, not only against the white back-
drop of the Jura. She had asked him to Malaga to watch the bullfights:
'Come in time for Corpus Christi, my dear, there's a fair for several
days, and the bullfights, so they say, will be the finest in Spain for years.
Be a dear and come.'[23] He could not come. But ageing, stricken, from
his suburban chair, he confided in Giselle: 'I have suffered in every way
during these last years: physical privations, hunger, cold, reverses of
fortune, anxiety of spirit and of heart, all the horrors of foreign and civil
war; I have been separated from all I loved, imprisoned, living in a
tomb, and now, the crisis over, I feel as it were a measureless lassitude
and it seems that the chariot of destiny has passed over me, so broken
are my bones. And then the weather is fearful: rain, wind and fog,
autumnal weather, miserably cold, and I need warmth, as at Malaga,
where I should love to be. Spain has always been the land of my
predilection and it is there I have built my castles, round about
Granada.'[24]

As the autumn of 1871 gave place to winter, as he sat cold and tense
by the unwarming fire, his thoughts raced unbearably to Carlotta in

he grateful warmth of the South; then back across the years to a glor-
ous Spanish summer:

'How fortunate you are [he told her] to be at Menton, on the blue sea
shore, among the orange trees and palm trees, warmed by the mild sun!
Here we are in the midst of fog and the last leaves are falling. Winter is
about to come upon us, the winter you are escaping with your young
daughter. You are going to find the swallows again! Oh, that I could
come with you! I, too, long for an atmosphere less cold than this climate
of France that men call temperate, this climate in which you shiver three
quarters of the year. I should have served you as guide and interpreter
in this land of Spain that you'll cross on your way to Madeira, the fortunate isle, the paradise of eternal spring: this land of Spain that I
know so well, whose language I speak, this land that is my true home.
For want of myself, I'm sending you a copy of *Voyage en Espagne*.
How sweet it would have been, in your company, to see the Alhambra
again, the Generalife at Granada, the Alcazar and the Giralda of Seville
and the white town of Cadiz that seems a silver crown on the blue brow
of the sea! You will also receive the book that I would have wished
myself to lay at your feet: *Tableaux de Siège*. It is the collection of all I
wrote in that *année terrible*, in which, with all the miseries and horrors of
invasion I felt the far greater grief of not seeing you, not receiving any
of your news. Turn these pages over in your leisure, if the journey
leaves you any, and think that as I wrote them I was dying of hunger
and the shells came to punctuate every phrase. . . . I feel nostalgia for
azure, sun and palms; I feel a trembling and a restlessness of wings
like birds feel in the season of departure; but the wings are shorn and I
must stay in the gutter with the sparrows.'[25]

As winter froze away the last of the *année terrible*, the flamboyant
partisan of *Hernani*, the author of *Voyage en Espagne* was once more, in
thought, in Spain: 'I think [he wrote gently, now, to Carlotta], I think
you will find Malaga to your liking; it's a charming town, lying non-
chalantly on the sea shore, where the temperature is as mild as it is in
Algiers. I enjoyed myself there so much. I stayed at the Hôtel des
Trois-Mores—it's thirty-one years ago, now. How time passes! You
can go from there to Granada through Velez-Malaga, Alhama, Cacin,
by mule, over admirable mountains. . . . I made this crossing once,
disguised as a smuggler, with a jacket which had a vase of flowers on
the back, a red silk cummerbund, trousers with filigree buttons, and
pricked-leather gaiters. How happy and proud I was! I thought myself
almost a thief!'[26]

The beloved blue-ciphered envelopes, with their copperplate writing,
sped back, like messengers of happiness, from Spain. Carlotta (anxious
now), enquired about his health, described her southern seas and
southern skies:

'How fortunate you are [he answered, gratefully], to be down there
on the blue sea shore, under a blue sky that sends down a drop or two
of rain to lay the dust! Here we are having the strangest, craziest
weather. Yesterday storms and flashes of lightning and rolls of thunder
as if it were summer. This morning a December mist, a yellow London
fog, so intense, so thick, that at noon we almost had to light the lamp
to find the food on our plates. And affairs are like the weather. Storms
and fogs and not the least little glimpse of blue in the future. One can
no longer resort to plausible conjecture; one has to stand in the slush,
waiting for destiny. Everything is provisional: government, public
fortune, commerce and, especially, literature. As for work, one might
still find some, but it's being paid that's not easy. The banks half open
for a moment and shut again with all speed. When you pass, it's always
too early or too late. Everyone keeps his money in a woollen stocking
or leather belt in case of some or other catastrophe. The pretenders are
agitating, the Commune dreams of revenge, the *députés* quarrel and slang
each other and don't make decisions. What is certain is that we're
crushed by taxes and the heavy feet of the Germans still profane our
country. God grant that the great subscription of the women of France
delivers us! As for me I have almost emerged from the affair and I have
survived this tempest when I thought I should promptly founder. All
the same it is hard to have to begin again instead of enjoying a rest after
forty years' work: especially when one's health, which had so far been
faithful, fails and grows capricious. But don't be alarmed; for the last
few days I've felt distinctly better; my breathing is easier and my heart
doesn't beat so hard. The thinness of the siege is beginning to disappear
and I have put on a little weight again. They are prescribing me arsenic
and brandy; it's the latest treatment and suits me pretty well. There's
my bulletin of health. So thanks to the spring that is coming with its
warm breezes, I can keep the hope of seeing you again; I confess that
this winter, on certain dark days when I felt sadder, more ill-at-ease, I
did not expect to see you again on earth. You will soon be leaving Malaga
for Seville which will certainly please you. There you will see the finest
arena in Spain, the best bulls and the most famous swords of Anda-
lusia. Why can I not be with you in your box that day! It would be so
simple. A question of 150 to 200 louis at most. Well! disbelieve me if you
like . . . at the moment I don't possess them. The festivities of Holy

Week are most curious in Spain; watch them carefully so that you can
describe them to me. . . .'[27]

Carlotta told him, in detail, of her journeys; entertained him with pen-
portraits of visitors at her hotel. 'You don't realize,' answered the
master of Flaubert and Baudelaire, 'that you write better than Mme de
Sévigné.'[28] Encouraged, she talked of Spanish art, sent him gossip and
comment on Spanish summers. Her letters had always been pedestrian,
but now, since she had seen the Gautier who had survived the Siege,
the Gautier bereft of health and almost of happiness, there was a new
tenderness about them.

*   *   *

On the afternoon of 18 June 1872, Eugénie Fort came again: 'He is
still in that torpor: it seems to me more serious than people think. He
is not in pain, but life is going.' Six days later came a heart attack, but
he recovered enough to write shakily to Régina Lhomme, suggesting
that he might see her soon.[29] And Eugénie was reassured: 'He's better,
he's talking more easily. He has left off all medicine. He must rest completely.' The improvement was brief: in the last days of June he suffered
another attack; and early in July Turgan expressed grave fears, and
Princess Mathilde sent Flaubert such despondent news that he felt he
had bidden Gautier farewell for ever. On 6 July Edmond de Goncourt
saw him.[30] He seemed like a sleepwalker. His silence was terrifying, his
absent-mindedness fearful, he was so prostrate that de Goncourt felt
compelled to speak to him to reassure himself that his mind remained to
him. On 31 July came yet another stroke; for nearly an hour Gautier
was speechless. Yet when de Goncourt saw him next day, he still clung
to life, and speculated on his literary future: if he were allowed to live
and not to vegetate, he would, he said, spend a year in Venice and write
about Venice in the days before the Revolution.[31]

Other journeys were suggested now: Émile Bergerat's mother invited
him and Lili to spend September with her at Veules;[32] and from
Guernsey came the grandiose invitation: 'My ground-floor room would
be filled with glory if my dear Théophile Gautier came to live in it.'[33]
But it was the spirit of Hugo whom Gautier visited: one day, with
Bergerat, he drove to the place Royale, dismounted from his carriage,
heavily. Then, holding his son-in-law's arm, he stood, for some minutes,
gazing.

'There is a swallow's nest over one of your windows,' Victor Hugo
had written (it had been the year of *Mademoiselle de Maupin*). 'It always
makes me think of you. You should certainly do as the swallow, and
come back and lodge there in the month of April.'[34]

40. *La Comédie de la Mort*

AND, IN a sense, Gautier had done so. In these last months, while all about him observed the outward signs of premature old age, watched illness take its slow, inexorable possession, he had made his supreme return to the Romantic world.

In February he had called on Hugo, asked for his place for the imminent revival of *Ruy Blas*: 'It made us young again,' wrote Hugo in his diary. 'It was like old times returned.' On 19 February Hugo added simply: '*Ruy Blas* this evening. A triumph like *Hernani.*'

Was it, perhaps, this evening that set Gautier, in March, to begin *l'Histoire du Romantisme*? Intermittently, through the painful spring and summer, he wrote his astonishing, happy, vigorous chronicle: remembering with young enthusiasm, brilliant clarity and authenticity; showing the incisiveness, the naïve pleasure in colour and in detail, of an illustrator of missals. Now, more than forty years after the *bataille d'Hernani*, he recalled the leading actors in Romanticism: Petrus Borel, magnetic, olive-skinned, with the manners of a grandee and 'the eyes of an Abencerrage dreaming of Granada'; Joseph Bouchardy, like a maharaja in disguise; Jules Vabre, *le compagnon miraculeux*, who turned English for love of Shakespeare; Gérard himself, original, restless, endearing; Célestin Nanteuil, recorded with a delicacy that only a miniaturist or Gautier could have shown: 'He had the air of one of those long angels, bearers of incense, players of the sackbut, who live in the cornices of cathedrals, an angel who had come down into the town, among the bustling *bourgeois*, still wearing his aureole upon his head, in the guise of a hat, without the least suspicion that it was unusual to wear one's nimbus in the street. . . . He was thin, tall, slender like the elongated columns of fifteenth-century naves, and his curls fairly suggested the acanthus on the capitals. . . .'[1]

The Romantic age was the age to which Théophile Gautier had frequently returned. Often and often, as his career had seemed increasingly depressing and conventional, he had returned in thought to that brief period in his youth when he was frankly Bohemian, not yet shackled by material responsibilities, when journalism had not yet taken its untiring hold upon him, and life and art might be enjoyed without restraint. Now, in this final work, which is, as he would have wished, his best comment upon literature, he returned to it again; for 'present generations must find it hard to imagine the spiritual effervescence of the time; there was a movement like that of the Renaissance. The sap of new life rushed into circulation. Everything was taking root, budding, bursting at once. Dizzying perfumes rose from the flowers; the air was heady, people were mad with lyricism and art. It seemed that the great lost secret had just been found again, and it was true: they had rediscovered poetry.'[2]

It was in August 1872, as he was recalling the first night of *Hernani*, that he ceased to be a critic: that the pen fell from his hand.

* * *

On the last day of August he was sixty-one. His family arranged a surprise for him: one of the firework displays that he so loved: 'To follow a colour in the sky at its most intense, most brilliant, flaming, sparkling, vivid like a star is simple ecstasy. Those blues and reds and greens which make sapphire, ruby and emerald seem earthy: that white and yellow of which silver and gold are but the shadows: as they rise and fall against the black curtain of night they give us enchantment beyond expression. It seems that Paradise should be set in the heart of a bouquet of fireworks, and Hell underground.'[3]

'His distraction,' wrote his son to Eugénie, 'will only last, I know, as long as our rockets.'[4] Next day his illness again took possession. He wandered from studio to *salon*, from *salon* to studio, relighting his cigar, though already he lacked the strength to draw on it.[5] He could not resign himself to illness: 'Does a man gaily renounce the pleasures he loves and stay pitifully indoors, when the sun is shining outside with ironic brilliance, when carriages are spinning the world to its business and its pleasure? Is it not humiliating to confess oneself weak, infirm, defeated by illness?'[6]

On 10 October he braced himself to write to Régina Lhomme: he apologized for being out when she called: he had been to see Ricord: 'The only legitimate excuse. Count on me at the first ray of sunshine. Thank you very much for not forgetting me.'[7] He was told he must not write. But the whole question, he said, was whether Sisyphus suffered more when he pushed his rock than when he did not push it. He had described to Banville, scene by scene, a tragedy classical in grandeur, modern in spirit, a tragedy in full flower in his mind: it needed only to be clad in poetry.[8] He had written enough in his lifetime to fill three hundred books; he forced himself, now, to try a few hesitant lines: 'I want to try to write bigger, now, with goose-quills, after a while I shall get into the habit and it will be more convenient for everyone. . . . I must form the letters more. . . . I am going to begin my writing immediately, except for dictating when my eyes or hand are tired. It is a beginning in literature. . . .'⁹ Save for the name of Carlotta, they were the last words he wrote.

*   *   *

On Thursday, 17 October, Feydeau came and asked him for a copy of *Tableaux de Siège*. Gautier promised him a copy a week hence. On the morning of Saturday, 19 October, Gautier had a fit of choking. The household were warned of his grave condition. Next day he dined with his family and, smiling, began with the words: 'When I'm well again . . .' It was the act of a man who did not want to frighten those he loved, who did not want to show his fear of death.¹⁰ Gautier had not believed in *malades imaginaires*. 'I should rather believe, myself,' he had said, 'in *les bien-portants imaginaires*, who hide their wounds from themselves and, when they are ill, make a joyous pretence of health. Did not Mazarin ask them to rouge his cheeks on his deathbed?' But when Puvis de Chavannes, who had called for an hour, was about to go, Gautier struggled out on to the landing: 'Go downstairs slowly,' he said. And when Chavannes asked why, he answered: 'I shall see you longer.'¹¹

*   *   *

On 21 October, Primoli came to see him, bringing a letter from Ernest Hébert in Rome:

'He was there, in the middle of the room, sitting painfully in a big armchair that he had not left for a fortnight. His stiff body was swathed in his vast blue flannel robe, the sort of nocturnal uniform of the guests at Saint-Gratien. On his head was a red knitted cap; the tassel drooping down on his curling hair gave it the appearance of a tarbouch and recalled our journey to Egypt, where we had all adopted the oriental fez. His waxen complexion, his hanging cheeks, his unkempt beard, his half-closed eyes gave him the look of a Christ in agony.

'A bloodless hand rested sadly against his heart and the other, on the arm of the chair, held a cigar half extinguished. The swelling of his legs, which constantly increased, paralysed the lower part of his body. As I entered, he came out of his torpor, recognized me and smiled. . . .

'He must in a flash have recalled the fine days at Saint-Gratien, the radiant sun of Cairo. . . . Perhaps, confusedly, he remembered our pilgrimage to the Virgin's Tree, when I had jumped from the carriage in a cotton-field, to pick him the flower he wanted. . . . For a moment he seemed happy to see me again. . . .

'On the back of his chair leant his pretty daughter Estelle. In a corner of the room were his two old sisters, Zoé and Lili: one of them, paralysed, shivering in a woollen wrap; the other sitting on a low divan with

. big white cat at her feet and a black cat in her arms. They tried to look unconcerned, but I saw their tears shining.

'When I mentioned your name and handed him your letter, his expressionless face lit up. . . . He opened the envelope with difficulty, turned the letter in all directions like a child who cannot read; he was astonished not to see and at once accused the digitaline of troubling his sight. I told him your writing was difficult to decipher. When his daughter asked him what you had written, he gave her the unfolded page and said to her: "The simplest thing is to take the letter and read it." The conversation lagged and the silence was only broken by vague words. The enchanting conversationalist I had known, or, rather, the enchanter whose winged and coloured words had borne us to distant or fantastic regions, like a magician's wand, sought painfully for the words that would not always come. . . .

'Little by little, I saw sleep fall upon him, and I had the impression that I watched the beginning of his agony. . . . I looked upon him with grief, and rose to go.

'His cigar fell, he opened his eyes, and, seeing me near him:

'"You mustn't think I'm sleeping," he said to me, smiling. "You must punch my head and wake me. . . . But it is a month now since I've been to bed."

'"As you don't go to bed," I answered, "it is only natural that you should feel drowsy now, and I'm going to let you sleep."

'"So I must sleep?" he asked, with the resignation of a child. "Good-bye, then!"

'"Good-bye till next time," I said, and turned to hide my grief.

'I took the hand he held out to me as if he would keep me, but I disengaged myself gently and went away, unable to hide my emotion any longer. It was the first time I had seen someone dying.'[12]

*   *   *

He had wanted, above all, in these last days, to reconcile and forgive in a Christian spirit; and of Mendès, the only man he had ever hated, he said simply: 'I had an enemy, once, but now I have lost him!' He gathered all those whom family dissension had divided, tried to unite them in affection, and only the fierce possessiveness of his sisters kept Carlotta and Ernesta from the door.[13] Other visitors continued to come; for there is, in farewells, as Gautier had once written, 'a melancholy and pervasive charm; it is like the scent of the last rose, whose whole aroma must be gathered in; it seems that one is leading a departing glory on the road to posterity.'[14] And so they came: Arsène Houssaye, every day remembering the Impasse du Doyenné; Maurice Dreyfous, who fled from the room to hide his tears. On the morning of 22 October they told Princess Mathilde that Gautier was growing worse and wanted to see her. She hastened to him, found him speechless. She pressed his hand, and he returned the pressure.

And then, that evening, Banville came to see him. 'He seemed to me exactly like a god. He sat in a big chair, the covering over his legs fell, naturally, in folds, like the noblest of classical draperies. He was calm, radiant, free at last of all care, and his beard, his magnificent hair, the certainty in his eyes, gave me exactly the idea of Zeus on Olympus. Of death, there was no question. It was something tacitly understood, something to which no human words applied. He said to me only: "I was expecting you," and he spoke to me of our art with serene and tranquil eloquence. All the words in the language obeyed him; it was like a symphony in which all the instruments sang in one great harmony. . . . That conversation was doubtless the lesson of lessons from the master to his pupil; yet it was something even nobler, even greater: it was the word of the traveller who, after a long and laborious journey in some unlighted labyrinth, sees the light at last.'[15]

'Dear mother [wrote Toto to Eugénie],
    'There is nothing new; father is still growing gradually weaker.
    'I think you can come tomorrow, which is your usual day. No one can object. Come as if there was nothing the matter, as if you knew nothing.'[16]

Next morning, just after half past eight, Gautier died in his sleep.[17]

41. Valediction

EDMOND DE GONCOURT, reading his paper over dinner, came across the announcement suddenly, and went at once to Neuilly. Bergerat led him into the room where Gautier lay. He noticed the dusky pallor of Gautier's face, framed in the long black hair. 'And so the poet appeared, rude and serene, like some man of centuries ago sleeping in oblivion. Nothing there suggested a modern death. Memories of the figures of stone in Chartres Cathedral mingled with memories of Merovingian times came back to me, but why I do not know. The room itself, with the oak head of the bed, the red velvet patch of a prayer-book, a sprig of box in an ancient jar, gave me the impression that I had entered a *cubiculum* in ancient Gaul, a primitive, grandiose, formidable, tragic room of Roman times. And the grief of a sister with ash-coloured hair, a grief that hid itself in a corner with the wild and frantic despair of some other age, added yet further to the illusion.'[1]

The procession of friends and disciples, poets and artists, past and present, drove out to the rue de Longchamps to record their homage: Leconte de Lisle, Banville, Emmanuel des Essarts, François-Victor Hugo, Baudry, Girardin, Monselet, Doré, Mallarmé and Coppée.[2] Maurice Dreyfous came, bewildered with grief; Feydeau came, remembering last week's promise. Armand Silvestre found the death-bed covered with late roses, and saw upon Gautier's face a strange solemnity. 'He had not been more handsome, even in the days of his legendary and vigorous beauty. "You would think him a saint!" said one of the servants, gazing, weeping. And never was word more just. He was a saint and a martyr to duty, this man who had just died careless of immortality; he slept as a lion sleeps, letting the last fires of the sun burn out in his eyes.'[3]

*   *   *

On Friday 25 October, at noon, the mourners assembled. 'He belongs to us no longer,' Maurice Dreyfous had said to Gautier's son. 'He belongs to France.'[4] And France gave Gautier his funeral. In the crowded church at Neuilly the Requiem was sung by members of the Opéra. Faure, who had come, five months earlier, to sing at Estelle's wedding, now came again; and, as he sang his solo, he wept bitterly. Then the congregation of three hundred set out on foot to the Cimetière Montmartre. The hearse was escorted by a detachment of troops, Gautier's privilege as an Officier de la Légion d'honneur; the coffin was almost hidden under violets and palm-leaves, and as the procession crossed the place Clichy, an onlooker cried with unconscious irony: 'C'est un richard!'

Feydeau, feeling too ill to attend, had spent the morning reading *Tableaux de Siège*. As the time of burial drew near, his reading grew strangely disturbed, Gautier seemed to reproach him for his absence; and, troubled, he sent for a carriage and drove to the little street that led to the cemetery, the avenue du Cimetière du Nord. Crowds were waiting along the boulevards. At about three o'clock, from his carriage, he saw the head of the procession, a bugler of the 12th battalion of *chasseurs*. He noticed the captain marching to the right of his detachment, a captain whose new epaulettes glinted silver in the pale sun. He noticed Théophile Gautier *fils* with Mendès and Bergerat. He recognized Nadar, tall, determined, bareheaded, his hair blown by the wind. He was carrying a light coat over his shoulder. And then the hearse drew level with the carriage; and Feydeau cried aloud: 'Adieu, Théo!'[5]

*   *   *

The cemetery was crowded with admirers, with nameless colleagues 'escorting the journalist—and not the poet, not the author of *Mademoiselle de Maupin*.' For the strange *guignon* which had followed Gautier all his life did not forget him now. Hugo was absent, Hugo who owed his disciple the last favour of his presence; Mendès had sent him a telegram, but he answered only with a brief note and a poem. Nor was Flaubert present: by some inexplicable destiny, Mendès' telegram had reached Croisset in a letter the previous morning; and Flaubert, assuming the funeral would be that day, had thought he could not reach Paris in time. 'So I went to Rouen, so as not to look *sensitive.* . . . Never, in all my life, have I been so nauseated by humankind. I thought continually of the love that *mon vieux Théo* had known for art, and I felt something like a tide of filth submerging me. For he died, I am sure, long suffocated by modern stupidity.'[6]

A like stupidity attended the burial: when Dumas and Chalamel had pronounced their orations, they found that the clergy had gone. There was no holy water to cast upon the coffin.[7] Auguste Marc tore a bough from a tree and threw it into the grave, and everyone followed him.

> *Oh! quel farouche bruit font dans le crépuscule*
> *Les chênes qu'on abat pour le bûcher d'Hercule!*
> *Les chevaux de la mort se mettent à hennir,*
> *Et sont joyeux, car l'âge éclatant va finir.*[8]

42. Afterwards

EVERY YEAR, after Gautier's death, on All Saints' Day, Puvis de Chavannes would make a pilgrimage to the Cimetière Montmartre and leave a bunch of flowers on his tomb. And in Poitiers, above the great staircase in the Hôtel de Ville, in the mural in which Fortunatus read his poems, the figure of Gautier, painted by Puvis de Chavannes, remained as listener and judge.[1] In 1873 Alphonse Lemerre published *le Tombeau de Théophile Gautier*: 'In years to come,' he wrote, 'men will no doubt be moved, as they turn the pages, to see that so many poets, French and foreign, differing in custom, tongue and spirit, have joined to praise a peaceful life and an exemplary work.' It is indeed touching, this tribute in five languages, paid by more than eighty poets: among them Banville and Coppée, Dierx and Glatigny, Heredia, Mallarmé and Leconte de Lisle. Mendès writes an epitaph, Swinburne offers six poems to 'the most luminous of all poets'.[2] And Hugo pays pontifical tribute to the most devoted and distinguished of his disciples, and declares that an age is ending. And, in a sense, the death of Gautier did mark the end of an epoch: with his death there died the finest symbol of Romanticism.

*   *   *

And then, of course, the forest of judgment, misjudgment and neglect grew about him. In the heated days that followed the Second Empire, he had already been accused of 'rallying late, but completely, to the government of 2 December. He allowed himself (a fat sinecure) to be appointed librarian to the Princess Mathilde; he became a Court poet.... He made the mistake of celebrating the Prince Imperial's birth in poetry. One would still condemn the verse if the chronicle did not recall that it was bought for 20,000 francs, a good round sum for little octosyllabic lines.'[3] Even Flaubert misjudged him: to Flaubert, he was the victim of his editors; and Flaubert suggested the theme for Feydeau's study.[4] Carlotta Grisi, with deplorable lack of understanding, increased the confusion by withdrawing Gautier's letters, in proof, from Bergerat's book. Bergerat, the devoted, heightened his comments. Indeed it seemed that Gautier's closest friends ill served him; for the Vicomte de Spoelberch de Lovenjoul, having amassed an astonishing Gautier collection (a collection which, in its early stages, had astonished the poet himself), continued to ban the most intimate correspondence not only from the public but from the serious Gautierist who, having duly gained permission from two members of the Institut de France, finally passed through the heavy double doors of the library at Chantilly. It was small wonder that biographers continued to republish platitudes and speculations, that interest in Gautier was moribund. After the 1880's his work (except for his poetry and his two major novels) was hardly ever republished; the vast preponderance of it still remains buried in nineteenth-century periodicals, and as Gautier's journalism forms by far the largest part of his writing, his literary achievement has never been appreciated. When, in 1880, Alice Ozy offered to pay for a momument in Paris, the *Conseil municipal* refused to erect it. Emile Faguet, in his guide to nineteenth-century literature, made the monumental statement: 'I think he will perish in his entirety.'[5] He remains today, more than eighty years after his death, '*ce grand méconnu*'.

*   *   *

Such neglect and misunderstanding seem the more curious when one considers Gautier's recognized status and influence. 'Gautier means the exclusive love of Beauty, with all its subdivisions, expressed in the most appropriate language [wrote Baudelaire in *l'Artiste* in 1859].

Now by his love of beauty, a love intense and fertile, renewed unceasingly, Théophile Gautier is a writer at once new and unique. . . . I am convinced that thanks to his innumerable articles and his excellent accounts of his travels, all young people possessed of a natural taste for beauty have acquired the complementary education they were lacking.'

Baudelaire's article in *l'Artiste*, his appreciation in the *Revue fantaisiste*, and the dedication of *les Fleurs du mal* are only the most obvious indications of his admiration for the *magicien ès lettres françaises*, for his dear and venerated master and friend. Bourget remarks that if Baudelaire undertook to discover the poetry of modern Paris and reproduced the *décor* in exact and detailed relief: 'Exact relief is the whole art of Théophile Gautier.'[7] And Baudelaire may well have been influenced by Gautier's thought as well as by his style. In the article in *l'Artiste* he declares his admiration for Gautier's 'immense innate understanding of *correspondence*'; and Baudelaire's theory of correspondences may well owe something to the correspondences that Gautier expressed in his criticism of music and, indeed, throughout his work. Mallarmé too, confessed that 'the deep-hidden treasure of correspondences, the intimate agreement of colours, the memory of inner rhythm and the mysterious science of the word' were stirred within him by Gautier's poetry. One may insist here on Gautier's belief that 'in heaven, one man shall touch his poetry, another hear his sculpture, a third shall see his music. All the arts will live together in a single work, and every work will swim in an atmosphere of light and perfumes, the atmosphere of this intellectual paradise!'[8] For this Platonic dream of the fulfilment of beauty, Gautier's dream of supreme correspondences, has been considered his highest achievement: 'What still imposes itself today as the magician's greatest achievement is this famous *fusion of the arts*, whose coming he prepared by his doctrines and by the living lesson implicit in his work. . . . He perceived it not as a philosopher, but as an artist: the unity of the sensual phenomena which remain at the base of all art. From this to the perception of their correlation, or, more justly, their *correspondence*, was but a step; the step still had to be taken. That was the real achievement of Théophile Gautier and his school: his biography and his work are there to bear witness to it.'[9]

Baudelaire was not the only major contemporary who was probably influenced by Gautier's thought and style. Writing of Flaubert, Antoine Albalat declares roundly that 'his real inspiration, his model and his master was certainly Théophile Gautier. . . . It is not only in Chateaubriand, but in Gautier that one must seek the origin of Flaubert's talent, his ideas, his character and turn of mind. It is the author of *le Roman de la Momie* who gave the author of *Salammbô* the terrible pessimism of *la Comédie de la Mort*, his descriptive vocation, his passion for colour, his doctrine of Art for Art's Sake, his exclusive cult of form, his truculent romanticism, and, finally, his hatred of the *bourgeois*. But what the example of Gautier taught, especially, to Flaubert, is the importance of description. . . . That Flaubert got his taste for description from Gautier is absolutely certain, and it is also very possible that the counsels of Gautier and the publication of *le Roman de la Momie* in 1857 directly inspired *Salammbô*.'[10]

Arsène Houssaye records more definitely that, after *Madame Bovary*, Flaubert wanted to find another Rouennaise heroine; 'but Théo said to him: "Draw an antique figure as I did in *le Roman de la Momie*. . . . Take a Carthaginian woman as heroine, it will be original." And, in bold strokes, Théo sketched the whole of *Salammbô* for Flaubert.'[11] When *Salammbô* was published in 1862, and Gautier reviewed it,[12] Flaubert answered with the admiration of the disciple: 'If someone had told me, twenty years ago, that the Théophile Gautier who filled my imagination would write about me like this, I should have gone mad with pride.'[13] And Bourget goes further: 'Flaubert believes he is obeying the rules of scientific psychology in building up his characters by a series of states of conscience, and these states of conscience by a series of mental images. Now it happens that Gautier gave the clearest formula and the most accomplished example of such character-painting.'[14]

The Goncourts followed the fashion that Gautier set for the eighteenth century: Edmond de Goncourt admitted that he had taken Gautier as a model. The letters of Banville indicate his eager respect for Gautier's judgment, his admiration for the critic whom he recognized as his master;[15] and time and time again, in Banville's *Critiques*, one seems to detect the influence of Gautier's dramatic criticism.

There is much indeed to confirm the contention that if Gautier had not existed, Baudelaire and the Parnassians, Flaubert and the Goncourts, Anatole France and Pierre Louÿs would probably have written their work; but certainly they would not have written it as we know it.[16] Saintsbury declares in 1886 that 'as Gautier has for years been one of the most influential of authors in forming the style of younger men of letters, his work is largely the key to modern French.'[17] And even Faguet, who, evidently, was not inclined to praise him, had revised his opinion by the centenary of Gautier's birth: 'Because he taught *artistic writing* he entirely created Banville and Banville's pupils. . . . But what is more important than Banville's school, and it has not been sufficiently remarked, is that Gautier had a decisive influence on the novel from 1850 to 1900; it is, above all, to Flaubert, the Goncourts, Alphonse

Daudet and Zola that he taught artistic writing, and it is them, above
all, whom he taught how to write *precisely*, that is to say to be very
precise about writing and never to be content with an approximation or
an analogy. That the novel should have become a work of art like the
epic fragment or the lyrical poem, is due precisely to Gautier.'[18] And
Faguet, in this unexpected eulogy, goes yet further: 'I have only wanted
to mark the place of Gautier in the evolution of poetic art and of all the
literary art of the nineteenth century. This place is most considerable,
and literary historians will meet Gautier at all the big turning-points
from 1830 to 1910.'[18]

And, as Emile Henriot points out, Gautier represented, 'in tangible
fashion, heroic Romanticism and the cult of Beauty. Hence the considerable influence of Gautier, an influence effective, direct, immediate.
It is he who makes the transition between the school of 1830 and the
school of 1860. And so, with his taste for vitality, his exuberant
life, his devotion to art, he is surely the father of realism, the grandfather
of naturalism (this, perhaps, despite himself), and it is through him that
these schools are connected to Romanticism. . . . Gautier's transforma-
tion was felt by literature at the same time, to the same rhythm. It will
not be the least of Gautier's glories that he so impressed on succeeding
generations the seal of his spirit, and the will of his eyes to see only
reality and extract its beauty.'[19]

Gautier might indeed be called the precursor of realism and naturalism; his absolute submission to the object, the exactitude and brilliance
of detail in his novels, his travel books, his poetry and criticism, were
examples to his contemporaries and to young writers preparing for a
career: 'He was the most prodigious objective writer who has appeared
in any literature,' wrote Xavier Aubryet. 'If we assessed all we owed to
Gautier, Paris would be insolvent; he invented modern description.'[20]
Indeed, after Gautier, naturalism and realism were inevitable: as Sainte-
Beuve pointed out, he made vague descriptions impossible: 'The word
indescribable is no longer French since this master of vocabulary could
say everything.'[21]

Nor was Gautier's influence purely national: Swinburne, Rossetti and
William Morris chose subjects evidently inspired by the works of
Gautier and Baudelaire. And Edmund Gosse declares that 'Swinburne
had been influenced by Théophile Gautier almost to excess.'[22]

*   *   *

As a poet, Gautier's chief contribution to literature is probably the
artistic writing that every critic hastens to discern in him. As a novelist,
he is remembered for more transpositions of art. *Mademoiselle de
Maupin* is an illuminated missal, and its glowing pictures may be

detached without damage to the tale. *Le Roman de la Momie* is an artist's diligent re-creation of ancient Egypt. *Le Capitaine Fracasse* (on Gautier's own admission) is purely picturesque: an excuse for some seven hundred descriptive pages. And Gautier's short stories (he was always more felicitous when he wrote briefly) leave a series of exquisite visions in the mind: the 1830 world of *les Jeunes-France* and *Fortunio*, the willow-pattern world of *le Pavillon sur l'Eau*. It is, again, by a torrent of verbal images, of transpositions of art, that we remember Gautier's books of travel; we remember them by their multiple impression of beauty. And Gautier's own achievement as a writer of topography may well be suggested when he comments: 'The real travellers are artists, and the smallest sketch, provided it be spontaneous and sincere, says more than the finest page of description. . . . Through the covering the artist reaches the inner meaning, and reveals the soul as he shows the body.'[23]

To dilate upon Gautier's poetry, his novels, short stories or travel books is, however, to repeat what may be found in any reliable history of French literature. Moreover, this work is only the fraction that appears above the surface; the vast bulk of Gautier's work looms under waters where few have cared to dive. Gautier's journalism, week by week, covers more than forty years and would fill (so he estimated himself) the better part of three hundred volumes. Gautier the journalist writes on all the arts and their leading exponents; he does not restrict himself to the arts of his country or his age, he touches on social history and current events, records his own life, shows the generation and later life of much of his poetry. Perhaps, then, one should linger for a moment on his journalism, for until we appreciate it, we cannot properly assess him.

*   *   *

Gautier's criticism is indeed (in Brunet's phrase) an organ of revivification; and it not only revivifies the drama, art and literature of the past but, as Gautier anticipated, it is a vast source of information about the arts, celebrities and events of the nineteenth century. Gautier's dramatic criticism reflects the French theatre from Marie Dorval to Sarah Bernhardt, from Hugo to Sardou. His music criticism embraces the performances of Chopin and of Liszt, the struggles of Berlioz and Wagner, the early work of Verdi. His criticism of art begins at a time when artists are still reacting from the neo-classicism of David, and it discusses the full flush of Realism. Gautier's literary criticism covers French literature from Béranger to Mistral. His topical reporting records, among much else, the great exhibitions of mid-century, the growing understanding between England and France, the coming of

the railways, the interest in air travel, the Siege of Paris. And his journalism, taken as an all-embracing whole, is a source of information for
any study of aesthetic thought in nineteenth-century France, for a
study of almost any figure in the contemporary French artistic world.

It helps, more particularly, to refute Emile Montégut's strange
statement that Gautier declined as a poet when he established himself
in journalism.[24] No student of *Emaux et Camées* would maintain that
these poems, nearly all of them written in mid-career or late in life, were
inferior in technique to the poet's early work; while if journalism
imposed life-long frustration on Gautier, poetry is born of sorrow,
weariness and anger as well as joy, and a study of his career confirms
that his regrets brought new elements into his work. Besides, some of
Gautier's verse was in all probability inspired by his prose; and growing
ideas for poems, and echoes of poems completed, may be found in
his journalism. It is also quite possible that frequent descriptive practice helped to change Gautier's poetry: that his critical work helped to
make this determined Romantic the master of the Realists of the Second
Empire. And he himself was not unaware of such benefits. When
Murger, after years as a journalist, won instant fame with *la Vie de
Bohême*, Gautier wrote: 'Let Murger not repent this broadcast scatter-
ing of the intellect from which, whatever people say, the poet gains
more than he loses. . . . Journalism has this advantage, that it mingles
you with the crowd, and saves you from the stupidities of solitary
pride; it is fencing which breaks you in and makes you supple.'[25]

Gautier's journalism is not only a guide to some of his poetry; it is
also a precious source of information for a study of his character and
career. It is, in the first place, abundantly clear from his aesthetic
sympathies and dislikes, from his attitude to life itself, that he was no
Parnassian. He was, instead, and unmistakably, a born Romantic of
1830. Whatever he told the Goncourts about repressing himself in his
work, whatever he told Eugénie Fort about his impersonality, it proved
impossible, naturally enough, to conceal himself from his readers for
some forty years; nor did Gautier desire to do so. Repeatedly he chose,
in Romantic fashion, to express his own unhappiness and frustration;
inevitably he revealed his hopes and his pleasures. And he published,
in his journalism, a considerable amount of autobiography, both open
and concealed.

And here it may be remarked that Gautier's business correspondence
does much to destroy Flaubert's contention that Gautier was the victim
of his editors. 'Make it quite clear,' Flaubert advises Feydeau, who is
about to write a biography, 'make it quite clear that he was exploited
and victimized in all the papers he wrote for; Girardin, Turgan and

Dalloz were torturers to the poor man. . . . When you write the biography of a friend, you should do it from the point of view of his
vengeance. . . . Be serious, be pitiless.'[26] It is clear from Gautier's
journalism that he knew financial hardship, felt himself oppressed by
editors and by the discipline of his profession. It also seems evident that
the editors and publishers suffered considerably from Gautier's lack of
discipline, his recurrent vagaries, his frank, indeed publicized distaste
for much of his work.

And it is this very distaste for journalism that explains Gautier's distinction and achievement as a journalist and critic. He did not consider
himself a man of letters; he considered himself an artist.[27] It was to his
early training in Rioult's studio that he claimed to owe his taste for art
and his feeling for beauty; and all his life, regretting that he had abandoned painting, he transposed it into literature. '*Anch'io son pittore!*'
he said in 1867. 'I've regretted all my life I abandoned my first career.
Since then I've done nothing but make transpositions of art.'[28]

In his *Pages de Critique et de Doctrine* Paul Bourget indicates, perceptively, the connection between the Gautier of *Mademoiselle de
Maupin* and the Gautier of this three-dimensional journalism, quoting
the words of d'Albert: 'My pictures are only coloured bas-reliefs. For
I like to touch what I've seen and to follow the curves of contours into
their most hidden folds. I consider everything from every aspect, and
I turn about it, a light in my hand.' Here again is Gautier the artist;
here again is a key to his journalism. For Gautier the critic confirms
Bourget's suggestion that Gautier makes, with words, the gesture of
d'Albert. To write is, for him, 'to follow the curves of contours into
their most hidden folds.'[29]

So it is that Gautier, the pupil of Rioult, sets out as a dramatic critic
not only to criticize but to produce 'a daguerrotype of the theatre'; and
in his dramatic criticism, at its best, we are given not only aesthetic
considerations, but three-dimensional figures re-enacting their parts.
It has been suggested that Gautier's plastic criticism of the theatre is
defective; that he has painted the scenery instead of analysing the plays.
Plastic criticism, if exclusive, might indeed be inadequate; but in
Gautier's work it lends charm to ephemeral performances, preserves
(as he had hoped) many fine ones, and both explains and enhances his
literary considerations. Gautier himself told Lovenjoul that he considered this plastic criticism highly important.[30] He went further: he
considered it a philosophy.[31]

Gautier's devotion to the visual arts inspired not only his writing
on the theatre but his happiest writing about music: the portraits of
Liszt at the piano, the imaginative commentary on Weber; and it

inspired, most significant of all, his brilliant, constant, influential use
of correspondences. Gautier sought to create the plastic criticism o
music, and his chief contribution to music criticism was happily indicated by Ernest Reyer: 'He spoke about it like a poet, translated the
pleasure it had given him into language rich with imagery.'[32]

The artist who wrote plastic criticism of the theatre and music
achieved his highest successes as a writer on literature when he re-
created, visually, his great and lesser contemporaries, or revivified, in
visual language that sometimes touched the height of a prose-poem
the impressions that poetry had made upon him.

And, naturally and deliberately, Gautier created the plastic criticism
of art. And here one might recall the perceptive appreciation with which
he declared himself so satisfied: 'Art criticism, the manner in which he
practises and understands it, is one of the innovations and special gifts
of Théophile Gautier [wrote Sainte-Beuve in 1863]. . . . Every painting
and fresco seems to appear in the light in which he describes it, and one
sees not only its project and disposition, but its effect, its tone and line.
Gautier's system of description is a system of transposition, an exact
equivalent reduction rather than a translation. Just as a symphony is
reduced for piano, so he *reduces* a picture to an *article*. It is not ink he
uses, but lines and colours; he has a palette and pencils. . . . These
accounts speak and live. In art, perhaps the most useful form of criticism is to show rather than judge.'[33] And the words of Sainte-Beuve are
confirmed and enhanced by those of an artist, Baudry: 'The description
of my pictures enchants me. No writer performs or will perform, like
you, this miracle of transposition and crystallization, as Stendhal called
it (though Stendhal only applied the term to love). It is true you love
painting as men love women. . . . When time has faded my paintings
something at least will remain in the magnificent veil you cast about
them. It is the story of the mummies of which, when life is gone, the
body almost vanished, only perfumes remain. . . .'[34]

'They often call me *fanciful*,' said Gautier to Sainte-Beuve, 'and yet,
all my life, I have only tried to see properly, to study nature, draw,
interpret, paint it, if I could, just as I saw it.'[35] He did not merely
observe outward appearances; yet throughout his work one finds the
constant preoccupation with the visual, the plastic and the three-
dimensional, and time and time again one recalls his comment to the
Goncourts: 'I am a man for whom the visible world exists.'[36]

Gautier was not, however, only an artist. He was also a poet; and he
constantly reminded his readers of the 'poor poet diverted from his art'.
They were reminded more happily of his vocation by the germs of
poetry scattered throughout his work, by the poems published in and

out of articles, and by the echoes of poems resounding in his criticism. They were reminded of his poetry, too, in numerous improvisations and asides; for the journalist, so he told them blandly, 'is a hybrid animal, half critic and half improviser'.[37] A comment on the farewell of Taglioni, on the transience of dramatic art, on the funeral of Decamps, may lift his prose to the level of a prose-poem; a sterile week in the theatre will allow him to improvise engagingly on the winter or the spring.

It is at such moments that Gautier's poetry touches his prose. Gautier's poetic (and Romantic) feeling is found in his love of colour and history, his affection for the exotic: the Spanish, Egyptian, Chinese and Japanese; it is found in his veneration for all religions and for the supernatural, even for superstition, it is found in his eager interest in the prospects of ballooning, in the prosaic notes he made on the undiscovered world of astronomy. It is found in the experiments with hashish, recalled in *le Club des Hachichins*,[38] in which he attempted to discover new dimensions of experience. And Gautier the poet is reflected not only in his love of the remote and strange. He is reflected (and here the poet and the artist meet) in the principle which guides his work, indeed his very life: in his evident and abiding search for beauty. 'I adore above all things the beauty of form,' he had written in *Mademoiselle de Maupin*. 'Beauty, for me, is visible divinity, it is palpable happiness, heaven descended on earth. . . . Who could not kneel before thee, pure personification of the thought of God?' And again: 'I ask only for beauty, it is true, but it must be so perfect, that I shall probably never encounter it.' Those few sentences hold much of the philosophy that informed his work.

One finds there what René Lauret defined as the Romantic longing for the impossible.[39] Yet if, as Lauret suggests, 'the thirst for the impossible is the mark of powerlessness,' it is still this very striving after the unattainable, this very regret of human inadequacy, that gives dignity to Gautier's philosophy, and to the criticism it inspires. 'The delights for which he yearns,' writes Lauret of Gautier, 'are esthetic; he wants them so fervently, his love of beauty is so candid that it ennobles his very insensibility, and sets him above the lovers of nameless beauty.' A study of Gautier underlines the contradiction: Gautier cannot be both fervent and insensible. Nor is he (as Lauret implies) a superior dilettante; nor can he be dismissed (as Lauret dismisses him) for 'his too ardent need of beauty'. The need of beauty cannot be too ardent; the religion of beauty, which Gautier professed, raises him far above the amateur of art, and gives him not only his fervour as poet and as artist but his distinction as a critic. Antoine-Orliac much more nearly

understands Gautier's philosophy[40] when he sees it as the Platonic
cult of beauty and relates it to 'the Greek dream which moves towards
the divine through beauty of form'.

Yet Antoine-Orliac sees Gautier's plastic ideal, his worship of form,
as his consolation for 'metaphysical disquietude'; and Gabriel Brunet
reaches much the same conclusion: 'Gautier discovered the balm for
every grief: consolation by the contemplation of appearance.'[41] Gautier
may indeed have consoled himself for the disappointments of life by the
contemplation of beauty in art and nature. But it must be emphasized
yet again (and his writing makes it abundantly clear) that though he
could not, to his sorrow, accept all the tenets of Catholicism, he was a
devoted pantheist. When he declares in *Mademoiselle de Maupin*
'Christ did not die for me. I am as pagan as Alcibiades and Phidias', he
is declaring himself a pantheist as much as a pagan. He worships beauty,
so he tells us himself in his novel and throughout his work, as the visible
form of divinity. He worships the beauty of nature and the beauty of
art. As he wrote once, himself, of Diderot: 'If he did not see God at a
particular place in the heavens, he saw Him everywhere in the beauty
of the universe.'[42] And as Emile Montégut so well expressed it: 'The
pleasures of dilettantism, usually so superficial, attain, in Gautier, the
power and nobility of the pleasures of mystic ecstasy. His eyes turn
towards the sun of art with the same burning desire as the eyes of a
Christian monk who seeks the invisible sun of morality; his whole
being is absorbed in the contemplation of beauty, undistracted by any
preoccupation foreign to the vision that possesses him, and never was
Brahmin, lost in his search for the place occupied by intelligence, more
separate from earth than Théophile Gautier by the ravishment into
which he is thrown by a Renaissance canvas and a fragment of Greek
art.'[43]

So it is that Gautier recognizes the work of an artist as an act of
devotion; so it is he maintains what all critics should maintain: the ideal
purpose and unattainable standards, the sovereign independence and
sacred nature of art. So it is that Gautier professes his belief in Art for
Art's Sake from his earliest criticism, from the moment he writes so
nobly, so sincerely: 'In art we have no religion but the religion of art
itself.'[44]

Critics have long indicated one of the obvious distinctions of
Gautier's journalism. Victor Fournel observed that 'criticism for him
was only a pretext for pictures, and, frankly, he was not asked for anything else'.[45] 'Nostalgia for the picturesque,' added Pontmartin,
'dominates his talent and his life.'[46] And Zola rightly confirmed: 'His
constant effort was to reduce written thought to the material nature of

the painted form. Théophile Gautier had, in brief, a painter's eye, and that was his dominant quality.'[47] Hugo indicated the other major characteristic of Gautier's criticism when he thanked him for an article on *Ruy Blas*. 'What a master you are, dear Théophile! What poetic prose! ... Your criticism has the power of creation.'[48] Yet none of these critics remarked that Gautier's distinction came from his dual nature: from the fact that he was artist and poet together. It is Sainte-Beuve who touches the heart and sums the significance of Gautier's criticism when he writes: 'After all, he is only a displaced artist and poet.'[49]

Here lie both the weakness and the extraordinary strength of Gautier's work for the Press. His love of art and poetry, it is true, often led him to be undisciplined, to indulge in his own prose-pictures, his own imaginings, instead of critical comment; to delegate the tasks he found unrewarding; to permit occasional plagiary; to be, throughout his career of some forty years, the desperation of his punctual editors. Artist and poet born, he must have been one of the most rebellious, least predictable contributors to any paper since journalism began. And there is, perhaps, another weakness in Gautier's love of art and poetry: an inherent weakness which he recognized. We cannot look to him for academic judgments, we cannot look to him for reasoned surveys, documented explanations. We must not expect him to explore a problem deeply, bring a vast weight of erudition to his theme. For Gautier is not an intellectual; he is, perhaps, by nature, the least critical of critics. He had written, once, of Diderot: 'He thinks with his heart as much as with his head.'[50] He himself appreciates the arts with his heart and soul rather than his intellect.

And yet, is this a weakness? When all is said, the arts, in their purest form, are inspired by emotion rather than intellect, and it is through the heart that they should be comprehended, and with the heart that they should be loved and described. It is, perhaps, the distinction of Gautier the critic, not his weakness, that he approached the arts in a loving, not an academic, spirit. His devotion to art and poetry may explain some of his failings; but it gave him, also, an intimate and unusual understanding. It gave him a broad and lofty conception of the arts and a superlative visual style: made his writing, at its best, a living record and a work of literature. Gautier tried, persistently, throughout his long career of some forty years, to make his daily work embrace both art and poetry, both the vocations he felt he had abandoned. And as we consider his journalism we often recall the theory he expressed in the early years of his career: 'Every art has its weakness, whence derives a part of its beauty. The measureless struggles of the poet who lacks a plastic form, the artist who lacks a succession of ideas, the sculptor who lacks

T

movement, the composer who lacks words, have produced the most wondrous works of the human spirit.'[51]

Gautier's journalism suggests one surely inescapable conclusion: that Gautier was an artist and a poet, not a conventional journalist or critic; and precisely because he was far more than a journalist or critic, he gave journalism a new significance and a new status. He made it, at its best, when poet and artist took over the common task, a work of literary art. And he did more: he wrote it with the eagle-eyed view of his time, the religion of art, the ideal and constant standards that alone can give criticism its value and its permanence. In an age when superficial values were too readily accepted and public taste was too frequently gratified, he maintained in his criticism the importance of the ideal, the permanent values of civilization. Coppée described him as 'the great and exquisite poet who has consented, in the interest of the Cause of Art, to become the first of contemporary critics'.[52] If Gautier's journalism and criticism are given their distinction by his artistic and poetic nature, they are also given their dignity by his militant, unswerving, religious devotion to art and beauty. It was with truth that he wrote to Sainte-Beuve: 'If I had possessed the least personal fortune I should have devoted myself entirely to *the love of the green laurel*; but in the prose into which I have fallen, I have always defended the interests of art and proclaimed the name of the sacred masters with my whole heart and soul.'[53]

Appendices

APPENDIX ONE

The Birth of a Poem

POETRY DOES not spring fully grown and ready armed from the mind of its creator. It is often the child of a long intellectual process; and posterity may sometimes have the good fortune to witness gestation and birth. Among the poems we may so follow is a favourite poem in French anthologies, a poem from *Emaux et Camées: Inès de las Sierras.*

Some critics maintain that Théophile Gautier was inspired by Charles Nodier's tale (which bears the same title). This is probably not the whole truth: indeed, Gautier suggests it himself by the dedication to la Petra Camara and by the last two verses of the poem. For the origin of this eminently Romantic work I think we should turn not to Nodier, but to Gautier, the dramatic critic of *la Presse*. The origin of *Inès de las Sierras* may well be traced to Gautier's announcement on 12 May 1851 that the Spanish dancers, on their way to the Great Exhibition in London, will perform in Paris. The dancers made their début on 13 May; on the 19th there appeared in *la Presse* Gautier's first impressions of la Petra Camara. It shows all his ardent nostalgia for Spain. It reveals a fascination, at once sensual and strange, which closely anticipates the feeling expressed in the poem. Some of the phrases recall lines of *Inès de las Sierras* that Gautier abandoned; and others come close to phrases in the accepted version of the poem:

'. . . El ole Gaditano est un pas seul qui permet d'apprécier plus à l'aise le talent de la Petra Camara, un peu perdu dans ce tourbillon éblouissant [writes Gautier in *la Presse*, 19 May 1851].

'La danseuse arrive du fond du théâtre nonchalamment, d'un pas lent et brisé; puis ses bras se déploient, *ses petites mains, où claquent des castagnettes d'ivoire, secouent un rhythme sec et nerveux* qui semble la réveiller de sa torpeur; ses mouvements deviennent plus vifs et plus rapides, mais sa tête conserve toujours son air endormi; *ses yeux baissés sont chargés de trop de langueur pour se lever, un vague demi-sourire entr'ouvre ses lèvres;* son rêve interrompu ne l'a pas quitté encore.

'Tout ce commencement de pas est presque somnambulique; on y sent *l'accablement voluptueux* et la lethargie bercée de rêves d'opium de l'Orient. . . .

'Rien n'est plus étrange et plus charmant.

'Connaissez-vous une tête de Velasquez à laquelle pendent, de chaque côté des joues, d'énormes grappes de perles mêlées aux boucles d'une chevelure d'ébène, comme des gouttes de rosée qui se seraient figées sur les cheveux de la nuit? Des sourcils d'un noir de peau de taupe, épais à ne pas les croire naturels, et que l'on dirait tracés avec du surmeh, comme les sourcils des femmes turques, surmontent des yeux d'un éclat extraordinaire avivés encore par deux petites plaques de fard. Cette tête, c'est le portrait de la Petra Camara fait par anticipation.

'Bientôt, l'animation la gagne; *ses paupières bordées de longs cils de jaïs palpitent comme des éventails noirs sur ses joues plus colorées;* le génie mystérieux de la danse s'empare d'elle; son sein se soulève, sa narine rose se dilate; un éclair blanc passe entre ses lèvres rouges; ses yeux, jusque-là baignés d'ombre, s'ouvrent et s'illuminent brusquement. . . .

'Comment rendre le reste de ce pas *si violent et si retenu, si voluptueux et si chaste*, cette grâce tendre et fière, cette souplesse d'Almée, cette cambrure des poses, cette rapidité étincelante qui succède aux langueurs et aux défaillances de la passion, cette gravité dans l'amour, toutes ces nuances si profondément espagnoles?

'*Il y a surtout un moment d'une grâce inimitable : la danseuse, appuyée sur un genou, se renverse et semble, avec ses bras qui rasent le sol, faire un raffle des coeurs et des bouquets* qu'elle ramasse dans un pli de sa jupe relevée. . . .'

On 18 August there appeared in *la Presse* Gautier's second impression of la Petra Camara: an impression refined and heightened and astonishingly close in feeling and expression to the poem in *Emaux et Camées*. It is indeed so close that one may suggest that some part or version of *Inès de las Sierras* was written about 18 August 1851:

'La Rosa Espert n'a pas la grâce sauvage, la passion enivrée et sombre, l'allure hautaine, jusque dans ses provocations voluptueuses, de la Petra Camara . . .; mais elle déborde de vie, de santé et d'entrain. Sa robustesse exubérante plaît et réjouit là où la Petra Camara troublait profondément. Vous souvenez-vous d'*un délicieux roman de Charles Nodier?* . . . *Ce roman est l'histoire de quatre militaires français qui passent la nuit dans un château hanté par des esprits et des apparitions* quand minuit sonne, à la grande terreur de ces braves à l'abri de toute crainte humaine. Du fond *d'un long couloir éclairé par une vague lueur,* s'élance une figure immobile et rapide, et qu'ils reconnaissent pour être l'original du portrait d'Inès de las Sierras, tuée, il y a trois cents ans, par le farouche maître de ce château maudit; elle est si pâle qu'on la croirait fardée avec du clair de lune, et *sur sa poitrine blanche étincelle, comme un rubis, le joyau de sa blessure.*

'*Elle danse avec une grâce languissante et morne, une nonchalance glaciale, une froideur de sépulcre, un charme de l'autre monde, effrayant et délicieux,* qui fait brûler d'amour les officiers glacés d'epouvante. *Elle semble avoir rapporté de la tombe de mystérieuses voluptés,* et les plis de *sa basquine fripée par l'humidité du caveau,* renferment d'irrésistibles séductions. Dans son extase endormie et sa danse somnambulique, elle lève de temps à autre ses paupières allourdies d'un sommeil de trois siècles, et il en jaillit un éclair si vif, si brûlant, si rempli d'ardeurs insensées et de folles promesses, qu'il entre dans le coeur comme un fer rouge dans la neige. Quand ce regard vous a touché, *il faut le suivre fût-ce au fond des catacombes, par des escaliers et des souterrains à la Piranèse, fût-ce au fond des enfers.* Vous avez l'inextinguible soif de l'impossible, le rêve d'amour dans la mort.

'La Petra Camara est la plus exacte réalisation d'Inès de las Sierras: le style de sa danse est la même. Elle aussi a été tuée il y a trois cents ans par un meurtrier pâle et morne: *elle aussi a sur la poitrine la raie rouge du coup de couteau; c'est le fantôme de la vieille Espagne qui nous apparaît du fond du passé, avec un frisson de tambour de basque et un babil de castagnettes* dont la joyeuseté vous navre; tout cela est si charmant, si bizarre, si surnaturel, qu'on sent bien que c'est la danse d'une ombre; et pourtant il y a dans cet œil ouvert et renfermé si vite un tel éblouissement de lumière, une telle phosphorescence d'amour qu' *on serait tenté de croire à la vie de cet adorable spectre* qui n'existe plus que dans les portraits de Zurbaran, de Murillo et de Velasquez. Ah! Petra Camara, comme je t'aurais aimée si tu n'étais pas morte depuis si longtemps!'

· · · · ·

A close comparison of this review and the final version of *Inès de las Sierras* shows the poem to be almost a transposition of the prose:

REVIEW	POEM
Vous souvenez-vous d'un délicieux roman de Charles Nodier? Ce roman est l'histoire de quatre militaires français qui passent la nuit dans un château	*Nodier raconte qu'en Espagne* *Trois officiers, cherchant un soir* *Une venta dans la campagne,* *Ne trouvèrent qu'un vieux manoir;*
	Un vrai château d'Anne Radcliffe, *Aux plafonds que le temps ploya,* *Aux vitraux rayés par la griffe* *Des chauves-souris de Goya,*
Des escaliers et des souterrains à la Piranèse	*Aux vastes salles délabrées,* *Aux couloirs livrant leur secret,* *Architectures effondrées* *Où Piranèse se perdrait.*
	Pendant le souper, que regarde *Une collection d'aïeux* *Dans leurs cadres montant la garde,* *Un cri répond aux chants joyeux;*
Du fond d'un long couloir éclairé par une vague lueur	*D'un long corridor en décombres,* *Par la lune bizarrement* *Entrecoupé de clairs et d'ombres,* *Débusque un fantôme charmant.*
	Peigne au chignon, basquine aux hanches, *Une femme accourt en dansant,* *Dans les banies noires et blanches* *Apparaissant, disparaissant.*
Une grâce languissante et morne . . ., un charme de l'autre monde, effrayant et délicieux. . . . Elle semble avoir rapporté de la tombe de mystérieuses voluptés. . . . Effrayant et délicieux	*Avec une volupté morte,* *Cambrant les reins, penchant le cou,* *Elle s'arrête sur la porte,* *Sinistre et belle à rendre fou.*
Les plis de sa basquine fripée par l'humidité du caveau	*Sa robe, passée et fripée* *Au froid humide des tombeaux,* *Fait luire, d'un rayon frappée,* *Quelques paillons sur ses lambeaux,*
	D'un pétale découronnée, *A chaque soubresaut nerveux,* *Sa rose, jaunie et fanée,* *S'effeuille dans ses noirs cheveux.*

Sur sa poitrine blanche étincelle, comme
un rubis, le joyau de sa blessure. Elle
aussi a sur la poitrine la raie rouge du
coup de couteau

Une cicatrice, pareille
A celle d'un coup de poignard,
Forme une couture vermeille
Sur sa gorge d'un ton blafard;

Et ses mains pâles et fluettes,
Au nez des soupeurs pleins d'effroi
Entre-choquent les castagnettes,
Comme des dents claquant de froid.

Elle danse, morne bacchante,
La cachucha sur un vieil air,
D'une grâce si provocante,
Qu'on la suivrait même en enfer.

Il faut le suivre . . . fût-ce au fond des
enfers

Les longs cils jouent comme des papillons
noirs, sur le fard de sa joue

Ses cils palpitent sur ses joues
Comme des ailes d'oiseau noir,
Et sa bouche arquée a des moues
A mettre un saint en désespoir.

Quand de sa jupe qui tournoie
Elle soulève le volant,
Sa jambe, sous le bas de soie,
Prend des lueurs de marbre blanc.

La danseuse semble faire un raffle des
coeurs et des bouquets. [Review of 19
May.]

Elle se penche jusqu'à terre,
Et sa main, d'un geste coquet,
Comme on fait des fleurs d'un par-
terre,
Groupe les désirs en bouquet.

On serait tenté de croire à la vie de cet
adorable spectre

Est-ce un fantôme? est-ce une femme?
Un rêve, une réalité,
Qui scintille comme une flamme
Dans un tourbillon de beauté?

C'est le fantôme de la vieille Espagne qui
nous apparaît du fond du passé, avec un
frisson de tambour de basque. . . .

Cette apparition fantasque,
C'est l'Espagne du temps passé,
Aux frissons de tambour de basque
S'élançant de son lit glacé,

Et, brusquement ressuscitée
Dans un suprême boléro,
Montrant sous sa jupe argentée
La divisa prise au taureau.

La cicatrice qu'elle porte,
C'est le coup de grâce donné
A la génération morte
Par chaque siècle nouveau-né.

J'ai vu ce fantôme au Gymnase,
Où Paris entier l'admira,
Lorsque dans son linceul de gaze
Parut la Petra Camara,

Impassible et passionnée,
Fermant ses yeux morts de langueur,
Et comme Inès l'assassinée
Dansant, un poignard dans le coeur!

The poem was probably ready—at least in part—in Gautier's mind in August 1851. And there, it seems it lay for another year. Gautier was born indolent; and only in 1852, when *Emaux et Camées* was about to appear, did he write the last nine verses. In the summer of 1852, when he stopped at Syra, in the Cyclades, on his way to Constantinople, he sent them to his friend and literary agent, Louis de Cormenin. It is characteristic of him that the vision of la Petra Camara remained long after he had crystallized it into poetry, and that he remembered it in his prose. On 1 February 1853, admiring Mme Guy-Stephan's dancing of the madrilena, he recalls it closely, in *la Presse*:

'Nous aimons ces emportemens passionnés, ces pétulances folles, ces langueurs pâmées, ces cambrures lascives, ces bras qui semblent recueillir les désirs comme une gerbe. . . . Qui admire plus que nous les sourcils de velours, les longs yeux, toujours baissés, et s'entr'ouvrant comme un nuage noir pour laisser passer un éclair de la Petra Camara, cette somnambule et vampire de la danse avec sa grâce effrayante et son charme inquiétant, irrésistible comme la mort ou comme cette Pedrina qui, sous le nom d'Inès de las Sierras, rend fous d'amour et de terreur Sergy et les officiers français dans le charmant conte de Nodier, dont nous avons traduit la prose en vers qui ne le valent pas.'

(Gautier then quotes four verses of his poem.) Fourteen years after he had seen la Petra Camara at the Gymnase, Gautier saw her again at the Variétés, and recorded her in phrases that by now were familiar:

'*Le ballet de Gitanos*, nous n'avons pas besoin de le décrire [he wrote in *le Moniteur universel*, on 26 June 1865]: un tourbillon de jupes qui volent, de jambes qui luisent avec des éclairs de soie, de bras pâmés rasant la terre, de sourires étincelants entre des lèvres de grenade, le tout au milieu du ronflement des tambours de basque, des *aye!* et des *oh!* du frou-frou des guitares et du cliquetis des castagnettes qui bourdonnent leur note obstinée comme des cigales aux plus chauds jours de l'été dans les environs d'Ecija, cette poêle de l'Andalousie. A travers ce fourmillement de paillettes et de dentelles et de roses posées sur l'oreille, se démène avec une verve endiablée la Petra Camara, toujours belle, toujours ardente, toujours souple, mais ayant pris une richesse de contours bien rare chez une danseuse. Ce n'est plus tout à fait la Petra Camara du Gymnase, qui dansait les yeux baissés et semblait, en les rouvrant, remplir la salle de flamme at de lumière, une almée ayant dans le coeur une goutte de sang de taureau et résumant toutes les poésies de l'ancienne Espagne; c'est égal, allez aux Variétés et applaudissez-la bien fort, cette belle Petra Camara dont se souviendront toujours les poètes.'

Théophile Gautier had good reason to remember her.

APPENDIX TWO

The *Correspondances* of Théophile Gautier

THE WORD *correspondances* brings one instantly on to the battlefield where supporters of Baudelaire and Rimbaud hotly dispute their poets' possible book-lists and probable influences. One insists that Baudelaire, and Rimbaud after him, were inspired by *Louis Lambert*. Another brushes Balzac aside and quotes the passage in *Roger* where Alphonse Karr points out the analogy of impressions produced by Gothic stained-glass windows and the seraphic sounds of the organ. A third quotes the remark attributed to Léon Gozlan: that piety is pale blue, resignation pearl grey, and joy is apple green. Someone recalls Flaubert's explanation: 'Dans mon roman carthaginois, je veux faire quelque chose de pourpre. Dans *Madame Bovary*, je n'ai eu que l'idée de rendre un ton, cette couleur de moisissure de l'existence des cloportes.' And a lover of the obscure might cite the case of Benjamin Lumley's friend, who was sensitive to corres-pondences to a quite ludicrous degree:

'Whenever this person listens to a singer, a colour corresponding to his voice becomes visible to the eyes:

Giuglini.	Maroon. The colour softened and well blended in its grada-tions. Substance, a rich velvet pile.
Patti.	Light and dark drab, with occasional touches of coral.
Clara Novello.	Tomata [sic]. Always the same, but a cold glaring colour.
Battu.	Yellow and white, but sometimes the two colours blend, and form (in idea) a daisy, which is really pretty—like whipped cream with little bits of dark spice in it.

Two clear facts emerge from the mêlée: there was a general interest in *corres-pondances* during the nineteenth century; and one important influence has been ignored: the influence of a regular critic in a popular daily paper: Théophile Gautier, of *la Presse* and *le Moniteur universel*.

The power of perceiving correspondences was, in Gautier, very highly developed indeed. The correspondences he recorded may be found in his travel books, in his novel *Spirite*, and in his criticism of art and literature. They are most often found when, his emotions stirred, his technical knowledge least strong, Gautier writes about music.

In *le Premier Visage de Rimbaud*, Noulet quotes Gautier's article on his hashish dream (1843) as the first expression in literature of a definite synopsis of the senses; but it was neither the first suggestion nor the first expression. As early as 1832 Balzac had discussed correspondences in *Louis Lambert*; and in 1836 Thoré suggested in *l'Art de Parfums*: 'Il faut les classer en tons et demi-tons, et quand vous aurez déterminé les parfums en notes, vous écrirez des lettres *en parfum*.'

Yet if Gautier were not the first to discuss a synopsis of the senses, he was certainly one of the first to use correspondences freely in his prose, and he began to use them at least as early as 1836, when, in *la Presse*, on 29 November, he gave a vivid impression of Rubens' picture of the Assumption: 'On dirait un énorme bouquet de roses effeuillées; cette peinture est si fraîche, si vermeille et si fleurie qu'elle sent bon, et jette dans l'église une ravissante odeur printanière.' This use of correspondences is only the logical development of the transposition Gautier had used when he wrote of Paul Huet's landscapes that 'chaque touche de son pinceau est une strophe de l'ode colorée qu'il chante: son coucher de soleil dans les montagnes est une Orientale.' In an article *Progrès dans les Arts*, Gautier further explores the correspondence between sight and sound, and discusses 'la musique visible', and he returns to the subject to maintain that ballet is 'une musique que l'on regarde', and returns to it yet again when he describes Auber's work as 'considérablement passée de ton. Ce n'est pas de la musique à l'huile, c'est de la musique au pastel; la poudre colorée se détache et ne laisse plus voir que la trame grenue de la toile'. He defines Perrot's dancing as 'la mélodie visible, et, si l'on peut parler ainsi, ses jambes chantent très-harmonieusement pour les yeux'; as he hears Liszt at the piano, his sense of touch and his visual sense are affected together: 'Ce sont des bouffées de notes qui passent sur le clavier avec la rapidité et le frissonnement d'un vent d'orage dans les ramures d'un forêt, des chants clairs et perlés.' Discussing Donizetti's *Lucrezia Borgia*, late in 1840, Gautier grows increasingly precise: 'Beaucoup de morceaux de cet opéra, qui devraient être verts de poison, s'encadreraient aisément dans la musique fraîche et rose d'un opéra buffa.' As he listens to *la Reine de Chypre* in 1841 he feels that 'le tremolo aigu des violons et le chant de la clarinette expriment à merveille la fraîcheur nocturne et le frémissement argenté de la lune sur les vagues. C'est de la musique azurée, si l'idée de la couleur peut s'appliquer à un son.'

But the idea that colour may correspond to sound seems increasingly possible to him: indeed, it comes to him so naturally and spontanément that years afterwards, in *les Vacances du Lundi*, he reverses the same correspondence when he notices, on the way to Zermatt, 'comme une vibration de lumière ascendante qui rappelait le tremolo de violons dans le *Lever de Soleil* de Félicien David', and in *l'Orient*, describing his excursion into Greece, he writes that 'le jour se levait lentement avec un *crescendo* de teintes plus délicatement ménagées encore que le fameux *crescendo* de violons du *Désert* de Félicien David'. The *Stabat Mater* of Rossini, reviewed in 1842, suggests a new correspondence between music and sculpture and, indeed, the germ of *Symphonie en Blanc Majeur* (which was to appear in 1849): 'C'est dans ce système italien d'élégance, de beauté et de mélodie qu'est écrit le *Stabat*,' writes Gautier: 'Quelque chose de blanc et de suave dans le goût de la Madeleine de Canova, où l'on pourrait désirer plus d'abattement, mais non plus de grâce et de beauté. . . . Toutes les roses mystiques semblent pleuvoir d'un ciel d'or sur les mots *paradisi gloria*.' At Thalberg's concert 'le chant reste toujours lumineux, scintillant, et le tremolo bourdonne à l'entour, en faisant palpiter ses ailes sonores comme un papillon autour d'un flambeau.' Watching Dreyschock at the piano in 1843, Gautier observes 'des notes lumineuses, claires comme l'argent" bursting from the instrument; and a few weeks later, hearing Mme Damoreau sing, he declares that 'jamais plus brillans feux d'artifice de gammes ne se sont évanouis dans le ciel musical en pluie d'or et d'argent.'

*   *   *

It seems, then, that Gautier's account of the hashish dreams in 1843, in which he heard colours, saw luminous and spiral music, and swam in an ocean of sonority, was not the first literary expression of a synopsis of the senses, but the logical development of a theory which he had long practised, the most extravagant expression of ideas which had long been natural to him. Though he did not invent either transposition or correspondences, though he was not the first nor the only writer to discuss them in his time, Gautier was surely among the first to practise them easily and naturally in his prose; and in this practice his creative imagination and his predominantly plastic way of thinking played a large and evident part.

Throughout his descriptions of music Gautier continued to express correspondences in striking fashion: he saw the voice of Mlle Thorn bursting 'en bouquets d'argent dans l'azur des mélodies de Palestrina'; and when, at the Club des Hachichins, the *voyant* played the piano, 'les notes m'entraient dans la poitrine comme des flèches lumineuses; mes doigts s'agitaient sur un clavier absent; les sons en jaillissaient bleus et rouges.' Gautier's growing interest in correspondences is clearly shown in his impression of Félicien David's symphony, *Christophe Colomb*: here, 'à la seconde partie, nous sommes au tropique. . . . L'orchestre murmure des extases d'une mélodie enivrante: tout ce qu' il y a de plus doux, dans les cuivres et les cordes, s'exhale comme un parfum, flotte et babille comme l'azur étoilé de la mer, et le chœur des génies de l'Ocean s'élève autour des navires en gerbes de notes perlées.' When land is about to be sighted, 'les oreilles et le coeur peuvent seuls apprécier l'incomparable mélodie que l'orchestre fait éclore: rien de ce que la plume verse en lettres noires, sur une feuille stupide, ne pourrait en donner une idée au plus intelligent de ses lecteurs. Il semble que les notes se parfument et s'épanouissent en gerbes odorantes; on devine que le Nouveau-Monde va se révéler, comme un jardin virginal.' There is a faint suggestion of Baudelaire's *Parfum exotique* in this tropical evocation.

These passages reflect an increasingly serious attitude to correspondences, an eager anxiety to express by correspondences those emotions beyond the reach of language, and to push back the frontiers of criticism. We see, too, the anxiety to record a transient art that Gautier shows in his criticism of the theatre. In 1849, in a significant article (*la Presse*, 12 March), he discusses the problems of evoking music in prose, and expresses the wish that a stylist would find the means of describing sonority, evolve 'la plastique du son' and triumph over the scholars who have discovered the form of vibrations and the colour of notes. Later this year, when he comes to describe the revival of *le Prophète*, he remarks: 'Nous ne savons pas s'il est permis d'assigner des couleurs aux sons, quoique Faraday en soit bien capable; mais les notes qui forment le chant des trois anabaptistes nous apparaissent toujours comme des chauves-souris noires voltigeant sur le fond clair de la musique.'

But the hopes and hesitations which Gautier expressed were in fact largely rhetorical. He had long discovered the plastic means of describing sound, of expressing the emotions that evaded definition. He had found the power of correspondences; and no technical terms could express what he expressed with them. Yet if these examples show the ease, the skill and constancy with which he transposed the arts and recorded correspondences, they do not entirely explain Gautier's purpose. He was attempting to break down artistic barriers, to overcome the weaknesses and enlarge the powers of each art; he was also attempting to push back the frontiers of criticism. But he was attempting yet more: to perceive the affinities of the senses and to be the *voyant* which he believed the true poet should be. He was trying to see not only the unity of the arts but the significance behind their expression. This dual purpose is explained by the passage in *Spirite* in which Spirite transposes poetry into music:

'Bientôt elle se remit au piano et fit jaillir du clavier une mélodie d'une puissance et d'une douceur incomparables, où Guy reconnut une de ses poésies . . . transposée de la langue du vers dans la langue de la musique. C'était une

nspiration dans laquelle, dédaigneux des joies vulgaires, il s'élançait d'un essor
désespéré vers les sphères supérieures où le désir du poète doit être enfin satis-
fait.—Spirite, avec une intuition merveilleuse, rendait l'au-delà des mots, le
non-sorti du verbe humain, ce qui reste d'inédit dans la phrase la mieux faite,
le mystérieux, l'intime et le profond des choses, la secrète aspiration qu'on
s'avoue à peine à soi-même, l'indicible et l'inexprimable, et tout le flottant, le
flou, le suave qui déborde du contour trop sec de la parole. . . .
   'Les mélodies s'échappaient du piano en vibrations visibles et colorées, se
répandant à travers l'atmosphere de la chambre par ondulations lumineuses
comme celles qui nuancent l'explosion radieuse des aurores boréales. . . .
Malivert sentait cette satisfaction qu'éprouvent si rarement les poètes . . . d'être
compris dans toutes les délicatesses et les profondeurs de son génie.'

*   *   *

   Gautier's use of *correspondances* confirms his artistic nature; it confirms, as
strongly as his support of contemporary composers, the progressive character
and the high purpose of his critical work. And it brings us back to the Baudelairean battlefield.
   In his article in *l'Artiste* in 1859, Baudelaire declares his admiration for
Gautier's 'immense intelligence innée de la *correspondance*'; it seems most
probable that Baudelaire became aware of *correspondances* through articles in
two popular daily papers written by a poet and critic whom he much admired.
Baudelaire's theory may well owe something to the frequent *correspondances*
that Gautier expressed in his criticism of music and, indeed, throughout his
journalism. And when Mallarmé confessed that 'le trésor profond des correspondances, l'accord intime des couleurs, le souvenir du rhythme intérieur et la
science mystérieuse du verbe' were stirred within him by Gautier's poetry,
perhaps he, too, may have been prepared by the prose of the journalist.

NOTES

MU=le Moniteur universel
JO=le Journal officiel

PART ONE

1. The Son of Artagnan

1. For the most detailed account of Gautier's early life, see Jasinski: *Les Années romantiques de Théophile Gautier*
2. *Mademoiselle de Maupin*, p. 156
3. Chantilly: C 1581 (ms 503) ff 4/5
4. Ibid.
5. *JO*, 19 July 1869
6. *La Presse*, 8 November 1852
7. Ibid, 20 October 1845
8. Sainte-Beuve: *Correspondance générale*, I, 155; and *le Constitutionnel*, 16 November 1863
9. *MU*, 2/3 November 1862
10. *Histoire du Romantisme*, p. 92
11. Ibid, p. 85
12. Hugo: *Correspondance générale*, I, 507, note 2.

2. The Green Season

1. *Quand on a Vingt Ans.* (*Revue du XIXe siècle*, 1 January 1867.)
2. *La Presse*, 2 October 1843
3. Letter of 15 January 1834. Quoted by Bergerat: *Entretiens*, p. 280
4. Gérard de Nerval: *Correspondance*, p. 48
5. Bergerat, op. cit., p. 279
6. Chantilly. C 482 ff 20/21
7. Chantilly. C. 482 ff 22/23

PART TWO

3. Fortunio the Critic

1. Charles Monselet in *l'Artiste*, 30 August 1857, pp. 380/1
2. *Les Annales romantiques*, t. vii, May-June 1910, 161 sqq.

3. Gautier: *Poésies complètes*, ed. Jasinski, pp. 90 and 98
4. Houssaye: *Les Confessions*, I, 347 sqq.
5. *La Presse*, 18 March 1837
6. Balzac: *Correspondance*, t. I, p. 387. Letter of 11 April 1837
7. *La Presse*, 1 March 1837
8. *La Presse*, 22 January 1838
9. Ibid, 17 February 1838
10. *L'Artiste*, lre série, t. 15, pp. 78 sqq.
11. *La Comédie de la Mort.* (*Poésies*, 1890 edition, pp. 46-7.)
12. *La Presse*, 19 May 1839
13. Chantilly: C 469 f. 13
14. *La Presse*, 11 March 1839
15. Ibid, 26 August 1839
16. Ibid, 9 November 1839
17. Chantilly: C 482 f. 11
18. Augustin Thierry, pp. 25 sqq.

4. Don Teofilo

1. Chantilly: C 469 f. 19
2. *La Presse*, 23 March 1840
3. *Le Laurier du Généralife.* (*España. Poésies*, 1890 edition, p. 139.)
4. *La Presse*, 20 January 1845
5. Ibid, 17 January 1853

5. *Giselle* and *la Péri*

1. *La Presse*, 5 July 1841
2. Ibid, 2 July 1842
3. *L'Eclair*, 26 June 1899
4. *La Presse*, 6 January 1842
5. *L'Artiste*, 2e série, VIII, 337/8
6. Chantilly: C 1581 (ms 503) f. 13
7. *The Times*, 14 March 1842
8. Lumley: *Reminiscences of the Opera*, p. 39

9. *La Presse*, 16 January 1843
10. Ibid, 25 July 1843
11. Ibid, 25 September 1843
12. Vaudoyer, 29 sqq.; Thiébaut, 70/71
13. The letters that Gautier received from Alice Ozy well suggest the forces at work behind the theatre. 'Mon cher Théo', she writes to him in an undated note (Chantilly: C 498 f. 120):

'J'ai été bien contrariée de ne pas voir le compte rendu de notre pièce dans votre feuilleton. Allons à Lundi. N'abîmez pas trop nos auteurs qui sont des gens aimables et à défaut de rôle dites que j'ai l'air d'une vraie Marquise et montre des formes agréables au Marquis. Ça me fera plaisir et ça te coûte si peu de mentir.'

A further note accompanies her own draft of an advertisement which Gautier is to publish (C 498 f. 123): 'Voici le réclame pour mon bénéfice *il faut* vous dépêcher de le faire mettre au milieu de votre presse.' A third undated letter from *l'Aspasie moderne* again asks the Gautier to use his influence (C 498 f. 139):

'Cher théo—Je t'en veux de n'être pas encore venu me voir 14 boulevard poissonnière dans mon nouveau logement. N'oublie pas cher ami de mettre dans ton feuilleton que je suis née le 6 août 1825 . . . et que j'ai débuté en 1840 . . . un impudent met dans un feuilleton Mlle Ozi que nous voyons depuis 10 ans; j'ai l'air d'une duègne. C'est à toi excellent ami de reparer cet outrage tu peux en même temps te révolter sur la manie qu'on a de vieillir les actrices, Mme Volnis et autres quie seraient grandmères [sic] du cèdre fameux, si on les écoutait. . . .'

14. Houssaye: op. cit., II, 238
15. Cf. letter of 11 April 1844 (in the possession of Mme Bergerat)

16. *The Times*, 26 September 1843
17. Ibid, 2 October 1843
18. Ibid, 18 November 1843
19. Ibid, 9 October 1843
20. Ibid, 10 October 1843

6. *Hernani* and others

1. *La Presse*, 21 May 1849
2. MU, 21 March 1864
3. *La Presse*, 30 November 1837
4. JO, 19 July 1869
5. *La Presse*, 27 November 1837 26 February 1838
6. Ibid, 30 April 1838
7. Ibid, 11 September 1837
8. Ibid, 28 December 1837
9. Ibid, 18 March, 1840
10. JO, 24 June 1869
11. *La Presse*, 20 December 1853
12. Ibid, 11 April 1843
13. Ibid, 22 April 1844
14. Ibid, 20 December 1842
15. MU, 25 March 1861
16. *La Presse*, 23 October 1848
17. Ibid, 15 October 1849
18. MU, 11 May 1863
19. Ibid, 19 September 1864
20. *La Presse*, 9 October 1841; MU 11 May 1863, 11 June 1866
21. Ibid, 3 December 1849
22. Ibid, 17 February 1851; MU, 6/7 April 1863
23. MU, 6/7 April 1863
24. *La Presse*, 24 June 1844; MU, 23 June 1862, 20 May 1863
25. MU, 1 August 1860
26. *La Presse*, 24 June 1850
27. MU, 13, 20 May 1863
28. Ibid, 5 March 1860
29. *Quarante Ans de Théâtre*, 194
30. *La Presse*, 28 March 1854
31. MU, 10 August 1857
32. *Italian Travel Sketches*, 176 sqq.
33. *La Presse*, 8 January
34. Arvin: 227 sqq.
35. *La Presse*, 27 April 1847
36. Ibid, 29 September 1837
37. Ibid, 8 August 1843
38. Ibid, 11 September 1843
39. Ibid, 15 July 1844

0. MU, 12 October 1863
1. *La Presse*, 21 September 1846
2. MU, 2 July 1855
3. *La Presse*, 18 March 1844
4. Ibid, 1 July 1850
5. Ibid, 9 March 1852
6. Ibid, 1 March 1843, and passim
7. MU, 12 January 1862
8. *La Presse*, 20 May, 29 July 1844
9. Ibid, 23 June 1851
0. Ibid, 8 January 1838
1. Ibid, 26 March 1849
2. Ibid, 29 November 1854
3. Ibid, 1 July 1850
4. *L'Artiste*, 14 December 1856
5. MU, 8 December 1856
6. *La Presse*, 23 December 1844
7. Ibid, 25 February 1850
8. Ibid, 1 January 1849
9. Ibid, 22 January 1844
0. Ibid, 11 January 1847
1. Ibid, 4 March 1850, and passim
52. MU, 14 December 1863
3. *La Presse*, 30 September 1844
4. Ibid, 14 July 1851
5. Ibid, 17 November 1845
6. MU, 20 July 1857
7. Ibid, 2 March 1863
8. JO, 19 July 1869
9. *La Presse*, 23 January 1843
70. MU, 9 July 1855
1. Ibid, 2 March 1863
2. *La Presse*, 14 February 1842
3. Ibid, 23 December 1844
4. Ibid, 4 September 1848
5. *La Presse*, 20 January 1851
6. MU, 1 October 1855
7. *La Presse*, 1 November 1852
8. MU, 5 May 1856
9. *Chronique de Paris*, 5 June 1836
0. *Figaro*, 19 January 1837
1. *La Presse*, 29 December 1841
2. Ibid, 27 April 1842
3. Ibid, 19 October 1842
4. Ibid, 6 December 1842
5. Ibid, 13, 14 March 1843
6. Ibid, 10 February 1841
7. MU, 12 January 1863
8. JO, 19 April 1870
9. MU, 30 May 1864
0. Ibid, 29 April 1861
1. Ibid, 7 July 1856

92. *La Presse*, 24 February 1845
93. Ibid, 7 March 1842
94. Ibid, 13 June 1843
95. Ibid, 10 February 1845
96. Ibid, 6 December 1847
97. Ibid, 15 August 1848
98. Ibid, 27 March 1855
99. MU, 18 November 1861
100. *La Presse*, 2 May 1843
101. Ibid, 14 March 1843
102. JO, 3 May 1869
103. *La Presse*, 7 June 1841
104. MU, 16 June 1856
105. Ibid, 7 July 1856
106. Ibid, 3 September 1855
107. Ibid, 6 October 1856
108. Ibid, 27 October 1856
109. Ibid, 21 August 1860
110. *La Presse*, 19 December 1854
111. Goncourt: *Journal*, II, 10/11
112. JO, 21 March 1870
113. *La Presse*, 6 August 1849
114. MU, 21 July 1862

7. Son of the Prophet

1. *La Presse*, 17 March 1845
2. Ibid, 5 May 1845
3. *Ghazel.* (*Poésies Diverses*, 1890 edition, pp. 70/1.)
4. *La Presse*, 6 January 1845
5. Chantilly: C 485 f. 99
6. Chantilly: C 407 f. 123
7. Chantilly: C 407 ff 126/7
8. *La Presse*, 15 September 1845
9. Sainte-Beuve: *Corr. gén.*, VI, 179/180
10. Ibid, 176/7
11. *Fatuité.* (*Poésies diverses*, 1890, p. 65.)
12. *L'Artiste*, 1 August 1867, p. 314
13. *La Presse*, 15 June 1845
14. Monselet: *Petits mémoires littér-aires*, pp. 6 sqq.
15. Feydeau: *Théophile Gautier*, pp. 11 sqq.
16. *Journal du Dimanche*, 22 August 1847
17. Sensier: *Souvenirs*, p. 159
18. Balzac to Mme Hanska: *Corr.*, III, 194 and 216/7

19. *La Presse*, 2 February 1846
20. Ibid, 18 May 1846
21. R. de Beauvoir: *l'Hôtel Pimodan*. *L'Artiste*, 1 September 1844
22. *La Presse*, 31 March 1846
23. Ibid, 16 June 1846
24. Chantilly: C 482 ff. 58/59
25. Chantilly: C 469 ff. 49/50

8. *Le Glas Intérieur*

1. *La Presse*, 1 February 1847
2. Du Camp: *Théophile Gautier*, pp. 85/6
3. Du Camp: *Mes Souvenirs*, II, 66/7
4. *La Presse*, 22 February 1847
5. Ibid, 22 March 1847
6. Ibid, 30 March 1847
7. Ibid, 12 July 1847
8. Ibid, 5 July 1847
9. *L'Artiste*, *Revue de Paris*, 2 January 1848
10. Houssaye: *Confessions*, II, 192
11. *L'Artiste*, 16 January 1848; cf. also *la France littéraire*, November 1834, p. 397
12. Du Camp: *Souvenirs*, I, 417
13. *Le Glas Intérieur*. (*Poésies nouvelles*. 1890, pp. 204/5.)
14. *La Presse*, 20 March 1848
15. Ibid, 22 April 1848
16. Ibid, 25 May 1852
17. Chantilly: C 485 ff. 405/6

9. Marie

1. *Illustrated London News*, 20 January 1849
2. *La Presse*, 19 February 1849
3. Delacroix: *Journal*, I, 348
4. *La Presse*, 8 April 1851
5. Ibid, 26 February 1849
6. I.L.N., 17 February 1849
7. Ibid, 24 February 1849
8. Blanguernon: *Revue de Paris*, July, 1914, p. 125
9. Du Camp: *Souvenirs*, I, 418
10. *La Presse*, 9 August 1849
11. Chantilly: C 493 f. 509 (undated)
12. It is characteristic of Gautier the philanderer that on 12 August he

had sent an erotic letter to Ernest Grisi, then staying at Fontaine bleau (Bergerat)

10. The Sorrows of Fortunio

1. Du Camp, op. cit., I, 440/1
2. Letter to De Vatry. Chantilly C 485 ff. 372/3 (26 December 1849.)
3. *La Presse*, 8 April 1850
4. *La Presse*, 25 February 1850
5. Ibid, 29 January 1850
6. Houssaye: *Confessions*, VI, 119
7. Du Camp: *Souvenirs*, I, 483 sq.
8. Ibid, I, 486
9. *La Presse*, 6 August 1850

11. *Séjour à Venise*

1. Letter of 4 September 1851
2. Chantilly: C 469 f. 62
3. *L'Artiste*, 15 September 1850
4. Letter of September 1850
5. Letter of 14 October 1850
6. Bédarida: *Théophile Gautier l'Italie*, pp. 35/6. Giuseppe Ricc ardi (1808–82) was a Neapolita man of letters; his turbulent cha acter and liberal opinions led hi to take part in the southern cor spiracies and he had to go int exile. He recorded some of h adventures in *My Memories as Rebel* (1857).
7. *La Presse*, 16 December 1850
8. Du Camp, op. cit., II, 1/3

12. *Un Ange chez Moi . . .*

1. *La Presse*, 20 January 1851
2. *Premier sourire du Printem* (*Emaux et Camées*, ed. Mator p. 29.)
3. *La Presse*, 17 June 1851
4. Letter of 31 July to Louis d Cormenin
5. *Coquetterie posthume* (*Emaux Camées*, ed. Matoré, pp. 24/5.)

13. Alarms and Excursions

1. *La Presse*, 18 August 1851
2. Chantilly: C 485 f. 61. When he visited London in 1862, Gautier stayed in Panton Street: no doubt at the Panton Hotel, 'un hotel français assez médiocre', where Edmond Got, the actor, was to stay in 1871.
3. Chantilly: C 482 ff. 122/3
4. *La Presse*, 25 August 1851

14. The Flight of the Swallow

1. Letter of 23 March 1852
2. Letter in the possession of Mme Bergerat. It is a further interesting comment on Gautier the philanderer, for only three days after it was written, Marie Mattei had invited him to the rue de Sèze to begin the new chapter in their liaison. On 23 March and 7 May Gautier again sent devoted letters to Ernesta. One recalls his note to Maxime du Camp about the lacquer box which contained the letters of 'Carlotta, Ernesta and la Mattei, those I have most loved and love the best'; and M. Vendramin, reprinting this in *Quo Vadis* (April–June 1954, p. 64), remarks that the box also contained certain letters sent to Gautier by Mlle Ozy at the beginning of an earlier liaison. In June 1852, as he left the arms of Marie for those of Ernesta, Gautier could still address an amorous letter to Alice (ibid.).
3. Letter of 28 May 1852
4. Letter of 6 May 1852
5. Letter of 24 June 1852 from Constantinople
6. Letter of 5 September 1852
7. Letter of 10 December 1852
8. Letter of 14 January 1853
9. *L'Hirondelle*. (*Poésies nouvelles*, 1890, p. 246)
10. Letter of 21 May 1852

15. A Turk of the Reform

1. Sainte-Beuve, op. cit., pp. 191 sqq.
2. Thiébaut: *Edmond About*, 40 sqq.
3. Ibid, p. 43. The diaries of Gautier's former mistress suggest that she did not remain fancy-free when the poet left her. According to family information, she had liaisons with Arthur Kratz and Edmond About.
4. *Revue de Paris*, August 1852, p. 155
5. Letter of 19 August, Chantilly: C 498 ff. 349/50
6. *L'Artiste*, 15 August 1852, pp. 24/5
7. Flaubert: *Correspondance*, III, 41
8. *La Presse*, 18 August 1852
9. Ibid, 13 September 1852
10. Ibid, 23 August 1852
11. *Revue de Paris*, September 1852, pp. 96 sqq.
12. *Les Matelots*. (*Poésies*. 1890 edition, p. 66)

16. The Impenitent Romantic

1. Lovenjoul, II, pp. 48–58
2. Monselet, *Petits mémoires*, p. 20
3. *Poètes et financiers. Poésies*, ed. Jasinski, III, 168
4. Lapauze: *Ingres*, 468 sqq.
5. *La Presse*, 25 April 1854
6. *MU*, 4 June 1854
7. *La Presse*, 11 July 1854
8. Letter in possession of Mme Alice Théo Bergerat
9. Letter in possession of Mme Alice Théo Bergerat
10. Joubin: *Chassériau*, insertion after p. 264
11. *La Presse*, 5 December 1854

17. Months of Moment

1. Du Camp: *Souvenirs*, II, 168 sqq.
2. *La Presse*, 30 January 1855
3. *L'Artiste*, 9 August 1857
4. *La Presse*, 6 February 1855

5. Chantilly: C 482 f. 75
6. Chantilly: C 495 f. 186, letter from Arsène Houssaye

PART THREE

18. L'Aigle du Moniteur

1. MU, 16 April 1855
2. Ibid, 10 September 1855
3. Joubin, III, 258
4. Chantilly: C 482 f. 76
5. MU, 11 May 1855 and 14 May 1856
6. MU, 14 May 1855
7. MU, 16 July 1855
8. Letter in possession of Mme Alice Théo Bergerat
9. MU, 2 July 1855
10. Chantilly: C 482 ff. 77/78
11. MU, 24 December 1855
12. ILN, 12 January 1856
13. MU, 28 January 1856
14. MU, 4 June 1855
15. Letter in possession of Mme Alice Théo Bergerat
16. Letter in possession of Mme Alice Théo Bergerat
17. Claudin: Mes Souvenirs, pp. 142/3

19. The Artist as Critic

1. Diderot: Oeuvres, t. x, 207 sqq.
2. L'Artiste, 1 December 1854
3. Ibid, 14 February 1858
4. La Presse, 28 July 1849
5. Ibid, 31 March 1846; see also MU, 9 June 1856
6. Tableaux à la Plume, p. 6
7. La Presse, 10 March 1837
8. Ibid, 2 May 1851
9. Ibid, 26 March 1844
10. Ibid, 3 April 1844
11. MU, 6 February 1860
12. La Presse, 26 March 1844
13. MU, 1 October 1855
14. La Presse, 28 March 1851
15. Ibid, 19 March 1836
16. Ibid, 13 October 1836
17. Etudes d'Art
18. La Presse, 2 July 1849

19. Ibid, 26 July 1849
20. MU, 3 June 1857
21. Figaro, 11 November 1836
22. La Presse, 27 December 1836
23. Journal officiel, 5 April 1870
24. L'Artiste, 24 August 1845
25. La Presse, 7 May 1851
26. Ibid, 9 December 1849, 5 February 1851
27. L'Evénement, 8 August 1848; reprinted in Souvenirs de Théâtre
28. Ibid, p. 203
29. MU, 24 December 1855, 2 February 1857, 4 June 1868, etc.
30. Ibid, 30 July 1861
31. La Presse, 9 December 1849
32. Ibid, 8 April 1846
33. Ibid, 3 April 1844
34. Ibid, 11 March 1837
35. Ibid, 4 April 1839; and see also, for example, Tableaux à la Plume, p. 9
36. Journal officiel, 26 June 1869
37. Les Beaux-arts en Europe, I, 32/36
38. Ibid, p. 42
39. Figaro, 17 December 1836
40. Moniteur universel, 7 January 1854
41. Ibid, 20 April 1866
42. La France littéraire, March 1833
43. La Presse, 8 March 1851
44. Joubin, III, 279/80
45. La France littéraire, March 1833
46. Ibid.
47. Lapauze, 519 sqq.
48. Meynell, 74 sqq.
49. Ariel, 19 March 1836
50. La Presse, 20 March 1837
51. L'Artiste, 25 October 1857
52. Moniteur universel, 29 July 1866
53. La Presse, 2 May 1848
54. Moniteur universel, 7 March 1860
55. Ibid, 6 July 1864
56. Moreau-Nélaton, II, 134
57. Chantilly: C 493 f. 92
58. Moniteur universel, 24 June 1865
59. Journal officiel, 18 July 1870
60. Roosevelt, p. 190
61. L'Artiste, 20 December 1857
62. Chantilly: C 493 f. 368
63. Moniteur universel, 18 May 1864
64. Ibid, 6 February 1860
65. La Presse, 10 January 1848

6. *Moniteur universel*, 15 December 1856
7. *Journal officiel*, 7 October 1871
8. *La Presse*, 10 January 1848
9. *Moniteur universel*, 13 July 1868
10. Ibid.

20. The Little Mark upon our Heart

1. *Journal* (1888 edn.), 164 sqq.
2. Letter in possession of Mme Alice Théo Bergerat
3. ILN, 28 February 1857
4. Baudelaire: *Correspondance*, ed. Crépet; pp. 142/3
5. Chantilly: C 500 ff. 107/9
6. *Journal*, t. 1, pp. 181 sqq.
7. MU, 29 July 1857
8. For Eugénie Fort's diary, on which so much of this book depends, I am very deeply indebted to M. Pierre Théophile Gautier.
9. *La Presse*, 21 May 1849
10. Reminiscences of Comte Joseph Primoli
11. *La Presse*, 20 November 1847
12. Chevillard: *Chassériau*, 29 sqq.
13. *La Presse*, 19 April 1852
14. *La Presse*, 11 February 1850
15. Lovenjoul, I xix/xx
16. Chantilly: C 499 f. 300

21. The Seal of Respectability

1. Bergerat: *Souvenirs*, I, 299. Billy: *les Frères Goncourt*, 142
2. Chantilly: C 485 f. 258
3. *L'Artiste*, 15 August 1858
4. Viel-Castel: *Mémoires*, IV, 319/20
5. Flaubert: *Corr.*, IV, 275
6. Chantilly: C 484 f. 339
7. Lovenjoul: *Histoire*, I, xi/xv
8. Letter in the possession of Mme Alice Théo Bergerat.
9. Feydeau, op. cit., 195 sqq.

22. The Tethered Poet

1. *L'Artiste*, 6 March 1859
2. Chantilly: C 485 ff. 375/6

3. Chantilly: C 492 ff. 118/21
4. Letter to Adolphe Gaiffe. Chantilly: C 484 ff. 225/6
5. Letter in the possession of Mme Alice Théo Bergerat
6. *Ce que disent les Hirondelles.* (*Emaux et Camées*, ed. Matoré, p. 96.)
7. ILN, 7 January 1860
8. MU, 13 February 1860
9. Toto's extensive part in *les Trésors d'Art de la Russie* is clearly shown in the letters he sent his parents from Russia, from February 1859–February 1860 (letters in the possession of M. Pierre Théophile Gautier)
10. Letter in the possession of Mme Alice Théo Bergerat
11. Du Camp: *Souvenirs*, II, 230/1
12. MU, 5 September 1860
13. Goncourt *Journal*, 24 August 1860

23. Return to Russia

1. Reminiscences of Comte Joseph Primoli
2. *Revue fantaisiste*, 15 July 1861
3. Chantilly: C 484 ff. 156/7
4. MU, 5 August 1861
5. Chantilly: C 484 ff. 238/9
6. Letter of 7/19 August 1861, in the possession of Mme Bergerat
7. Lovenjoul: *Histoire*, I, xv–xviii
8. Letter in the possession of Mme Bergerat
9. Letter in the possession of M. Pierre Théophile Gautier.
10. Chantilly: C 497 ff. 493/4. *La Revue du XIXe siècle*, 1 December 1866, announces that Gautier has been created Commander of the Order of St. Stanislas of Russia. I have found no other record that Gautier received this decoration.
11. Letter in the possession of M. Pierre Théophile Gautier
12. *Après le Feuilleton.* (*Emaux et Camées*, ed. Matoré, pp. 100–1)

24. The Displaced Contemporary

1. ILN, 11 January 1862
2. MU, 27 January 1862
3. *Journal*, II, 10
4. MU, 10 March 1862
5. ILN, 3 May 1862
6. Ibid, 10 May 1862
7. MU, 4 May 1862
8. Gautier visited Thackeray on 8 June (*Letters and Papers of W. M. Thackeray*, ed. Ray, IV, 402). He had evidently known him for some years, for in *la Presse*, 14 January 1850, he had written: 'Nous nous souvenons d'avoir dîné à Londres avec Thackeray, le colossal et spirituel auteur de la *Foire aux Vanités*. L'on parlait d'Espagne, et on lui demandait s'il connaissait ce pays. "Pardieu! si je le connais", répondait-il; "j'ai passé une fois deux heures à Cadix!" Ce mot n'est pas si paradoxal qu'il en a l'air.'
9. *L'Artiste*, 1 July 1862
10. *Loin de Paris*, pp. 137/8
11. Goncourt *Journal*, II, 43/4
12. Ibid, 45/6
13. MU, 8 September 1862
14. *Le Château du Souvenir*. (*Emaux et Camées*, ed. Matoré, 110)

25. The Widening Rift

1. ILN, 8 January 1863
2. Houssaye: *Confessions*, IV, 54
3. *Musée des Familles*, March 1863
4. *L'Artiste*, 15 February 1863
5. *L'Artiste*, 1 April 1863
6. MU, 11 May, 7 June 1863
7. Goncourt *Journal*, II, 89 sqq.; and passim
8. Ibid, II, 105 sqq.
9. MU, 16/17 August 1863
10. Goncourt *Journal*, II, 116 sqq.

26. *Le Capitaine Fracasse*

1. Feydeau, op. cit., 210–11
2. *L'Artiste*, 1 November 1863

3. MU, 29 October 1863
4. *L'Artiste*, 15 November 1863
5. *Reliquiae*, II, 208 sqq.
6. Flaubert: *Correspondance*, V, 116
7. *Le Constitutionnel*, 16 November 1863
8. Letter in the possession of Mme Alice Théo Bergerat. Gautier, to give him his full title, was a member of the Conseil supérieur d'enseignement institué près l'Ecole impériale des Beaux-Arts (Chantilly: C 1581 (ms 503) ff 26/48). Other papers at Chantilly (C 1581 ff. 50 sqq.) show that he was on the Jury of the *Salon* in 1867 and 1868

27. The Quest for Happiness

1. See previous note.
2. *L'Artiste*, 1 March 1864
3. MU, 25 April 1864
4. MU, 5 June 1864
5. *Poésies* (1890 edition), I, 299–300. Notre Dame
6. MU, 4 September 1864. Gautier's articles on this visit to Spain were reprinted in *Quand on Voyage*, pp. 239/336
7. Charles de Boigne: *Petits Mémoires de l'Opéra*, pp. 248 sqq.
8. Letter in the possession of M. Emile Henriot
9. *Dernier Voeu*. (*Emaux et Camées*, ed. Matoré, p. 124.)
10. *Symphonie littéraire. L'Artiste*, 1 February 1865
11. Article reprinted in *Nos Morts contemporains*

28. *Poète mathildien*

1. *L'Artiste*, 1 May 1869, p. 281
2. Ibid, 15 January 1862
3. Ibid, 15 March 1862
4. Primoli
5. Ibid
6. Ibid
7. *Mille Chemins, un seul but.* (*Poésies*. 1890 edition, III, 254)
8. Primoli

29. Spirite

1. Chantilly: C 496 ff. 77/78
2. *La Petite Revue*, 3 September 1864
3. Goncourt *Journal*, II, 211
4. Quoted by Bergerat, *Souvenirs*, p. 365
5. *La Petite Revue*, 2 September 1865
6. *Le Constitutionnel*, 12 June 1865
7. Judith Gautier: *le Second Rang du Collier*, pp. 333-4
8. MU, 26 July 1865
9. *Spirite*, pp. 65/6
10. *Spirite* was serialized in the MU from 17 November—1 December 1865.
11. Typescript in the possession of Mme Alice Théo Bergerat
12. Ibid
13. Ibid
14. Ibid
15. Chantilly: C 484 f. 190
16. Letter to Albert Dardenne de la Grangerie. Chantilly: C. 484 ff. 133/4. The de la Grangeries were welcome visitors at Neuilly, and it was for Mme de la Grangerie that Gautier had recently improvised his *Sonnet à Marguerite* (19 July 1865; *Poésies*, 233) and would write a further sonnet the following year (ibid, 234).

30. The Great Punchbowl

1. *Revue de Paris*, December 1851
2. Suffel: *Anatole France*, pp. 125/6
3. *Revue de Paris*, March 1852
4. Loliée: *La Païva*, 184/5
5. Houssaye: *Confessions*, IV, pp. 97/8
6. MU, 25 May 1867
7. *L'Artiste*, 31 January 1858
8. Ibid, 1 April 1868
9. Ibid, 1 March 1868
10. Arthur Meyer: *Ce que je peux dire*, pp. 179 sqq.
11. *L'Artiste*, 1 March 1868
12. *L'Artiste*, 1 May 1870
13. Houssaye: *Confessions*, V, 341

14. Roosevelt: *Doré*, 262 sqq.
15. *La Petite Revue*, 12 March 1864
16. Chantilly: C 493 ff. 188/9
17. *Gazette anecdotique*, 15 April 1882

31. The Marriage of Judith

1. ILN, 13 January 1866
2. Goncourt *Journal*, III, 9
3. *Mercure de France*, 15 May 1929, pp. 120/1
4. Calmettes, 134 sqq.; and family information
5. Letter of 9 December 1863. (Chantilly: C 485 ff. 413/4)
6. *La Nue.* (*Emaux et Camées*, ed. Matoré, pp. 117/18)
7. *La Fleur qui fait le Printemps.* (*Emaux et Camées*, ed. Matoré, pp. 121/3)
8. Letter in the possession of M. Pierre Théophile Gautier
9. Letter of 25 March 1866, in the possession of M. Pierre Théophile Gautier
10. Letter of 3 April 1866, in the possession of M. Pierre Théophile Gautier
11. Goncourt *Journal*, III, 34
12. Calmettes, op. cit. There is a sidelight on Judith's early married life in an unpublished letter from Théophile Gautier *fils* to his father (letter in the possession of M. Pierre Théophile Gautier). Writing on 19 September 1866, Toto records:
   'Je suis allé deux fois à Neuilly où tout m'a paru régulier. Estelle est toujours gentille et d'une excellente tenue. Il n'en est pas de même de Judith qui se promène à Barbizon, parmi les paysages et les paysagistes, en pantalon et blouse de toile, à califourchon sur un âne et fumant des cigares! Ces excentricités ont été faites trop bien par Mme Sand pour qu'on puisse les égaler et l'on n'arrive par là qu'à se rendre grotesque. Le père Mendès est en faillite. Enfin nous avons fait

The Marrage of Judith—*continued*.
faillite! cela arrangera peut-être
leurs affaires.'
For the disastrous consequences
of Judith's marriage, see Camacho: *Judith Gautier*, pp. 100/7

32. The Sanctuary
Saint-Jean of

1. MU, 23 April 1866
2. Letter in the possession of M.
   Emile Henriot
3. Letter of 29 April 1866, in the
   possession of M. Pierre Théophile
   Gautier
4. *L'Impassible. Poésies* (1890 edition), III, 235
5. Primoli
6. MU, 1 October 1866
7. Du Camp, *Souvenirs*, II, 436/7.
   Gautier also laments de Cormenin's death in a letter to Carlotta on 22 November 1866
8. Letter in the possession of M.
   Emile Henriot
9. Letter in the possession of M.
   Emile Henriot
10. Letter of late September 1866
11. Letter in the possession of M.
    Emile Henriot
12. Decree of 18 February, recorded
    in the MU, 1 May 1867
13. MU, 3 May 1867
14. *L'Année littéraire*, 1868, p. 430
15. Goncourt *Journal*, III, 97
16. Ibid, III, 101
17. MU, 10/11 June 1867
18. *L'Artiste*, July 1867
19. Chantilly: C 484 ff. 12/13
20. Primoli
21. Ibid, 68
22. Ibid, pp. 335/6
23. *Poésies* (1890 edition), III, 256
24. Primoli
25. Ibid
26. Goncourt *Journal*, III, 127

33. Librarian to Her
Highness

1. MU, 4 January 1868
2. Letter to Ernest des Vallières.
   Chantilly: C484 ff. 164/5
3. *L'Artiste*, January 1868, pp. 144/5
4. In an unpublished letter to his
   mother, on 21 March 1868,
   Théophile Gautier *fils* remarks:
   'Tu vas être bien seule. . . .
   Pourquoi n'accepterais-tu pas la
   proposition du père et n'irais-tu
   pas un peu à Neuilly? Cela pourrait être un premier pas vers une
   grande solution. Quant à moi, je
   te le conseille vivement.' This
   advice makes an interesting footnote to the diaries of Eugénie
   Fort, and one cannot help thinking that the 'grande solution' of
   which mother and son both
   dreamed would have been bene-
   ficial to Gautier in his later years.
5. Letter in the possession of M.
   Emile Henriot
6. Two unpublished letters from
   Théophile Gautier *fils* (in the
   possession of M. Pierre Théophile
   Gautier) cast a sadly revealing
   light on his installation as sous-
   préfet. In the first letter, dated 17
   October 1868, he observes to his
   mother that not only has Gautier
   failed to give him a present on the
   occasion but he has tried 'to
   extirpate 40 francs a month' from
   him: 'that's to say what he earns
   from 50 or 60 lines of copy'.
   Gautier's financial difficulties
   hardly need to be recalled, but his
   demands on his son seem both
   selfish and exorbitant. In the
   second letter, dated 27 November, the sous-préfet justly rebukes
   his father: 'You see me begin a
   career that assures my future—
   indeed, our future—and you remain a benevolent onlooker . . .
   you don't give me anything, even
   a trifling souvenir—and then you

come and ask me for 40 francs a month because you say you cannot produce them. If someone wanted to stop me from succeeding they would do exactly the same as you. . . . You know very well that if I have gone into the administration it is with the idea that in ten years or so I shall be in a position to give you some peaceful, calm and comfortable corner when you want to retire. Literature wouldn't give me the means to do it, so I've tried another way. And I shall succeed, if I am not stopped by my family.'

7. Gautier reassured Sainte-Beuve on 9 April: 'Je suis très fatigué, grippé, courbaturé, mais nullement en danger'; and on 8 April we find him writing to Dumas *fils*: 'Je ne suis pas si crevé que le Figaro me représente et j'ai passé hier soirée avec toi, en lisant le premier volume de ton théâtre complet . . . tu es sûr maintenant que je ne suis pas mort. dis le aux amis' (Chantilly: C 484 f. 188). To the Emperor he explained that he had merely suffered from 'une indisposition passagère' (C 485 ff. 423/4). None the less, he was probably suffering from cardiac trouble: one of the causes of his death in 1872.

8. The seriousness of Gautier's illness is suggested by an unpublished letter from Théophile Gautier *fils* to Eugénie Fort on 25 April 1868 (a letter in the possession of M. Pierre Théophile Gautier): 'Tout ce que tu m'écris du père m'attriste un peu; si la maladie s'installe et que le découragement arrive, je ne sais pas ce que deviendra cette maison. Pourquoi ne cherche-t-il pas à marier Estelle, avec un honnete homme qui puisse lui devenir un gendre sérieux? La princesse lui en a parlé un jour à St Gratien et il a fait le grimace et la pirouette que tu connais.'

9. Gautier's boredom with this *scie patriotique* is, alas, clearly seen. Viollet-le-Duc declared that the report was 'un exercice littéraire de grand collégien'. It does not (as Maurice Dreyfous claimed) show the influence of Romanticism on French poetry; and the modern reader, observing the two pages accorded to Amédée Pommier or to Calemard de la Fayette, the five pages given to Pierre Dupont, the space that is granted to such ephemera as Mme Ackermann and Mme Blanchecotte, may indeed be surprised and disappointed to find Verlaine a mere name, Heredia and Mallarmé each dismissed in a phrase, and Vigny hardly discussed. The appreciation of Baudelaire sometimes echoes, almost phrase for phrase, the obituary of 1867 (which itself owed much to an earlier study) and the more extensive work of 1868; and the eulogy of Hugo is embarrassing in its blind and blatant hero-worship.

10. Goncourt *Journal*, III, 166/7

11. *Les Vacances du Lundi. Tableaux de Montagnes* first appeared in book form in 1881, and suggests its chief and familiar distinction in its title. It is a series of romantic landscapes graced by very few figures or buildings, and there is a sameness about mountain scenery which does not make for variety in reading. These collected articles have little of the fire that inspires the early travel books; they betray the weariness of a journalist forced to write copy even on his holidays.

12. Letter in the possession of M. Emile Henriot

13. Letter of 1 October 1868

14. Letter of 3 October 1868

15. Letter of 10 October 1868

16. Letter undated, but late 1868
17. Letter of 18 October 1868
18. Letter of 23 October 1868
19. Chantilly: C 497 f. 152
20. Goncourt *Journal*, III, p. 181

34. The Vagabond Librarian

1. Viollet-le-Duc; *Lettres inédites*, 77 sqq.
2. Ibid
3. Letter in the possession of M. Emile Henriot
4. Goncourt *Journal*, III, 183/4
5. Letter of 27 April, in the possession of M. Emile Henriot
6. Goncourt *Journal*, III, 220/1
7. Gautier to Carlotta Grisi, 4 May 1869. Letter in the possession of M. Emile Henriot
8. Primoli
9. Goncourt *Journal*, III, 221
10. Gautier to Carlotta Grisi, 4 May 1869. Letter in the possession of M. Emile Henriot
11. Primoli
12. JO, 6 June
13. Letter of 1868
14. Idem
15. Chantilly: C 498 ff. 37/38
16. Letter of October 1869 in the possession of M. Emile Henriot
17. Letter of October 1869
18. Idem
19. Idem
20. Letter of 25 October 1869, in the possession of M. Emile Henriot
21. Letter of 13 November 1869, in the possession of M. Emile Henriot
22. Letter of 22 October 1869, in the possession of M. Emile Henriot
23. Letter of 13 November
24. Primoli
25. Letter of 28 November 1869, in the possession of M. Emile Henriot
26. Primoli
27. JO, 16 June 1870

35. The Royalty of Literature

1. Letter of February, quoted by Bergerat, op. cit., p. 315
2. JO, 14 February 1870
3. Ibid, 7 March 1870
4. Ibid, 28 March 1870
5. Chantilly: C 470 ff. 208 sqq.
6. JO, 9 May 1870
7. Letter of 5 February, in the possession of M. Emile Henriot
8. Maxime du Camp, op. cit.
9. Charles Yriarte: *les Portraits cosmopolites*, pp. 61/74
10. Houssaye: op. cit.
11. *L'Artiste*, 1 April 1870

PART FOUR

LA COMÉDIE DE LA MORT

36. A Descent into the Maelstrom

1. JO, 6/7 June
2. Letter of 22 June 1870, in the possession of M. Emile Henriot
3. Letter of 14 July 1870, in the possession of M. Emile Henriot
4. Letter of 27 July 1870, in the possession of M. Emile Henriot
5. Letter of 12 August 1870, in the possession of M. Emile Henriot
6. Letter of 14 August 1870, in the possession of M. Emile Henriot
7. JO, 29 August 1870
8. Goncourt *Journal*, IV, 13
9. Primoli
10. Idem

37. Ugolino's Tower

1. Goncourt *Journal*, IV, 77 sqq.
2. MU, 1 April 1867; *L'Artiste*, 1 October 1867; Delacroix *Journal*, I, 377

3. Primoli
4. Letter of 31 October 1870, in the possession of M. Emile Henriot
5. Letter of 30 November 1870, in the possession of M. Emile Henriot
6. Bergerat, op. cit., p. 319
7. *La Presse*, 17 March 1839
8. Du Camp: *Souvenirs*, II, 441
9. Banville: *Mes Souvenirs*, 454 sqq.
10. Silvestre: *Au Pays des Souvenirs*, p. 40
11. Dreyfous: *Ce que je tiens à dire*, 229 sqq.
12. Goncourt *Journal*, IV, 172/3. The Armistice was signed on 28 January 1871.
13. Letter of 12 February 1871
14. Letter of early 1871

38. The Ruins of Sodom

1. Letter of 22 February, in the possession of M. Emile Henriot
2. Dreyfous, op. cit., pp. 253/4
3. Letter of 5 March 1871
4. Letter of 26 March 1871
5. Letter of 6 April 1871
6. Unpublished letters from Théophile Gautier *fils* and Olivier de Gourjault cast further light on the proposed Belgian visit. Toto made preliminary enquiries of Bérardi, editor of *l'Indépendance*, to see if Gautier could pay his way in journalism; he also asked his father to be godparent (with Princess Mathilde) of the infant Paul Gautier. But Gautier did not reach Brussels until the Princess had returned to Saint-Gratien (Primoli, op. cit., 361)
7. Letter at Chantilly
8. Calmettes, op. cit., pp. 161/2
9. Letter of 21 April 1871, in the possession of M. Emile Henriot
10. Letter of 6 May 1871 in the possession of M. Emile Henriot
11. Letter in the possession of M. Pierre Théophile Gautier
12. Bergerat, *Entretiens*, 331/2
13. Chantilly: C 485 f. 113

14. *Le Vingt-sept mai.* (*Poésies*, 1890 edition, p. 271)
15. Letter of 14 June 1871
16. Du Camp: *Souvenirs*, II, 522/3

39. Fine Autumn

1. *L'Artiste*, July/August 1871
2. Flaubert: *Correspondance*, VI, 274
3. Goncourt *Journal*, IV, 272
4. Ibid, 278
5. Primoli
6. Edmond de Goncourt, in the Introduction to Bergerat, *Entretiens*, xvi sqq.
7. Chantilly: C 485 ff. 379/80
8. Théophile Bergerat, *Nouvelle Revue*, January 1904, 3 sqq.
9. *La Comédie de la Mort. La Vie dans la Mort*, I. (*Poésies*, 1890 edition, I, 10/11)
10. Bergerat: *Souvenirs*, I, 291 sqq., and *Entretiens*, 1/2
11. Flaubert: *Correspondance*, VI, 356
12. Goncourt *Journal*, V, 29
13. Bergerat, *Souvenirs*, I, 359 sqq. Ibid, 343 sqq.
14. Flaubert: *Correspondance*, VI, 368
15. Ibid, VI, 373
16. Chantilly: C 497 ff. 174/5
17. *La Presse*, 23 February 1846
18. *Figaro*, 3 October 1836
19. *La Comédie de la Mort*, loc. cit.
20. Goncourt *Journal*, V, 38/39
21. Chantilly: C 485 ff. 550/1
22. Bergerat, *Souvenirs*, I, 374 sqq., and II, 85 sqq.
23. Letter in the possession of M. Pierre Théophile Gautier
24. Letter in the possession of M. Emile Henriot
25. Letter of 14 November 1871, in the possession of M. Emile Henriot
26. Letter of 1872 in the possession of M. Emile Henriot
27. Letter in the possession of M. Emile Henriot
28. Letter of November 1871 in the possession of M. Emile Henriot
29. Letter of 29 June. Chantilly: C 485 f. 82

30. Goncourt *Journal*, V, 47/48
31. Ibid, V, 50
32. Chantilly: C 485 ff. 442/3
33. Hugo: *Corr. gén.*, III, 319/20. Letter of 12 August.
34. Bergerat, *Entretiens*, 227

40. *La Comédie de la Mort*

1. *L'Histoire du Romantisme*, pp. 53/54
2. Ibid, p. 2
3. *La Presse*, 6 May 1850
4. Letter in the possession of M. Pierre Théophile Gautier
5. Bergerat, op. cit., 227 sqq.
6. MU, 7 January 1856
7. Chantilly: C 407 f. 130
8. Banville: *Mes Souvenirs*
9. Chantilly: C 407 f. 138
10. Bergerat, op. cit., 228/9
11. Vachon: *Puvis de Chavannes*, 170 sqq.
12. Letter of 24 October to Hébert in Rome
13. Bergerat: *Souvenirs*, II, 85/86
14. *La Presse*, 1 July 1844
15. Banville: *Mes Souvenirs*
16. Letter in the possession of M. Pierre Théophile Gautier
17. Bergerat, op. cit., 229

41. Valediction

1. Goncourt *Journal*, V, 59/60
2. Chantilly: C 1581 (ms 503) ff. 87 sqq.
3. Silvestre, op. cit., 47 sqq.
4. Dreyfous, op. cit., 332/3
5. Feydeau, op. cit., 333 sqq.
6. Flaubert: *Corr.*, VI, 432/3. Letter of 25 October 1872
7. A draft letter from Théophile Gautier *fils*, presumably to the Archbishop of Paris, complains of the clergy's behaviour at Gautier's funeral: 'A l'arrivée au cimetière, le clergé s'est placé devant la tombe; je ne saurais affirmer qu'il ait donné l'absoute: on trouverait certainement peu de témoins pour

le certifier. Quoiqu'il en soit, immédiatement après cette cérémonie, le clergé a disparu, et lorsque je me suis avancé pour jeter sur le cercueil de mon père une dernière goutte d'eau bénite on n'a plus trouvé de bénitier. . . . Vous serez juge, Monseigneur, de la conduite du clergé de Neuilly, qui a produit une impression douloureuse sur la famille et sur l'assemblée.' (Letter in the possession of M. Pierre Théophile Gautier.)
8. Hugo: *A Théophile Gautier*. (*le Tombeau de Théophile Gautier*)

42. Afterwards

1. Vachon: op. cit., 170 sqq.
2. Letter to Ed. Stedman, 23 February 1874
3. *Grand Dictionnaire universel du XIXe siècle*, pp. 1090/91
4. Flaubert: *Corr.*, VI, 448/9
5. Faguet: *XIXe Siècle, Etudes littéraires*, 295 sqq.
6. *L'Artiste*, 13 March 1859
7. Bourget, op. cit.
8. *La Musique*, 262
9. Paul Flat: *le Centenaire de Théophile Gautier*. *Revue bleue*, 14 October 1911. And see Appendix Two
10. Albalat: *Gustave Flaubert et ses Amis*, 42 sqq.
11. Houssaye: *Confessions*, III, 96
12. MU, 22 December 1862
13. Flaubert: *Corr.*, IV, 71
14. Bourget, op. cit.
15. Banville: *Mes Souvenirs*, 454
16. Boschot: *Théophile Gautier*, p. 9
17. Saintsbury: Preface to *Scenes of Travel* (translated selections from Gautier's travel books), 1886
18. Faguet: *De l'Influence de Théophile Gautier*. RDDM, 15 July 1911
19. Emile Henriot: *Théophile Gautier, poète. Annales Romantiques*, t. ix, 1912
20. Aubryet: *Chez Nous et chez nos Voisins*, 68 sqq.

21. *Le Constitutionnel*, 30 November 1863
22. Gosse: *Life of Swinburne*, 207
23. MU, 15 January 1866
24. MU, 6 March 1865; and see Appendix One
25. *La Presse*, 26 November 1846
26. Flaubert: *Corr.*, VI, 448/9
27. *L'Artiste*, 14 December 1856
28. Primoli, op. cit., p. 345
29. Bourget: *Pages de Critique et de Doctrine*, I, 66 sqq.
30. Lovenjoul: *Histoire*, I, 124
31. Sarcey: *Quarante Ans de Théâtre*, 91 sqq.
32. Reyer: *Notes de Musique*, 408 sqq.
33. *Le Constitutionnel*, 30 November 1863
34. Chantilly: C 491 ff. 322/3
35. *Causeries du Lundi*, XIV, 73
36. Goncourt *Journal*, I, 141/2
37. *La Presse*, 12 May 1851
38. Reprinted in *Romans et Contes*
39. *Mercure de France*, 16 May 1911
40. Ibid, 15 August 1928
41. Ibid, 15 October 1922
42. MU, 7 January 1854
43. MU, 17 January 1865
44. *Le Cabinet de Lecture*, 19 March 1836
45. Fournel: *Figures d'Hier et d'Aujourd'hui*, 47
46. Pontmartin: *Causeries littéraires*, 303
47. Zola: *Documents littéraires*, 140
48. Hugo: *Corr. gén.*, III, 306
49. *Le Constitutionnel*, 30 November 1863
50. MU, 7 January 1854
51. *La Musique*, 262
52. Chantilly: C 492 ff. 582/3
53. Lovenjoul, op. cit., I, xix/xx

SELECTED BIBLIOGRAPHY. I

The following are among the books consulted. English
books are published in London, French books in
Paris, unless otherwise stated.

ALBALAT, Antoine, *Gustave Flaubert et ses Amis* (Plon 1927)
ARNOLD, Matthew, *Essays in Criticism* (Macmillan 1865)
AUBRYET, Xavier, *Chez Nous et chez nos Voisins* (Dentu 1878)
AVENEL, H., *Histoire de la Presse française depuis 1789 jusqu'à nos Jours*
   (Flammarion 1900)
BALZAC, H. de, *Correspondance, 1819–1850* (Calmann Lévy 1876)
   Lettres à l'Etrangère (Calmann Lévy 1899)
BANVILLE, T. de, *Mes Souvenirs* (Charpentier 1883)
   Critiques (Charpentier 1917)
BARBEY D'AUREVILLY, J., *XIXe siècle. Les Œuvres et les Hommes.* Ire série,
   3e partie. *Les Poètes* (Amyot 1862)
   IIe série. *Journalistes et Polémistes* (Lemerre 1895)
BAUDELAIRE, Charles, *Œuvres posthumes et correspondances inédites.* Précédées
   d'une étude biographique par Eugène Crépet (Quantin 1887)
   L'Art romantique suivi de *la Fanfarlo.* Introduction, éclaircissements et notes
   de Blaise Allan (Lausanne. La Guilde du Livre 1950)
   Théophile Gautier. Notice littéraire, précédée d'une lettre de Victor Hugo.
   (Poulet Malassis et de Broise 1859). Reprinted from *l'Artiste*, 13 March 1859
BÉDARIDA, Henri, *Théophile Gautier et l'Italie* (Boivin 1934)
   Théophile Gautier, poète et critique d'art, en face du Corrège (Leroux 1934)
BERGERAT, Emile, *Souvenirs d'un Enfant de Paris. I. Les Années des Bohème.*
   II. La Phase critique de la Critique (Charpentier 1911, 1912)
   Théophile Gautier. Entretiens, Souvenirs et Correspondance. (Bibliotheque
   Charpentier. Fasquelle 1911)
BOSCHOT, Adolphe, *Théophile Gautier méconnu* (Monaco. Imprimerie de
   Monaco 1925)
   Théophile Gautier (Desclée de Brouwer 1933)
BOUCHER, Henri, *Iconographie générale de Théophile Gautier* (Leclerc 1913)
BOURGET, Paul, *Pages de Critique et de Doctrine* (Dentu 1885)
   Etudes et Portraits (Lemerre 1889)
CALMETTES, Fernand, *Leconte de Lisle et ses Amis* (Librairies-Imprimeries
   réunies 1902)
CAMACHO, M. Dita, *Judith Gautier. Sa Vie et son Œuvre* (Droz 1939)
CARRE, J. M., *Voyageurs et écrivains français en Egypte.* (Le Caire. Imprimerie
   de l'Institut français d'archéologie orientale 1932)
CASSAGNE, Albert, *La Théorie de l'Art pour l'Art en France* (Hachette 1906)
CASTILLE, Hippolyte, *Emile de Girardin* (Sartorius 1858)
   Les Journaux et les Journalistes sous le règne de Louis-Philippe (Sartorius 1858)
   Les Journaux et les Journalistes depuis 1848 (Sartorius 1858)
CHAMPFLEURY, *Grandes Figures d'Hier et d'Aujourd'hui* (Poulet-Malassis et
   de Broise 1861)
   Souvenirs et Portraits de Jeunesse. 2e édition (Dentu 1872)
CHEVILLARD, Valbert, *Un Peintre romantique : Théodore Chassériau* (Lemerre
   1893)

CLARETIE, J., *La Vie à Paris* (Charpentier 1896 &c.)
CLAUDIN, Gustave, *Méry : sa Vie intime* (Bachelin-Deflorenne 1868)
 Mes Souvenirs. Les Boulevards de 1840–1870 (Calmann Lévy 1884)
CORMENIN, Louis de, *Reliquiæ* (Pillet 1868)
CUVILLIER-FLEURY, *Voyages et Voyageurs* (Michel Lévy 1854)
DAUDET, Ernest, *Souvenirs de mon Temps, Débuts d'un Homme de lettres*, 1857–1861 (Plon 1921)
DE BOIGNE, Charles, *Petits mémoires de l'Opéra* (Librairie nouvelle 1857)
DE BONNIÉRES, Robert, *Mémoires d'Aujourd'hui* (Ollendorff 1883)
DELACROIX, Eugène, *Correspondance générale*. Publiée par André Joubin (Plon 1935–1938)
 Journal. Notes par MM. Paul Flat et René Piot (Nourrit 1893–1895)
DE PONTMARTIN, Armand, *Causeries littéraires*. 3e édition (Michel Lévy 1862)
DE RÉGNIER, Henri, *Portraits et Souvenirs*. 3e édition (Mercure de France 1913)
DES ESSARTS, Emmanuel, *Portraits de Maîtres* (Librairie académique Didier. Perrin 1888)
DREYFOUS, Maurice, *Ce que je tiens à dire*. 1862–1872 (Ollendorff 1912)
 Ce qu'il me reste à dire (Ollendorf 1913)
DU CAMP, Maxime, *Théophile Gautier* (Hachette, s.d.)
 Théophile Gautier. Tr. by J. E. Gordon. Preface by Andrew Lang (Fisher Unwin 1893)
 Souvenirs littéraires (Hachette 1882–3)
DUFAY, Pierre, *Autour de Baudelaire* (Au Cabinet du Livre 1931)
EVANS, R. L., *Les Romantiques français et la Musique* (Champion 1934)
FAGUET, Emile, *XIXe Siècle. Études littéraires* (Boivin 1893)
FEYDEAU, Ernest, *Théophile Gautier. Souvenirs intimes* (Plon 1874)
FLAUBERT, Gustave, *Œuvres complètes. Correspondance*. Nouvelle édition augmentée (Conard 1926 sqq.)
 Œuvres complètes. Correspondance. Supplément. Recueillie, classée et annotée par MM. René Dumesnil, Jean Pommier et Claude Digeon (Conard 1954)
 Lettres inédites à la Princesse Mathilde (Conard 1927)
 Lettres inédites à Tourguéneff. Présentation et notes par Gérard Gailly (Monaco. Editions du Rocher 1946)
FOURNEL, Victor, *Figures d'Hier et d'Aujourd'hui* (Calmann Lévy 1883)
FOURNIER, Ed., *Souvenirs poétiques de l'Ecole romantique* (Laplace, Sanchez. 1886)
FROMENTIN, Eugéne, *Correspondance et fragments inédits*. Biographie et notes par Pierre Blanchon. 2e édition (Plon 1912)
 Voyage en Egypte (1869). Introduction par J.-M. Carré (Editions Montaigne. Fernand Aubier 1935)
FUCHS, Max, *Théodore de Banville*. Thèse pour le doctorat ès lettres présentée à la Faculté des lettres de l'Université de Paris. 1910. (No publisher given)
GAUTIER, Judith, *Le Collier des Jours, Souvenirs de ma Vie* (Félix Juven 1907)
 Le Collier des Jours, Le Second Rang du Collier. Souvenirs littéraires (Félix Juven 1909)
GAUTIER, Théophile.

Poetical Works

L'España. Ed. René Jasinski (Vuibert 1929)
Emaux et Camées. Introduction de Jean Pommier, Notes et Lexique de Georges Matoré (Genève. Droz 1947)

Poésies complètes. Publiées par René Jasinski (Librairie de Paris. Firmin Didot 1932)
Poésies (Lemerre 1890)

Theatre

Théâtre de Poche (Librairie Nouvelle 1855)
Théâtre. Mystère, Comédies et Ballets (Charpentier 1872)

Travel Books and Topical Journalism

Voyage en Espagne (Tra los Montes) (Charpentier 1881)
Voyage en Italie (Italia) (Bibliothèque-Charpentier. Fasquelle 1896)
Voyage en Russie (Bibliothèque-Charpentier. Fasquelle 1912)
L'Orient (Charpentier 1881)
Constantinople (Charpentier 1883)
Quand on Voyage (Michel Lévy 1865)
Loin de Paris (Michel Lévy 1865)
Caprices et Zigzags (Victor Lecou 1852)
Les Vacances du Lundi (Charpentier 1881)
Tableaux de Siège. Paris, 1870–1871 (Charpentier 1871)

Collected and Reprinted Criticism

Salon de 1847 (Hetzel. Warnod 1847)
Les Beaux-Arts en Europe (Michel Lévy 1856)
L'Art moderne (Michel Lévy 1856)
Abécédaire du Salon de 1861 (Dentu 1861)
Trésors d'Art de la Russie ancienne et moderne (Gide 1861–1862)
Guide de l'Amateur au Musée du Louvre, suivie de la vie et des œuvres de quelques peintres (Charpentier 1882)
La Musique (Bibliothèque-Charpentier. Fasquelle 1911)
Victor Hugo (Charpentier. Fasquelle 1902)
Honoré de Balzac (Poulet-Malassis et de Broise 1860)
Les Grotesques (Michel Lévy 1859)
Les Maîtres du Théâtre français de Rotrou à Dumas fils (Payot 1929)
Portraits contemporains: littérateurs, peintres, sculpteurs, artistes dramatiques (Bibliothèque-Charpentier. Fasquelle s.d.)
Portraits et Souvenirs littéraires (Michel Lévy 1875)
Souvenirs romantiques (Garnier 1929)
Souvenirs de Théâtre, d'Art et de Critique (Charpentier 1883)
Histoire du Romanticisme, suivie de Notices Romantiques et d'une Etude sur la Poésie française 1830–1868 (Librairie des Bibliophiles. Flammarion 1929)
Tableaux à la Plume (Charpentier 1880)
Fusains et Eaux-Fortes (Charpentier 1880)
Histoire de l'Art dramatique en France depuis vingt-cinq ans (Hetzel 1858–1859)
Théophile Gautier: critique artistique et littéraire (Larousse 1929)

Novels, Short Stories, etc.

Jean et Jeannette (Baudry s.d.)
La Croix de Berny (In collaboration) (Librairie Nouvelle 1855)
Les Deux Étoiles (Bruxelles. Tarride 1848)

Les Jeunes-France, romans goguenards, suivis de contes humoristiques (Charpentier 1880)
Le Roman de la Momie (Bibliothèque-Charpentier. Charpentier & Fasquelle 1898)
Spirite. Nouvelle fantastique (Charpentier 1886)
Mademoiselle de Maupin (Charpentier 1922)
Mademoiselle de Maupin. Avec une Introduction et des Notes par Adolphe Boschot (Garnier 1955)
La Préface de Mademoiselle de Maupin. Edition critique par Georges Matoré (Genève. Droz 1946)
Le Capitaine Fracasse (Librairie Garnier 1930)
Partie carrée (Charpentier 1914)
Un Trio de Romans (Charpentier 1888)
Nouvelles (Bibliothèque-Charpentier. Fasquelle 1923)
Romans et Contes (Bibliothèque-Charpentier. Fasquelle s.d.)

Miscellaneous

La Peau de Tigre (Michel Lévy 1866)
Ménagerie intime (Lemerre 1869)
A Domestic Menagerie. Translated . . . with an Introduction by M. Strachey (Elliot Stock 1899)
La Nature chez Elle (Charpentier 1891)
Œuvres érotiques. Poésies libertines. Lettres à la Présidente (Arcanes 1953)
De la Mode (Poulet-Malassis et de Broise 1858)
GIRARDIN, Mme Emile de, *Le Vicomte de Launay.—Lettres parisiennes* (Michel Lévy 1857)
GONCOURT, Edmond & Jules de, *Journal* (Flammarion. Fasquelle 1935–6)
    Charles Demailly (Charpentier 1896)
    L'Art du XVIIIe siècle. 3e édition (Quantin 1880–83)
    Etudes d'Art (Librairie des Bibliophiles. Flammarion 1893)
GOSSE, Edmund, *The Life of Algernon Charles Swinburne* (Macmillan 1917)
Grand Dictionnaire Universel du XIXe siècle (Larousse 1872)
GUILLAUME-REICHER, G., *Théophile Gautier et l'Espagne* (Hachette 1935)
HALPÉRINE-KEMINSKY, E., *Ivan Tourguéneff d'après sa correspondance avec ses amis français* (Charpentier 1901)
HEGERMANN-LINDENCRONE, L. de, *In the Courts of Memory, 1858–1875.* From contemporary letters (N.Y. Harper Bros. 1912)
HENRIOT, Emile, *Livres et Portraits. (Courrier littéraire.)* 2e série (Plon 1925)
HERVIER, Marcel, (*Les Écrivains français jugés par leurs contemporains.* IV. XIXe siècle (2e partie.) (Mellottée 1942)
HOUSSAYE, Arsène, *Les Confessions. Souvenirs d'un demi-siècle. 1830–1880* (Dentu 1885–91)
    Souvenirs de Jeunesse, 1830–1850, 1850–1870 (Flammarion 1896)
HUGO, Victor, *Correspondance générale* (Albin Michel. 1947 sqq.)
JASINSKI, René, *Les Années romantiques de Théophile Gautier* (Vuibert 1929)
    Histoire de la littérature française (Boivin 1947)
JULLIEN, Adolphe, *Ernest Reyer, sa Vie et ses Œuvres* (Laurens 1909)
KARR, Alphonse, *Le Livre de Bord.* IIIe série (Calmann Lévy 1880)
LAPAUZE, Henry, *Ingres : sa Vie et son Œuvre (1760–1867).* D'après des documents inédits (Imprimerie Georges Petit 1911)
LARGUIER, Léo, *Théophile Gautier* (Tallandier 1948)

LEMERRE, Alphonse (ed), *Le Tombeau de Théophile Gautier* (Lemerre 1873)

LESCURE, M. de, *François Coppée. L'Homme, la Vie et l'Œuvre* (Lemerre 1889)

LIFAR, Serge, *Carlotta Grisi*. Tr. Doris Langley Moore (Lehmann 1947)

LOLIÉE, Frédéric, *Les femmes du Second Empire. Papiers intimes* (Juven 1906)
Les femmes du Second Empire. La Fête impériale (Juven 1907)
La Païva (Tallandier 1920)

LOVENJOUL, Vicomte de Spoelberch de, *Histoire des Œuvres de Théophile Gautier* (Charpentier 1887)
Les Lundis d'un Chercheur (Calmann Lévy 1894)

LOVIOT, L., *Alice Ozy* (Les Bibliophiles fantaisistes 1910)

LUMLEY, Benjamin, *Reminiscences of the Opera* (Hurst & Blackett 1864)

MARCEL, Henri, *Essai sur Théophile Gautier* (Société d'éditions littéraires et artistiques. Ollendorff 1903)

MENDÈS, Catulle, *Rapport à M. le Ministre de l'Instruction publique et des beaux-arts sur le mouvement poétique français de 1867 à 1900* (Imprimerie Nationale 1902)

MÉRIMÉE, Prosper, *Lettres inédites*. Introduction de Félix Chambon. (Printed for private circulation 1900)

MEYER, Arthur, *Ce que je peux dire* (Plon. 1912)

MIRECOURT, Eugène de, *Théophile Gautier* (Faure 1867)
Emile de Girardin (Faure 1867)
Gérard de Nerval (Faure 1867)
Scribe (Librairie des Contemporains 1869)
Ricord. 3e édition (Librarie des Contemporains 1869)

MONSELET, Charles, *La Lorgnette littéraire. Dictionnaire des grands et des petits auteurs de mon temps*. 2e édition. (Poulet-Malassis et de Broise 1859)
Petits mémoires littéraires (Charpentier 1885)

MONTÉGUT, Émile, *Nos Morts contemporains*. 2e série (Hachette 1884)

NERVAL, Gérard de, *Correspondance* (1830–1855). Avec une introduction et des notes par Jules Marsan. 3e édition. (Mercure de France 1911)
La Bohème galante. Nouvelle édition (Calmann Lévy 1882)

NICOLARDOT, Louis, *L'impeccable Théophile Gautier et les sacrilèges romantiques* (Tresse 1883)

NOULET, E., *Le Premier Visage de Rimbaud*. (Académie Royale de Langue et de Littérature Française de Belgique. Palais des Académies. Bruxelles 1953)

PATCH, H. E., *The Dramatic Criticism of Théophile Gautier* (Bryn Mawr. Pennsylvania 1922)

POTEZ, Henri, *Théophile Gautier* (Armand Colin 1903)

REYER, Ernest, *Notes de Musique* (Charpentier 1875)

RICHARDSON, Joanna, *Rachel* (Reinhardt 1956)

ROOSEVELT, Blanche, *Life and Reminiscences of Gustave Doré* (Sampson Low 1885)

RUDRAUF, Lucien, *Eugène Delacroix et le problème du romantisme artistique* (Laurens 1942)

SAINTE-BEUVE, C. A., *Portraits littéraires* (Garnier 1862–4)
Premiers lundis (Michel Lévy 1874–5)
Nouveaux lundis (Michel Lévy 1863–70)
Les grands écrivains français. Etudes des Lundis et des Portraits classées selon un ordre nouveau et annotées par Maurice Allem. XIXe siècle. Les poètes. II. Victor Hugo-Musset-Théophile Gautier (Garnier 1926)
Correspondance générale. Recueillie, classée et annotée par Jean Bonnerot (Stock 1935 sqq.)

SAINTSBURY, George (ed.), *Théophile Gautier. Scenes of Travel* (Oxford. Clarendon Press 1886)

SAND, George, *Catalogue de la Bibliothèque de Mme George Sand et de M. Maurice Sand* (Ferroud 1890)

Correspondance entre George Sand et Gustave Flaubert (Calmann Lévy 1904)

SARCEY, Francisque, *Quarante ans de théâtre. Feuilletons dramatiques*. (Bibliothèque des annales politiques et littéraires 1900)

SILVESTRE, Armand, *Au Pays des Souvenirs. Mes Maîtres et mes Maîtresses* (Librairie illustrée 1893)

SPRONCK, Maurice, *Les Artistes littéraires. Études sur le XIXe siècle* (Calmann Lévy 1889)

SWINBURNE, A. C., *Letters to John Morley*. Ed. Edmund Gosse (Printed for private circulation 1914)

The Letters of Algernon Charles Swinburne, with some personal recollections by Thomas Hake and Arthur Compton-Rickett (Murray 1918)

THACKERAY, W. M., *Letters and private papers*. Collected and edited by Gordon N. Ray (Cambridge. Mass., Harvard University Press 1945–6)

THIÉBAUT, Marcel, *Edmond About* (N.R.F. Gallimard 1936)

TILD, Jean, *Théophile Gautier et ses Amis* (Albin Michel 1951)

TOURNEUX, Maurice, *Théophile Gautier. Sa Bibliographie* (Baur 1876)

TROUBAT, Jules, *Sainte-Beuve intime et familier* (Duc 1903)

Souvenirs du dernier secrétaire de Sainte-Beuve (Calmann Lévy 1890)

TUIN, H. van der, *L'évolution psychologique, esthétique et littéraire de Théophile Gautier. Etude de caractérologie littéraire* (Nizet et Bastard 1933)

VACHON, M., *Puvis de Chavannes* (Socétié d'éditions artistiques 1900)

VANDAM, Albert D., *Undercurrents of the Second Empire* (Heinemann 1897)

VAUDOYER, J.-L., *Alice Ozy ou l'Aspasie moderne*. (Editions M.-P. Trémois 1930)

VIEL-CASTEL, Comte H. de, *Mémoires sur le règne de Napoléon III, 1851–1864*. 2e édition (Chez tous les libraires 1883)

VILLEMESSANT, H. de, *Mémoires d'un Journaliste* (Dentu 1872–8)

VIOLLET-LE-DUC, E.-E., *Lettres inédites*. Recueillies et annotées par son fils (Librairies-Imprimeries réunies 1902)

YRIARTE, Charles, *Les Portraits cosmopolites* (Lachaud 1870)

ZOLA, Emile, *Documents littéraires. Etudes et Portraits* (Charpentier 1881)

ANONYMOUS, *An Englishman in Paris. Notes and Recollections. The Reign of Louis-Philippe and the Empire* (Chapman and Hall 1893)

SELECTED BIBLIOGRAPHY. II

Articles

The following are among the articles consulted:

BARJAC, Claude, 'Écrivains et directeurs de Journaux' (*Grande Revue*, January 1936)

BERGERAT, Théophile, 'Théophile Gautier. Souvenirs de Famille' (*Nouvelle Revue*, January 1904)

BERNARD, Paul, 'Théophile Gautier. Le Rêve de la Beauté (*Etudes*, 5 February–5 June 1912)

BERTAUT, Jules, 'Théophile Gautier, voyageur' (*Grande Revue*, 25 August 1911)

BLANGUERNON, Edmond, 'Une Amie inconnue de Théophile Gautier. Documents inédits' (*Revue de Paris*, July 1914, pp. 123 seqq.)

BOSCHOT, Adolphe, 'Théophile Gautier, critique d'art' (*Revue de Paris*, 1 January 1932)

BOUCHER, Henri, 'Lettres familières de Théophile Gautier' (*Mercure de France*, July/August 1914, tom. CX, pp. 23 sqq.; 15 May 1929, pp. 108 sqq.; 1 June 1929, pp. 319 sqq.)

BOURGET, Paul, 'L'influence de Théophile Gautier' (*Revue Française*, 22 October 1922)

BRANCOURT, R., 'Théophile Gautier, critique musical' (*Ménéstrel*, 20 September–1 November 1913)

BRUNET, Gabriel, 'Sur la Critique' (*Mercure de France*, 15 April 1922) 'Théophile Gautier, poète' (*Mercure de France*, 15 October 1922)

FAGUET, Emile, 'De l'influence de Théophile Gautier' (*Revue des Deux Mondes* 15 July 1911)

FLAT, Paul, 'Le Centenaire de Théophile Gautier' (*Revue Bleue*, 14 October 1911)

FONTAINAS, André, 'Les Poésies de Théophile Gautier' (*Mercure de France*, September/October 1911)

HENRIOT, Emile, 'Théophile Gautier, poète' (*Annales Romantiques*, t. ix. 1912)

JARRY, Paul, 'Théophile Gautier à Neuilly' (Extrait du Bulletin de la Commission historique de Neuilly-sur-Seine. Imprimerie de Neuilly. Roche 1922)

LAURET, René, 'L'âme romantique de Théophile Gautier' (*Mercure de France*, 16 May 1911)

LUX, J., 'Théophile Gautier' (*Revue Bleue*, 1911)

MALLARMÉ, Stéphane, 'Symphonie littéraire' (*L'Artiste*, 1 February 1865)

MAUREVERT, Georges, 'Des Sons, des Gouts et des Couleurs' (*Mercure de France*, 15 June 1939)

ORLIAC, Antoine, 'Essai sur le Pessimisme chez les Parnassiens' (*Mercure de France*, 15 August 1928)

PILON, Edmond, 'L'évolution du journalisme français' (*Nouvelle Revue*, 1901. tom. vi)

PRIMOLI, J. N., 'La Princesse Mathilde et Théophile Gautier' (*Revue des Deux Mondes*, 1 November 1925, pp. 47–86; and 15 November 1925, 329–66)

RICHARDSON, Joanna, 'The Genesis of Gautier's Variations sur le Carnaval de Venise' (*French Studies*, Vol. VIII, pp. 338 sqq.) 'Une Semaine à Londres. Théophile Gautier en Angleterre' (BBC French Service scripts, 13 January, 25 March 1954)

SERVIÈRES, Georges, 'Les relations d'Ernest Reyer et de Théophile Gautier' (*Revue d'Histoire Littéraire de la France*, 1917)

TORCHET, J., 'Théophile Gautier, critique musical' (*Le Guide Musical*, 9, 16, 23 October 1904)

VENDRAMIN, Lorenzo, 'Mlle Ozy et ses Amis' (*Quo Vadis*, January–March and April–June 1954) 'Cinq lettres inédites de Théophile Gautier' (*Quo Vadis*, April–June 1954)

ANON., 'Une lettre inédite de Théophile Gautier' (*Revue de l'Agenais*, 30 September and 31 October 1889)

Periodicals

The following are among the periodicals consulted:

L'Abeille Politique et Littéraire (1848)
Les Annales Romantiques (1904–1914)
Ariel, Journal du Monde Élégant (1836)
L'Artiste (1831–1872)
L'Année Littéraire et Dramatique (1859–1867)
Bulletin du Bibliophile et du Bibliothécaire (1926–1951)
Le Cabinet de Lecture (1832, 1836)
La Charte de 1830 (1836)
La Chronique (1841–1846)
Chronique de Paris (1836–)
Figaro (1836–1838)
Figaro-Livre (1837)
La France Littéraire (1830–)
Le Journal Officiel (1869–1871)
Le Magasin Pittoresque (1833–1850)
Le Mercure de France (1892–1953)
Le Moniteur Universel (1855–1868)
Le Musée des Familles (1834–1872)
La Nouvelle Revue (1879–1953)
La Petite Revue (1863–1866)
Philological Quarterly (1922–1954)
La Presse (1836–1855)
La Revue Indépendante (1841–1848)
La Revue de Paris (1851–1858)
La Revue des Cours Littéraires (continued as *La Revue Politique et Littéraire*),
    3e, 4e and 5e séries
La Revue des Deux Mondes (1 and 15 November 1925)
La Revue du XIXe Siècle (1857–1867)
La Revue Nationale et Étrangère (1861–1862)

INDEX